Facing the Abusing God

Facing the Abusing God

A Theology of Protest

DAVID R. BLUMENTHAL

Westminster/John Knox Press
Louisville, Kentucky

Book design: The HK Scriptorium, Inc.

Cover design: Laura Lee

Cover illustration: Käthe Kollwitz, "The Survivors," Rosenwald Collection © 1993, National Gallery of Art, Washington, D.C. Used with permission.

First edition

Published by Westminster/John Knox Press
Louisville, Kentucky

This book is printed on acid-free paper that meets the American National Standards Institute Z39.48 standard. ∞

PRINTED IN THE UNITED STATES OF AMERICA

9 8 7 6 5 4 3 2 1

Library of Congress Cataloging–in–Publication Data

Blumenthal, David R.
  Facing the abusing god : a theology of protest / David R.
Blumenthal. — 1st ed.
    p.   cm.
  Includes bibliographical references and index.
  ISBN 0–664–25464–0 (alk. paper)

  1. Holocaust (Jewish theology) 2. God (Judaism) 3. Holocaust survivors—Religious life. 4. Adult child abuse victims—Religious life. I. Title.
BM645.H6B58   1993
296.3'11—dc20   93–19484

*to the many who have suffered —
they are like gnarled trees growing in the wilderness*

*and to the few who help —
they are those who cultivate wild plants*

*in memory of Tante Rüthchen —
survivor and therapist*

"You shall love your neighbor as yourself, I am the Lord . . ."
"You shall love the Lord, your God, with all your heart, with all your soul, and with all your might" (Lev. 19:18 with Deut. 6:5, cited in Mark 12:28-31).

"'You shall love your neighbor as yourself' — Rabbi Akiva said, 'This is a great principle in the Torah'" (Sifra, cited in Rashi, ad loc.).

"'With all your heart' — with your impulse to do good and with your impulse to do evil; another interpretation: with your heart not divided on the subject of God'" (Sifre, cited in Rashi, ad loc.).

Rabbi David says: "How do you love your neighbor as yourself? By allowing yourself to be silenced by your neighbor's pain, a silence of awe and of openness. And by *not* allowing yourself to be silenced by your neighbor's pain, by speech which is powerful and comforting. And how do you love the Lord, your God, with all your heart? By allowing yourself to be silenced by the presence of God, a silence of amazement and of receptivity. And by *not* allowing yourself to be silenced by God, by speech which is strong and just."

Contents

Foreword

THE SHEER HORROR of human suffering in this century, its intensity, diversity, and magnitude, has shaken theology to its core. To respond, theologians have had to come to terms with that horror without minimizing it, without escaping into cynicism or hollow pieties, and without making the victims either invisible or balkanized competitors for justice. This book takes up that challenge with courage and sensitivity.

David Blumenthal's work is remarkable and bold in its examination of horror through the eyes of two groups who have not before been joined — the survivors of the holocaust and the survivors of child abuse. This linking is not done, however, by muting the distinctive voices of the two groups into a neatly harmonized whole, but by respecting their outrage and their distinctive cries for revenge, retribution, and restitution. At the same time as he looks for common aspects, Blumenthal is careful to uphold and honor the unique aspects of suffering created by the different experiences of holocaust survivors and survivors of sexual and domestic violence. In both linking and separating, he negotiates creative and fructifying tensions and illuminates the shadowy corners of evil.

Blumenthal's willingness to avoid a quick resolution of the tensions involved makes this an emotionally honest and disturbing book: disturbing in the best sense, for it challenges one's most basic theological assumptions — including the nature of theology as a discipline. At the same time, it nurtures one's sense of the importance of undertaking theological ventures. A journey through this book is likely to leave one with new questions and answers, with open ends and resolutions, and with disquiet as well as comfort. It is an essential journey.

To address the sexual abuse of children requires a revolution in theological thinking, in ways parallel to the revolutions in Judaism following the Babylonian exile and the destruction of the temple by the Romans. While Blumenthal's book emerges out of the Jewish response to the holocaust, he stretches the emotional and disciplinary envelopes of theology and challenges Christian theologians to confront more honestly the profound evil we find in the everyday midst of human life. He lays common ground for this challenge by basing his exploration of evil and God's role in it on biblical commentary.

Blumenthal's work is also remarkable because few male scholars in any theological tradition have seen the implications of viewing theology from the perspective of survivors of sexual abuse, partly perhaps because to do so honestly and respectfully requires attention to the devastating implications of male hegemony. Fewer still have achieved the level of insight and thoughtfulness found in this book. That level is achieved because Blumenthal does not subsume feminist perspectives forged in the crucible of women's experience into his own scheme and does not jump to facile theological solutions he has not lived in his own experience. He lets the dissonances of various voices coexist without denying the challenges to his own work and without smoothing over painful tensions.

Blumenthal refuses to tie up his theology into systematically neat or comforting packages. He focuses acutely on the ambiguities and pain of profound suffering as they are experienced by those grounded in biblical faith. He wades resolutely into the conflicts and attends to the confusion of voices that emerge from tragedy that rips human life apart at its very heart. He is persistent in listening, patient with the confusions created by torture and abuse, courageous in facing horrifying examples of human evil, and outraged by God's silence or possible complicity. His courage and sensitivity make this an emotionally powerful and profoundly pastoral book.

At confessional moments Blumenthal identifies the limits of his experience and ability to comprehend the world of survivors of abuse. He places in the text itself alternative perspectives and experiences from those survivors and feminist theologians with whom he is in intense conversation. This integrity makes Blumenthal a trustworthy dialogue partner for feminists, for he does not placate or pretend. He listens, argues, struggles to understand, is compassionate, does not take over what is not his, and refuses to label falsely. He is respectful of feminist issues, but he is honest about his limits as he endeavors to maintain his own need for authentic religious expression as a Jewish man.

The concreteness of Blumenthal's struggle is what makes this book so valuable to those of us outside the parameters of Jewish theology, even as it is distinctively and wonderfully Jewish. Blumenthal takes a traditional medieval Jewish form of textual commentary, in which conflicting interpretations are set side by side, and uses it to create a postmodern, multivocal form that enables the reconstruction of compassion. With these conflicting juxtapositions, hope for healing emerges in the multiplicity of voices that convey complex and nuanced energies. This Jewish way of doing theology is rich and breaks new methodological ground. It will, I hope, become more common in Christian theology. It is grounded in textual traditions, respecting the rootedness of people in their distinctive histories, and it works within that grounding toward new religious horizons.

Few theological works will touch us as widely or as deeply as this exploration into the heart of human suffering. It draws its truths from a complex and nuanced analysis of the lessons learned from listening to the survivors of horrifying evil. Blumenthal asks important theological questions and unsettles us by requiring that we reconsider our theologically comfortable assumptions in the face of profound horror. He gives no singular or final answers, but, as the best theologians do, he requires us to examine our presuppositions and most dearly held beliefs. Where his challenge leads us will depend on our own answers as we struggle with life in this and the next century. The journey begins with the excruciating joy of reading this book.

Rita Nakashima Brock
Feast of Weeks/Pentecost, 1993
St. Paul, Minnesota

Roadmap

How Did We Get Here?

WHEN I WAS in high school (1952–1956), we did not talk about the holocaust.[1] When I was in college (1956–1960), which included a year in divided Jerusalem a scant few hundred yards from Jordanian gun emplacements, we did not talk about the holocaust. When I was in rabbinical school (1960–1964), which again included a year in divided Jerusalem, I heard one lecture on the holocaust. It was not until my third year as an active rabbi (1967) that the holocaust was mentioned, and then in a liturgical context. During these years, too, my great uncle Max, the only member of the family to survive and to come to America, lived half an hour from us; but I did not know him. The curtain of silence hung heavily around him, as it hung around the years he represented.

It was the unbelievable Six Day War (1967), combined with the aging of the survivor generation, that slowly opened the floodgates of knowledge. Jews felt confident that history could be mastered, that might would make right; and survivors began to realize that, if they did not tell their stories, no one would ever know and the past would be lost. Books were written, speeches given, memorials created, chairs of holocaust study established, newsletters started; even American liberators who had known total silence were brought into the picture. Holocaust literature and studies flourished and became a small industry.

Holocaust and post-holocaust theology also flourished. On the Jewish side, theological reflection ranged from the denial of the God of history and morality, to a repetition of the traditional theodicies, to asserting that the holocaust was God's punishment of the Jews for the sin of moderniza-

---

[1] On not capitalizing "holocaust," see p. xxii below.

tion.[2] On the Christian side, it ranged from the assertion that the holocaust was the punishment of the Jews for their continued rejection of Christ to viewing the Jews as the truly crucified.[3] Liturgies were created and annual holocaust memorial services were held.

Having been under the seal of silence in my earlier years, I did not want to teach the holocaust. My Christian colleague Jack Boozer persuaded me, after visits to campus by Elie Wiesel and Simon Wiesenthal, that I owed it to the victims, to the future, and even to God to engage this subject. Another Christian colleague, Fred Crawford, persuaded me that we needed to do serious research in this area. And so our courses on the holocaust and the Witness to the Holocaust Project were created. From exposure to the material, I was drawn into wrestling with the questions and, as a theologian, I was particularly drawn to the question of God and the holocaust: If we believe in providence, that is, in God's active participation in human history, how can we account for God's activity in the holocaust? Was God active, inactive, indirectly active? present, absent? silent? angry? powerless? punitive? Years of study and reflection in biblical, rabbinic, and medieval religious thought prepared me to look at the question but not to answer it. This book is an attempt to answer the question of God's responsibility in the holocaust, granted that humans must assume their responsibility too. This is one path leading us to this place.

Jews in America, particularly in academia, went through a phase of acculturation, of adapting Jewish civilization to western culture. We learned how to study and act in an appropriate manner; we assimilated to the dominant culture. Martin Luther King, Jr., and the civil rights movement liberated us. King taught us that it was legitimate to be openly Jewish, that we need not hide our Jewishness any more than he needed to hide his blackness and African-American culture. I was at the great civil rights demonstration in 1963 and, by one of those strange acts of providence, I was in the press section, a scant one hundred feet from King when he gave his "I Have a Dream" speech. The speech and the whole occasion were liberating.

The permission to be outspokenly ethnic given us by Martin Luther King, Jr., was followed by the surge in ethnic pride after the Six Day War, and Jews came out of the closet. In academia, chairs of Jewish studies were created, whole departments and programs were generated, enrollments jumped, publications appeared, and student and professional associations were formed. The same happened among African Americans. Eventually, the women's movement took on momentum and the same thing happened there. Asians, Hispanics, homosexuals, and others joined in this liberation. Everyone began to seek affirmation of one's group—not just individual civil rights but recognition of one's

[2] One thinks of the works of R. Rubenstein, E. Berkovitz, I. Greenberg, E. Fackenheim, S. Katz, and others.

[3] One thinks of the works of F. Littell, R. and A. Eckhart, R. Ruether, J. Moltmann, and others.

integral group identity by others. This tendency has recently coalesced under the banner of "multiculturalism" (earlier called "pluralism"), and its goal is to demand and to extend recognition to previously marginalized groups. Multiculturalism seeks to find a way not only to treat others as equal under society's regulations but to honor the culture, the commitments, indeed the identity of the other as a community of history and concern. Academicians hope that the multicultural thrust of the campus of today will be the ideology of the world of tomorrow.

For Jews, multiculturalism meant finding topics and practices that flow out of Jewish civilization and writing about them, especially in a way that would shed light on the dominant culture and other cultures. The Jewish contribution to human civilization shifted from recasting Jewish culture in the mold of the dominant culture to analyzing the special modes of Jewish identity and holding those modes up to the scrutiny of others to see if something general could be learned from them for other cultures and civilizations. Jews, for instance, have been studying texts and interpreting them for millennia. Is there anything noteworthy in that process that needs to be displayed to the world as a way worth walking? Jews have also been doing theology for millennia. Is there anything special to their way of thinking that needs to be shared with others—so that it may be honored, but also so that others may learn a new way to think about theology? This quest for an "authentic" Jewish identity which will be recognized and honored by others and which may even serve as a model for others is another path leading us to this place.

In the course of our liberation and discovering the otherness of other people, we stumbled upon battered women, women who lived in violent and abusive conditions. And, in the course of talking with battered women, we discovered child abuse—children who had been beaten, burned, raped, emotionally abused, and some even killed. Beatings, even torture; rape, even incest; young children and crippled adults, some striving mightily to recover their sense of self and healing. How did one survive child abuse? How did one put one's life back together? How did one face God?

Adult survivors of child abuse have much in common with survivors of the holocaust. First and foremost, the abuse was real, physical; it was not a bourgeois act of fantasy. And the abuse was extended, not a single incident. And it was massive, not incidental or trifling. There are dissimilarities, too. Abuse for children went on for a long time, longer than the usual stay of an inmate in the camps. And it was interspersed with moments that were more or less normal, not a continuous terrorization. And it was usually suffered without support, no one with whom one could share the terror. Worst of all, child abuse comes from those one is supposed to love—indeed from those whom one does love in some way, not from the identifiable enemy. By contrast, abuse in the holocaust was national, not personal; racial, not generational. And it was part of history and ideology, not just an aberration of personal psyche. There are also similarities and dissimilarities in the life distortions of these two groups of survivors and in the therapeutic protocols.[4] The intersection of these communities, of their abuse and their life-reconstruction, is another path leading us to this place.

This book, then, is an attempt to address the question, How can one speak responsibly of God and the holocaust without excluding God's action from that event? It is also an effort to answer this question in a Jewish way, in forms that grow out of and correspond to Jewish modes of theological reflection. Finally, it is an undertaking that seeks to answer the question by understanding and working from the experience of survivors of the holocaust and child abuse.

How Should the Reader Proceed?

Part 1 is titled "Beginning Somewhere"; it contains five chapters. In "Introduction" I address issues of language about God, finding one's theological voice, and I set forth the intellectual structure of the unit. I also identify myself as fully as I can so that the reader will know the place from which I write. In "Personality" I justify using this category as a way to describe God, deal with the Freudian challenge to this mode of discourse, and then set forth six personalist attributes of God as they flow from the classic Jewish sources and as they are rooted in a "theology of image" shared by the divine and the human (Gen. 1:26). I address the Freudian challenge only briefly because this has been dealt with fully by others. In "Holiness" I justify using this category as a way to describe God and make some suggestions about the group of words that describe holiness. I also set forth an interpretation of the Jewish teaching on *kavvana* (focusing of consciousness) and describe the interrelationship between holiness, fear, and joy.

Having expounded the two essential attributes of God, I turn to methodological issues. In "Universes of Discourse" I elaborate a theory of language usage involving the universes of aesthetic, moral, personal, rational, and spiritual discourse. I also speculate on the interrelationship of these discourses. Finally, in "*Seriatim,* or Sailing into the Wind," I develop the basic dynamic image of my theology: a movement that advances by turning first one way and then another. This is applied to life and to texts.

This part is written is expository prose. However, after the holocaust, as L. Langer and S. Shapiro have argued, nothing should be written without

---

[4] See D. Blumenthal, review of J. Leehan, *Pastoral Care for Survivors of Family Abuse* (Louisville, Ky.: Westminster/John Knox Press, 1989); E. Gil, *Treatment of Adult Survivors of Childhood Abuse* (Walnut Creek, Calif.: Launch Press, 1988); and P. Marcus and A. Rosenberg, *Healing Their Wounds: Psychotherapy with Holocaust Survivors and Their Families* (New York: Praeger Publishers, 1989), *Religious Studies Review* 18:3 (July 1992), 209–11, where I have suggested some of these points. See also pp. 259–261 below, for a fuller discussion of this issue.

caesura, without the disruptive in-breaking in the fullest terms possible of that event.[5] I have tried to honor this by concluding each chapter with something of the dissonance that the holocaust brings into our most thoughtful reflections; hence, the closing sections titled "Meditative Postscript," "Second Thoughts," "Cognitive Dissonance," and "Counter-image." The reader, thus, encounters ideas and counter-ideas, expository theology and irruption of the holocaust.

Part 2 is titled "Text-ing"; it is composed of an introduction and four psalms, each of which has four commentaries. In the introduction, titled "Intimations," I explain the nature of text, interpretation, intertextuality, and the special method by which these psalms and commentaries are written and composed on the page. This method is composed of two parts: commentary as a genre of theological reflection and the "grouped textual field" as a method of text presentation. There are four commentaries. One addresses the philological questions; it is named "Words." One presents spiritual readings of the text drawn from that tradition of commentation; it is called "Sparks." One articulates the ongoing emotional attitudes ("affections, dispositions") of the psalms; it is named "Affections." And one attempts readings across the meaning of the psalm drawn from deconstruction, psychoanalysis, psychotherapy, and the world of child abuse and the universe of the holocaust; it is called "Con-verses." The "grouped textual field" method of text presentation involves nesting the psalm on the page, surrounding it by each of its commentaries. This practice has only recently made its debut in English-language books on theology. It is, however, the classical and standard method of printing Jewish texts, and it is the method I have chosen. This unit, then, addresses the second task of this book: to articulate a Jewish way to do theology through multiple commentaries and a grouped textual field. At the end of "Intimations," I make suggestions on how to read this text.

Psalm 128 defines happiness. "Affections" develops such themes as fear of God, blessedness, erotic and covenantal love, and hierarchies of holiness. "Con-verses" develops such motifs as terror and power, the dangerous woman, womanly blessedness, and the desacralization of hierarchy.

Psalm 44 deals with national rage. "Affections" interprets the rage by reference to the holocaust. It also deals with the motif of land and concludes with a full appreciation of the stance of the psalmist in the closing lines of the psalm. "Con-verses" extends the rage yet further with other meditations on the holocaust. It concludes with the discourse of transgression as a response to the psalm as read in the post-holocaust context.

Psalm 109 is an imprecatory psalm, a text of personal rage. "Affections"

---

[5] See pp. 8–9 below. A similar, though ritual, step was taken after the destruction of the second temple: ceremonies were introduced to commemorate that terrible moment in Jewish history; the most well known is the breaking of a glass at Jewish wedding ceremonies.

interprets the outrage and the rage, enhancing the performative language of the text. It also follows the psalmist into his prayerful resolution. "Con-verses" suggests the theme of abuse and reads the psalm as a response to abuse, including a self-destructive reading. It concludes by returning to the theme of abuse, especially in the relevant scriptural passages, and by rejecting the psalmist's solution as deeply wrongheaded.

Psalm 27 is a text of healing. "Affections" expounds the methods of religious healing as they flow from the psalm and the traditional literature. "Con-verses," drawing upon the literature of psychotherapy, suggests another mode of healing, not always consonant with the religious mode. I address the psychotherapeutic literature only briefly because there are others who deal with it more thoroughly, some of whom are listed in the bibliography.

Having encountered expository prose consciously fragmented by the irruption of the holocaust in part 1, the reader of part 2 will have engaged commentative prose in various styles consciously displayed in a grouped textual field, both of which are distinctively Jewish ways to write theology. The reader will also have come face to face in commentary form with the problem of the book: abuse, God, and our response.

Part 3 is titled "Re-sponse"; it is composed of an introduction and four chapters. This part continues the process of bringing the reader closer to the problem of the book. In "Dialogue with an Adult Survivor of Child Abuse," I share an edited version of correspondence with an academic colleague who is herself a survivor of child abuse and who read the commented psalms in part 2 very carefully over an extended period of time. In her letters, Diane questions my attempting the voice of the abused, sets forth her deep distrust of God, and expresses her skepticism about the possibility of healing for the abused.

In "Dialogue with a Systematic Theologian," I share an edited version of correspondence with a Christian academic colleague who also read the psalms material carefully. In her letters, Wendy questions my understanding of covenant and raises very serious ethical, spiritual, and theological questions to the stance I took in the commentaries. She concludes by wondering if I have really addressed the problem of healing. The reader will, thus, encounter yet another genre of writing, that of correspondence, in which ideas are shared, serious objections raised, and partial answers proposed. In "Beth's Psalm" the author, a student who had been raped, shares her searing exegesis of parts of Psalm 27. With this, the response to part 2 is completed and the reader is ready to return to expository theology, this time dealing directly with the question of the book: How can we speak responsibly of God and to God in situations of child abuse and the holocaust?

Part 4 is titled "Con-templation"; it, too, is composed of an introduction and three chapters. In "The Abusing God," I first explain that the task of the theologian is to stand between God, the tradition, and the people; it is to interpret each to the other. I then return to the biblical texts and suggest that God is abusive. Finally, I address forthrightly the question of abusiveness as an attribute of God.

In "Facing the Abusing God," I draw from the book of Job and Elie Wiesel to suggest that a theology of protest and suspicion, coupled with the religious affections of distrust and challenge, is the proper post-holocaust, abuse-sensitive theological stance. I then present a new form of religious healing rooted in psychotherapeutic method. Finally, I deal with several psychological and theological problems that the proposals in this book have raised.

In "Addressing the Abusing God," I turn from the genre of expository theological writing to prayer and liturgy because all religious thinking must come into the presence of God if it is to be true. I propose a stance from which to address God. I then present five more psalms. Next I offer a universal prayer and several modifications of the traditional Jewish liturgy for the Day of Atonement and the daily penitential prayers. I close with a personal meditation.

The reader of this book, then, will have encountered expository prose, consciously fragmented by the irruption of the holocaust in part 1; will have engaged commentative prose in various styles, consciously displayed in a grouped textual field in part 2; will have met correspondence and poetic commentation as a response to the psalms in part 3; and will have returned to confront expository prose and liturgy in part 4. The range of literary genres is great but important because commentation, grouped textual field, and liturgy are distinctively Jewish modes of expression, thus accomplishing the second task of this book—to display Jewish modes of doing theology. In addition to a serious literary voyage, however, the reader will also have approached, first obliquely and then increasingly more directly, the problem of this book—abuse and God's responsibility in it—and my proposed resolution of this problem. The path, then, is a spiral, moving inexorably inward.

The book closes with indexes, a glossary, and a bibliography.

The map the reader needs to follow is clear. There will be, however, many detours because this reading is hard going, emotionally more than literarily. It is very upsetting to confront the problem of this book, even in its avowedly spiraled presentation. Reading this material forces us to feel rage at gross injustice. It compels us to see aspects of our selves that we would rather not see. And it pushes us powerfully toward a hard look at God, at faith, at sacred texts, and at the dark side of our spiritual lives. At some points, the reader will feel close to an internal abyss. At others, the reader will experience being at the edge of acceptable belief. Probing this material is frightening—emotionally and theologically. It took many years to write this book, and I too approached the abyss more than once. I have only patience, perseverance, and inner courage to offer to those willing to travel this road.

On Matters of Style

To talk about God is to be sensitive to the language we use. As shared consciousness has grown, many have come to realize that the use of exclusively male pronouns to refer to humanity and to God creates the impression that the male reference is somehow more authentic, or better. This is false and, hence, the privileging of male pronouns for general reference seems now unjust. It also excludes women from identifying with the texts and the God portrayed in them. I have, accordingly, adopted the inclusive style of language with reference to fellow human beings and with reference to God. The latter may seem stilted to some, but what is gained in spiritual integrity and in equalizing access to God more than outweighs any stylistic discomfort.[6]

When I discovered myself capitalizing "Golden Calf," I realized the absurdity of grammatically singling out the epitome of idolatry. This led to a decision, motivated by spiritual principle, that I would capitalize only the word "God," together with pronouns and substitute nouns referring to God. Thus, I capitalize God, Lord, Presence, Face, Name, Glory, King, Ayin, Nothing, He or She (where relevant), and similar terms. By contrast, words that are sometimes capitalized but do not need to be, I do not capitalize; hence, for instance: holocaust, messiah, temple, and halakha. I have, however, retained the usual capitalization of names of books, places, and holidays.

Some Hebrew words are basic to understanding Jews and expressing Judaism; for instance, halakha, Shabbat, Torah, sefirot, tikkun. If we are to take the interfaith setting of our work seriously, we must become accustomed to these terms; they ought not to be foreign words. Hence, I do not italicize them.

Together with most young people of my age, I was taught to think in orderly fashion; the "Harvard outline" was the model of clear thinking and writing. Years of experience have taught me, however, that life is not so orderly; neither are the human mind and spirit. Rather, life is like a backstitch; one progresses forward by circling backward. The backstitch is also one of the strongest methods for sewing parts of a garment that really belong together. I have, therefore, followed this method in this book. Ideas appear and reappear; motifs surface in different contexts, with different emphasis; the fabric as a whole actually becomes clearer that way.

Finally, for ease of reference, I have given a full bibliographical reference for each book cited at the first occurrence in each chapter.

---

[6] See, by contrast, my *God at the Center* (San Francisco: Harper & Row, 1988), p. xxx and below, pp. 40–41 and 64, where I have chosen for reasons explained there, to preserve masculine references to God while rigorously using inclusive language for humans.

Personal Acknowledgments

There is no way to thank adequately the people who have helped to make this book possible. First and foremost, I want to acknowledge my profound debt to the students who participated in the seminar in which I first taught this material. They struggled with it, responded to it, and supported me even where they disagreed forcefully with my ideas. I am particularly grateful to Beth, Amy, and Michele Foust, who have given me permission to include some very powerful material they wrote.

Over the years student colleagues have had an enormous influence on one. My gratitude goes out to Maggie Wenig and Naomi Janowitz (then of Brown University) and Ellen Umansky (formerly of Emory University) for their patience in guiding me to a careful consideration of the womanly other. They have suggested books, discussed, and argued over many years, and without them I should be very much the poorer.

I want, particularly, to acknowledge colleagues who have read this material thoughtfully. I am especially grateful to Wendy Farley and Diane for the courage and strength they have shown in their continued correspondence with me. Thanks also go to the many colleagues who commented on drafts of parts of this book: Reverend Jim Leehan, Professor "Tess" Tessier, Father Benedict Groeschel, and Rabbi Avis Miller. My very special thanks to Carl-A. Keller of Lausanne, to Paul Courtright and Michael Broyde of Emory University, and to Alexa Smith of Westminster/John Knox, who read the text very carefully, made many corrections, and gave excellent advice.

Finally, I express my gratitude to the Georgia Council on Child Abuse, which permitted me to attend the monthly supervision session for those brave psychotherapists who daily face the terrible stories of abuse and its repercussions. This book is dedicated to the many who have suffered *and* to the few who help.

The woman to whom this book is dedicated, Dr. Ruth Stein, was a survivor of the holocaust. Tante Rüthchen, as she was known to us, was born in Berlin and lived for a time in Amsterdam. From there she was deported to Bergen Belsen, which was one of the worst camps; the film clips of bulldozers pushing mounds of corpses come from Bergen Belsen. Tante Rüthchen had many stories about the camp. My favorite was when she put a rag on her arm and declared herself a camp nurse though she had no training and, of course, no medications. One night she went out and the guard called, "Halt! Who goes there?" "The nurse," she answered firmly, and he let her pass. After the war, Tante Rüthchen became a psychologist, making it clear to her training analyst that she would not discuss anything of her experience in the camp. Notwithstanding this, Dr. Stein developed into one of the most respected psychologists in St. Gallen and Zurich, where she dealt particularly with children, many of whom came from abused backgrounds. As a survivor and fellow sufferer, Tante Rüthchen knew how to help them, using her own unique mixture of understanding, insight, and humor. Her facial expression, her infectious laugh, and her body language were as much a part of the healing process as her love and professional skill. There are thousands who owe their healing to her. Tante Rüthchen died as I read the proofs for this book; I think she would have approved of it. It is an honor to dedicate it to her memory. May her memory be a blessing to those she helped and an inspiration to all those who survive, who heal, and who are healed.

The ideas put forth here and the genres used are only a beginning, an open door. I welcome correspondence at the Department of Religion, Emory University, Atlanta, GA 30322.

This book contains the holy Name of God in Hebrew. Please treat it with respect and dispose of it properly.

Hanuka, the Feast of Lights, 5753
Winter 1992
Atlanta, Georgia

Acknowledgments

Grateful acknowledgment is made to the following for permission to reproduce copyrighted material.

Jessica Benjamin, *The Bonds of Love.* Copyright © 1988 by Jessica Benjamin. Reprinted by permission of Pantheon Books, a division of Random House, Inc.

Chopp, Rebecca S., *The Power to Speak: Feminism, Language, God.* Copyright © 1989 by Rebecca S. Chopp. Reprinted by permission of The Crossroad Publishing Company.

Primo Levi, *Survival in Auschwitz.* Copyright © 1959 by The Orion Press, Inc., translation. Original copyright © by Guilio Einaudi editore S.p.A. Used by permission of Viking Penguin, a division of Penguin Books USA Inc.

Elie Wiesel, *Night,* translated by Stella Rodway. Originally published in French by Les Editions de Minuit, copyright © 1958. Copyright © 1960 by MacGibbon & Kee. Copyright renewed © 1988 by The Collins Publishing Group. Reprinted by permission of Hill and Wang, a division of Farrar, Straus & Giroux, Inc., and Georges Borchardt, Inc., for the author.

Gisella Perl, *I Was a Doctor in Auschwitz.* Copyright © 1948 by Dr. Gisella Perl. By permission of International Universities Press, Inc.

Alice Miller, *For Your Own Good,* translated by Hildegarde and Hunter Hannum. Translation copyright © 1983 by Alice Miller. Reprinted by permission of Farrar, Straus & Giroux, Inc., and Faber and Faber Ltd.

Naomi Janowitz, "Mizmor Rivka." Reprinted by permission of *Response.*

Personal material written by Beth, Amy, Diane, Wendy Farley, Michele Foust Broemmelsiek, Flora Keshgegian, Margaret Moers Wenig.

Beginning Somewhere

Introduction

Talking About Talking About God

TO BE A THEOLOGIAN is to be on the boundary.

To be a theologian is *to be a voice for the tradition*. It is to speak its words, to teach its message, and to embody its authority. However, there is no single entity one can call *the* tradition. There is no one message, no sole authoritative voice. Rather, the tradition is multivocal, multifaceted; and some of it has been repressed. Hence, no one can speak for the tradition in its entirety.

The voices of the tradition are also conditioned by their contexts. They are male, learned, heterosexual; and they are older voices. They are also rational, mystical, legal, exegetical, and poetical. No one can speak in all these voices, least of all those who are not within the circle of voices which the tradition has, traditional-ly, accepted.

To be a theologian, then, is to accept a prior commitment to speak from out of the tradition and on behalf of some segment of it, with whatever authority one's voice can muster. It is to acknowledge one's limitations, but it is also to listen to the inner resonances of the tradition and to measure one's own music against its inner tones—as best one can.

To be a theologian is also *to speak for God*. It is to have a personal rapport with God, to have a sense of responsibility for God and for how God is understood and related to by our fellow human beings. It is to mediate between God, as one understands God, and those who listen. It is to create an echo of God in the other.

To be a theologian is to defend God, to put back together the pieces of broken awareness and shattered relationship. Great is the suffering of our fellow human beings, and deep is the estrangement between them and God. The theologian must be a healer of that relationship, a binder of wounds, one who comforts.

To be a theologian is also *to speak for one's fellow human beings*, for we are infinite in our complexity, suffering, and ecstasy. It is to have listened to joy, confusion, and despair. It is to have heard praise, rage, and helplessness.

To be a theologian is to be in solidarity with one's fellow human beings before God. It is to take the heart of the other to God. To bless and to share blessing, to be angry and to share rage, to talk the despair of the other to God. It is to talk to God for the people, to address God on their behalf. It is to be angry with God, for them. It is to praise God, with them.

To be a theologian is also *to speak the "ought."* It is not enough to explain, to explicate, and to exegete. It is to make a prior commitment to formulating a vision and to preaching that vision as an ideal toward which humanity should, indeed must, strive. Theology is not a value-free discipline; it is, rather, a value-laden discipline and it should be so consciously, unashamedly.

To be a theologian, then, is *to have prior commitments* — to the tradition, in whatever form one can appropriate it, while acknowledging its multivocity; to the experience of God, in whatever form one experiences that most fully, while acknowledging the difference of the experience of the other; to one's fellow human beings, in their concreteness and in as much of their variety as one can grasp; and to the form of the ought, to the human search for meaning formulated as the ought, taught with passion, involvement, and as much coherence as possible.

To "do theology" is to reflect and to share one's thoughts about, and one's experiences of, God, tradition, community, and meaning. All such theology is confessional, though not in a sectarian sense. It is teaching about God — as embedded in the particular theologian who is, in turn, embedded in his or her tradition and community. To do theology is to create a dialogue between forebear, teacher, and listener. It is to talk from the intertextuality of the traditions, the collective readings of the traditions, the selves of the theologians, the persons of the hearers, and the presence(s) of the divine. Theology flows from the confluence of these "texts." Theology is the intertextual forming of these elements into an interpersonal medium; it is creation. To be a theologian is to create — in the midst, and on the boundaries.

Confessional theology begins in acknowledgment of one's own voices. I am male, middle-class, middle-aged, Jewish, heterosexual, educated in rabbinic tradition, and an academic raised in a bicultural world. And I am committed to the calling of the theologian as a voice for God, for the tradition, for the Jewish people, and for humanity, with a mission to speak the ought. These voices will figure my work; they will set its parameters and generate its metaphors. My theology will be a dialogue between the texts of life, as I experience them, and the texts of the tradition, as I know them. Life will inform my understanding of the tradition, and the tradition will act as an inner resonance against which to measure life. I will speak from within the tradition, as I understand it, but I will speak from within the life of the communities in which I participate, as I understand that. Mine will be an intertextual, confessional theology.

Voice

I did not design my life. I worked hard at each stage but the inner pattern has emerged by itself, sometimes becoming clear only in retrospect.

After early schooling in an intensive religious setting, I attended the University of Pennsylvania (B.A.) and the Jewish Theological Seminary of America (M.H.L., Ordination), where I was dazzled by, and at the same time trained in, the finest traditions of Jewish scientific historical study. My teachers— Professors E. A. Speiser, Moshe Greenberg, Yehezkel Kutscher, Shelomo Dov Goitein, Saul Lieberman, David Weiss-Halivni, Shalom Spiegel, and others— were among the giants of Jewish scholarship of this century. The world of scholarship was followed by the world of the practical rabbinate, and I served for four years as rabbi, teacher, leader, and pastor to a small congregation. Then I returned to *Wissenschaft des Judentums* for my doctorate in medieval Jewish philosophy and mysticism (Columbia University and Ecole pratique des hautes études) with Professor Georges Vajda. I spent the first twelve years of my career working in this field, publishing seven books and numerous articles and reviews. As I look back, I realize that my past work proceeded from Bible to Talmud to medieval thought—a natural, historical progression. Throughout, I had studied the modern period, but I had not done scholarly work in that area.

Years of teaching undergraduates, coupled with the death of my father and most of my teachers, moved me to take up the modern period. It was not, however, historical scholarship about the modern period that attracted me but a deep desire to make an intellectual, theological contribution. I discovered that this impulse, while not common among Jewish scholars, is recognized and indeed carefully cultivated by Christian, particularly Protestant, thinkers under the rubric of constructive or systematic theology. The shift of fields was not simple. When Christians "do" theology, they do it differently; they have different issues and styles. I have had to create a set of issues, as well as a style, which is "Jewish." The task is difficult and far from complete.

My method in this new area of work has been three-pronged. First, I attempt a return to the vocabulary of the holy, the spiritual, as a realm of human experience not reducible to any other realm. In the traditional texts, the vocabulary for the holy is highly nuanced, and I have sought to expose this. Second, I attempt a return to the personalist, psychological language of the tradition. Thus, when speaking of God, I have tried to use the mixture of commonsense and personalist language which characterizes Scripture and many rabbinic sources. Finally, I attempt to set my work in the form of commentary on, and a response to, classical texts. As I see it, a book or an article must be an act of intertextuality, an interplay between a text of life and a classical, traditional text. These three elements help to make what I do "Jewish," in content and style, though Christians could use this method as well.

This book follows my most recent work, *God at the Center,* which, in turn, follows my earlier works *The Place of Faith and Grace in Judaism;* "Mercy"; "Creation: What Difference Does It Make"; "Speaking About God in the Modern World"; and *Understanding Jewish Mysticism.* It takes up the three-pronged approach and advances a step further by including a critical element lacking in the earlier work. At the same time, I continue to write articles, lead conferences, present papers, and, together with my colleagues, develop a program at Emory University which trains students, Christian and Jewish, in an integrated approach to theological thinking. I also remain an active member of the Jewish community and serve on various holocaust and Jewish–Christian task forces.

God's Two Essential Attributes and the Theology of Image

In the middle ages, thinkers debated the question of whether God has any qualities that are crucial to our understanding of God, that are part of God's very essence. Maimonides taught: God is so unlike anything we can think that God cannot have any attributes at all. At our most coherent, therefore, we can only say that God is not a member of the class of beings that possess any given trait or its contrary. This is "negative theology."[1] Saadia Gaon taught: God must have some attributes; the evidence of the tradition and of logic points to this, for otherwise we could not talk of God at all. Hence, there are some qualities that are of God's essence, and others that are just words we use to relate to God. The former are called "essential attributes"; the latter are called "accidental attributes."[2]

In many of the classical sacred texts of the tradition, God walks and talks. God feels anger, despair, and joy. God exercises moral judgment. God even laughs. "Personality" is the quality that best conveys the person-ness of the subject who engages us. It is that congery of emotion, intellect, moral

---

[1] Maimonides, *Guide of the Perplexed,* trans. S. Pines (Chicago: University of Chicago Press, 1963), I:50–58.

[2] Saadia Gaon, *The Book of Beliefs and Opinions,* trans. S. Rosenblatt (New Haven, Conn.: Yale University Press, 1948), II:1–4, 13. For a more complete exposition of these two schools of thought, see D. Blumenthal, "Croyance et attributs essentiels dans la théologie médiévale et moderne" (forthcoming).

judgment, and personal presence that identifies each of us to ourselves and to others. God, too, has personality, according to the texts of the tradition; or, to phrase it more systematically, personality is integral for the understanding of God, according to several major streams of the tradition.[3] Through personality, God is what God is. Through personality, God acts, God relates, God becomes.

Put differently, an important part of the tradition teaches, and our own personal experience confirms, that there is an experience of one's self and of the self-ness of others that enables one to interpret life and the world around one, and to direct oneself toward certain goals. This sense of self has great range and power; it encompasses a complexity that is unimaginable. The depth and fullness of being are clarified in the richness of personality. God too, according to several major streams of the tradition, possesses this depth of personality with all its complexity and grandeur. A trans-personal God, as in some eastern traditions or in certain philosophical understandings of Judaism, is, in my opinion, an incorrect reading of the texts of God's Presence.[4] It contradicts the tradition, as well as common Jewish experience.

In the classical sacred texts of the tradition, God is also holy. God is the spiritual, the numinous. God is the ineffable, the source of awe, the fountain of trembling silence. "Holiness," sometimes called "wholly otherness," is a quality we sense in moments, in people, in texts, and in places. It is our cue to the presence of God in that context. Through holiness, God is utterly remote and also intimately near. Holiness is the quality that best conveys our sense of the sacred. It is an awareness *sui generis;* it is not an extension of the aesthetic or the moral, or a psychological projection.

Put differently, the tradition teaches, and our own personal experience confirms, that there are experiences of the holy; that they are accessible to all persons, some being more sensitive to the holy than others; and that, for people molded by the Jewish tradition, these experiences are located in the sensed presence of God. All the power, eerieness, and sublimity that are entailed in the various experiences of the holy are experienced in God.

Using the language of the medieval thinkers, we can say that God has two essential attributes: holiness and personality. God is incarnate in personality and holiness; so is humanity. God becomes through personality and holiness; so does humanity. God is known and manifest through personality and holiness; so is humanity. Holiness and personality are attributes (Hebrew *yeḥasim*); they are relation and relatedness (Hebrew *yaḥas*).

"And God created humanity in God's image; in the image of God, God created it; male and female, God created them" (Gen. 1:27). This verse

---

[3] For example, Scripture, midrash, liturgy, Talmud, and the Zohar; in contrast to the medieval and modern philosophical-rationalist theological stream. See also pp. 39–43 below.

[4] See the works of A. J. Heschel and M. Kadushim cited below, p. 12 n. 2.

generates "the theology of image" and, for all the streams of Jewish tradition, it is at the core. From it knowledge flows about God and about humanity. From it revelation and piety, obedience and redemption follow. The theology of image, as I understand it, also states the principle of dialogue, of reciprocal addressability. The theology of image implies mutuality of demand and claim. Humanity, in its individual and collective existence, is created in God's image and hence struggles, together with God, to live the depth of that image.

Holiness and personality are the *imago Dei,* the *selem 'Elohim,* the image of God in which humanity is created. God put that image into us (Gen. 1:26–27). God stamped (Hebrew *hitbi'a*) it into us. It is our coin/mold (Hebrew *matbe'a*), our nature (Hebrew *teva'*). It is what God and we have in common. It is that which enables us to talk about, and with, God. Holiness and personality are the core of the theology of image. To do theology faith-fully is to ponder and understand that image, to work with that stamp and that mold, to grasp that nature, and to speak those attributes.

The essential attributes of personality and holiness, then, em-body the theology of image. They reflect the depth, the complexity, the richness, and the otherness of the image. Through them, the image is formed and expressed — for God and for humanity. The theology of image, of God and humanity struggling to articulate personality and holiness, is what an important part of the tradition teaches.

It is this "personalist" theological stream that I shall follow. Perhaps there is more; I do not know.

Irruption

In a series of articles, Susan Shapiro has argued that, in the aftermath of the holocaust, one cannot simply speak; that discourse has been shattered by the irruption of the holocaust into modern consciousness; that language has been ruptured by the in-breaking of the holocaust into common speech.[5] Lawrence Langer, too, has made this point: that the holocaust stands unresolved and unintegrated into the lives of survivors and those who study the holocaust; "a lexicon of disruption, absence and irreversible loss."[6] Others have made the point too.[7] How *can* one speak of beauty or meaning with six million ghosts hovering in the background? How *can* one write poetry or paint in

---

[5] See Susan Shapiro, "Hearing the Testimony of Radical Negation," *Concilium* 175 (1984), 3–10; eadem, "Failing Speech: Post-Holocaust Writing and the Discourse of Postmodernism," *Semeia* 40 (1984), 65–91; and eadem, review of Fackenheim, *Religious Studies Review* 13:3 (July 1987), 204–13.

[6] See L. Langer, *Holocaust Testimonies: The Ruins of Memory* (New Haven, Conn.: Yale University Press, 1991), p. xi.

[7] One thinks of the works of E. Wiesel and Y. Greenberg.

the shadow of the holocaust? How *can* one do theology in the presence of one million burning children?

Caesura, brokenness, fragmentation are all we have to express the disjuncture of normal discourse with the reality of the holocaust. Dissociation, rupture, a sudden veering away are all we have to preserve the holocaust in the midst of normal speech. Thought itself must be broken, shattered, fragmented — like a nightmare; for writing theology after the holocaust is living in a nightmare with its sudden turns, its flashbacks. To do theology is to remember, in pieces, in horrible pieces.

I have tried to capture the nightmare-flashback quality of reasoned reflection in the post-holocaust era by appending a holocaust meditation to each of the chapters in this part; hence, "Meditative Postscript," "Second Thoughts," "Cognitive Dissonance," and "Counter-image." Each consciously seeks to break the flow of thoughtful deliberation. Each intentionally tries to disrupt and fragment the smoothness of the theological discourse. Each is an irruption of that suppressed reality into the careful considerations of reasoned theology. To do otherwise is to repress, to make believe that we can talk now as if there were no ghosts.

Caesura. Fragmentedness. Irruption.

Personality

Personality as an Attribute of God

PERSONALITY[1] HAS many components: each person's individual character—for instance, whether one is intelligent, understanding, verbal, shy, or aggressive; each person's sensitivities—for instance, whether one is musical, insightful, spiritual, or insensitive to suffering; each person's individual history—for instance, whether one was loved well, neglected, traumatized, successful, or abused. There are more.

Personality also includes the ability to make complex moral judgments, to define and to act on right and wrong, good and evil, and all the shades in between. Moral judgment has a vocabulary and conceptuality of its own, but it is an integral part of personality. Moral consciousness runs parallel to, and interacts in very complex ways with, each person's individual character and history.

God, as understood by the personalist stream of the tradition and experience, is personal. So God too must have a character, sensitivities, an individual history, and a moral capacity. These together identify God as a distinct person. The purpose of theology is to get to know this holy person, God.

A substantial segment of the tradition, particularly the philosophical rationalist stream, teaches that no human language can be used of God, that all language about God is metaphoric or analogical. This claim has been strongly rejected, mostly on the grounds that Scripture and rabbinic literature do not use this abstract language. In its place the use of clearly anthropopathic language has been advocated.[2]

---

[1] I have chosen "personality" and not "personhood" because the latter sounds more abstract while the former, because of its connections with psychology, evokes the actual structures of human existence.

[2] See, e.g., A. J. Heschel, *The Prophets,* 2 vols. (San Francisco: Harper & Row, 1962), vol.

The Attribute of Personality and Freud

The problem of describing God's personality and building a theology upon it is complicated by the important social-psychological fact that a large number of theologians and clergypersons have read Freud or, more importantly, have undergone some form of psychotherapy or psychoanalysis. Those of us who have been through this know from deep personal knowledge that our understanding of God, particularly the personal aspect of God's being, has been forcefully molded by our own personalities. We know that we have twisted God's personality to fit our own, and we are wise enough to recognize that others have done this as well, and continue to do so. This raises the question of whether, or to what degree, one can speak of God in a personalist mode. It evokes the problem of transference distortion, which requires a few words.

There is a difference between Freud's metapsychology and his methodology. Freud's metapsychology includes such powerful constructs as the Oedipus complex, ego–id–superego, and eros–thanatos. His methodology includes such potent analytic concepts as transference, resistance, anxiety, countertransference, counterresistance, and counteranxiety. There has been considerable debate about the relationship between these two areas of Freud's enterprise: Are the various metapsychologies consistent? Must the therapeutic field include all of them? Can one use the methodological concepts without the metapsychological constructs?[3]

I share the following opinion:

> In conducting therapy, well trained psychoanalysts of various metapsychologies continue to observe and define relatively similar processes and patterns of relatedness and communication. . . . [D]isagreements [among psychoanalysts] do not arise, strictly, from differing structures of empirical and systematic inquiry. They arise, rather, from conflicting philosophies about life, about which there is still room to differ among rational men [sic].[4]

2; M. Kadushin, *The Rabbinic Mind* (New York: Jewish Theological Seminary, 1952; reprint, New York: Bloch Publishing, 1977), pp. 194–324; D. Blumenthal, review of D. Klemm, *Hermeneutical Inquiry* (AAR Studies in Religion; 2 vols.; Atlanta: Scholars Press, 1986), and R. Chopp, *The Praxis of Suffering* (Maryknoll, N.Y.: Orbis Books, 1986), in *Religious Studies Review* 15 (1989), 122–125; A. Green, "Rethinking Theology: Language, Experience, and Reality," *The Reconstructionist* (Sept. 1988), 8–13; and idem, *Seek My Face, Speak My Name* (Northvale, N.J.: Jason Aronson, 1992; reviewed by me in *Modern Theology* 9:2 [April 1993] 223–225), pp. 25–27. See also Y. Muffs, *Love and Joy: Law, Language, and Religion in Ancient Israel* (New York: Jewish Theological Seminary, 1992), especially chap. 1.

[3] See B. Wolstein, *Theory of Psychoanalytic Therapy* (New York: Grune & Stratton, 1967).
[4] Ibid., pp. 29, 41.

I accept, then, the judgment that, practically, in the therapeutic situation, it is the analysis of phenomena using methodological concepts that is primary and that allows change while the metapsychological constructs provide supplementary, multidimensional structures of interpretive insight.

For theology, this has two implications: First, it is generally *not* useful to engage Freud on the level of his metapsychology. Theology has its own metasystem and it is not clear that Freud's metasystem is inherently any better, or worse, than that of traditional theology. Theologians need not claim Freud's metapsychology as their own; they need only probe their own metasystem utilizing all the modes of analysis available, including those of Freud. For this reason, it can be enlightening to apply Freud's metapsychology to certain religious narratives and rituals (e.g., the stories of the fall or the binding of Isaac, or the rituals of *Kol Nidre* or the Mass) because theologians learn something of the hidden dimensions of meaning in these acts. But this type of study does not lead very far and is, in any case, not a serious discussion of the basic insights of either metasystem.[5]

Second, it *is* very useful to engage Freud on the level of his methodological constructs. Such an encounter forces us to confront the way we project our own parents into our understanding of God. Put differently, God's personality is portrayed by the tradition in its texts. Yet we read God's personality through the screen of our understanding of our own parents. This is our individual transferential distortion of the personalist God of the tradition. The task here, then, is to identify and reduce our own personal distortions of the personalist God portrayed in the sacred texts. This process is very difficult—indeed, it is impossible to separate completely our personal perceptions from our understanding of the tradition. But the task of identifying and reducing our transferential distortions is clear, and it is useful because it yields a deeper personalist theology in which God can possess the most vibrant personality one can allow. It is also an ongoing process, not a one-time effort.

To the task of reducing individual transferential distortions must be added the ongoing task of reducing social-historical distortions, that is, those which are embedded in the formation and transmission of the tradition,[6] as well as the contemporary-communal distortions, that is, those which shape the meanings a given contemporary community will accept.[7] The goal of doing an

---

[5] See, e.g., T. Reik, *Ritual: Four Psychoanalytic Studies* (New York: Grove Press, 1946); idem, *Mystery on the Mountain* (New York: Harper & Row, 1959); and C. Jung, *Answer to Job,* trans. F. C. Hull (Princeton, N.J.: Princeton University Press, 1958).

[6] See the work of H. G. Gadamer and particularly that of the feminist interpreters (e.g., P. Trible, M. Bal), who have shown clearly that the tradition itself is subject to the cultural distortions of its creators, editors, and transmitters.

[7] Three examples: Contemporary scholarship shows clearly the Christian reading of Jewish sources, and vice versa; it shows the occidental bias in reading texts; and it is almost exclusively formulated in the Enlightenment mode, which is not recognized as valid by serious

"objective" theology becomes impossible in light of these tasks; indeed, only local theologies can be articulated, and they must be formulated with as much dignity, honesty, and integrity as possible. The responsibility of the theologian committed to the personalist stream of religious understanding, then, is to try to articulate a relationship with, and an understanding of, God with the realization that no completely objective personalist theology can be written and that any personalist theology must be formulated with the conscious recognition of and reduction of the transferential, as well as the historical and the communal, distortions each person brings to the theological enterprise.

Theology, then, is an exercise in intertextuality. Theology takes the texts of the tradition, as told and modified over the centuries, and reads them over against, and with, the texts of the life of the individual theologian, as that narrative takes shape under the influence of reflection and of the vicissitudes of life, always within the social and psychological contexts of the theologian. One's knowledge of life, community, and tradition become deeper and more nuanced with age and vary from person to person. Life is a never-ending narrative; so is one's appreciation of the tradition. For this reason, the personality of God as disclosed by one thinker differs from that disclosed by another. Moreover, the God one comes to know as a teenager is not the same as the God one knows in mid-life.

The intertextual approach to theology cannot yield an absolute truth, valid for all. It can only lead to partial coherence. Furthermore, the intertextual approach can only lead to partial integration, for we are never whole, nor are we ever at one with the tradition, which is too varied to be fully absorbed in one person. Jewish theology is a theology of fragments, of brokenness. It is an incomplete knowledge, as indeed one's knowledge of oneself and of life is always incomplete. Fragmentedness does not, however, stop one from living, from acting, from enjoying, and from suffering. Nor does it stop one from worshiping, studying, wrestling with, and contemplating God.

Six Personalist Attributes of God

What, then, can a contemporary Jewish theology say about God's personality, given a prior commitment to the personalist understanding of the tradition and of human experience, and bearing in mind humankind's personal and communal distortions?[8]

---

fundamentalist or spiritualist interpreters. One's reading community is highly determinative of what one will accept as readable.

[8] Personalist theology and human psychology remain wary of rigid hierarchies; personality is too flexible, in theory and practice, for such understandings. Hence, these six attributes of God are arranged in no particular hierarchic order.

First, God must be fair. In American English, the word "just" is too strong, for it conjures up the stereotype of a God of law who punishes severely, except insofar as God's mercy overrules the strict requirement of the law. It conjures up, too, the person compulsively pursuing the letter of the law, ignoring the spirit thereof. The word "grace" is also too strong, for it evokes a God who has no standards of justice, who forgives all wrongdoing, thereby undermining God's own teaching of justice. "Fairness" has just the right connotation in American English. God must act fairly, appropriately punishing the wicked, including ourselves, and appropriately rewarding the faithful, including our enemies. "Loving justice" or "just compassion" are also ways to express God's fairness.

In a theology that affirms God's ongoing providence, God's presence in all events, there is, however, the problem of acts of God which are not fair, which do not embody God's just compassion: the suffering of the innocent and the just; natural and human disasters, which strike good and evil persons indiscriminately; child abuse, infant death, debilitating pain, holocaust. This problem is not new, and many answers—theodicies—have been proposed. The beginning of a "solution" to the problem of theodicy in personalist theology is to say that fairness implies dialogue; that there is a standard by which to judge and a means of accumulating credit and debit in all relations, even in our relationship with God and in God's relationship with us. All humankind's acts are debatable; all God's judgments are arguable. Faithfulness, trust, and openness to dialogue are basic. Text, life, and moral dialogue are intertwined.

The texts in the tradition supporting God's fairness and the implied dialogue between humanity and God are numerous: Abraham arguing with God over the destruction of Sodom (Genesis 18), Job's uncompromising defense of his innocence, Levi Yitzhak's defense of the sinners of Israel.[9] All these texts teach that God is bound by fairness and, hence, is committed to moral dialogue. Not that there is some external force inherent in nature or being that compels God to be fair, for there is no force external to God in monotheistic thought; God, unlike God's creatures, is totally autonomous. Rather, morality is an integral part of all personality. Hence, it is integral to the being of God and, then, to God's creation.

Second, God addresses, and can be addressed by, humankind. Although God is totally autonomous, God can be influenced. God can be angered or pleased by what humans do. In the words of the medieval thinkers, God is passible. Ultimately, this means that God can be induced by human words

---

[9] On Levi Yitzhak, see S. Dresner, *The World of a Hasidic Master* (New York: Shapolsky, 1986); and D. Blumenthal, *God at the Center* (San Francisco: Harper & Row: 1988). On the tradition of moral dialogue with God, see Anson Laytner, *Arguing With God: A Jewish Tradition* (Northvale, N.J.: Jason Aronson, 1990; reviewed by me in *Modern Judaism* 12:1 [Feb. 1992], 105–110).

and behavior to change God's mind, to reverse a decision, to alter a judgment. This insight is sometimes formulated as "the efficacy of prayer" or "original repentance."

God can, and did, also address humankind; for creation, majestic and beautiful though it is, does not have the power of judgment. It is natural, morally neutral. Hence, there is no "natural moral law." For guidance, God addressed humankind, and God's presence continues to draw humanity onto the path God wishes. Furthermore, God's guidance causes humans anguish, joy, guilt, and satisfaction. Human beings, too, are passible.

This com-munication, this mutual addressing of one another, is central to the dialogic nature of creation-revelation-piety. It constitutes the interrelatedness of humankind and God. It is the ground of the intertextuality of divine and human existence.

Third, God is powerful but not perfect. God makes mistakes and admits it, as after the flood of Noah (Gen. 8:21–22). God lets Godself be seduced by Satan, as in the prologue of Job. God is unnecessarily short-tempered with the Jewish people, as Moses reminds God (Ex. 32:7–14; Num. 14:11–20). And God repents (Gen. 6:6; Ex. 32:14; 1 Sam. 15:11, 35; 2 Sam. 24:16). Some argue that all such incidents are just acting, that they are a testing of humankind, but that does not seem to be the simpler meaning of the texts. Zoharic and Lurianic mysticism, too, seem to have left room for God's imperfection.[10]

God, however, does have power. God's power is absolute, but God cannot use it absolutely. For, having created a being also capable of moral judgment, God must limit God's own power so as to empower the being God created. Humankind too, thus, has power, though not as much as God. Power is dialectical. It is the intertextuality of God's and humankind's expectations.

Fourth, God is loving. There are many ways to love. There is erotic love—passionate, searing, erratic. There is virtuous love—ongoing, nurturing, morally rooted. There is parental love—protective, demanding, guiding even in its anger.

Sometimes love is unilateral; sometimes it is dialogic. Sometimes love is sacrificial; sometimes it is commanding, imperial. Sometimes love is open, articulated clearly; sometimes it is hidden, veiled.

Love is a breast—warm, comforting. Love is smooth ivory—alive, vibrant. A pounding heart—breathless, terrified. A glance deep into another's eyes, into being beyond existence. The innocent embrace of a child. The gratitude of an elderly person not forgotten.

Love is the affirmation of the other, given and received in wholeness. And forgiveness. Love is the presence of moral truth and goodness.

---

[10] See D. Blumenthal, *Understanding Jewish Mysticism* (New York: KTAV Publishing House, 1978), vol. 1, pp. 101–184. For other passages, see pp. 263–264 below.

Love is also the commitment to lead a life dedicated to truth and goodness. It is the stubborn perseverance on the way, no matter what the obstacle, the temptation, the sin.

Love is not smooth. It wrenches, it drags one along, it demands. And love frustrates; it causes deep anger. How does one love one's parent without superimposing that image on the child? How does one love one's child who rebels forcefully? How does one love the dying other?

Love is exclusive, dedicated to special persons in special ways. And love is inclusive, reaching from one to an-other, seeking to embrace the stranger.

Love does not tolerate injustice; it impels one to action. Love forces one from security and lethargy into the world of the impersonal and evil. Love demands confrontation, risk, and danger; not foolhardiness but courage.

Because it is many and varied, love is contradictory. Love is not monolithic. It cannot be rationalized into a coherent whole, into a system or a single theology. Love is much more complex than its metaphors.

God loves all humanity, and individual human beings, in all these ways— as human beings love others and seek to be loved, in all these ways. Life moves; love leads, and follows. Human beings touch the text of God's love and of human love. We enter it. We read it and ponder it. And it touches us, permeates us, puzzles and pains us, gives us life and demands death. Love, in all its complexity, makes us blossom and become that which we are destined to be. Even unilateral love is intertextual.

Fifth, God gets angry. There is anger that is righteous indignation in the face of moral iniquity. This is God's anger spoken by the prophets and the prophets' anger spoken on behalf of God; an interface, an intertext. "Woe unto the pinnacle of the crown of the drunkards of Ephraim!" (Isa. 28:1). "Shall one steal, kill, fornicate, swear falsely, make offerings to Baal, and follow other gods whom you do not even know; and then come and stand before Me, in this house upon which My name is called, and say 'We are saved,' only to go and do again those abominations?!" (Jer. 7:9–10). "You are the man!" (2 Sam. 12:7).

The anger of righteous indignation is rooted in covenant and, because covenant is rooted in mutuality, when human beings feel righteous indignation toward God, they speak it to God, for the sake of the covenant.[11] "Why do You ignore my soul, Lord? Why do You hide Your Face from me? You have alienated lover and friend from me, my acquaintances are darkness" (Ps. 88:15, 19). "Have we forgotten the name of our God? Have we spread our hands in prayer to a foreign deity? God may probe this, for God knows the hidden things of the heart. In truth, we have been killed all day long because of You; we have been treated as sheep led to the slaughter. Awake! Why do You sleep,

---

[11] There is a general covenant with all humanity, through Adam and Noah, and a specific covenant with the Jewish people, through Sinai. Both are the ground for the appeal to God's fairness.

Lord?!" (Ps. 44:21–24). "Why do You forget us forever? Why do You desert us for days without end?" (Lam. 5:20). If there is a post-holocaust Jewish theology, it is this theology of anger and protest, of righteous indignation, rooted in the intertext of the covenant, in mutual expectations and obligations.[12]

There is, however, also an anger which flows from bitterness, which springs from deep frustration and wells up from the recesses of the subconscious. God creates humankind and humanity turns rotten, "the instincts of the heart of humanity being evil from its earliest days" (Gen. 8:21). God brings the Jewish people out of Egypt with signs and wonders, and they rebel, building themselves a golden calf, murmuring against God and Moses, challenging Aaron, refusing the assault on the land and then leading one against God's wishes. Moses knows they will sin again. And, later, they ask for a king—not realizing that they already have a King. Neither the rod of Babylon nor the scourge of Rome teaches the lessons. God gets angry at God's stiff-necked people and punishes them.[13]

The people do not understand. Their anger, too, springs from bitterness, from frustration, from the depths of the unconscious. They ask God's vengeance upon their enemies. "Pour out Your wrath against the nations who have not acknowledged You" (Ps. 79:6). "Happy is he who will grab your children and smash them on the rocks, Oh Babylon" (Ps. 137:9). Many, many rabbinic responsa from the holocaust end with the angry imprecation, "May God avenge the blood of the innocent."

There is nothing wrong with these kinds of anger. If one loves passionately, zealously, one expects great things. God loves humanity and humanity loves God. The anger of righteous indignation has its place. So does the anger of bitterness and vengeance.

There is, however, a particularly human kind of anger that does not apply to God. Human beings sometimes displace their anger; that is, they express anger at one person when they are really angry at something or someone else entirely. Tension in one's work can sometimes spill over into anger against one's children or spouse; or tension in a marriage can spill over into one's workplace. This displaced anger, while natural to human beings, is not known to God. The texts do not speak of it, and the unfairness of it mitigates against it being a part of the personality of God.[14]

[12] See D. Blumenthal, *The Place of Faith and Grace in Judaism* (Austin, Tex.: Center for Judaic-Christian Studies, 1985); and idem, "Mercy," in *Contemporary Jewish Religious Thought,* ed. A. Cohen and P. Mendes-Flohr (New York: Charles Scribner's Sons, 1987), pp. 589–595. See also E. Wiesel, *The Trial of God* (New York: Schocken Books, 1979); and Laytner, *Arguing With God,* 196ff. For a fuller discussion, see pp. 249–257 below.

[13] See H. Fisch, *Poetry with a Purpose: Biblical Poetics and Interpretation* (Bloomington, Ind.: Indiana University Press, 1988), pp. 140–142, that God wrestles with God's anger against Israel as it is undermined by God's love. See my review in *Midstream* (August–September 1992), 41–43.

[14] This is the basis for the argument in the book of Job. I disagree with Jung (*Answer to Job*)

Sixth, God chooses; God is partisan. No one likes to hear this, but God chooses and, having chosen, God jealously guards that which is God's; and God demands loyalty from those whom God chooses.

God chose to create the world. It is God's possession; it belongs to God. For exactly that reason, no one may abuse it or lay absolute claim to it.

God chose the Jewish people. They too, in their flesh, are God's possession; they belong to God. For exactly that reason, no one may abuse them or lay claim to absolute authority over them.

God chose the holy land. God resides in it. God's people reside in it. The holy land, in its mountains and valleys, in its rocks and trees, is God's possession; it belongs to God and to God's people. For exactly that reason, no one may abuse the land or the people's right to it. The people must respect God's land because the land is theirs, from God.

The election of the Jews was always a scandal, an incomprehensible thought. How could a universal God elect one people from among the myriads of creation? Non-Jews never understood, and they have hated Jews because of the claim — especially Christians and Muslims, who trace their own chosenness to the same God. Jews have differed in their reactions. Some have rejoiced in their specialness; others, particularly modern Jews, have been embarrassed by it. But, if God has personality, of course God has preferences. All persons have preferences for certain other people. Personality means having a character and a history, and character and history mean having preferences, being partial, partisan. One need not always act on one's preferences. And one must always carefully consider one's preferences and the consequences of acting on them. But preference is core to personality. Therefore, the scandal of particularity is core to theology.[15]

There is no real reason for one's preferences. It is chemistry, history, the template of the face, a look in the eye. It is biological, corporeal; it may be spiritual. It is blood. In real life, preference is balanced by culture, reason, and religion — it may not be used to justify a misuse of power — but preference itself is real, unreasoned.

To be partisan is to be loyal and to demand loyalty. It is to accept the election and to remain faithful to the elector. It is to acknowledge that the one who chooses has a right to demand fidelity. Choosing creates a bond. Among humans, partiality is almost absolute; in God, preference is inalienable. Among humans, a marriage can end in divorce; not so God's marriage to humanity

---

on this, though it is possible — indeed probable — that, in a personalist-image theology, God's personality includes a subconscious.

[15] See M. Wyschogrod, *The Body of Faith: Judaism as Corporeal Election* (New York: Seabury Press, 1983; reviewed by me in *Association for Jewish Studies Review* 11 [1986], 116–121); and D. Hartman, *A Living Covenant* (New York: Free Press, 1985; reviewed by me in *Association for Jewish Studies Review* 12 [1987], 298–305). One can even read the book of Genesis as an essay in chosenness and rejection.

in general and, more specifically, to the Jews. The Jews are God's bride, God's children, God's bloodline. There is no escape, either for God or for the Jewish people. God does, and must, guard the Jews and the Jews do, and must, remain loyal to God.

One may challenge certain acts of loyalty or protection; indeed, the blessing of moral judgment obligates one to this. One may question specific demands of the covenant; indeed, the blessing of mind obligates one to this. Revelation and creation empower, and make it one's duty, to question, to challenge, and to disagree. One may even disown a demand or disclaim an act, but never the bond. Election and covenant demand faithfulness, even as the specifics are debatable.

The joy of chosenness is the knowledge that one is special. It is the joy of the firstborn, the comfort of knowing one is elected, forever, absolutely. The pain of chosenness is the sureness of being hated by everyone else, the certainty of persecution at the hands of others independent of one's behavior toward them. Nothing I can do will change my status; this is joy and burden.

Meditative Postscript

A suckling infant stares at its mother's face; a senile person follows a face as it moves through the field of vision. Face is the first thing we see; it is also the last act of full recognition that we experience. Face is the basic template of personhood. Face is presence, and presence is face.

The Face of God is God's Presence; God's Presence is present in God's Face—which is why Face, and only Face, is capitalized.

We seek the Face of God, we look for it, we search for it, we long for it: "As a deer yearns for a stream of water, so my inner being yearns for You, God. My innermost self thirsts for the living God; when shall I come and see / be seen by Your Face" (Ps. 42:2–3).

We study God's Face, we look at it, we ponder it, we question it: "Study the Lord and the Lord's mightiness; seek God's Face in all times and places" (Ps. 105:4). What kind of Face does God have? What does it communicate? What do we read when we read God's Face, God's Facial expression?

We rejoice to see God's Face; it is a light for us, it shines upon us and we are jubilant: "May the Lord cause the Lord's Face to shine upon you, and may God be gracious unto you" (Num. 6:25).

We also fear God's Face, we flee God: "Where can I go away from Your spirit and where can I flee from Your Face" (Ps. 139:7). We hide our face from God: "Moses hid his face because he was afraid to look upon God" (Ex. 3:6). Jonah.

God hides God's Face from us and we are left existentially alone, isolated, without Presence. This undermines our presence, our orientedness; it constricts our face: "You hid Your Face; I was terrified" (Pss. 30:8; 104:29). And we yearn even more deeply to see God's Face again, to be seen by God's Face again, to return to God's Presence: "My heart echoed You saying, 'Seek My Face'; I do seek Your Face, Lord" (Ps. 27:8).

A face, God's Face, has many facets: anger, joy, shame, pain, light, severity, humor, doubt, kindness, waiting, expectation. There are as many facets to F/face as there are modes of relatedness.

F/face has ten special expressions: inexpressibility, wisdom, understanding, grace, power, judgment, timelessness, beauty, fundamentality, and majesty (Zohar).

F/face is the meeting point of the inner self and the outer world. F/face is the welling-forth of inexpressibility and inner depths into the stream of manifest consciousness. It is the majestic portal of expression of, and access to, grace, power, judgment, and beyond. F/face is the veil which renders the invisible visible. It is the gateway to the S/soul, the allusion to P/presence (Zohar).[16]

But, what does one say when the F/face is cold, angry, forbidding? Where does one look when one is too intimidated to look upon the F/face?

'God, Full of Compassion'[17]

'God, full of compassion' —

Were it not for the God, full of compassion,

there would be compassion in the world, and not just in Him.

I, who picked flowers on the mountain

and gazed into all the valleys,

I, who carried corpses from the hills,

know and tell that the world is empty of compassion.

I, who was the king of salt by the side of the sea,

who stood without decision by my window,

who counted the steps of the angels,

whose heart lifted weights of pain

---

[16] See also Green, Seek My Face, pp. 28–37.

[17] A poem by the Israeli poet Yehuda Amihai, taken from his collection Shirim, 1948–62 (Jerusalem: Schocken Books, 1976), pp. 69–70 (my translation). The title and initial words are drawn from the liturgy for the dead, and the second line involves a play on words that cannot be captured in English.

in terrible competitions,
I, who use only a small portion
of the words in the dictionary

I, who am compelled against my will to solve riddles,
know that, were it not for the 'God, full of compassion,'
there would be compassion in the world,
and not just in Him.

CHAPTER
3 *Holiness*

Holiness as an Attribute of God

HOLINESS IS A QUALITY. One senses it in objects, in moments, in texts, and in certain people. It is not a feeling like joy or anger. It is not a commitment like love or loyalty. It is not a state of mind like happiness or gloom. It is not a thought or concept. It is an awareness of the sacred, a consciousness of the spiritual. It is an experience of the *mysterium tremendum et fascinans,* a contact with the numinous. It is a perception of otherness, an intimation of the beyond.[1]

> The truly "mysterious" object is beyond our apprehension and comprehension, not only because our knowledge has certain irremovable limits, but because in it we come upon something inherently "wholly other," whose kind and character are incommensurable with our own, and before which we therefore recoil in a wonder that strikes us chill and numb.[2]

> [H]oliness is the abstract term taught man [*sic*] by God to mark God's difference and the nature of everything that comes to be included . . . within his difference. . . . That which enters the class of things of which he is a member ("holiness") loses its provenance in nature and history at the moment it is restored to the precinct of divinity. . . . From the standpoint of human experience, therefore (the point of view

---

[1] R. Otto, *The Idea of the Holy* (New York: Oxford University Press, 1958), chap. 27. Otto, following Schleiermacher, characterizes these moments as *Gefühle,* usually translated as "affections." However, the English translator, following the popular German usage, renders this as "feelings." "Feelings," as I see them, are more transient, while "awarenesses" or "moments of consciousness" are more intense and less the product of psychological stimuli. I also distinguish "feelings" from "dispositions" or "sustained emotional attitudes," the latter being more enduring and constituting virtues to be cultivated (see D. Saliers, *The Soul in Paraphrase: Prayer and the Religious Affections* [New York: Seabury Press, 1980] and p. 59 below).

[2] Otto, *Idea of the Holy,* p. 28.

of language), holy is not in the ordinary sense a predicate, a word that asserts something about a term, but the sign of withdrawal of all reference into its source, a determinator of the radical disablement of metaphor and the absolute preemption of the truth of discourse at the supremely privileged moment of reference to reality.[3]

The holy is encountered in many places and moments: in the grandeur of nature, in the still, small voice of conscience, in the silence of the soul, and in the rapture of beauty. It can be found in creativity of the mind, in gentleness of the heart, in the eye of a lover, and in the innocence of a child. The holy meets one in the depth of sacred texts, in moments of prayer, and in those rare moments when one truly meets an-other.

The holy approaches when one is weak or when one is strong. It draws near when one is least expecting it. The holy can be sought but it cannot be found. It breaks in upon awareness. It interrupts.

In the language of the tradition: "Holy, holy, holy is the Lord of hosts; the fullness of the universe is God's Glory. . . . And I said, 'Woe unto me; I am struck dumb, for I am a man of impure lips and I live among a people of impure lips, and now my eyes have seen the King, the Lord of hosts'" (Isa. 6:1–8). "You are holy, God Who dwells above the praises of Israel" (Ps. 22:4). "Holy are You and awesome is Your Name; there is nothing divine other than You. . . . Blessed are You, the holy King."[4]

Words That Go in Circles

There are no words; or rather, the words go in circles. The holy is a quality *sui generis*. One knows it intuitively, as one knows beauty. It is irreducible. It can only be described by synonyms or by the traces it leaves. The holy is ineffable, yet it is identifiable. One can point to it and say, "This is holy," without being able to say what, or how, or why. One can identify the holy without being able to describe it, except by the word "holy" and its synonyms.

The circle of the holy superimposes itself on other circles as one tries to grasp the holy and to live within it. As one integrates the holy into life, one needs other words. One reaches outward: King, Lord, Name, justice, beauty, purity, Shabbat, Israel, You. One probes inward: awe, wonder, radical amazement, sublime, love, joy, bliss, bless, worship. One gropes for forms: holy day, temple, mitsva, liturgy, charity, study, Torah, acts of kindness, martyrdom. The failure of language is transformed into a rich vocabulary of response,

[3] A. Grossman, "Holiness," in *Contemporary Jewish Religious Thought,* ed. A. Cohen and P. Mendes-Flohr (New York: Charles Scribner's Sons, 1987), pp. 389–390. See also A. Green, *Seek My Face, Speak My Name* (Northvale, N.J.: Jason Aronson, 1992; reviewed by me in *Modern Theology* 9:2 [April 1993] 223–225).

[4] The New Year liturgy, in *The Authorized Daily Prayer Book,* ed. J. Hertz (New York: Bloch Publishing, 1960), p. 850.

always haunted by its own muteness. Silence overflows into words, an echo of an unfathomable depth.

The holy is intimately related to the beautiful, the personal, and the moral.

The holy need not be beautiful: "Here is Behemoth which I have made; in comparison with you . . ." (Job 40:15); Behemoth was ugly, yet holy as creature. However, the beautiful can be holy, and the holy can be beautiful: "Bow down to the Lord in the beauty of holiness" (Pss. 29:2; 96:9). And yet, the holy is more than the beautiful; it enfolds it.

The personal and the holy overlap: "You are my God; I search everywhere for You; my soul thirsts for You; my body yearns for You. . . . Indeed, I have visions of You in the holy place" (Ps. 63:2–3). "You are holy and Your Name is holy. . . . Blessed are You, the holy God."[5] But the holy is more than the personal; it envelops it.

The moral and the holy are coterminous: "The holy God is made holy by righteousness" (Isa. 5:16); "You shall be holy for I, the Lord your God, am holy" (Lev. 19:2). The holy cannot be immoral or amoral. Still, the holy is more than the moral; it encompasses it.

The holy, the beautiful, the moral, and the personal overlap and interact with one another. The beautiful may be holy but, if the beautiful is immoral or unnatural, it is not holy, no matter how beautiful it is. The personal can be holy but, if the personal is immoral or unnatural, it is not holy, no matter how intense it is. The moral must be holy but it need not be beautiful, perhaps not even personal.[6]

Kavvana and the Attribute of Holiness

How does one integrate the unintegratable? How does one live within that which is wholly other? There are two kinds of kedusha (holiness).[7]

There is hierarchical kedusha. It is "a sensed mystical quality of certain objects, days, and persons."[8] The tradition ranks these in hierarchies; for example, the sequence of locations within the holy land, the set of sacrifices, the ranks of priesthood, and the degrees of impurity and purity.

There is also nonhierarchical kedusha. It is created by an individual act of will.[9] By it, one declares an object consecrated to God. Through it, one

---

[5] The daily liturgy, in Authorized Daily Prayer Book, ed. Hertz, p. 137.

[6] See pp. 33–43 below, where I have set forth these universes of discourse and their overlapping.

[7] The following discussion is based on M. Kadushin, Worship and Ethics (Chicago: Northwestern University Press, 1964), pp. 216–237. See also A. J. Heschel, God in Search of Man (New York: Meridian Books, 1951), part 3.

[8] Kadushin, Worship and Ethics, p. 216.

[9] See also J. Neusner, Judaism: The Evidence of the Mishnah (Chicago: University of Chicago Press, 1981), pp. 270–281.

dedicates an act to God. It is a function of mitsva, of commanded act, and
of the intention to fulfill that command. Holiness is generated by *kavvana*,
by intent to holiness.

> Rather than just a mystical quality alone, *kedushah* is now something that must
> be achieved through effortful personal conduct. . . . The *kedushah* achieved through
> fulfilling the *mizwot* is throughout, therefore nontheurgical. Instead, it is an
> experience in normal mysticism, an experience of a close relationship with God. . . .
> Such an experience of relationship can take place, of course, only when a *mizwah*
> is fulfilled with *kawwanah*. Indeed, *kawwanah* in this connection, we have noticed,
> itself implies an awareness of a relationship with God, a consciousness that a
> particular *mizwah* is a communication by God here and now. . . . During the process
> of performing a *mizwah* with *kawwanah*, a person has an experience of *kedushah*.
> It is a mystical experience and yet, being normal mysticism, it is in some degree
> describable.[10]

Holiness, then, is a matter of experience. It is an awareness that humans
bring to the performance of the acts of daily living. Holiness is focused openness to holiness. It is numinous otherness within the mundane same; the
ineffable within the effable.

Kavvana is the mode of consciousness by which one performs ordinary acts
yet remains alert to the dimension of holiness concealed in them. *Kavvana*
is the method by which one holds the presence of the holy in one's mind while
doing everyday deeds: "I sleep but my heart waketh."[11] *Kavvana* is the process
by which one opens one's consciousness to the multiple levels of reality that
are implicit in any act, particularly to the sacred dimensions of action. *Kavvana*
is the way one transforms routine acts into moments of awareness of the
ineffable. *Kavvana* is the key to nonhierarchical holiness, to the holiness which
does not greet one but which, rather, one must achieve.

"Normal mysticism" comes closest to describing the way one integrates the
unintegratable. Everyday acts with everyday objects, when handled with an
intent to be aware of the holy, yield a mysticism that is not ecstatic, not
annihilative, and not theurgical, but "normal," habitual, usual. Life, which
is composed of commonplace events, when approached with a willingness to

---

[10] Kadushin, *Worship and Ethics*, pp. 224–225, 232. I have not changed the spelling to conform to my own. Thus: *kedushah=kedusha; mizwah=mitsva;* and *kawwanah=kavvana.*

[11] The quotation is from Song of Songs 5:2 and is used by Maimonides in his *Guide of the
Perplexed* III:51, trans. S. Pines (Chicago: University of Chicago Press, 1963), p. 623, to allude
to the ongoingness of *kavvana*. For a fuller discussion of the levels of *kavvana*, see D. Blumenthal,
Understanding Jewish Mysticism (New York: KTAV Publishing House, 1982), vol. 2, pp. 112–116,
reprinted in idem, *God at the Center* (San Francisco: Harper & Row, 1989), pp. 186–190 (see
also the index there) and in *News Notes* ([Fellowship of United Methodists in Worship, Music,
and Other Arts, Atlanta] summer 1989), 3–5. When I wrote this passage, I was not yet sensitive
to inclusive language but it should be read in that style and tone.

be open to the sacredness of all existence, yields a spirituality that is customary, regular, familiar.[12]

The holy is, thus, encountered in the wholly other, at the edge of human existence. But the holy is also met in the confluence of the wholly other with the wholly mundane, at the center of normal existence. The holy is ec-static, standing outside; it is also famili-ar, standing within. God is holy person; humankind, created in God's image, is holy person.

Holiness, Fear, and Joy

Holiness overwhelms. It compels; it frightens. And holiness also comforts; it draws forth; it embraces. Holiness pervades existence and consciousness. There is no escape—neither from the *tremendum* nor from the intimate holiness of God's presence. The holy engenders fear, but the holy does not frighten God.

The human flees the holy. Moses pleads inexperience (Ex. 3:11–4:17). Isaiah pleads impurity (Isa. 6:5). Jeremiah pleads youth (Jer. 1:4–10). Ezekiel must be coerced (Ezek. 2:8–3:3). Jonah takes flight. The psalmist cries:

> Where can I go away from Your spirit and where can I flee from Your face? If I rise to heaven, You are there; if I plunge into the netherworld, You are there. If I travel on the wings of dawn or dwell at the end of the world, there too Your hand will rest upon me and Your right hand seize me. If I say, "Let darkness envelop me and let night be light for me," even darkness is not dark for You and night is as lit up as day; like darkness, like light. For You have possessed my insides; You encompassed me even in the womb of my mother. (Ps. 139:7–13)

Sin leads one away from the holy; it tempts. The forms of temptation are as many as the imagination: the tasks of daily living, sexual fantasy, ambition, despair. Purity and sin fluctuate; hope and despair alternate.

> Be generous to me, God, according to Your gracious love; in the abundance of Your compassionate love, wipe away my rebellion. . . . Truly, I know my rebellion; my sin is before me always. I have sinned before You alone and I have done evil in Your eyes. . . . Let me hear joy and gladness; let my bones which You have oppressed rejoice. . . . Hide Your Face from my sins and wipe away my iniquities. . . . Do not cast me away from before You, nor take Your holy presence away from me." (Ps. 51:3–14)

Holiness and sin are lovers; fear and flight are indissolubly linked to the call of holy presence. To know one is to know the other; to be attached to one is to cling to the other. Humankind struggles to incarnate the one and to resist the other, but they are a pair. God, too, struggles to let the one

---

[12] M. Kadushin, *The Rabbinic Mind* (New York: Jewish Theological Seminary, 1952; reprint, New York: Bloch Publishing, 1977), esp. pp. 20–23.

preponderate over the other: "May it be My will that My compassionate love predominate over My anger, overwhelming My other qualities, so that I comport Myself with the quality of compassionate love toward My children, engaging them beyond the requirements of the law."[13]

Joy is not happiness.

Happiness comes from setting goals and achieving them. Happiness is social. It is a state of well-being derived from those around us. Not everyone is happy, and no one is happy all the time; yet we all know happiness from time to time.

Joy is an inner awareness, a moment of insight through our selves into that which is beyond. It is a connectedness between our inner being and that which transcends it.

Happiness requires contention, fighting for what one believes, compromise; joy is a moment of wholeness, and purity. Happiness is rooted in time and space; joy suspends us in a realm beyond ourselves.

Joy can strike us at any time. But it is more likely to come to us in moments of service, at times when we see ourselves within the larger meaning that embraces reality. Joy derives not from accomplishment but from centeredness within the greater whole.

> The rule is that, when a saint worships God, even the simple people have joy because the pious, by performing their mitsvot, bring blessing and joy to all the worlds. Thus, it happened that the people of the city of Shushan who were not Jews also had joy even though they did not know its cause, for Mordecai's stewardship brought blessing and joy on *all* the people, as it says, "the city of Shushan" — that is, its people, the non-Jews — "was cheerful and joyous" (Esther 8:15–16). But the Jews had special reason to be joyous because they had been saved from Haman. And the rule is that, when a person knows the reason why he or she is happy, then he or she experiences a joyous light, for reason enlightens them as to the purpose of things. Therefore, it also says, "and the Jews had light and joy" (ibid.)[14]

There are many kinds of joy.

There is the joy of knowing that God loves us, of knowing that we are objects of God's grace. And there is the joy of having served God, of having done a mitsva simply because it brings pleasure to the Creator.

> By the acts which people had to do — to plant and to sow, to raise cattle and to sacrifice — the Creator, blessed be He, caused the flow of blessing to descend upon them. . . . When Israel was in the desert, however, they were in the state that the Holy One, blessed be He, showered His blessing upon them because of His great

---

[13] Talmud, Berakhot 7a, used in modified form in the High Holiday liturgy, in *Authorized Daily Prayer Book,* ed. Hertz, p. 882; see also below, pp. 263 and 290–291.

[14] See D. Blumenthal, *God at the Center,* p. 205. Levi Yitzhak was a nineteenth-century hasidic master beloved by all. He wrote a compilation of homilies entitled *Kedushat Levi.* This quotation is taken from that compilation. On Levi Yitzhak, see *God at the Center,* pp. xiv–xvi; and S. Dresner, *The World of a Hasidic Master* (New York: Shapolsky, 1986).

grace as in the case of the manna and the well of water for, in these, there was no action of humans at all.[15]

There is the joy of seeing the solution to a problem, and the joy of actually solving it.[16]

There are also the joys of worship:

One should tremble and faint when standing to pray before the great King. And it is proper that one's limbs shake. Similarly, after praying, one should think, "How can I dare to bring out of my mouth useless words and enjoy them? Have I not just spoken before the great and awesome King? And will I not have to speak again before Him Whose Glory fills the universe?"[17]

For when one meditates well on the greatness of the Creator, may He be blessed, — that He is the root and principle of all worlds, that He encompasses and fills all reality, that no thought can grasp Him at all, and that all the worlds, souls, and angels are all annihilated and as nothing and emptiness before Him — then one's soul is awakened to yearn and to be consumed in the flame of sweetness, bliss, and love. Then, one desires and has a passion to worship God at all times . . . one's heart is enflamed to worship God.[18]

Even God experiences joy.

A person, in his or her worship of God, may He be blessed, through Torah and mistvot, brings great joy above. And so, when a person wants to know if God, may He be blessed, has joy from this worship, the criterion is this: If one sees that one's heart burns like a fire and that one feels religious enthusiasm always to worship Him and that one has a passion and a will to worship the Creator, then it is certain that God, may He be blessed, has joy from that person's worship.[19]

The holy is joy-ful, even as it is fear-ful.

Second Thoughts

Does one have a right to speculate about God this way? Has the holocaust not intervened to force a distortion of categories, a rupture of language itself?

On the march to work, limping in our large wooden shoes on the icy snow, we exchanged a few words, and I found out that Resnyk is Polish; he lived twenty years at Paris but speaks an incredible French. He is thirty, but like all of us, could be

[15] Blumenthal, *God at the Center*, p. 75, quoting Levi Yitzhak's *Kedushat Levi.*
[16] Ibid., p. 197.
[17] Ibid., p. 37, quoting Levi Yitzhak's *Kedushat Levi.*
[18] Ibid., pp. 152, 148–150, 183–185, quoting Levi Yitzhak's *Kedushat Levi.*
[19] Ibid., p. 56, quoting Levi Yitzhak's *Kedushat Levi.* See also Heschel, *God in Search*, p. 199 (italics in the original: "The mystic experience is an ecstasy of humanity; revelation is *an ecstasy of God*").

taken for seventeen or fifty. He told me his story, and today I have forgotten it, but it was certainly a sorrowful, cruel and moving story; because so are all our stories, hundreds of thousands of stories, all different and all full of a tragic disturbing necessity. We tell them to each other in the evening, and they take place in Norway, Italy, Algeria, the Ukraine, and are simple and incomprehensible like the stories in the Bible. But are they not themselves stories of a new Bible?

Silence slowly prevails and then, from my bunk on the top row, I see and hear old Kuhn praying aloud, with his beret on his head, swaying backwards and forwards violently. Kuhn is thanking God because he has not been chosen.

Kuhn is out of his senses. Does he not see Beppo the Greek in the bunk next to him, Beppo who is twenty years old and is going to the gas chamber the day after tomorrow and knows it and lies there looking fixedly at the light without saying anything and without even thinking any more? Can Kuhn fail to realize that next time it will be his turn? Does Kuhn not understand that what has happened today is an abomination, which no propitiatory prayer, no pardon, no expiation by the guilty, which nothing at all in the power of man can ever clean again?

If I were God, I would spit at Kuhn's prayer.[20]

May one understand God as wholly other, as sacred, after Auschwitz? May one think of God as holy, if the holy cannot be immoral? Does one have a right to say that God is fair, addressable, possessed of power, loving, and choosing? Is not speaking of God's anger blasphemous in the context of the holocaust? Can one talk of God's essential attributes as holiness and personality after hearing the testimony of the distortion of personality and transcendence? Is any language adequate after the rupture of all human communication in the camps?[21]

And yet, can one not talk of God? Can one abandon God Who, for better or for worse, is the creator and judge? Can one cast even God into the abyss of silence? Can one deny one's own experience of God's holy otherness and of God's intimate personal presence?

And, can one close one's ears to the other testimony — the testimony of faith, the witness to the Jew's love of God? "Yea, though God slay me, I turn expectantly to God" (Job 13:15).[22]

*

The theology of image, a personalist theology, proposes, in humility and embarrassment, that there is no choice but to retrieve the hermeneutic of

---

[20] Primo Levi, *Survival in Auschwitz*, trans. S. Woolf (New York: Summit Books, 1960), pp. 65–66, 129–130.

[21] See pp. 8–9 above for references to Shapiro and Langer on this.

[22] For stories of Jewish religious heroism, see M. Prager, *Sparks of Glory* (New York: Shengold Publishers, 1974). For Christian stories, see C. Ten Boom, *The Hiding Place* (Old Tappan, N.J.: Spire Books, 1971). There are other examples of this genre.

personal and of holy language; that one must speak, as best one can, always aware of the silence that haunts one's speech, of God and of humankind as holy person, in dialogue. The theology that understands God's essential attributes as personality and holiness teaches that there is no alternative to forming a vision of God and humankind that is rooted in personality and holiness; that one must do this, as clearly as possible, even as one must remain aware of the darkness that encompasses and threatens humanity.

Universes
of Discourse

The General Theory with Four Examples

CONSIDER the following narrative: "As the runner rounded third base and headed for home, the crowd stood up and roared. But before he could make it, the forward guard came in from right field, tackled him, grabbed the puck, and streaked the length of the field to score a goal." Even for people familiar with the special jargon of the sports pages, this narrative is incomprehensible. It is unintelligible precisely because it mixes universes of discourse. It mixes the universe of discourse of baseball with that of hockey and football; hence, it is incomprehensible. It is nonsense, not as an essay in English syntax and grammar, but as a description of something which we know from our experience. The language of each of the games mentioned is mutually exclusive; no one could play all three games at once, given the current rules. In this example, then, there are clearly defined games, with clearly defined languages, and we always use only one language at a time.

The example from the world of sports can be generalized to a hypothesis about common language usage, with certain modifications, as follows: First, words more or less faithfully reflect our life experience and that of others; that is, words stand for experiences we have. Second, words come in groups and, within each group, the terms mutually define one another, without clear reference to a term or terms outside the group; that is, the words of each group relate to one another by contrast and similarity without our being able to formally define those words. Such a group of terms can be called a "universe of discourse." Third, though each universe of discourse is discrete, referring to a distinct dimension of human experience, common usage allows them to overlap. Several examples.

First, there is *the universe of aesthetic discourse.* This universe of discourse is composed of those words which characterize acts, events, objects, or persons aesthetically. The terms of this universe of discourse are, at one end of the spectrum: "beautiful, pretty, harmonious, graceful." At the other end of the spectrum, the terms are: "ugly, jarring, hideous, odious, loathsome." And in the middle of the spectrum the terms are: "homely, plain, graceless, artless, dingy." There are many more terms, as the entries in a thesaurus under "beauty" and "ugliness" indicate.

These words conform to the three criteria for a universe of discourse: (1) They form a group and have in common one dimension of human existence—the realm of the aesthetic. (2) They define one another by similarity and contrast, without recourse to terms outside the shared universe of discourse and without formal definition. Thus, one would say, "This sonata is beautiful and that one is not." But one would not normally say: "The act of poisoning her husband was beautiful, or graceless, or jarring"; or: "Being kind is harmonious, or artless, or ugly." Similarly, a painting can be said to be beautiful and have no other function while a chair can be functional, independent of its aesthetic qualities. (3) Words from the universe of aesthetic discourse can sometimes be used with a nonaesthetic meaning as, for example: "The crime of genocide is ugly"; or: "The act of saving the child's life was beautiful." When we do that, we are mixing universes of discourse; we are really making moral and not aesthetic judgments, even though we are using the language of aesthetics.

Second, there is *the universe of moral discourse.* This universe of discourse is composed of those words which characterize acts, events, objects, or persons morally. The terms at one end of the spectrum are: "good, just, virtuous, dutiful, morally significant." At the other end, the terms are: "evil, unjust, bad, wicked, foul." And in the middle of the spectrum, the terms are: "neutral, inconsequential, unimportant." Here, too, there are many more terms.

These terms, too, conform to the three criteria for a universe of discourse: (1) They form a group and have in common one dimension of human existence—the realm of the moral. (2) They define one another by similarity and contrast, without recourse to terms outside the shared universe of discourse and without formal definition. Thus, one would say, "Being kind is good"; or: "Evil deeds are wicked." But one would not normally say: "That painting is virtuous, or wicked, or unethical"; or: "Prayer is fair, or wrong, or foul." Similarly, when we say of a person that he or she is "good" or "bad," we are not passing judgment on that person's aesthetic qualities but on his or her moral qualities. Or, an act can be pregnant with moral meaning and yet be unaesthetic or antisocial. Thus, too, we know people who are physically ugly yet are morally without peer, and we can think of acts that are morally courageous yet which have no inherent aesthetic meaning. (3) Words from the universe of moral discourse can sometimes be used with a nonmoral meaning, as when we say, "Beauty is good." When we do that, we are mixing universes of discourse; we are really couching an aesthetic judgment in moral language.

The reason for the overlap of moral and aesthetic vocabularies lies in the historical usage of western culture in which the beautiful and the good are said to overlap, even though each is a separate realm of discourse with its own vocabulary and its own judgments. This tradition has deep roots in western culture, beginning in Plato and continuing through the middle ages and into modern philosophy. Note, however that, in the prophetic tradition, morality and aesthetics did not overlap. Rather, classical prophecy (and later rabbinic teaching) put primary emphasis on the universe of moral discourse and saw the aesthetic realm as secondary. Justice is not always beautiful, while the beautiful can sometimes be very evil—for the prophet.

Third, there is *the universe of personal discourse.* This universe of discourse is composed of those words which characterize acts, events, objects, or persons personally. The vocabulary here, too, is familiar; it is drawn from our knowledge of human psychology. Thus we speak of people being "loving, kind, supportive, happy" or "aggressive, critical, constructive, productive" or "angry, destructive, sad, uncommunicative." There are many more words we use to describe people.

These words, too, conform to the three criteria for a universe of discourse: (1) They form a group which describes a common dimension of human existence—the realm of the interpersonal. (2) They define one another by similarity and contrast, without recourse to terms outside the shared universe of discourse and without formal definition. Thus, one would say, "He is loving, or critical, or angry"; or: "She is happy, or aggressive, or uncommunicative." But one would not normally use aesthetic or moral terms when trying to describe someone psychologically. (3) Words from the universe of personal discourse can sometimes be used together with terms from the moral and aesthetic realms, even though they are coherent unto themselves. Thus, a person can be said to be aggressive and moral, yet not beautiful; or, sad yet beautiful and/or moral. A person could even be loving, yet unethical or ugly.[1]

Fourth, there is *the universe of rational discourse.* This universe of discourse is composed of those words which characterize acts, events, objects, or persons rationally. The terms at one end of the spectrum are: "reason, proof, analysis, logic." At the other end, they are: "sophistry, inconsistency, unreasonableness, invalid argument." And in the middle of the spectrum, they are: "probable, likely, hypothesis, plausible." These words are derived from strictly logical thinking (e.g., mathematical proofs), but they apply also to more intuitive rational thought, the former, however, being regarded as the paradigm for the entire universe of rational discourse.

These words, too, conform to the criteria for a universe of discourse: they form a group of words that describe a single dimension of human existence;

---

[1] The concentration camp guard who is loving toward his family or even toward certain inmates is an example.

they are self-defining and hence self-consistent; and their universe of discourse sometimes overlaps with that of other universes of discourse, as in the statement, "That is an elegant solution." In western culture in particular, the universe of rational discourse overlaps with the universes of moral and aesthetic discourse, as in the extended medieval argument about the simultaneity of the good, the rational, and the beautiful.

To summarize: (1) In everyday speech, we use words to describe various aspects of experience. (2) These words have a tendency to group themselves into units, called "universes of discourse," in which the terms define one another by similarity and contrast. (3) The primary sense of these universes of discourse can be distinguished, and we use them coherently to describe persons, events, objects, moments in time, and texts. (4) Despite the discreteness of each universe of discourse, common usage, particularly in western tradition, permits a certain overlap of terms, creating hybrid usages. (5) The four universes of discourse noted here are the aesthetic, the moral, the personal, and the rational. Each has its own interrelated vocabulary. Each, despite the semantic overlap, describes a specific aspect of human experience. And each enables us to exercise active judgment in its respective dimension of human living; each enables us to characterize persons, objects, places, texts, and events with the range of terms specific to that universe of discourse.

The Universe of Spiritual Discourse

Religious persons of all ages and all cultures have occupied themselves with the problem of seeking to find words and categories and to arrange them so that they describe the realm of the religious. Scholars in the field of the history of religions have also taken up the task.[2] Casting around in the mind by using the technique of free association, one discovers that this universe of discourse is, indeed, a rich one. There are such words as "holy, transcendent, spiritual, sacred, awe, fear of the Lord, love, ecstasy, worship, piety, saintliness." And there are such words as "demonry, ghost, curse, unholy, weird, sacrilegious, fiendish, blasphemous." There is also a group of words that are specific to given religious traditions and institutions: "sacrament, worship, idolatry, love, mass, sh'ma, born-again, teshuva." The number of words available is considerable, and it is only secular habits of thought that limit our use of such words. It is useful to return to a few of these words to see how they are used, how they relate to one another, and to catch a glimpse of the realm of human experience to which they allude.

What does the word "holy" mean? "Holiness," as noted in the previous

---

2 See, most notably, R. Otto, *The Idea of the Holy* (New York: Oxford University Press, 1958) (available in many languages).

chapter, is a quality we become aware of in certain events, texts, objects, or people. It is not an awareness of the aesthetic. Nor is it an awareness of deep moral rectitude. It is a sense of something "other," of the presence of something that is qualitatively different from everything else we are aware of. It is an awareness of the dimension of the sacred in the event, text, object, or person before us.

"What is the matter with you, O sea, that you flee? with you, O Jordan, that you reverse your course? with you, O mountains, that you dance like lambs? and with you, O hills, that you spring about like young sheep?" (Psalm 114). Can one say that these are "good" metaphors or that this is "good" poetry? Usually, one does not, even in poetry, think of the sea fleeing or the mountains dancing like lambs. Usually, even in a metaphor, a river does not reverse its course, or the hills spring about like young sheep. The idea of nature being stood on its head, so to speak, makes sense particularly in the context of the creative power of God. God, after all, set the character of nature by God's power. And God could reverse or change it. Under God's influence, the sea could flee, the river could reverse itself. In God's presence, the mountains and the hills could act like young animals. To the psalmist, nature is not an object of perception. Certainly, it is not an object of exploitative instincts. To the psalmist, nature is not even a beautiful entity. Rather, nature is an expression of a power that is beyond us, which we perceive through a glass darkly. Nature is an expression of another realm in which our association and logic do not apply. For, as the psalmist says in the next verse: "It is before the Lord, Who formed the universe; before the God of Jacob, Who turns a stone into a pool of water and a flint into a fountain." The word "holy," then, is the word for that realm which transcends humankind with a power and a majesty that we only glimpse from time to time.

What does the word "spiritual" mean? "Spirituality" is a quality we become aware of in certain events, texts, objects, and people. It is not an awareness of the moral dimension of the person before us. Nor is it an awareness of the aesthetic dimension of the event or object contemplated. "Spiritual" is a word used to describe an event, text, person, or place which is holy, that is, which participates in that realm of otherness.

Who is the most spiritual person you know? Not the most practicing, nor the most communally active, nor the most professionally involved, nor the most ethical. Who is the person who, in your opinion, most has that quality that is called "spirituality"? One can almost always answer this question. There are such people, and we know who they are.[3] Put another way: We do know what we mean by the word "spiritual." We do know what we mean by the word "holy." We are at a loss when we must produce formal definitions; yet

---

[3] Unfortunately, the group of people whom we know and whom we would characterize as holy often does not include religious professionals, which has a message of its own.

we can, and do, use these words. It is even likely that there exists a consensus on their usage.

What is the "sublime"? A. J. Heschel defined it as follows:

> The sublime is not opposed to the beautiful, and must not, furthermore, be considered an aesthetic category. The sublime may be sensed in things of beauty as well as in acts of goodness and in the search for truth. The perception of beauty may be the beginning of the experience of the sublime. The sublime is that which we see and are unable to convey. It is the silent allusion of things to a meaning greater than themselves. It is that which all things stand for. . . . Just as no flora has ever fully displayed the hidden vitality of the earth, so has no work of art, no system of philosophy, no theory of science, ever brought to expression the depth of meaning, the sublimity of reality in the sight of which the souls of saints, artists, and philosophers live. The sublime, furthermore, is not necessarily related to the vast and the overwhelming in size. It may be sensed in every grain of sand, in every drop of water. Every flower in the summer, every snowflake in the winter, may arouse in us the sense of wonder that is our response to the sublime.[4]

What is the meaning of the word "mystery"? Again Heschel: "It [i.e., mystery] is not a synonym for the unknown but rather a name for a meaning which stands in relation to God."[5]

What is "wonder"? Again Heschel:

> Wonder is a state of mind in which we do not look at reality through the latticework of our memorized knowledge; in which nothing is taken for granted. Inquire of your soul . . . [and] it will tell you . . . each thing is a surprise; being is unbelievable. We are amazed at seeing anything at all; amazed not only at particular values and things but at the unexpectedness of being as such, at the fact that there is being at all.[6]

Such, then, are the words of the universe of spiritual discourse. They, too, fulfill the three criteria for a universe of discourse: (1) They form a group of words and have in common one dimension of human existence—the realm of the spiritual. (2) They define one another by similarity and contrast, as they articulate the realm of humankind's experience of the holy, without recourse to terms outside the shared universe of discourse and without formal definition. (3) Words from the universe of spiritual discourse can sometimes be used in overlapping fashion with terms from other universes of discourse. Thus, one can speak of a religious experience as being beautiful, or good.

Language about God, even in the post-holocaust world, must begin with the words that describe, or at least allude to, the realm of the holy, the spiritual, and the transcendent. If one speaks of God only in terms of social action,

---

[4] A. J. Heschel, *God in Search of Man* (New York: Meridian Books, 1951), p. 39.

[5] Ibid., p. 74.

[6] A. J. Heschel, *Man Is Not Alone,* Harper Torchbooks (New York: Harper & Brothers, 1951), p. 12.

one is not true to God's transcendence. If one speaks of God only in terms of morality, one is not true to God's holiness. Holiness is God's, and there can be no talk about God without using these terms.

Furthermore, there can be no talk about God without the experience of the holy that pervades the use of this vocabulary. If no religious experience lies behind the use of the word "God," one is using a word that has no spiritual meaning. If theology loses its root in the realm of the spiritual, it is mere manipulation of dogmas. As Heschel put it so clearly: "Religion begins with the sense of the ineffable, with the awareness of a reality that discredits our wisdom, that shatters our concepts. It is, therefore, the ineffable with which we must begin, since otherwise there is no problem; and it is its perception to which we must return since otherwise no solution will be relevant."[7]

The awareness of the spiritual is, however, only the beginning. It is only the first step. From this basic awareness, one must develop a sense for the variants, the nuances, for the different faces of the holy.[8] One must develop, too, a sense for the all-pervasiveness of the holy. After a while, when one becomes accustomed to living with the holy, one learns to regard all of reality from the point of view of the holy. One learns to see all of life from within the perspective of the spiritual.[9] Eventually, the spiritual becomes the central focus for seeing, and living, life. As Heschel put it: "Those to whom awareness of the ineffable is a constant state of mind know that the mystery is not an exception but an air that lies about all being, a spiritual setting of reality; not something apart but a dimension of all existence."[10] Actually, that is what we mean when we say someone is a saint. We mean that he or she lives always in the awareness of the holy; that she or he somehow is a part of the stream of sacred consciousness that envelops all of us but which we usually veil from ourselves.

The Relationship Between the Spiritual and Other Universes of Discourse

Having established that we use various universes of discourse and that among them is the universe of spiritual discourse, and having made the point that, in developing a way to talk about God, it is the vocabulary of the realm of religious language and experience that must be primary, it is also necessary

---

[7] Ibid., p. 59.

[8] See, e.g., D. Blumenthal, *Understanding Jewish Mysticism*, 2 vols. (New York: KTAV Publishing House, 1982); idem, *God at the Center* (San Francisco: Harper & Row, 1988).

[9] This was the point of Heschel's oeuvre, which proceeded from *Man Is Not Alone* to *God in Search* to his spiritual ethics, *The Insecurity of Freedom* (New York: Schocken Books, 1959).

[10] Heschel, *Man Is Not Alone,* p. 64.

to state that, for the three western religious traditions, language about God begins in the ineffable but includes other universes of discourse.

The psalmist and the prophets recognize that God is holy; however, they also teach that God is a person, and hence they invoke the universe of personal discourse as an addition to the universe of spiritual discourse. To put it differently, God is not only a being Whose Presence can be sensed in holiness; God is also a being Who has a personal Presence. God is a "You," and this means that God can be addressed by humankind, and that God addresses us. God's personal-ness means that there is a dialogue between God and us, a reciprocity that is to be found in revelation and piety, in covenant and prayer, and in study. To expose oneself to the holy is to expose oneself to the personal; God's Presence is, inextricably, both.

The language of the universe of personal discourse, taken in connection with the language of the holy and the spiritual, also means that God is a "He" or a "She." At first blush, the idea of God as She may seem offensive to persons steeped in the traditional conceptualities and usages which favor the masculine image. But all personhood, as we experience it, God's included, is gendered, even though personhood is not limited to gender. No person we know is gender-less, though gender is not the totality of any person's being. Personhood is a function of one's full personal consciousness, including but not limited to, one's sexuality. Personhood uses the entire range of the language of the universe of personal discourse. Therefore, whether male or female, God (and humankind) can be loving, kind, and supportive; or aggressive, critical, and productive. She or He (and we) can be angry, sad, and uncommunicative; or joyous, powerful, and compassionate.

The following prayer is written in the style of Rabbi Levi Yitzhak of Berditchev, a nineteenth-century hasidic master who was known for his great love of the Jewish people and for his special style of prayer, which was a form of arguing with God. Over and over again, Levi Yitzhak would challenge God, openly, on behalf of the Jewish people. The style is Levi Yitzhak's; the formulation is contemporary:

Ruler of the Universe

I Sarah, daughter of Ruth, come before You as a mother.

When my child is sick,

    I care for her with all my soul and with all my body.

I use my lips to recite prayer for her.

I use my legs to fetch good foods to sustain her.

I use my voice to sing her soothing songs.

I use my hands to hold her close.

And You, Who are the Creator of all flesh
   and the Mother of Your people Israel,
What have You done to soothe Your children
   who are sick with longing for Jerusalem?
You have given us life and Your slightest movement
   would be enough to sustain and nourish that life.
How can You withhold that help
   and not be shamed before Your children?[11]

Personalist language and transcendent power, both of which characterize language about God in Jewish tradition, are clearly present in this meditation.[12]

As talk about God must begin in the language and experience of the ineffable, with all its variations and subtleties, and in the language and experience of the personal, with all its variations and subtleties, for Judaism talk about God must also include the language and experience of the universe of moral discourse. Ever since Abraham, perhaps ever since Adam, holiness, personality, and morality have been inextricably intertwined. God is not only holy, God is not only person, God is also moral—deep though the problems are that that statement entails and, in the post-holocaust age, those problems are truly horrendous. Job did not say that God is immoral or amoral; rather, that he, Job, was innocent. Levi Yitzhak did not say that God did not care; rather, that the Jews did not deserve the punishment God had meted out to them.[13]

There are long debates in the history of religions on whether there exists a realm that is beyond the ethical. Scholars in far eastern religions and in mysticism maintain that such a realm does exist; that one could transcend the moral in one's religious praxis and in one's spiritual experience. From the point of view of most of Jewish tradition, such a transethical realm is out of the question. God is the ultimately real, the ultimately holy, *and* God is moral. God's acts may appear unjustified, even deranged; but the postulate of God's moral holiness remains. This unwillingness to remove talk about God from the universe of moral discourse led to very strong pressure placed upon Jewish philosophy by classic rabbinic Jewish teaching. Maimonides, for instance, while he wrote of a philosophic-mystical experience of God that was beyond morality,

[11] M. Wenig and N. Janowitz, *Siddur Nashim* (unpublished), p. 37.

[12] The alternative to gendered language is inclusive or neutral language. I am of two minds on the subject; see p. xxii above and p. 64 below.

[13] See also A. Laytner, *Arguing With God: A Jewish Tradition* (Northvale, N.J.: Jason Aronson, 1990; reviewed by me in *Modern Judaism* 12:1 [Feb. 1992], 105–110).

nonetheless taught that God must act through moral categories and that humankind must reach God through ethical discipline.[14] This need to unite the holy and the moral also put Jewish mysticism under pressure by classic rabbinic tradition. Thus, the *Zohar,* for instance, teaches about the *Ein Sof,* which is beyond the sefirot which are moral in character, but also teaches that the divine emanation of energy cannot proceed to humanity without passing through the moral sefirot and, vice versa, that humankind cannot reach the ultimate without passing through the ethical dimensions of the Godhead.[15]

Language about God, then, even in the post-holocaust period, must have deep roots, in the first instance, in the universe of spiritual discourse with its vast and varied vocabulary. Such language, however, must, for Jewish (and probably for Christian) tradition, also have firm roots in the universes of personal and of moral discourse, with their respective vocabularies.

Jacob Neusner has written:

> Mishnah's purpose is so to construct the disciplines of every day life and to pattern the relationships among men [*sic*] that all things are made intelligible, well regulated, and trustworthy. Its view is that order and rationality are not man's alone. Man is made in God's image. And that part of man which is like God is the thing that separates man from beast — [rational] consciousness. It is when we use our minds that we act like God. . . . The modes of learning are holy because they lead from earth to heaven, as synagogue-prayer or fasting or other tolerated holy rites cannot. Reason is the way, God's way, and the holy person is the one who is able to think clearly and penetrate profoundly into the mysteries of Torah and, especially, of its most trivial laws. In context, those trivialities contain revelation and serve to impart to the one who grasps them the fully realized experience of transcendence.[16]

In taking the position that mind is the common bond between humankind and God, Neusner stands in a tradition which reaches deep into classical antiquity and which enjoyed a genuine efflorescence during the middle ages. It is the stream of the tradition which argues that God is "mind thinking itself" and that the "image of God" in humanity is the intellect. In this stream of the tradition, the universe of rational discourse overlaps with — indeed becomes synonymous with — the universe of spiritual discourse. It claims that the fusion of the rational and the spiritual vocabularies represents the highest form of

---

[14] Maimonides, *Guide of the Perplexed,* trans. S. Pines (Chicago: University of Chicago Press, 1963), III:51 with I:54 and III:54. See also p. 43.

[15] See, e.g., Blumenthal, *Understanding Jewish Mysticism,* part 2. See also the relevant parts of I. Tishby, *The Wisdom of the Zohar,* trans. D. Goldstein, 3 vols., Littmann Library (London: Oxford University Press, 1989).

[16] J. Neusner, "Transcendence and Worship Through Learning: The Religious World-View of Mishnah," *Journal of Reform Judaism* 25:2 (Spring 1978), 27–29. This theme is found also in Neusner's *Invitation to the Talmud* (New York: Harper & Row, 1973) in the foreword and especially in chap. 7; and in his *The Glory of God Is Intelligence* (Salt Lake City, Ut.: Brigham Young University Press, 1978), especially chap. 1. I have indicated only the first instance of gendered language.

talk about God, the supreme expression of humankind's perception of the divine. In this synthesis, mind is God and God is mind, and humankind's mind is a "chip off the old divine block," ontologically. It follows logically, within this stream of the tradition, that the universes of moral and personal discourse are accorded only pedagogic, functional value.[17]

This claim for the superiority of the philosophic-rationalistic mode of theology has been challenged.[18] The cornerstone of this counterargument is that the Bible, the midrash, and the liturgy—that is, the Jewish sources which antedate, and perhaps are more basic than, the rabbinic medieval synthesis—speak of God as a fusion of the holy, the personal, the moral, and the rational (in its looser sense of intuitive knowledge or wisdom). These materials do not speak of God in the rationalist-intellectual sense that that word acquired in the later philosophic Jewish tradition. Worded differently: the "image of God" in humankind, up to the intellectualization of Judaism in the rabbinic medieval synthesis, was a capacity for moral-personal judgment in the presence of the holy, which is not "intellectual" in the systematic philosophic sense. Rather than assert the superiority of the philosophic-rationalist view of spirituality, then, contemporary Jewish theology and scholarship need to recognize that, even at its most powerful moment, rational discourse was only a means for expressing the holy or a path to the holy.[19] Further, contemporary Jewish theology needs to take cognizance of the fact that the universe of rational discourse overlaps with the universes of spiritual, moral, and personal discourse in describing God, but not in any essentialist or exclusive way.[20]

[17] Neusner has assembled the material from Jewish late antiquity. For the medieval material, see, e.g., Maimonides, Guide of the Perplexed, passim.

[18] See the works of M. Kadushin, especially The Rabbinic Mind (New York: Jewish Theological Seminary, 1952; reprint, New York: Bloch Publishing, 1977); and A. J. Heschel, The Prophets, 2 vols. (San Francisco: Harper & Row, 1962), on divine pathos and concern. See p. 12.

[19] See D. Blumenthal, The Philosophic Questions and Answers of Hoter ben Shelomo (Leiden: F. J. Brill, 1981), pp. 55–72; and, more completely, "Maimonides: Prayer, Worship, and Mysticism," in Approaches to Judaism in Medieval Times, ed. D. Blumenthal (Atlanta: Scholars Press, 1988), pp. 1–16.

[20] Contrary to Mordecai Kaplan, various Reform theologians, and Neusner, who have consistently argued that the discovery of the well-regulated pattern of nature, society, and history through Torah study is itself revelation. See H. Fisch, Poetry with a Purpose: Biblical Poetics and Interpretation (Bloomington, Ind.: Indiana University Press, 1988; reviewed by me in Midstream [August–September 1992], 41–43); see especially chap. 2, for a good analysis of the relation of the beautiful and the holy.

Cognitive Dissonance

Praying Next to a Survivor

Yom Kippur, 5745   *For Alex*

We recited confession
I was astounded
What was he confessing, and why?
Who was asking forgiveness from whom?

We recited the penitential prayers
I saw
the shadow that crossed his face
memories welling up from the depths.

"Therefore, put fear of You into all Your creatures" —
an anger hidden in his body
Why were they not afraid?
Why did He not put fear into them?

We recited the Sh'ma
I was ashamed
Who am I to recite Sh'ma next to him?
What is my faith next to his?

"Our Father, our King" —
he has the advantage
Job, faithful servant
'How horrible are the terrible deeds You have set aside
    for those that fear You
an eye other than Yours has seen, O God.'

"Act for the sake of suckling infants who have not sinned" —
Were they my children?
Woe unto the eyes that saw such things.

I do not want to see; I cannot.

He too does not want to see but he is compelled,

   and I am compelled in his compulsion

My son . . .   my daughter . . .

"If as children, if as servants" —

Lord, we really and truly only wanted to be

   good children, loyal servants

Even now,

   "we are Your children and You are our Father"

   "we are Your servants and You are our Sovereign"

Have mercy on us; have pity.

Heal us, and we shall be healed.[21]

*

Then, why talk about God at all?

First, the realm of the holy is there. We do sense it. We are aware of it. And, as with any other realm of human experience, humankind owes it to itself to relate to this realm and to incorporate it, in some way, into its life, just as it does with the realm of the beautiful, or the realm of the mind.

Second, and perhaps more important, Heschel has said, "The opposite of humanity is brutality, the failure to acknowledge the humanity of one's fellow human being. . . . Humankind has reached a point of no return to animality. Humanity turned beast becomes its opposite, a species *sui generis*. The opposite of the human is not the animal but the demonic."[22] Or, as Heschel again put it:

> The secret of being human is care for meaning. Humankind is not its own meaning, and if the essence of being human is concern for transcendent meaning, then humankind's secret lies in openness to transcendence. Existence is interspersed with suggestions of transcendence, and openness to transcendence is a constitutive element of being human. . . . From the perspective of the Bible: Who is humanity? A being

[21] Poem in Hebrew and English, *Emory Studies on the Holocaust,* ed. S Hanover and D. Blumenthal (Atlanta: Emory University, 1988), vol. 2, pp. i–iii. The quotations in the poem are taken from the Day of Atonement liturgy and the citation in single marks is a rereading of Ps. 31:20 and Isa. 64:3, understood by rabbinic sources to allude to the bliss of the world to come (see, e.g., Maimonides, *Mishne Torah,* "Hilkhot Teshuva," 8:6–8).

[22] A. J. Heschel, *Who Is Man?* (Stanford, Calif.: Stanford University Press, 1965), pp. 47, 101. I have taken the liberty, since I believe it to be in Heschel's spirit, of changing the style to inclusive language in this and in the following quotation.

in travail with God's dreams and designs, with God's dream of a world redeemed, of reconciliation of heaven and earth, of a humankind which is truly God's image, reflecting God's wisdom, justice, and compassion.[23]

It is by talking about God; it is by deliberately using the language of the universes of religious, personal, moral, and rational discourse; it is by fighting mightily to hold ourselves open to the realms of human experience expressed by these words that humankind may be able to save itself from a fate as bad as, or worse than, the holocaust.

[23] Ibid., pp. 66, 119.

CHAPTER
5 *Seriatim, or*
Sailing into the Wind

The Images

IT IS NOT POSSIBLE to sail directly into the wind. A sail must have wind blowing across it, or into it, in order to propel a boat. Hence, if one turns a sailboat directly into the wind, the sail flutters uselessly and the boat cannot advance. If one must move in the direction from which the wind is coming, one must advance in a zig-zag fashion, always sailing at an angle to the wind. This strategy is called "tacking." Ideally, one sails at forty-five degrees to the wind in one direction and then tacks ninety degrees to sail at forty-five degrees to the wind in the other direction, repeating the procedure as often as necessary to reach an up-wind destination. If the ideal cannot be achieved, one sails as close to the wind as one can, advancing into it toward one's destination as well as one is able.[1]

Seriatim: medieval Latin, "one after another, one by one in succession."

The Images and Life

Living life is sailing into the wind.[2]

Sometimes the wind is strong; sometimes, light. Sometimes the trip is a pleasure; sometimes it is hard, even dangerous, work.

Always, life is a moving into, an advance toward love, success, understanding;

[1] My thanks to my sailing friends in Larchmont, New York, who taught me these important lessons.

[2] The index of John Bartlett's *Familiar Quotations*, 15th ed., revised and enlarged (Boston, Mass.: Little, Brown & Co., 1980) has twelve columns of listings for "life" and another six columns for "live/lives/living." I did not see the metaphor of sailing.

peace, accomplishment, friendship—goals that are not easily attained, yet are worth striving for.

Sometimes life pulls and pushes us; we are caught up in the wind. Sometimes we are in control, or, more accurately, we have some control; we develop a useful relationship with the wind, with life.

When we articulate a goal worth achieving, rarely can we attain it by direct assault. Life, in its variety, complexity, and in its very integrity, is not given to simple, straightforward acquisition. We cannot sail directly into the wind of life. So, we learn to tack, to advance obliquely. In order to get where we want to go in life, we set our eyes on a goal, we test the winds, and we set off on an indirect course, perhaps one that is at forty-five degrees from our goal. We continue on that course for a while, until we seem to be getting off course. Then we tack, we "come about" and we set off on another oblique course, always with the goal in sight—the goal that can only be reached by indirect advance. And we repeat the procedure—check the goal, check the forces we must engage, set an oblique course, sail, recheck and set another course—as often as necessary. "If at first you don't succeed, try, try again" — but with method, with subtlety, with indirection.

We sail through life, by tacking into the wind of life. This accounts for the seemingly erratic nature of the human endeavor. For, to achieve our life goals, we must do contradictory things; to get where we are going, we must sail in different directions.

We live *seriatim*. We live in sequences of acts, and they do not form a straight line; rather, they err, they wander, in a rough direction. We walk the path of life not as an unswerving highway but as a meandering road that gets to where it is going, but indirectly. We walk the path of life not as a concrete ribbon but as a path that wanders through meadows and fields and cities, yet arrives at its destination, in due time. To act *seriatim* is to err with vision. It is to start, to stop, to get lost, to find the path once more, and to start again; and it is to repeat this process as often as necessary, as long as we have strength. Life is a walk, not a march; a walk errs, even as it heads toward a destination.[3]

*

Universes of discourse are tacks, paths in different directions which enable us to live life in all its variety without losing our sense of direction. Thus, one may explore the universe of aesthetic discourse—its terms, its varieties,

---

[3] I have used the term *seriatim* in my previous work to express this idea. See the index of my *God at the Center* (San Francisco: Harper & Row, 1988). *Erring: A Postmodern A/theology* is the title of a book by Mark C. Taylor (Chicago: University of Chicago Press, 1984), which proposes a nonlogocentric theology. See, however, my review of it, "But Rabbi David Says," *Cross Currents* (Winter 1988–89), 468–474.

its nuances, and the points where it overlaps with other universes of discourse. One learns about art, music, dance, and the other muses and draws on them for an understanding of life. The arts serve as a fundament of metaphor for what life is all about.

One never exhausts the aesthetic; rather, one tacks and chooses another course. Then one may explore the universe of moral discourse — its terms, its varieties, its difficulties, and the points where it overlaps with other universes of discourse. One learns about goodness, evil, justice, compassion, and suffering and draws on them for an understanding of life. Moral judgment serves as a way to see and express one core of human existence.

One never exhausts the moral; rather, one tacks and chooses another course. Then one may explore the universe of personal discourse — its concepts, its tools of interpretation, its subtleties, and the areas where it overlaps with other universes of discourse. One learns about character, transference and countertransference, trauma, and healing and one draws on these, too, for an understanding of life. Personal psychology serves as a way to comprehend the depth and power of humanness and of life.

One never exhausts the personal; rather, one tacks and chooses another course. Then one may explore the universe of rational discourse — its structures, its power, its usefulness, and the areas where it overlaps with other universes of discourse. One learns about logic, about reason as a way to order reality, about rational communication as a tool for conflict resolution and one draws on these, too, for an understanding of life. The intellect serves as a way to see the world and our relationship to it.

One never exhausts reason either; rather, one tacks and chooses another course. Then one may explore the universe of spiritual discourse — its otherness, its comforting power, its inspiration, and the points where it overlaps with other universes of discourse. One learns about holiness, ritual, sacred time, and sacred space and one draws on these insights for an understanding of life. The numinous, too, serves as a way to see the world, life, and our fellow human beings.

There is no true starting place. On the contrary, one heads off into the wind of life and one tacks, from one universe of discourse to another. One sails into what life has to offer us, and one shifts course from one realm of human experience to another.[4]

This shifting of courses creates contradictions: The spiritual may move us toward meditative retiring from the world, while the moral may move us to social action. The aesthetic may blind us to evil, while the personal may sensitize us to the same evil. Each course, each path, has its integrity, its

[4] See A. Green, *Seek My Face, Speak My Name* (Northvale, N.J.: Jason Aronson, 1992; reviewed by me in *Modern Theology* 9:2 [April 1993] 223–225), pp. 217, 224, for the Hebrew equivalent, *ratso' va-shov.*

meaning-fulness. However, we cannot experience everything at once, nor can we act in consonance with all of our experience; so we alternate our contradictions, we live them fully but *seriatim*.

To be open to everything, even if one does it *seriatim,* is to run the risk of having no center. It is to have identities, in place of identity. It is to defy the logocentric thrust of western tradition. But logocentrism is not the only way to see life. Life need not have only one center, and we who live it need not have only one identity. Drawing from the universe of personal discourse, we know that, in different situations, we have different "identities." I am father to my children, husband to my wife, teacher to my students, member of committees in some circumstances, rabbi in others, young in some contexts and old in others. Such multiple existence is true of all of us. One might say that these are roles, as distinct from identities; but we are our roles or, to put it differently, we live our roles fully, so fully that we fuse with our roles.[5]

Furthermore, many of us are comfortable without the logocentric assumption of a single center. Our lives are rich and full and meaningful precisely because we tack and set new courses—professionally, personally, morally, aesthetically, intellectually, and spiritually. Change—repentance, being born again—results from not "being in a rut," from tacking to new courses in life.

Finally, to live *seriatim* is not to be completely without focus; there is still the wind into which one sails. Life lived on multiple paths still has a general direction, a compass setting, toward which one orients oneself from time to time. Life lived in many universes of discourse still has language and subjectivity.

The Images and the Text(s)

A text has historical meaning; it also has moral and personal meaning, and aesthetic value, and rational coherence. To read a text is to be open to all the dimensions embedded in the text. Life is also a "text"; to live life is to be open, *seriatim,* to all the dimensions of the text of life.

Scripture, as the text par excellence in western culture, is a model of shifting perspectives. Parts of it are narrative—personal, moral. Parts are legal—rational, moral, cultic. Parts are prophecy—moral, aesthetic. Parts are pietistic—spiritual (in the western sense of the word), personal. And parts are cultic—holy, rational. To read Scripture is to sail into the wind of the text. To read the Bible is to tack, to set a new course every few chapters.

The rabbis debate which is more important, study or action. In one place

---

[5] There is a substantial amount of research on social conformity which shows that people become the roles they live. See, e.g., H. C. Kelman and V. L. Hamilton, *Crimes of Obedience* (New Haven, Conn.: Yale University Press, 1989).

(Mishna, Avot 1:17) they say, "Study is not the essential; rather, deed." And in another place (Mishna, Pe'ah 1:1), they list many deeds and say, "But study weighs as much as all the others taken together." The issue of the relative importance of various commandments is widely discussed in rabbinic literature. The answer lies in tacking, in living life *seriatim*.[6] One engages the path of one mitsva; then one tacks and sets out on the path of another mitsva. One devotes time and energy to study; then to prayer; then to charity; then to acts of social justice and kindness; and the course keeps shifting. That is life. If life, then, seems disorderly, then it is that; but it is full, rich, deep, even if it seems "unprioritized."

Maimonides, in his philosophical work, teaches that prophecy is an emanation of pure intellectual-spiritual energy that comes from God to the prophet. That emanation is passed on to the rational and imaginative faculties of the human soul which give the emanation form; they transform it into concepts, words, and images. Prophecy, then, has a preverbal, preconceptual state which is only later converted into narrative, law, poetry, and ethics. Maimonides further teaches that, on Mount Sinai, the people heard only a loud indistinguishable noise. Moses, however, who was also present, because he was physically, morally, and intellectually prepared for revelation, was able to receive the intellectual-spiritual emanation in its preverbal, preconceptual state and to give it form; that is, Moses was able to take the revelation at Sinai and turn it into Torah, as we know it. In his thirteen principles of the faith, Maimonides takes a slightly different position. He teaches there that the Torah is word for word — indeed, letter for letter — the binding Word of God; it is not (just) the Mosaic rendering of the divine emanation but the "speech" of God in a very literal way.

Why does Maimonides have this tension in his system? This, too, is a function of living life *seriatim*. From the point of view of phenomenology, prophecy is a religious experience, an influx of divine consciousness which must be construed in human terms by the human subject. Yet from the point of view of social reality, prophecy is the authoritative revealed text, the "constitution" of the people. In this perspective, prophecy is the covenant with God, not a mixing of divine and human intellectual-spiritual consciousness. One needs both approaches in order to articulate a coherent socio-spiritual view of religion, and one lives first one, then the other, *seriatim*.[7]

---

[6] M. Kadushin suggests that the variety of rabbinic stances on this issue reflects the variety of the human personality as it chooses to express its own character (*The Rabbinic Mind* [New York: Jewish Theological Seminary, 1952; reprint, New York: Bloch Publishing, 1977], chap. 4). That is not far from my position.

[7] I have dealt with this topic in a thorough way in "Maimonides' Intellectualist Mysticism and the Superiority of the Prophecy of Moses," *Studies in Medieval Culture* 10 (1977), 51–67; reprinted in *Approaches to Judaism in Medieval Times*, ed. D. Blumenthal (Chico, Calif.: Scholars Press, 1984), vol. 1, pp. 27–52.

"For everything there is a moment, and a time for every need under the heavens. There is a time to . . . and a time to . . ." (Eccl. 3:1ff.). We start with enthusiasm, we waver, and then we reaffirm—in all things: in marriage, in parenting, in career, in faith, even in theology. In matters of belief, there is a time for unyielding protest (on the subject of the holocaust) and there is a time for submission (on the subject of our own recalcitrance). There is a time for an absolutely omnipotent God (in humiliation and disaster) and there is a time for a fragile Lord[8] (in building a community or family). There is a time to repress the dissonance (in moments of danger) and a time to cultivate it (in prayer, poetry, study, and reflection). There is a time to demythologize (when history and literature beckon) and a time to live the myth fully (in seeking the depth of one's soul within one's people, one's Torah, and one's God). The polar structure of my rhetoric does not begin to grasp the complexity of the real-life movement; reality undermines the trope itself.

Other Voices

Rebecca Chopp, in *The Power to Speak: Feminism, Language, God,*[9] shows that the very structures by which we think and relate to one another reflect unstated assumptions that are inherent in our culture. In her words, "Language, subjectivity, and politics: these three realms, dimensions, common places, form today the structuring of the dominant social-symbolic order." Chopp then proceeds to "name the economies that dominate the basic themes and rules in modernity: in language, representational discourse; in subjectivity, narcissistic patterning; in politics, self-preservation." The answer to oppressive structuring of language, subjectivity, and politics into a dominant social-symbolic order lies, according to Chopp, in "resistance to and transformation of the rules, principles, orderings, and substance of language, subjectivity, and politics."[10]

After identifying two unsatisfactory types of feminist response, Chopp proposes a turn to the Word "not as primal referent for monotheistic ordering but as perfectly open sign that blesses specificity, difference, solidarity, embodiment, anticipation, and transformation."[11]

> This requires, of course, that any reflection on women begin not by securing an
> essence of experience or by trying to make women into something that they are not

---

[8] Jon D. Levenson, *Creation and the Persistence of Evil: The Jewish Drama of Divine Omnipotence* (San Francisco: Harper & Row, 1988; reviewed by me in *Modern Judaism* 10 [1990], 105–110), p. 139.

[9] R. Chopp, *The Power to Speak* (New York: Crossroad, 1989; reviewed by me in *Religious Studies Review* 15 [1989], 122–125).

[10] Chopp, *Power to Speak,* pp. 104, 105, 107.

[11] Ibid., pp. 107–115, 116.

and cannot be, but by considering the position of women in the present social-symbolic order and likewise standing in this position to try to transform the social-symbolic order. It again must be emphasized that to describe women's marginality is to deny any claim about the essence of woman's subjectivity, to forego a quest for the identity of "woman" as a universal singular. . . .

To further, then, the proclamation of emancipatory transformation, feminism . . . must pursue the richness of women's marginality to push against the ordering of language, subjectivity, and politics and to find new images, ways, forms, expressions of language, subjectivity, and politics.[12]

Chopp then goes on to propose several areas in which women's experiences can lend new meanings and emphases to the religious understanding of life: the caring for the wounded, the birthing of children, the feeding of souls and bodies.

Many women have found satisfaction in expressing their piety and knowledge of God in the language of caring for and being with rather than *mysterium tremendum et fascinans,* wholly other and ultimate concern. The nexus of religious experiences, at least for many women, is in and through relationships, friends, families, memories of the dead.[13]

Chopp also stresses women's understanding of time and space, adornment and *jouissance,* corporality.[14] Most important, though, she concludes:

From this place feminism questions the constant emphasis on identity and sameness at the expense of difference and specificity. . . . [S]he lives in the difference and specificity in the ongoing relationality of women and women, women and children, women and nature, women and creation, women and beauty . . . *a subjectivity, a language, and a politics that desires and embraces otherness, multiplicity, and difference.*[15]

Chopp's public call for openness and multi-possibility in life has been echoed by other feminists. Catherine Keller has called for "composite selfhood," "composite subjectivity," "momentary subject," and "polyvalency," and Jessica Benjamin has called for "intersubjectivity" and "conscious ambivalence."[16] I understand this multi-possibility to be not very different from the claim for a life rooted in the images of sailing and *seriatim.* Indeed, for many men, the entire call for a nongendered or womanist/feminist reading of texts and life is itself a new tack, a new course in understanding the self and the other, which leads to greater openness and polyvalency of meaning.

---

[12] Ibid., pp. 116–117.
[13] Ibid., p. 119.
[14] Ibid., pp. 120, 121, 123.
[15] Ibid., p. 122 (emphasis added).
[16] Catherine Keller, *From a Broken Web* (Boston: Beacon Press, 1986), pp. 163, 186, 187, and 206, respectively; Jessica Benjamin, *The Bonds of Love* (New York: Pantheon Books, 1988), pp. 15ff., 179. See also pp. 177 and 257–259 below.

Counter-image

*Everybody in the block had typhus. . . . [I]t came to Belsen Bergen in its most violent,
most painful, deadliest form. The diarrhea caused by it became uncontrollable. It
flooded the bottom of the cages, dripping through the cracks into the faces of the
women lying in the cages below, and mixed with blood, pus and urine, formed a
slimy, fetid mud on the floor of the barracks. . . .*

*Urine and excreta poured down the prisoners' legs, and by nightfall the excrement,
which had frozen to our limbs, gave off its stench. We were really no longer human
beings in the accepted sense. Not even animals, but putrefying corpses moving on
two legs. . . .*

*The location was slippery and unlighted. Of the thirty men on this assignment
[to clean the latrines], an average of ten fell into the pit in the course of each night's
work. The others were not allowed to pull the victims out. When the work was
done and the pit empty, then and then only were they permitted to remove the
corpses. . . .*

*The men could not bring themselves to obey this devilish order [to drink out of
the toilet bowls]; they only pretended to drink. But the block-fuehrers had reckoned
with that; they forced the men's heads deep into the bowls until their faces were
covered with excrement. At this the victims almost went out of their minds—that
was why their screams had sounded so demented. . . .*[17]

*

"Excremental Assault" is what Terrence Des Pres called it and, together with
the gas chambers and the crematoria, it is the counter-image. Auschwitz is
the incarnation of our century and the image thereof will haunt generations
of men, women, and children.

Concentration camp inmates—the victims—did not have the luxury of
tacking, of living *seriatim*. Survival, physical and moral, was all one could
manage, if that much. How, then, can we wallow in that luxury?

One of the paths of our life is walking with the victim—beyond endurance,
into suffering that cannot be told—as best we can. One tack in our lives is
to confront what we would rather avoid, with as much courage as we can
muster. Not so that we, too, will suffer, but as an act of solidarity; not in guilt,
but as an act of remembrance. We must do this in our texts, in our deeds,
in our commitments. We must do this in every universe of discourse we use.
As we tack, we need to bring the ghosts with us. As we move *seriatim* through
life, we need to carry history with us. Language, subjectivity, and politics must
confront the counter-image, if life is to be true.

[17] Quoted from Perl, Weiss, Weinstock, and Szalet in Terrence Des Pres, *The Survivor: An
Anatomy of Life in the Death Camps* (Oxford: Oxford University Press, 1976), pp. 53, 57, 59, 66.

TEXT-ING

Intimations

Text

"IT IS A SIGN between Me and the children of Israel forever" (Ex. 31:17).

That which is between is that which binds; a bond which holds, heals; and gives unity, meaning. It is also that which separates, which divides; a barrier between. And, being in the middle, it is that which is remote from both, beyond reach; in-between.

A "sign" is between. It is the bond which binds, the barrier which separates, and the in-between. A sign embraces, rejects, and is beyond reach; simultaneously.

A "sign" (Hebrew *'ot*) is a "letter" (Hebrew *'ot*), the atom of the written and spoken w/Word. The letter is the bond that binds, the barrier which separates, and the in-between. Torah-teaching/the organized letter/the Word/the sign par excellence embraces, rejects, and is beyond reach; simultaneously.

Me . . . you . . . and the sign, in-between.

Interpretation

"Reading" (Hebrew *qeri'ah*) is "calling" (Hebrew *qeri'ah*). To read is to call to the text, to attend to the voice, to listen to the word. To read is also to be called by the text, to be spoken to by the voice, to be addressed by the word. "Reading" (Hebrew *qeri'ah*) is also "proclaiming" (Hebrew *qeri'ah*). To read is to speak, to address, to communicate. Hence, to read is to receive and to give; simultaneously. It is also to give and to receive; simultaneously. Text is voice, and voice is text.

But there are many texts and many voices; simultaneously. "The Torah has six hundred thousand faces corresponding to each of the six hundred thousand

persons who stood at the foot of Mt. Sinai" (following Rabbi Isaac Luria).
Each voice is a sound in the symphony, and the symphony is cacophanous.
Each text is woven into the fabric of the text-ile, and the text-ile is mottled.

Reading is an entry into the fourth dimension, and beyond.

Reading is entering a room, known and unknown, blind; feeling the outlines,
groping toward the meanings, sensing the forms, forming a sense of the
room-text.

This part has six voices. The first is *the received Hebrew text*. All we have
is the echo which has reverberated through a period of time so long as not
to be believed; the scratched signs carefully transmitted by sensitive (and
insensitive) souls; the text as it was read-proclaimed.

The second voice is *the English translation*. It is a bearing-across (Latin
trans+ferre/latus) of meaning(s), a con-veying of the echo, a com-munication
of the scratched sign. It is a standing-under of the in-between, for readers of
English. It is a translation (Hebrew *tirgum*), which, in other semitic languages,
means a speaking. To speak is to translate, to carry meaning. This translation
is new. It has evolved from a study of the text and a comparison with other
translations into English, German, French, and Arabic. It must be new because
to read is to proclaim, and to translate is to speak.

The remaining four voices are given the literary shape of commentaries.
Each accomplishes a separate task, though the repetition of the dream is one.
One could attend to one voice and ignore the others, but plurivocity lends
depth, harmony, and disharmony; like a dream.

The first commentary is entitled "*Words*." It is a philological commentary
intended to justify the translation. It is a re-sound-ing of the voices of my
distinguished academic teachers. This commentary, however, is also meant
to demonstrate the plurisignification of the text, for the text can often be read
in more than one way. To translate is to determine what I consider to be the
best way, although I know it is not the only way, to render the text. "Words"
preserves the flexibility of meaning, the studied ambiguity, of the original.
It is an acknowledgment of the generations of interpreters whose voices have
joined the echo.

The second commentary is entitled "*Sparks*." It contains brief comments
on the psalms from the spiritual tradition of hasidism, sparks of the divine
hidden in the already-sacred text. It is the re-sound-ing of the voice of our
revered teacher, Abraham Joshua Heschel. These texts are offered because the
spiritual reading is often an inversion of the other meanings of the text.
Inwardness and outwardness become reversed; the spiritual reading proves more
profound than the "plain" reading. This is also a way of reading-calling, an
alluding to the great gap between the H/holy and the W/word. It is a pointing
to a different kind of fissure in the text-intepretation.

The third commentary is entitled "*Affections*." It is an attempt to point to
and interpret the sustained emotional attitudes which the psalmist-tradition

wishes us to cultivate. Don Saliers, in *The Soul in Paraphrase,* distinguishes between "emotions" or "feelings" which are transient (even if intense) and "affections" or "dispositions" which are ongoing emotional attitudes or feelings-concepts that we are *supposed* to feel, even to cultivate:

> Being angry and feeling angry are different in many cases, just as being thankful and feeling thankful may be. . . . What we are in our intentions and actions, is more adequately revealed by referring to the dispositions which constitute a "sense" of the heart than by referring to what we feel or what ideas we have at the time. To say that a person has a deep sense of gratitude is to remark upon his or her character. . . . The evidence of such gratitude will be found in his or her actions, perceptions, and feelings. Such a deep sense is what we shall call . . . an affection. It is not a feeling as such since it cannot be an episodic event "inside" the person. Neither can it be a mood . . . [it] is a disposition. Such emotions, when found in the context of teachings about God, are religious affections in this "dispositional" sense, rather than complex sensations, feelings, or moods.[1]

In this perspective, "to choose a certain moral or religious view of the world and to adopt a way of life congruent with it *is* to take up a particular set of passions and emotions. . . . [T]he function of literature and poetry, and much of Scripture as well, is to arouse, sustain, and articulate deep emotions, not by 'causing' certain subjective feelings, but by offering evaluative images and descriptions of reality . . . metaphors, images, symbols . . . stories, concepts, and practices. . . ."[2]

The Hebrew word for affection-disposition is, I think, *midda.* It means a measure, a virtue, a standard by which one judges one's behavior, one's ideas, and even one's feelings. A *midda* is conceptual, affectional, emotional, and moral. It is both judge and expression, text and voice; it is a sign, in-between.

"Affections" attempts to spell out the ongoing religious emotional attitudes of the psalms, to explicate the "dispositional" meaning(s) of the text. It engages the s/Self on the most nuanced levels possible for me, for I believe we must take seriously the theology of image, that is, that humanity is created in the image of God and that God wishes to be understood in the image of humanity. It is the human personality, in all its complexity ("The heart is more labyrinthine than anything; it is human; who can truly know it" [Jer. 17:9]), that constitutes this image. To study it, to identify with it, to resist it, and to incorporate it are *imitatio Dei.* This commentary, then, is the re-sound-ing of the voice of Saliers as well as of many years of psychoanalytic reflection. It goes beyond Saliers, however, in two ways. First, it deals with the affections of personal and national anger, even rage. Second, the commentary always remains within the consensual understanding of the rabbinic tradition. It is the voice—

---

[1] Don Saliers, *The Soul in Paraphrase: Prayer and the Religious Affections* (New York: Seabury Press, 1980), pp. 15–17.

[2] Ibid., pp. 12, 18, 19.

powerful, sometimes even offensive—of the accumulated centuries of self-measurement. It is the tuned echo.

The fourth commentary is entitled "*Con-verses*." It is an attempt to respond to Jacques Derrida, Michel Foucault, Sigmund Freud, Alice Miller, Carol Gilligan, Jessica Benjamin, Elie Wiesel, and others in the calling-reading-proclaiming of the psalms. Psychoanalysis, literary-philosophical criticism, the women's movement, the holocaust, child and spouse abuse, radical skepticism, and many other strands of modern and postmodern culture have challenged our reading of both the classical texts and the text of life. "Con-verses" is an overturning of the literary, social, and ethical hierarchies of the text. It is a counter-reading, a deconstruction (though not in the contemporary technical sense of the term). It is an attempt to dis-close the closure, to present and perform plurisignificative readings of the text. It is a pointing to the fissures and gaps between the text and the conscious-unconscious of the contemporary reader. It is an under-understanding, an inversion of the text-tradition. It is the re-sound-ing of the voices of my students and my colleagues.

"Convérse" means "to pass one's life, to live, to dwell in or with"; it comes from the later Latin *conversari*, which means "to turn oneself about, to pass one's life, to live." Later, it comes to have the contemporary meaning "to speak, to communicate; to hold inward communion." "Cónverse" means "intercourse, familiar interchange, communion." It can also mean "turned around, opposite, transposed." Both are intensive forms of the Latin *convertere*, "to turn about." "Turning about" leads to "familiar interchange"; to be "trans-posed" is to be "op-posite." "To turn oneself about" is "to dwell in, to live with." "To communicate" is the intensive form of "to turn about."

"Con-verses" is the "turning about" of the verses, which are already turned in a direction. "Con-verses" is the intensive form of the verses; they are transposed, op-posite. And yet they are "a dwelling within, a comm-union" with the already-oriented. To read them is to be con-verted, turned in the direction of new truths. Sometimes, "Con-verses" produce "contro-vers-y," especially when the verses turn in upon themselves.

It is difficult, perhaps impossible, to distinguish rigorously among the voices of these commentaries. They overlap, as do the images in a dream or the events and people of one's life. They fold into each other.

Inter-text-uality

The text is in-between; it is intertext.

The text is a fabric, woven (Latin *texere/textus*) from many threads. One thread is the received text—signs scratched, erased, and re-inscribed in eternity by many hands. One thread is the tradition—many conflicting voices echoing in the same eternity. One thread is the interpreter—gathering in, com-prehending, the threads into one fabric, but differently at different times. And one thread is the reader—calling and called to.

All text-fabrics are created from other text-fabrics. Every reading is a gathering-in of older threads into a new tissue; an interweaving of the particular life of the reader with the tissue of the tradition.

The text-fabric is never finished. It is a cloth with loose ends; a tissue which varies in transparency, color, and text-ure. Woven; re-woven; always being-woven.

Hence, all texts are plurisignificative; they mean more than one thing. All texts are plurivocal; they say more than one thing. And all texts are polysemous; they have more than one meaning/seed; they are genetically bountiful and divers(e). Significations and voices, therefore, are always in dys-harmony. Text-intepretation contains variegation and inconsistency—like a dream, like life.

The text does not have only one voice. The tradition does not have only one voice. I do not have only one voice. Plurivocity and ambiguity, not univocity and consistency, are the norm. Coexistence of meanings, not monolithic teaching, is the norm. Text-interpretation, like life, must be read *seriatim:* following one line of thought and following (returning to follow) another.

The six voices of this part—the received text, the translation, and the four commentaries: "Words," "Sparks," "Affections," and "Con-verses"—are the threads of a woven, and still weaving, text-person. I could not re-create these voices; even I can only hear their echoes and follow the melodies. At times, the voices fight violently with one another, the page burns in my hand. I think the reader will be similarly disoriented. Some readers will favor one commentary; others, another. Some will be horrified by the heresy; others touched by the spirituality; and yet others astounded at the psychology. The reader is the seventh voice—the sabbatical, messianic voice—for the reader, in pondering polysemous texts, determines their purpose, their meaning-fulness. The reader, together with the voices of the text, weaves the tissue of salvation.

Context is as important as text because context discloses the politics of text. Con-text is autobiography: I tend toward meaning, not one meaning but many; nonetheless, toward meaning. I reject literary, philosophical, and ethical nihilism. I am also male. I try to be egalitarian, to be included and inclusive, but I cannot have intellectual and emotional reflexes that are not mine. I urge my women colleagues to write their own multiple commentaries. I am also Jewish and, within that, rabbinic and American. I am also middle-class, middle-aged, heterosexual, and an active member of the Jewish community. Decades of training and action have set deep patterns.

I am also critical in a prophetic-intellectual sense. I feel a call to counter-read, to search for truth where others assume it is not; to de-center the stabilized interpretations and institutions. Correlated to this bias is the compulsion to speak and to write strongly. The psalmist and the prophet spoke, wrote, and acted with passion and strength, with power and might. To engage them is to do the same, to continue that tradition. I see myself, too, as a spokes-person, a messenger sent to teach, a rabbi-rebbe concerned with the redemptive meaning of texts and textuality. The teaching is complex because truth and the texts in which one finds it are woven. But teaching-with-authority—even if nonconsensual—is, as I see it, the commandment, the responsibility, of the theologian. And then there is the "I" that I do not know: the subconscious I. It is interwoven with each of the voices in this book, but the work is not identical only with them. The reader will have to draw lines and exercise judgment.

Ultimately, I try to engage God—to approach, to contend with, to rejoice in, to seek comfort from, to fear and to love . . . God. Jonah's flight and Abraham's persistence.

The text (and this part) is a sign between you and me—a sign which binds, separates, and is between; which embraces, rejects, and is in-between. . . . It is also between You and me.

W-rite-ing

Jacques Derrida has noted that, in order to accomplish the deconstruction of the language of any text, it is necessary to create a "grouped textual field."[3] By this, he means that, in order to pursue simultaneously several lines of reflection upon a given text, one needs to create several layers of commentation and response, each of which has a different purpose, and to present them together. The Derridean corpus includes two examples of this technique: "Living On: Border Lines" and *Glas,* the latter being a truly multiple-field text.[4]

For Jews versed in traditional texts, Derrida's grouped textual field is quite familiar. The standard rabbinic texts for Bible and Talmud study are always printed with multiple commentaries on the page. The recent edition of the Talmud by A. Steinsaltz is a contemporary example of a traditional text illustrated by multiple layers of commentation (in this case all by the same author).[5] A typical page from Steinsaltz's Hebrew edition of the Talmud contains the following units: the vocalized and punctuated text of the Talmud, which, because it is punctuated and vocalized, is already an interpretation; a

[3] Jacques Derrida, *Positions,* trans. A. Bass (Chicago: University of Chicago Press, 1981), p. 42.

[4] Idem, "Living On: Border Lines," trans. J. Hulbert, in *Deconstruction and Criticism* (New York: Continuum, 1986), pp. 75–116; and idem, *Glas,* trans. J. Leavy, Jr. (Lincoln, Neb.: University of Nebraska Press, 1987). Brown University has a computerized writing program that enables students to switch "windows" and hence achieve a multifield text, though I do not know if the various fields can be displayed simultaneously in print. A new type of children's book has also been published which allows the readers to choose an ending and to return to a certain spot and choose another ending several times in succession.

[5] *Talmud,* ed. A. Steinsaltz (Jerusalem: Israel Institute for Talmudic Publications, 1967–).

translation of the Aramaic text into modern Hebrew; a linguistic commentary; reflections on matters of substance; a summary of the actual law; comments on biographies, variants, and realia; Rashi; a later medieval commentary; and cross-references. Steinsaltz's *Talmud* has also been published in English, and the grouped textual field approach has been preserved.[6]

The main differences between such traditional Jewish texts and the Derridean texts is that the thrust of Derrida's work is to overturn the hierarchies of language, to release dissonance, and to allow the text to deconstruct itself, while the goal of rabbinic commentation is to overturn hierarchies of meaning and release dissonances so as to explicate and interpret the source text within rabbinic religious thinking.

This part is a w-rite-ing; a ritual of committing thoughts to paper; a rite which establishes a temporary beginning, middle, and end to an ongoing text which is itself an intertextual process. For this to be a "Jewish" w-rite-ing, it must be presented as a grouped textual field. Hence, all the voices must be scored on the same page; all the threads must be visible so that the fabric-text be whole. This is disorienting to the reader but, with practice, the rite of this writing can be read/entered.

The pages of this part, following the model of the traditional Jewish grouped textual field, contain the text in English translation, prominently displayed, nested among the voices which comment upon it. Furthermore, in Jewish fashion, the nested pages are set up as mirrors of one another, as the reader will quickly perceive. For convenience, each commented psalm — that is, each set of pages in a grouped textual field — is preceded by the received Hebrew text opposite the English translation.

The Hebrew of psalms does not lend itself easily to the rules of English grammar and syntax. First, it is very lapidary, which means that a verse, or at most two or three, forms a unit. A psalm is, then, a stringing together of short powerful units. There are no paragraphs in the sense in which we use that term. Second, the voice changes every few lines, as if the psalmist had another thought, or string of thoughts. Third, the style is elliptical, which means that antecedents are not always clear. Further, images are used where we might use concepts.

I have tried to use the following rules in this w-rite-ing:

1. I have used as little punctuation as possible. A superscripted number marks the beginning of a scriptural verse, but inside the verses and between them I have used punctuation as needed by the sense.

2. I have omitted "and" in most places. I have also substituted antecedents for pronouns where that seemed to clarify the meaning.

3. To catch the change of voice, I have used indentation.

[6] New York: Random House, 1989–.

4. The titles and subtitles of the psalms epitomize the interpretation and have been added by me.

5. I have used egalitarian language wherever possible, except with reference to God, Who is always referred to in the masculine. I have done this for three interrelated reasons. First, Hebrew does not have a neuter gender form. Second, given the personalist trope I have chosen, I need to use gendered language. And third, the male pronouns speak to my own masculine identity and understanding of God. I do not speak for women's experience of God.

6. The following Hebrew words are almost always translated as follows: Tetragrammaton—"the Lord"; *Elohim,* "God"; *ki,* "truly, surely, for, because"; *shir,* "song"; and *mizmor,* "psalm." Hebrew words that occur frequently enough to be part of the common parlance are treated as such and are not set in italics.

A *seder* is a ritual order, an order of battle: hence, the Passover *seder,* which is the liturgy for the table celebration of the deliverance of the Jewish people from bondage; the six orders (*sedarim*), which are the editorial structure of the Mishna; the *siddur,* the prayerbook, the order of the daily and holiday liturgy; and the *sidra,* the weekly lectionary from the Torah. The psalms interpreted in this part do not follow the order of the received text; rather, they have a *seder* of their own. I begin with Psalm 128, which is the psalm that defines blessing and blessedness. I then move to Psalm 44, which is a psalm of national anger, and then to Psalm 109, which is a psalm of personal rage. Finally, I conclude with Psalm 27, a psalm of healing. The whole is set off by this introduction, entitled "Intimations," and the concluding parts of the book, entitled "Re-sponses" and "Con-templation."

How to Read This Part

This is a difficult part to read for three reasons.

First, there are two major technical difficulties: (1) The nesting of texts, while typically Jewish, is not common in western w-rite-ing, and following the "text" will be confusing to the uninitiated reader. To facilitate the reader's task, two type sizes are used. In addition, each commentary is placed in the same location on the page (see figure 1). For even-numbered pages: "Affections" in the upper left-hand corner; "Con-verses" in the upper right-hand corner. "Words" occurs usually in the bottom half of the page, in two columns, and is followed by "Sparks" in two columns. For odd-numbered pages, a mirror image is used. However, since the amount of material in each commentary varies from page to page, the commentaries are sometimes out of place. To ease these confusions, each occurrence of each commentary is labeled for the reader's convenience. Finally, shortened titles of sources are given in parentheses and the sources are cited in full in the bibliography.

(2) Because the commentaries are nested around the text, there are several

Even-numbered Page   Odd-numbered Page

AFFECTIONS CON-VERSES	CON-VERSES AFFECTIONS
TEXT OF PSALM	TEXT OF PSALM
WORDS	WORDS
SPARKS	SPARKS

Figure 1

ways to read this material: One can read each verse with all the commentaries pertaining to that verse. Or one can read a particular commentary on the whole psalm, return to the beginning, and read another commentary on the same psalm. Or one can skip and choose according to one's interest and taste. At times, the material in one of these commentaries carries over to the next page; in that case, the reader need only follow and then return to complete the reading of the other commentaries. All this will seem disorienting at first but it *is* the traditional Jewish way of reading classical texts, and the reader will adjust to the method with practice.

Second, there is the matter of content. This part contains some very powerful psalms which deal with anger and rage. To give them the full range of expressiveness they already contain, they will need to be read out loud, more than once. Anger and rage, however, are difficult emotions to deal with. Reading about anger and rage evokes feelings and fantasies that can scarcely be controlled. Moreover, I have dealt with anger and rage in very sensitive contexts—holocaust, child and spouse abuse, feminist perspectives, cursing, the Bible, and our intimate relationship to God—and have used strong imagery and language, as indeed the psalmist does. Disturbing thoughts and feelings on these subjects generated by the very reading of the texts and the commentaries will need to be confronted.

Third, as I have taught and shared this material, it has become clear that, because the material touches on matters that run deep in our understanding of ourselves and the people around us, the reader needs an opportunity to participate in this part, a way to keep track of his or her feelings and thoughts. Accordingly, I recommend the use of a diary or log. One's response might be poetry, or a letter, or a commentary on one of the comments or psalms. The following rules were used to produce the depth writing that characterizes parts of the commentary: Use short choppy sentences. Use association freely. Use metaphors and images. Favor the counter-intuitive. Face the material directly. Center concentration before beginning to write. Eliminate transitional language and extra words. Avoid conceptual terms. Don't be afraid of ugly thoughts. Have courage.

Reading this part, then, is a voyage—not only into the world of Jewishly structured texts but also into the inner world of anger and rage. It is, however, also a voyage through that world into the realm of healing; for, in the commentaries on Psalm 27, I expound two types of healing—religious and psychotherapeutic. We live in angry and dangerous times, and we must make the voyage even if it is stormy.

*

A book has an introduction and a conclusion; a text has intimations and after-thoughts. "To intimate" is "to make known indirectly, to indicate." It is also "to imply, to allude to something that is not made known." An "intimate" is "a close friend, one who knows what is made known and what is not made known." An "intimate" is one who knows the intimate: the secret, the innermost recesses—not from reading the words of the book but from calling to, and being addressed by, the text; from being in-between; from inter-text-ing.

Psalm 128

WITH
FOUR
COMMENTARIES

שִׁיר הַמַּעֲלוֹת

אַשְׁרֵי כָּל
יְרֵא יְיָ
הַהֹלֵךְ בִּדְרָכָיו:

יְגִיעַ כַּפֶּיךָ כִּי תֹאכֵל
אַשְׁרֶיךָ
וְטוֹב לָךְ:

אֶשְׁתְּךָ כְּגֶפֶן פֹּרִיָּה
בְּיַרְכְּתֵי בֵיתֶךָ
בָּנֶיךָ כִּשְׁתִלֵי זֵיתִים
סָבִיב לְשֻׁלְחָנֶךָ:

הִנֵּה כִי כֵן יְבֹרַךְ
גָּבֶר יְרֵא יְיָ:

יְבָרֶכְךָ יְיָ מִצִּיּוֹן
וּרְאֵה בְּטוּב יְרוּשָׁלָ͏ִם
כֹּל יְמֵי חַיֶּיךָ:

וּרְאֵה בָנִים לְבָנֶיךָ
שָׁלוֹם עַל יִשְׂרָאֵל:

A Psalm of Virtues

in which happiness is defined
some biblical virtues are expounded
and a blessing is given

¹A song to be sung on the steps

Happy is each person
who has an ongoing fear of the Lord,
who persists in walking in His ways.

²If you eat by the sweat of your hands,
you will be happy
and goodness will be yours.

³Your wife will be as a fruitful vine
in the intimate recesses of your house;
your children will be as olive saplings
around your table.

⁴This is how a man who has an ongoing fear of the Lord
will be blessed.

⁵May the Lord bless you from Zion
May you see good for Jerusalem
all the days of your life.

⁶May you see children of your children.
Peace upon Israel.

AFFECTIONS

This psalm is divided into two parts. The first defines happiness by expounding certain biblical virtues (vv. 1–4), and the second is a blessing offered as a response (vv. 5–6). Virtue leads to blessing; the house of Israel is the greater family.

Happy is each person who has an ongoing fear of the Lord

"Fear of God" is an ongoing attitude; it is not a momentary emotion. It is a biblical virtue.

Fear of God is, first of all, fear of punishment. We experience this when we have done something we know deep inside ourselves is morally wrong. →

---

¹A song to be sung on the steps

Happy is each person
who has an ongoing fear of the Lord,
who persists in walking in His ways.

CON-VERSES

an ongoing fear of the Lord

The language of oppression is fear; sublimated into respect, rooted in awe. . . . Fear of God overwhelms, by terror. It is of the Other, of the holy, of the repressed returned to haunt us, of the "grue" in "gruesome". . . . The unspoken primal deed, so terrible that it is numinous, so terrifying that its memory terrifies; an archetype, a projection that roots us to our place in awe-fear-respect. . . . Law and Order! Keep humanity down! Keep the lid on tight! . . . The rhetoric of oppression, from within and from without; the fight against the sublimated self. →

WORDS

on the steps

Both great temples in Jerusalem had stairs leading from the upper to the lower courtyards. At various moments in the liturgical year, the priests and levites would assemble and form a procession using the steps, on each of which a psalm was sung (Mishna, Sukka 5:2). This psalm is sometimes wrongly called a "song of ascents"; it was actually used while descending the stairs. The subtitle, "a song of degrees," is based on a later meaning of the Hebrew word.

each person

Rashi points out that the word *kol* ("each") appears redundant. This teaches that women, too, are included in this insight.

ongoing . . . persists

For this translation, see "Affections."

SPARKS

ongoing fear . . . walking in His ways

The Talmud says that there are three blessings that are dependent not on merit but on "luck": life, children, and sustenance (Mo'ed Katan 28a). The Sefat Emet takes this talmudic text and reads it intertextually with this psalm, generating a structure for the psalm and a typology of holy behavior, as follows:

[Since the first verse has two stichs,] the text must be speaking of two types of persons. The first is one who "has an ongoing fear of God," does not sin, and observes God's mitsvot. The latter is one who occupies himself with the Torah and of him it is said, "he walks in His ways."

Scripture then explains the reward of the first. His reward is that he shall be providentially blessed with sustenance which will not end,

CON-VERSES

Yir'ah=fear-awe-respect; *yir'eh*= h/He will see and in seeing H/he will know, the terrible secret. . . . "*Sod ha-Shem lirei'av*=the secret of the Name for/belongs-to those who have an ongoing fear of Him" (Ps. 25:14). It is the secret He/we suppress: that we resent His rule, that He deprives us of our narcissistic freedom; the secret of anger. Only those who have an ongoing fear of Him know it. It is the secret of His (w)hol(l)y other Name, the Name that names us and thereby creates us and controls us. . . . "*Be'er la-ḥai ro'i*=the well to the life of Him Who sees me" (Gen. 16:14). To be seen is to live, to draw from the well; the well of the life of my fear. . . . "*Retson yerei'av ya'aseh ve-'et shav'atam yishma' ve-yoshi'eim*= He will do the will of those who have an ongoing fear of Him and He will hear their cry and will save them" (Ps. 145:19). Cognitive dissonance from pits of burning children. All of Jewish history is theodicy, rereading

AFFECTIONS

Everyone sins; that is, every person commits acts that are seriously wrong. Such acts have real social consequences. They disrupt our careers, destroy our human relationships, and undermine our self-image. They also desecrate the Name of God, casting a shadow over Him and our service to Him. We fear retribution for such acts. This fear is called *yir'at ha-'onesh,* "the fear of punishment."

When we sin seriously, however, we are also seized by anxiety. We know we have been untrue to our inner calling. We have violated our highest vision of ourselves. Such acts are incompatible with the presence of God in our lives. They are "the other impulse" in us seeking expression. We are frightened by the sense that some ugly truth in us has already partially surfaced, and we fear that it will permanently alienate us from the deeper truth of the presence of God. This is fear of God in its most basic sense, the fear that He will exact from

SPARKS

as it says, "you eat by the sweat of your hands." Further, he shall have a beautiful and modest wife, as it says, "your wife shall be as a fruitful vine." And he will merit beautiful and proper children, as it says, "your children will be as olive saplings." These three blessings are for one who "has ongoing fear of the Lord," as it says, "This is how. . . ."

As for the second type of person, he who occupies himself with Torah, he is worthy of greater blessings. Of him it says, "May the Lord bless you from Zion," that is, may such a person merit being an authorized interpreter of the Torah, as it says, "For from Zion shall go forth the Torah" (Isa. 2:3) and as it says, "may you see good for Jerusalem," for "good" denotes "Torah," as it says, "and the word of God from

Jerusalem" (Isa. 2:3). Further, [such a person will be blessed with] "may you see children of your children," meaning student-sages who will bring "peace upon Israel," as the sages have said, "Student-sages bring peace to the world, as it says, 'and all your children shall be learned of the Lord'" (Talmud, Berakhot 64a, citing Isa. 54:13).

Note that the Sefat Emet has taken the original talmudic saying out of context and has divided the psalm into two parts (vv. 2-4, 5-6, with v. 1 as an introduction). He has also beautifully woven other verses into the fabric of his meditation and has developed a typology of proper religious piety which values Torah-work more than fearing God.

AFFECTIONS   CON-VERSES

us a psychological and/or physical price for our sins, that He will desert us. We fear that He will allow our sinfulness so to alienate us from Him that we will stay psychologically, morally, and existentially lost. Such fear is called *yir'ah tata'ah,* "lower fear."

Our fear of God, however, is mitigated by two factors; otherwise we would be terrorized into compulsive pacification of a tyrannical deity. First, we know that we have certain merits. Even in our most sinful moments, we remember that we have performed acts of loyalty and dedication to Him and we have confidence that these deeds will mitigate His judgment of us. We also know that we have a continuing commitment to His presence and to the work He has asked us to do. In spite of our stumbling, we affirm this commitment and we trust the future it implies. We are as a ship that has gone off course but which will right itself by its own natural force when the storm has passed. This confidence in the deeper patterns of our being comforts us and enables us to live with our fear of God.

We also know from Scripture, the tradition, and our own experience of God that He is fair—indeed, kind and loving; that He will see our sinfulness as a sidestep, a temporary digression, from the more basic pattern of our faithfulness. We trust that He will understand. Even those sins within us which are compulsive, which repeat themselves without our being able to stop or eradicate them, He will look upon with a compassionate eye. He too knows anger, frustration, and fear for His creatures. He too "sins," that is, strays from the path of loving justice

catastrophe to fit the promises that have been broken, and the gnawing suspicion that after the Night they will never be kept. If the promises are not good (even, if they *may* not be good), the text and its interpretation are a farce, a game played with oneself and with Him and with the entrenched institutions that claim His Name. . . . The language of oppression doubles back on itself, binding the sacrifice without ever making it, yet without ever releasing it. . . . The Name names further, extending its power, em-bodying itself in oppression; proleptic illusion.

Re-spect, look back. Look back over one's shoulder at the grue-Presence, the haunting ghost, the unNameable terror and power. . . . "Be Happy, persist in walking in His ways": the funeral march, not the skipping of the lambs and the gamboling of the goats. . . . The margin, the limen of the repressed, the unstable border held in check by the forced march, through the wilderness of metaphysical oppression, of moral topsy-turvy; counter-commonsense; mark the border. . . . The ways: the straight path for His Name's sake; the absent Name, present in walking; the path with the blind pathfinder who is "happy," who persists on the path knowing it leads nowhere. . . . Gap, aporia; a spiderweb covering the hole; a way that leads to the circle of oppression-fear-re-spect; a path back to the gap. . . .

Din-Torah, the trial of God. Who is right? Why was the sacrifice made? Will the promise be kept? Why has it not been kept? . . . He should fear Our wrath, Our judgment. . . . Does He fear Himself? His own Judgment? . . . →

CON-VERSES

Judgment is embodied in us, incarnated in those who have no fear-awe-respect, in those who assert the primal crime as a step forward for humanity. He should fear *us*. Judgment is ours, unashamedly; it is our covenantal *right*. . . . *Yir'ah / yir'eh / yeira'eh*=fear / He will see / He will be seen. . . . "*Yir'u 'et Adonay kedoshav ki 'ein mahsor lirei'av*=fear/ see God, His holy ones, for there is no lack for those who have an ongoing fear of/who see Him" (Ps. 34:10) . . . *yeira'eh,* He Will Be Seen; We will be seen.

AFFECTIONS

which is His way because of these stresses, as do all parents. He is compassionate. This knowledge, too, helps us live with our fear of God.

However, we must be careful not to let the mitigating factors so encompass the fear that the fear ceases to be fear and becomes an excuse for our own weakness. The weakness of the other does not justify our own inadequacies.

Happiness requires that each person have an ongoing, true fear of God and His punishment, even if it does not always keep us from sinning.

Fear of God has another sense. It is a respect for the authority residual in the sacred tradition, in its scriptures, its rituals, its institutions, and in the ultimate Authority that lies behind religion. One may never idolize institutions, not even Scripture. But the authority of God is not detached from the concrete; it flows into the human-made. Happiness requires this basic respect for God and His authorized revelatory mechanisms.

Fear of God has, also, a fourth sense. It is a response to the awe one feels in the presence of the holy and the transcendent. We all experience God's present otherness, and we all respond to it with a sense of our own inadequacy. Happiness requires that we hold ourselves open to this Presence and to the feelings of radical amazement, awe, unworthiness, and fear that the awareness of God calls forth. Such fear is called *yir'ah 'ila'ah,* "upper fear."

who persists in walking in His ways

"Walking in God's ways" is not a happy, long promenade, nor is it a victorious march. Rather, it too is an

AFFECTIONS

ongoing attitude, a pattern of commitment. It too is a biblical virtue. To walk in God's ways is to persevere in the fear of God in spite of our sin, in spite of our reservations about the instantiations of His authority, and in spite of the dullness of spirit that keeps us from experiencing His presence. To walk in God's ways is to call to memory the joy of His presence and the glory of His manifestations in nature, in sacred time, and in people. It is to live in those memories. To walk in God's ways is to always seek God anew, even when we are depressed by sin and life. "To walk" is to persist in walking.

Neither fear of God nor walking in His ways is easy. They are interrelated virtues, affections, goals of the religious life. They are the key, the psalmist tells us, to the deepest levels of happiness.

If you eat by the sweat of your hands, you will be happy

2If you eat by the sweat of your hands, you will be happy and goodness will be yours.

"Labor is highly valuable because it brings honor to those involved in it" (Talmud, Nedarim 49b, cited in Feuer). "He who benefits from the sweat of his hands inherits two worlds [this world and the next]" (Talmud, Berakhot 8a, cited in Rashi). "The most pious thing a craftsman can have in mind is simply: 'I wish to do the best job possible to serve my customer or client. I want every stitch to be as tight as possible'" (Yisroel Salanter, cited in Feuer).

Not working is not good for us; it is a sign of depression, and depression is a form of introverted anger. A slow burning anger can bring no happiness. Taking up a task and working at it, the harder the better, will restore a sense of

WORDS

sweat
Lit., "fatigue"; hence, "labor" and then "sweat."

SPARKS

by the sweat of your hands
The rabbi of Shidlovtsi said, "It says specifically 'hands,' that the effort shall be 'by the sweat of your hands.' But the mind shall be holy unto God. For even when one is doing one's work, one should think of the Torah and wor-

ship. Then, 'you will be happy'—in this world, and 'goodness will be yours'—in the world to come." The rabbi of Kotsk said it this way, "The hands should do, but the head should be toward heaven" (Rosenwald).

CON-VERSES

AFFECTIONS

your wife will be as a fruitful vine

It says "*'esh(te)kha*=your fire," not "*ishtekha*= your wife." "Your fire will be a fruitful vine": semen, fire, fruit, children; orgasm, family, the fruit of fear-awe and work-society; planted olive trees, gnarled, masculine, strong; olive trees live for centuries.

Lost: fire for fire's sake, Prometheus's fire; "his intestines are a column of smooth ivory, adorned with sapphires" (Song 5:14). The joy of a body well and properly used—without fear, without encumbrance. Commitment to relatedness, not posterity—body to body, self to self. Fullness of physical being, verbal silence—bodily language. Touch; release. . . .

Aristotle distorted nature in labeling touch the evil sense. Paul castrated Christian sexuality. The rabbis nodded toward the body but worshiped the soul. Christian and Jewish disciples twisted creation and pulled up one of its roots in making touch-body the touchstone

> 3Your wife will be as a fruitful vine in the intimate recesses of your house; your children will be as olive saplings around your table.

competency, of setting a goal and achieving it.

It is best if the task one takes up benefits someone else, too, for then it also serves God. Doing good is spiritually, as well as psychologically, therapeutic. In the concentration camps, inmates made gifts for one another. The giving of a gift creates a moral bond, a human obligation. Work, particularly for others, is the source of happiness and goodness. It too is a biblical virtue, a religious affection.

Your wife . . . around your table

"When she remains in the intimate recesses of your house, she will be as a fruitful vine" (Rosenwald, based on Talmud Yerushalmi, Kil'ayim 1:7). Fruitfulness and modesty are ongoing attitudes, patterns of commitment. They are biblical virtues.

How, then, do we read the verses "I took off my clothes; how could I wear them?! I washed my body; how could I let it be dirty?! My beloved placed his

SPARKS

as a fruitful vine . . . as olive saplings

What were the analogies in the minds of the rabbis that made these two metaphors work? What does a wife have in common with a vine, and children with olive saplings?

The vine is fruitful. It is beautiful. It grows on a family plot. And the vine is one of the few plants on which one cannot graft anything except another type of vine. This latter quality makes the vine a symbol of purity. So it is with the wife of the God-fearing person. She is

fruitful, beautiful, modest, and undefiled.

The olive tree is beautiful. It is green all year long. And it, too, does not accept grafts except from its own kind. So it is with the children of the God-fearing person. They are beautiful. They do not wither but remain fresh all year. And they remain undefiled by the impurities of the sinful life. They shall be "around your table," under your influence, and not around the table of others (Rosenwald).

AFFECTIONS

CON-VERSES

hand on the hole and my insides were aroused because of him. I moved to open for my beloved, my hands dripping, scented. My fingers, overflowing with scent, passed over the surface of the closure" (Song 5:3–5)? What is sexual erotic love? Is it, too, a biblical virtue?

The tradition, following psalms and the prophets, affirms the sexual and condemns the sexually erotic. Sexuality is deemed a right, but is carefully contained by the laws of purity and the preachments of modest practice. Sexuality is commended, but firmly channeled into marriage. The psalmist's passion for God is preserved, and the Song of Songs is canonized as an allegory of the love of God and Israel for each other. Love, in the sense of sexual passion, is an emotion, not a virtue. Love, in the sense of commitment to family and modesty, is an abiding good, an ongoing attitude, a religious affection.

In a more subtle vein, the tradition, again following psalms and the prophets, understands the erotic in a covenantal, spiritual sense. God's love for Israel is like the erotic love of man and woman for each other. God's election of the people is carnal, jealous, irrational, passionate. So too the people's love of God is passionate, irrational, mad. The Jews love their God, His Torah, His land, and His children jealously, desperately, even unto death. During the holocaust, oftentimes, even godless Jews chose martyrdom rather than betray God and His people. The individual, too, can have an erotic relationship with God, yearning for Him and being enwrapped by Him, in His love. In the mystical traditions, the Jew can even

of evil and ethereal-soul the fountain of good in western theology. . . . The language of repression, the rhetoric of control, the compulsion of sublimation. . . . Lost, gone, an evaporated dream, a trace of memory, an unfulfilled wish; a phant(org)asm, repressed. . . .

yarketei=intimate recesses, the feminine form of *yarekh* (cf. Ben Iehouda)= thigh: "put your hand under my thigh," "gird your sword on the thigh of the hero," "your rounded thighs are like jewels" (Gen. 24:2; Ps. 45:4; Song 7:2).

The woman is the receptacle for the seed, the fertile ground for the fruitful vine; the enfolding flaps (of) the inner recesses of the tent; the lover-receiver, the mother-bearer.

But what of the spinster? the widow? the non-nubile woman? the barren woman? the not-yet-married woman? What of the woman who, by lack of opportunity, remains celibate? And what of the woman who, by conscious decision, chooses a chaste existence? the woman who is loving but infertile, intimate but chaste? And what of the woman who is lover, but not mother, perhaps not married? the woman who understands fullness of body but who does not fill her body with children? And what of the woman who finds love in the care of another woman? "Bless me, too, my F/father. . . . Have you not saved a blessing for me? . . . Have you but one blessing, my F/father? Bless me, too, my F/father" (Gen. 27:34, 36, 38). Blessedness is not fertility, though fertility is one kind of blessing.

"A Woman of Valor" (Proverbs 31) is an efficient manager of spoils. She is like a merchant ship; who fructifies the fields by her work; whose husband is well respected; who girds her hips with

CON-VERSES

strength and flexes the muscles of her arms. She too has an ongoing fear-awe of God. This also is the language of oppression, patriarchal mirror image, hidden matriarchy. There is no mention of love, no W/word of person; neither of body nor of self. Rather, there is virtue, valor, victory of sub-pression, rape. . . .

"I will tell you a story about my beloved: My beloved had a vineyard in the horn of the son of oil. He broke the ground, cleared the stones, planted it with the best vines, built a watchtower, and even constructed a winepress. He hoped it would yield grapes but it produced rotten fruit" (Isa. 5.1–2).

"Blessed are You, Lord, King of the universe, Who has created the fruit of the vine". . . . Noah planted a vineyard, drank from the wine, got drunk, and rolled around shamelessly in his tent (Gen. 9:18–27). . . . The nazirite must abstain from wine, from wine vinegar, from anything steeped in grape juice, from dry and moist grapes, even from the seeds and the skin (Num. 6:1–21). . . . Woman is the fruit of the vine, a dangerous (yet created) in-toxic-ant, in the intimate recesses.

But is this so? Intimacy is person-to-person, not an intoxicant. In person-to-person-ness is wholeness. To love is to look into the eyes of the other, freely, without the fruit of the vine. To be loved is to have the other look into one's eyes, not to ab-stain from the fruit of the vine. Woman is person, not fruitful vine. Person is wholeness, not intoxicant.

Lost: fire for fire's sake. Lost: woman for woman's sake.

your children will be as olive saplings

And: as lilies of the valley, as roses of

AFFECTIONS

touch God, intertwine with Him and, temporarily, become one with Him. However, erotic love — in the spiritual or mystical sense too — is an emotion, a moment: creation, Sinai, mystical ecstasy. A flash of lightning, a spiritual embrace. Always remembered, always returned to, but not ongoing.

Love as a virtue is rooted in family. It is the fruitfulness of the vine, abundant and regular. It is the youthfulness of the olive sapling, full of promise, requiring cultivation and attention. Love as a virtue is rooted in the future, in the seed, in the intimate recesses of one's home. This love is not sexually erotic.

Passionate, sexually erotic love is a moment of grace which illuminates the day. "Satisfy us in the morning with Your gracious love and we will sing and be happy all our days" (Ps. 90:14). There must be such moments in every human life, as indeed they occur in the life of God. But love as a virtue is an ongoing pattern. It is a commitment to till, to plant, to weed, to water, to prune, and to harvest.

And yet there is sin. The fires of erotic passion are very real. They vary in direct proportion to fantasy. "Do not go astray and follow your hearts, nor follow your eyes" (Num. 15:39). Temptation and sin always lie at the door (Gen. 4:7) of the mind and the heart. Imagination, which is the root of fantasy, is limitless and very clever. Real life is composed of people who do not always fulfill our expectations and situations which leave us disillusioned. Real life is very fickle, it disappoints, it frustrates. Ongoing living itself evokes fantasy and calls forth escape. Real life leads to sin, and sin tempts; strongly, always. →

AFFECTIONS   CON-VERSES

Yet, when one is alone, what does one have? If one is to live in the presence of God, what makes sense? In the end, what matters? Only family, if there has been the love which is commitment and the modesty which avoids the erotic. Emotions of all kinds seduce; virtues are building blocks.

⁴This is how a man who has an ongoing fear of the Lord will be blessed.

Emotions lead one astray; virtues elicit commitment. Emotions fade in and out; virtues persist. Happiness, the psalmist tells us, requires love as a virtue, love as a religious affection: a dedication to labor, fruitfulness, and modesty.

This is how a man . . . will be blessed

There are three kinds of blessing. God blesses creation, granting us abundance of rain, food, sun, shelter, children, and security. He satisfies us from His goodness and makes this year as blessed as the good years (daily liturgy). He accepts our prayers and offerings. He fulfills the wishes of our hearts. He blesses the work of our hands. These are the blessings of Joseph.

God also blesses us as partners in the covenant. He grants us the ability to study and to teach, to know and to decide. He gives us the wisdom, courage, and strength to judge, to build, and to lead. He sustains, through us, the dialogue between Himself and His people which is the covenant. These are the blessings of Judah.

And God blesses us as His children. He causes the light of His face to shine upon us. He lifts His face toward us. He

sharon. And: as weavers of the cloth of human relatedness, as nurturers, and as healers.

This is how a man . . . will be blessed

The virtuous human being is *de facto* a man with a fruitful, beautiful, modest, undefiled wife. He is rewarded for his ongoing fear of God with a pleasant and exclusive baby machine. He is recompensed for persisting in walking in h/His ways with a woman who sweeps his path in all domestic ways. Woman, in this view, is the tool which makes man's blessings possible. Her blessing is to be a blessing to him. She has no blessing of her own, no way of her own to God, the Man served by man and woman.

As a man, I cannot speak the blessedness of women. But some women have spoken as follows:

Happy is the woman
    who rejoices in God,
    who greatly delights in God's ways.
Security and self-knowledge
    shall be in her dwelling,
    her sharing shall endure forever.
                                    Michele Foust

Mizmor Rivkah
For flute and strings

My G-d, I cannot bear
this child and this pain.
I stagger like a drunkard
yet no wine has passed my lips.
My child struggles
as if she too gives birth.
She twists and turns
and I cannot comfort her.

CON-VERSES

My body, my breasts, my womb
have no more strength.
Who will be our strength?

G-d will be our strength.
For She too has carried
the pain of motherhood
and seen Her children do evil
and been rent asunder.

As She brought the world into existence
through contraction
my contraction too will create.
And when I am prostrate
She will be upright
so that my child will be born
into a world knowing of justice.

I weave
Her praises into my life
my life into Her praises.
She strews brilliance about the earth
and causes softness to take root.
She wraps the desert in strength
and nurses the plains with rain.
Praise Her.

                                        Naomi Janowitz

My mother has abandoned me,
Who will hold me, who will feed me?
I am empty and exposed.
Who will calm me?

The Lord is warmth.
She will cradle me.
The wings of the Lord will cover me.
Her breath will soothe me.

Who will explain to me
The waxing and waning of the womb?
From whom will I inherit the strength
To bear the pain of labor?

The form of the Lord is round and soft
Her mouth is broad and moist.
I depend on the Lord
For She alone will teach me.

                                        Maggie Wenig, 1974

AFFECTIONS

sets His presence before us. He puts His
spirit into our hearts. These are the
blessings of David, the psalmist.

We bless other human beings as God
blesses us. We give charity and provide
employment. We help in the work of the
community. And we pass on to others
the Presence we have received, acting as
a conduit for the holy otherness that has
been given to us.

We also bless God! "Bless God Who
is blessed," says the leader. "Blessed be
God Who is blessed forever," responds
the congregation (daily liturgy). To
"bless" God is to acknowledge that He
is the source of all blessings. It is also
to return to Him the energy He has
given us. Mostly, it is to acknowledge
His blessed Presence as itself blessed
and ourselves as aware of that blessedness. Blessing is dialogic, reciprocal. It
is more than covenantal; it is a reading
of the texts of His existence and ours,
reflected in one another as one text.
Blessedness is the intertextuality of true
existence.

The psalmist now gives voice to the
antiphon. The levites speak it from the
steps. God speaks it from the holy of
holies.

**May the Lord bless you from Zion . . .
peace upon Israel**

God's elections are concentric. He
chose the world. Then He chose the
holy land. Then He chose Jerusalem,
Zion. Then He chose the holy of holies,
the navel of the universe, the point
where heaven and earth meet. From
Zion His blessing goes forth; from
nowhere else does it truly proceed. The
priests in the name of God, God
through the priests, bless the virtuous
person from Zion. The greatest bless-

AFFECTIONS   CON-VERSES

ing is to see the goodness, prosperity, **May the Lord bless you from Zion . . .**
and safety of Jerusalem, for if Jerusalem **the good of Jerusalem**
is secure, so is the world. What a great
privilege for our   Concentric circles,
generations to see   of holiness, of
goodness for Jeru-   5May the Lord bless you from Zion. Power: the world,
alem! Will it last   the holy land, the
all the days of our   May you see good for Jerusalem   holy city, the holy
lives? We can   all the days of your life.   site, the holy of
scarcely believe   holies; humanity,
what our eyes   the Jewish people,
have seen! We are as in a dream (Ps.   the levites, the priests, the high priest;
126:1)! I, for one, regret that I do not   and later the rabbinic sleight of hand:
own land in Jerusalem, that I do not pay   humanity, the Jewish people, the levites,
taxes to those who see to its walls, that   the priests, the rabbis, the court, Moses
I do not occupy myself enough with the   our Rabbi—hierarchies of oppres-
welfare of Jerusalem.   sion. . . . Everything touched or named
Even Jerusalem would have no mean-   by the temple must go to the temple; it
ing if there were no Jews, no descen-   is holy. . . . Con-secrate, de-secrate, ex-
dants. First, there is the blessing of the ecrate [to utter curses upon]; in and out
body, the incarnation of the covenant.   of the holy; the hierarchy, the hier-archy
Then there is the blessing of those who   (the holy order). Order, ordure, law and
are worthy, for not everyone is able to   order, ordered cosmos, maintained by
receive all the blessings, as Jacob found   hier-archy, the holy order. . . . H/holi-
out (Genesis 50). Everyone gets some-   ness implies P/power, a reverse cosmo-
thing, for all are the holy seed. But some logical argument for the existence of
get more, not because we love them   God. P/power maintains O/order which
more, nor even because God loves them   turns to itself and sus/main-tains I/it-
more, but because they merit it; or   self. . . . Zion is the source of P/power,
because they are more sensitive, as some   "for from Zion shall go forth the Torah"
children are sensitive to art or gifted in (Isa. 2:3). Jerusalem is the wellspring of
music. There is the child who is an heir   O/order, blessing. The blessing goes
of the flesh, which is a blessing. And   forth to those who submit to the hier-
there is the child who may or may not   archy, violent hierarchy. Blessing does
be of the flesh but who is an heir to one   not spill down indifferently upon the
of the special blessings. To see two   "wicked" and the "righteous." The righ-
generations of blessing is itself a great   teous who walk the path of the holy
blessing.   Order are blessed. To be righteous is to
To see goodness for Jerusalem and   be virtuous, to be blessed, to be part of
the transmission of blessing is happiness   the holy order, to be the object of the
given in response to happiness. It is the   holy Power.
blessing of the virtuous, a just circle.   What is the "good" for Jerusalem?
If there is peace for Israel, there is Good-ness is peace, security, order, holy
peace for the world. If there is no peace   placed-ness. Good-ness is blessed-ness,
for Israel, there is no peace for the world. being within the holy Order. Good-ness

CON-VERSES

is unity, at-one-ness with the Holy One, suppressed rebellion, purified sin, purged guilt. Good-ness is a spiritual enema which cleanses the inner parts, the kidneys [the seat of the emotions], by "Him Who knows the kidneys and the heart." Good-ness is to be I/image and S/self, mirror in a mirror, holiness, wholeness, *shalom* (peace), *shalem* (whole). . . . Who would not prefer narcissistic holi/whole-ness to division, guilt, rebellion, independence, thought, criticism, stress, sin? Who would not prefer good-ness to alienation, to hole-ness? . . . Seductive hier-archy, comforting mirrority. The self is a known item, its re-flection is re-cognized. Even the symmetric O/other s/Self is a known quant/quality. . . . To be cut off/loose from the hier-archy, to be alien to the mirrored S/self, to be A/self, a/Self. This is sin, her(r)esy, Free-dom, free-dumb, struck dumb and free; a-lone(r), a-metaphoric, outside the pail/pale; F/face to f/Face, p/Presence to P/presence.

Is it "good" for Jerusalem to be split into dis-Ordered neigh/nay-borhoods? into poly-ticalities? Can Pales/Philistinians dwell in the holy city of oneness? Can the non-conformists to the hierarchy (called secularists) dwell in the city of O/order and P/power? Can an unclean Tamar or Rachel enter the holy precincts? Split hairs! Apply P/power! Tell me who may stay and who must go! Holy S/selfhood perpetuating neigh/nay-borhood; poly-ticks wearing down time, killing time. . . . If Jerusalem is polysemic [has varied seed], O/order is polysemic and it is no longer order. If the holy seed [the Jewish people] is polysemic, O/order is polysemic and it is no longer totalistically hier-archy. The chaos factor, the freedom of creation

from its C/creator, undecidability, undeicidability, the plurisignification of existence, *différance*. Polysemy is good for Jerusalem.

children of your children . . . peace upon Israel

Banim (sons, children)=*ba-sam* (in the medicine/poison)=*bala'* (H/he swallowed)=*ba-kaf* (in the palm of the hand)=*ba-sekhakh* (in the roofing)= *'avekha* (your clouds)=*'emunah* (faith)=*meivin* (h/He understands)= *hasidekha* (your righteous ones)=*hamdan* (one who covets)=*ve-'avdekha* (and Y/your servant) [the Hebrew letters of all these words have a numerical value of 102]. He swallows your children; your children swallow Him: "for on the day you eat of it, your eyes will be open and you will be like God(s) knowing good and evil; behold the human has become like one of Us knowing good and evil and now, lest it send forth its hand and take also of the tree of life and eat of it and live forever" (Gen. 3:5, 22).

His mother's eyes, his father's gestures, his great uncle's intuition, his grandmother's insight; four generations. . . . A spiritual child bears the knowledge. But knowledge was/is gained by sin; it is life eternal, sin against the Eternal, the F/fear of the Eternal. Such a child, bearing knowledge born of and in sin, is a seed in and of Eternity. He or she cannot be swallowed, digested, and assimilated. Rather, she or he swallows and digests and assimilates Eternity. A child of a child, so conceived, is being, born again.

"My son, Absalom; my son, my son, Absalom; Would that I myself could

CON-VERSES

have died in your place; Absalom, my son, my son" (2 Sam. 19:1). . . . Absalom, 'av shalom=the father of peace is the son of rebellion; shalom 'al Yisrael=peace on Israel, peace on the son who "fought with God and with men and who has prevailed" (Gen. 32:28); shalom=Peace is one of the Names of God: the Name be upon the son who fights with God and men, God be upon him; M/my son wants war, I/i want to be upon him, which will yield P/peace, O/order, hierarchy. . . . A rebellious son—misnamed 'av shalom=the father of peace, bo' shalom=come peace, shalom ba'=peace comes/has come—is still a son. He is his father's hope, his father's alter ego; therefore he can never die, never be inwardly alien. The father mourns him(self), he would die for such a son. . . . Absalom must rebel; he must leave his father— in anger or in peace which is a being of the-father-upon-the-son, which is really anger. The father of peace arrogates to himself the six days of creation (the vav [the "o" which has a numerical value of six] of shalom) so that he can be shalem, whole. Such a son is not a sacrifice, Absalom is not Isaac. . . . Absalom had three sons, but their names have been repressed, and one daughter, whose name was the

6May you see the children of your children. Peace upon Israel.

WORDS

peace on Israel
    The second part of the psalm, the blessing, begins with "May the Lord bless" and concludes with "peace." This may be an imitation of the priestly blessing, "May the Lord bless you and keep you . . . peace" (Num. 6:24–26; Hacham).

SPARKS

children of your children
    The rabbi of Buczacz said, "Every parent gives to his or her child beyond his or her strength. Yet every child feels that the parent has not even fulfilled his or her basic duty. When will there be peace between them? When the child has children, and the child gives to his or her child beyond his or her strength while that child feels that its parents have not even fulfilled their duty. Then, the first child will realize the righteousness of his or her parents in what they did do and will ask forgiveness of them. This is the meaning of 'may you see children of your children'—that your children should have children. Then there will be 'peace upon Israel,' for because of this, your child will acknowledge what you have done for him or her" (Rosenwald).
    The Talmud teaches (Ta'anit 5b–6a) as follows:
    When Rabbi Yitzhak was about to leave Rav Nahman to return to Israel from Babylonia, Rav Nahman said to him, "Bless me, master." Rabbi Yitzhak replied to him, "I shall tell you a parable." →

CON-VERSES

same as his sister's, the one who was raped by his brother whom the father of peace later murdered (2 Samuel 13 with 14:27). . . . A margin, a gloss in the holy His-story: "he shall be cut off"; "He re-members the sin of the fathers onto the sons, onto the sons of the sons, and onto the sons of the sons of the sons as My enemies" (Ex. 20:5, the Second Commandment).

The blessing is proleptic; it takes the future as past; it expresses hope, merging the future with the present. Jerusalem is not Absalom's Jerusalem; it is not even David's Jerusalem, or Solomon's, and certainly not Herod's. It is "Jerusalem of gold". . . . *Yerushalayim* is always written as a singular noun but with a dual ending. There is a hidden Jerusalem which is spoken but not written, which is seen and heard simultaneously. It is the heavenly Jerusalem, which hovers above the earthly Jerusalem. In it, sages study Torah and the righteous eat at the banquet of God. It casts a messianic, apocalyptic shadow over the earthly Jerusalem. . . . The children in the blessing, and in the popular Israeli song set to it, are not the children of today or a real tomorrow. The Jerusalem of the blessing, and of the song, is not the Jerusalem of today or the likely Jerusalem of tomorrow. For the children of today are Absaloms and the Jerusalem of today is a political city; it was always so. Rather, the blessing and the songs evoke the double mirror. The blessing/invocation is a messianic song. That which is on the margin is displaced to the center, and the center is overturned toward the margin, and hope hangs between them caught in the interval.

SPARKS

"To what may the matter be compared? To a man who was walking in the desert and was hungry, tired, and thirsty. He found a tree whose fruits were sweet, whose shade was pleasant, and under which there flowed a stream of water. He ate of its fruits, drank of its waters, and sat in its shade. When he was ready to go, he said, 'Oh tree, oh tree. How can I bless you? If I say "May your fruits be sweet," they are already sweet. And if I say, "May your shade be pleasant," it is already pleasant. And if I say, "May a stream of water flow under you," it already flows under you. Rather, I shall say, 'May it be God's will that all the saplings that come from you be like you.'"

"So you too," said Rabbi Yitzhak to Rav Nahman. "With what can I bless you? If with Torah, you are already a scholar. If with wealth, you are already well off. And if with children, you already have children. Rather, I shall say, 'May it be God's will that all your descendants be like you.'"

Psalm 44

WITH
FOUR
COMMENTARIES

לַמְנַצֵּחַ לִבְנֵי קֹרַח
מַשְׂכִּיל:

אֱלֹהִים בְּאָזְנֵינוּ שָׁמַעְנוּ
אֲבוֹתֵינוּ סִפְּרוּ לָנוּ
פֹּעַל פָּעַלְתָּ בִימֵיהֶם
בִּימֵי קֶדֶם:

אַתָּה יָדְךָ גּוֹיִם הוֹרַשְׁתָּ
וַתִּטָּעֵם
תָּרַע לְאֻמִּים וַתְּשַׁלְּחֵם:

כִּי לֹא בְחַרְבָּם יָרְשׁוּ אָרֶץ
וּזְרוֹעָם לֹא הוֹשִׁיעָה לָּמוֹ
כִּי יְמִינְךָ וּזְרוֹעֲךָ וְאוֹר פָּנֶיךָ
כִּי רְצִיתָם:

אַתָּה הוּא מַלְכִּי אֱלֹהִים
צַוֵּה יְשׁוּעוֹת יַעֲקֹב:

בְּךָ צָרֵינוּ נְנַגֵּחַ
בְּשִׁמְךָ נָבוּס קָמֵינוּ:

A Psalm of National Anger

in which God's support is recalled
His abandonment bitterly remembered
and His help angrily evoked

[1]From the leader's collection, by the Koraḥ family,
for contemplation.

[2]God, with our own ears we heard,
our ancestors told us
how You did mighty deeds in their days,
in days of old.

[3]You, with Your power, disinherited nations;
then You settled our ancestors;
You acted against nations, sending them forth.

[4]Truly, our ancestors did not inherit the land with their
    sword,
nor did their arm save them;
it was Your right hand, Your arm, and the light of Your
    Face
for You were pleased with them.

[5]You are my king, God,
command the victory of Jacob.

[6]With You, we will gore our enemies;
with Your Name, we will trample our foes.

כִּי לֹא בְקַשְׁתִּי אֶבְטָח
וְחַרְבִּי לֹא תוֹשִׁיעֵנִי:

כִּי הוֹשַׁעְתָּנוּ מִצָּרֵינוּ
וּמְשַׂנְאֵינוּ הֱבִישׁוֹתָ:

בֵּאלֹהִים הִלַּלְנוּ כָל הַיּוֹם
וְשִׁמְךָ לְעוֹלָם נוֹדֶה סֶלָה:

אַף זָנַחְתָּ וַתַּכְלִימֵנוּ
וְלֹא תֵצֵא בְּצִבְאוֹתֵינוּ:

תְּשִׁיבֵנוּ אָחוֹר מִנִּי צָר
וּמְשַׂנְאֵינוּ שָׁסוּ לָמוֹ:

תִּתְּנֵנוּ כְּצֹאן מַאֲכָל
וּבַגּוֹיִם זֵרִיתָנוּ:

תִּמְכֹּר עַמְּךָ בְלֹא הוֹן
וְלֹא רִבִּיתָ בִּמְחִירֵיהֶם:

תְּשִׂימֵנוּ חֶרְפָּה לִשְׁכֵנֵינוּ
לַעַג וָקֶלֶס לִסְבִיבוֹתֵינוּ:

תְּשִׂימֵנוּ מָשָׁל בַּגּוֹיִם
מְנוֹד רֹאשׁ בַּלְאֻמִּים:

כָּל הַיּוֹם כְּלִמָּתִי נֶגְדִּי
וּבֹשֶׁת פָּנַי כִּסָּתְנִי:

⁷Truly, I do not put trust in my bow,
nor will my sword give me victory.

⁸Truly, You have saved us too from our enemies;
You have also disgraced those who hated us.

⁹Through God we praise all day,
we give thanks to Your Name forever. Selah.

¹⁰But now, You desert and shame us.
You do not go out with our armies.

¹¹You put us to flight from our enemies.
Those who hate us tear us to pieces at will.

¹²You hand us over like sheep to be devoured.
You cast us among the nations.

¹³You sell Your people for nothing.
You do not make a profit on their sale price.

¹⁴You make us an object of shame for our neighbors,
a thing of scorn and derision for those around us.

¹⁵You make an example of us to the nations,
an object of head-shaking among the peoples.

¹⁶All day, my humiliation confronts me,
my shame covers me,

מִקּוֹל מְחָרֵף וּמְגַדֵּף
מִפְּנֵי אוֹיֵב וּמִתְנַקֵּם:

כָּל זֹאת בָּאַתְנוּ
וְלֹא שְׁכַחֲנוּךָ
וְלֹא שִׁקַּרְנוּ בִּבְרִיתֶךָ:

לֹא נָסוֹג אָחוֹר לִבֵּנוּ
וַתֵּט אֲשֻׁרֵינוּ מִנִּי אָרְחֶךָ:

כִּי דִכִּיתָנוּ בִּמְקוֹם תַּנִּים
וַתְּכַס עָלֵינוּ בְצַלְמָוֶת:
אִם שָׁכַחְנוּ שֵׁם אֱלֹהֵינוּ
וַנִּפְרֹשׂ כַּפֵּינוּ לְאֵל זָר:

הֲלֹא אֱלֹהִים יַחֲקָר זֹאת
כִּי הוּא יֹדֵעַ תַּעֲלֻמוֹת לֵב:

כִּי עָלֶיךָ הֹרַגְנוּ כָל הַיּוֹם
נֶחְשַׁבְנוּ כְּצֹאן טִבְחָה:

עוּרָה
לָמָּה תִישַׁן אֲדֹנָי
הָקִיצָה
אַל תִּזְנַח לָנֶצַח:

לָמָּה פָנֶיךָ תַסְתִּיר
תִּשְׁכַּח עָנְיֵנוּ וְלַחֲצֵנוּ:

¹⁷from the sounds of the taunter and the blasphemer,
from the fantasy of revenge on the enemy.

¹⁸All this happened to us
yet we did not forget You,
nor did we betray Your covenant.

¹⁹Our hearts did not retreat,
nor did our steps deviate from Your way.

²⁰Though You crushed us into a desolate place
and covered us with deep darkness,
²¹did we forget the Name of our God
or spread our hands in prayer to a strange deity?

²²Let God Himself investigate this
for He knows the hidden recesses of the heart.

²³Truly, for Your sake we are killed all day long,
we are considered sheep to be butchered.

²⁴Wake up!
Why do You sleep, Lord?!
Arise!
Do not abandon forever!

²⁵Why do You hide Your Face?
Why do You forget our persecution and our oppression?!

כִּי שָׁחָה לֶעָפָר נַפְשֵׁנוּ
דָּבְקָה לָאָרֶץ בִּטְנֵנוּ:

קוּמָה
עֶזְרָתָה לָנוּ
וּפְדֵנוּ לְמַעַן חַסְדֶּךָ:

²⁶For our souls have been pounded into the dirt,
our stomachs are stuck to the ground.

²⁷Get up!

Help us!

Redeem us for the sake of Your gracious love.

AFFECTIONS

This psalm is divided into five parts: a recalling of God's miraculous acts in the distant past (vv. 1–4), a remembering of His saving deeds in the lifetime of the psalmist (vv. 5–9), a confession of shame at the current defeat of the people (vv. 10–17), a strong protest of innocence (vv. 18–23), and an angry cry-prayer for immediate help (vv. 24–27). The psalm as a whole teaches us how to deal with anger against God.

our ancestors told us . . . saved us too

Memory is the core of Jewish existence. We, as a people, saw the miracles with our own eyes. We, as a people, saw the miracles with our own eyes. My parents told me, and their parents told them, and their parents told them, and so on back through centuries of time. And I shall tell my children, who will

CON-VERSES

This psalm is a psalm of rage. It calls to the surface our own feelings of fury. Try reading it out loud; not as a pious prayer but in the fullness of its rage.

Our generation reads this psalm in the shadow of the holocaust. It is not a survivor's psalm but a victim's psalm; and we identify with the victims. It expresses our rage— for them, for their suffering, for our own suffering through them. We rage at our enemies. We rage at those who betrayed us, by action and by inaction. And we rage at God. Otherwise, we have not confronted the holocaust.

"Affections" takes this stand, too, magnifying the anger, bringing it close to our reading of our post-holocaust situation. "Con-verses" reads this psalm in its utmost fury—against the text, against the tradition, even against God. Other texts are cited, but those that read against the psalm are in "Con-verses."

---

¹From the leader's collection, by the Korah family, for contemplation.

²God, with our own ears we heard, our ancestors told us how You did mighty deeds in their days, in days of old.

WORDS

from the leader's collection

Fifty-five psalms have this superscription. The evidence from Chronicles and Ezra suggests that the word *menaseah* denotes "a leader"; hence, *la-menaseah,* "from the leader's collection" (Kirkpatrick, p. xxi).

by the Korah family

According to Num. 16:32–33, Korah and his family were swallowed up by the earth in a rebellion against Moses. According to Num. 26:11, the sons of Korah did not die. In any case, here and in Chronicles, the Korah family

appears again. To account for this confusion, Ibn Ezra (Ps. 42:1) says they were descended from Heyman, who in turn was descended from Samuel the prophet, while Rashi (Ps. 42:1) cites the midrash that three of Korah's sons did descend into the earth but they truly repented and were saved. When they returned, they wrote these psalms under the influence of the holy spirit.

for contemplation

The term *maskil* occurs in the superscription to thirteen psalms. As a verb occurring variously

AFFECTIONS

tell their children, who will tell their children, and so on through more centuries of time. Further, I have seen many historical moments (the holocaust, the establishment of the State of Israel, the wars of the Middle East, etc.). I recount these moments to my children, who will tell their children, who will tell their children. And the story will continue. There is, thus, a continuous chain that is the witness to God's presence and His promise among us. Without that witness, there would be no promise. Without the witness and the promise, there would be no Jewish existence.

WORDS

in the Tanakh, it means "to instruct," "to enlighten"; hence, a psalm for "contemplation" or "instruction" (Ibn Ezra, Ps. 32:1; see also Kirkpatrick, p. xx, "a psalm with specially delicate and artistic character"). The term as a superscription, however, may refer to a musical instrument (Meiri, Ps. 32:1, cited in Feuer, ad loc.). In this case, it should not be translated since we do not know what instrument is meant.

SPARKS

our ancestors told us . . . in their days, in days of old

In the symbolism of the Zohar, Abraham is Hesed, Isaac is Gevura, and Jacob is Tiferet. The interpretation of the first part of this verse, then, is as follows:

"Our ancestors" — Hesed, Gevura, and Tiferet "told us" — indicate to us

"how You did a mighty deed in their days" — that, beginning with Hesed, the seven days of creation were accomplished.

The lower seven sefirot (Hesed, Gevura, Tiferet, Nesah, Hod, Yesod, and Malkhut), then, correspond to the seven days of the week and their coming-into-being is "creation."

The second part of the verse, however, presents a problem because the repetition of "in their days, in days of old" seems needless. The zoharic sources, however, interpret as follows:

"in days of old" — Prior to the creation of the world (before the seven sefirot), there are "days of old" (i.e., other sefirot; to wit, Keter, Hokhma, and Bina). These sefirot are "in days of old" (i.e., logically prior to "in their days").

The upper three sefirot (Keter, Hokhma, and Bina), then, precede the others in the sefirotic realm. They are, in this special sense, "before" creation.

Theologically, the ancestors teach the existence of the higher realm. Without the world of the ancestors, we would not know of the even higher worlds. Meditatively, it is through the lower realms that one reaches the higher realms. It is through time (the days of the week/history) that one reaches beyond time.

(Based on the Tiferet Shelomo, cited in the Imrot Tehorot; Rosenwald)

AFFECTIONS

with Your power, disinherited . . . settled

The claim of the Jewish people to the holy land derives from God. It is He Who created the whole universe and, because that is so, it is He, and only He, Who can dispose of any part of it. He designated the Jews to live in the holy land and, hence, they have a claim to it. The claim of any other people to the land, thus, cannot be rooted in conquest or in a history of settlement. Rather, non-Jews may occupy the holy land, but only temporarily, their claim being always subject to the authority of God, Who has actually willed the land to the Jews.

Because the claim of the Jewish people to the holy land is grounded in God's will, it too is not rooted in conquest or settlement. It is, rather, valid even if there is no Jewish state or physical Jewish presence in the land. Further, the claim of the Jewish people to the holy land is not rooted in merit. God gave the Jews the holy land because He wanted to, because He was "pleased with them," because He wished to fulfill

³You, with Your power, disinherited nations;
then You settled our ancestors;
You acted against nations, sending them forth.

⁴Truly, our ancestors did not inherit the land with their sword,
nor did their arm save them;
it was Your right hand, Your arm, and the light of Your Face
for You were pleased with them.

His oath to their ancestors (Deut. 9:5). No sin can remove that claim, even though sin can cause the Jews to be expelled from the land for longer or shorter periods of time (Lev. 26:33, 42–45). The metaphor of "planting" (here rendered as "settled") is, thus, a very good one, and it appears elsewhere in Scripture in this meaning (Ex. 15:17; 2 Sam. 7:10; Amos 9:15).

This rooting of the claim of the Jewish people to the holy land in the will of God as Creator is a scandal. The nations of the world do not admit this claim, as Rashi in his commentary on Gen. 1:1 notes. Indeed, it is part of the larger scandal of the chosenness of the Jewish people. The adamant resistance of the world notwithstanding, it is an affection—an ongoing emotional attitude, a feeling that is to be cultivated and sustained—that God chose the Jews and that He also chose the holy land for them. His loyalty to the Jews and to His promise to them of seed and of the holy land, and their loyalty to God, to His land, and to His teaching, are core affections in Jewish religious understanding.

WORDS

sending them forth

Ibn Ezra and the English translations take this clause to refer to the nations who are "driven out." The French and German translations take it to refer to Israel, whose roots are "sent forth." The latter preserves the symmetry of the four clauses. My translation tries to preserve the double meaning.

CON-VERSES

we will gore our enemies

Life is not a cup of tea with crumpets. Life is goring one's enemies, as an ox gores another ox or a person. Life is fierce loyalty to one's family and people. Life is also watching out for, and actively combatting, those who would do you in. Life is a jungle. Hatred and jealousy, not love, motivate life.

Why should I forgive my enemy?! especially if he or she has done nothing to indicate any feeling of genuine remorse?! Better to be wary, to return hostility. People rarely grow spiritually, psychologically. Sibling jealousy, fear of death, economic envy, racial prejudice—these do not go away. Better to

> 5You are my king, God, command the victory of Jacob.
>
> 6With You, we will gore our enemies; with Your Name, we will trample our foes.
>
> 7Truly, I do not put trust in my bow, nor will my sword give me victory.

know and acknowledge one's enemies, to be ready to gore them.

Christians often preach that the only way out of the jungle of life is love. Jews know that Christians have preached love but have not always practiced it. Almost twenty centuries of Christian persecution of Jews has convinced us that love is no way to act in the jungle of life. Living under the white Christian man's burden has convinced most of the rest of the non-Christian world, too, that Christian preaching and action are not always one, that Christian love is not effective in the jungle.

"I am peace; but, when I speak, they are for war" (Ps. 120:7). . . . "With You, we will gore our enemies."

WORDS

You are my king . . . we will gore

Note the effective shifting back and forth of singular and plural pronouns in this section, indicating an interweaving of personal and national consciousness.

I do not put trust

The shift in pronouns motivated Ibn Ezra and Radak to interpret this verse as the words of each individual fighter (Feuer). These commentators seem to be suggesting that this section was meant as an antiphon, or publicly recited prayer.

SPARKS

bow . . . sword

The commentators noticed that, after invoking the victory of Jacob (v. 5), the psalmist declares that neither his bow nor his sword can save him (v. 7). This stands in contrast to Jacob himself, who invoked precisely his bow and his sword to justify the special portion given to Joseph (Gen. 48:22). They point out, however,

that since the sword was the blessing of Esau (Gen. 27:40), it cannot have been the blessing of Jacob. Hence, the true interpretation of "bow and sword" here (in the invocation of Jacob's victory) and in Jacob's blessing to Joseph is "prayers and supplications," as the Targum to Gen. 48:22 suggests (Talmud, Bava Batra 123a; Feuer).

8Truly, You have saved us too from our
   enemies;
You have also disgraced those who
   hated us.

9Through God we praise all day,
we give thanks to Your Name forever.
Selah.

WORDS

saved us too . . . also

The words "too" and "also" are added, following Ibn Ezra and Radak. It strengthens the meaning to say that the army claims to have personally experienced miraculous salvations which, in turn, confirm the stories of the earlier redemptions.

Through God we praise

The prefix *b-* is unusual; compare Ps. 56:5, 11 also in the context of trust. The meaning is: "Through," or "because of" God's deeds, we are able to sing God's praises all day, which fits well with the context. The usual rendering, "In God we glory," is less precise.

Selah

This word is a great puzzle. Radak, together with most modern commentators and the Septuagint (where the Greek word is also unclear), teaches that this is a musical sign with no substantive content. It may signify an increase in musical volume (from the root "to raise"), or a musical interlude, or an antiphon. Ibn Ezra, on the other hand, takes it to be an affirmation that whatever preceded it is true and certain.

The term occurs, strangely, in rabbinic liturgical texts (three times in the daily morning liturgy). There it clearly means "forever, without end," a meaning reflected in the Talmud (Eruvin 54a): "Wherever the words *neṣaḥ, selah, va'ed* are used, they mean 'forever, without an end.'" This interpretation is also reflected in the Targum, Aquila, Jerome, and elsewhere (Feuer, on Ps. 3:3; Radak and Ibn Ezra, Ps. 3:3; Kirkpatrick, pp. xxii–xxiv).

SPARKS

Through God we praise all day

Rabbi David says, "Were it not for God Who enables us to say His praises, we could not even praise Him, as it says, 'Lord, open my lips and let my mouth speak Your praises' (Ps. 51:17)."

CON-VERSES

But now, You desert us and shame us

"Never shall I forget that night, the first night in the camp, which has turned my life into one long night, seven times cursed and seven times sealed. Never shall I forget the little faces of the children, whose bodies I saw turned into wreaths of smoke beneath a silent blue sky.

"Never shall I forget those flames which consumed my faith forever.

"Never shall I forget that nocturnal silence which deprived me, for all eternity, of the desire to live. Never shall I forget those moments which murdered my God and my soul and turned my dreams to dust. Never shall I forget these things, even if I am condemned to live as long as God Himself. Never" (Wiesel, *Night*, p. 32).

Those who hate us tear us to pieces at will

"One day when we came back from work, we saw three gallows rearing up in the assembly place, three black crows. Roll call. SS all round us, machine guns trained: the traditional ceremony. Three victims in chains—and one of them, the little servant, the sad-eyed angel. →

> 10But now, You desert and shame us.
> You do not go out with our armies.
>
> 11You put us to flight from our enemies.
> Those who hate us tear us to pieces
> at will.

AFFECTIONS

But now, You desert us and shame us

Having recalled the glories of the far and the recent past, the psalmist turns to the present—the immediate defeat of the people and their degradation at the hands of their enemies. The psalmist minces no words but speaks forcefully, with powerful images, and in short, choppy sentences.

You desert us . . . my humiliation confronts me

(Winter, 1944):
"You desert and shame us"—as they cut our beards and mass-rape our women.

"You do not go out with our armies" —with our resistance.

"You put us to flight from our enemies"—in mass exodus and transports.

"Those who hate us tear us to pieces at will"—using our skins for lampshades and our flesh for soap.

"You hand us over like sheep to be devoured"—in the gas chambers, crematoria, and mass burning-pits.

"You cast us among the nations"— as stateless and displaced persons. →

WORDS

But now

The context requires a disjunctive term (cf. Koehler-Baumgartner). For an almost exact parallel, see Ps. 60:12. The usual meaning of 'af, however, is conjunctive. Those who take this conjunctively read: "Although You desert us . . . yet we did not forget You" (with v. 18) or: "Through God we praise all day . . . although You desert us . . ." (with the previous verse).

AFFECTIONS

"You sell Your people for nothing" — we are worth less than slaves, less than animals.

"You do not make a profit on their sale price" — our value is precisely calculated for work, starvation, and death.

"You make us an object of shame for our neighbors" — so that no one touches us, in the camps and even after liberation.

"A thing of scorn and derision for those around us" — they toss scraps of bread into the trains of our starving people; they make us defecate in our clothing.

"You make an example of us to the nations" — of degradation and dehumanization, a sign par excellence and a symbol of Jew-hatred.

"An object of head-shaking among the peoples" — in disbelief that something like this is happening to anyone, much less to us, Your chosen people.

CON-VERSES

¹²You hand us over like sheep to be devoured.
You cast us among the nations.

¹³You sell Your people for nothing.
You do not make a profit on their sale price.

" . . . All eyes were on the child. He was lividly pale, almost calm, biting his lips. The gallows threw its shadow over him . . .

"The three victims mounted together onto the chairs. The three necks were placed at the same moment within the nooses.

"'Long live liberty!' cried the two adults. But the child was silent.

"'Where is God? Where is He?' someone behind me asked.

"At a sign from the head of the camp, the three chairs tipped over. Total silence throughout the camp. On the horizon, the sun was setting . . .

"Then the march past began. The two adults were no longer alive. Their tongues swollen, blue-tinged. But the third rope was still moving; being so light, the child was still alive . . .

"For more than half an hour he stayed there, struggling between life and death, dying in slow agony under our eyes. And we had to look him full in the face. He was still alive when I passed in front of him. His tongue was still red, his eyes not yet glazed.

"Behind me, I heard the same man asking, 'Where is God now?' And I heard a voice within me answer him: 'Where is He? Here He is — He is hanging here on this gallows . . .'" (Wiesel, *Night,* pp. 61–62)

WORDS

cast us among the nations

Some take this as evidence of a post-exilic composition. It need not be so. The reference could be to any number of population dislocations following war, or to the sale of prisoners of war (Kirkpatrick).

CON-VERSES

You do not make a profit on their sale price   **my shame covers me**

Was it really worth it, Hashem?

You did pay the price—of righteous ones, of innocent ones, of infants . . . Their Blood, Your Glory and Name, Your Honor . . . not just blood but humiliation, cruelty, attempted dehumanization.... "Profit"?! there was no profit at all, only loss—of us and of You. . . . The State of Israel is no compensation;

14You make us an object of shame for our neighbors, a thing of scorn and derision for those around us.

15You make an example of us to the nations, an object of head-shaking among the peoples.

16All day, my humiliation confronts me, my shame covers me, 17from the sounds of the taunter and the blasphemer, from the fantasy of revenge on the enemy.

"Why, but why should I bless Him? In every fiber I rebelled. Because He had had thousands of children burned in His pits? Because He kept six crematories working night and day, on Sundays and feast days? Because in His great might He had created Auschwitz, Birkenau, Buna, and so many factories of death? How could I say to Him: 'Blessed art Thou,

we do not accept that, either for them, or for ourselves, or for You. . . . There is no greater profit, esoterically hiding behind the holocaust. . . . Some people even capitalize that word "Holocaust" to give it status equal to Your Name. . . . You *did* pay the price; was it worth it, Hashem?

Eternal, Master of the Universe, Who chose us among the races to be tortured day and night, to see our fathers, our mothers, our brothers, end in the crematory? Praised be Thy Holy Name, Who hast chosen us to be butchered on Thine altar?'" (Wiesel, *Night*, p. 64).

WORDS

do not make a profit

Ibn Ezra points out that the verse has two meanings: (1) God did not keep raising the price on the life of the Jews, and (2) God made no profit from the deal. The latter seems stronger, more in keeping with the bitter tone of the psalm.

shame . . . scorn and derision

For the same phrase, see Ps. 79:4 and 1 Kings 9:7.

humiliation . . . shame

Shame is said to cover or clothe the body (Ps.

35:26; 49:7; 132:18). The Malbim points out that "humiliation" is experienced when one is degraded by others, while "shame" is felt when one realizes how disgracefully one conducted oneself, even under extreme pressure (Feuer).

fantasy of revenge on the enemy

Literally, "because of the enemy and the avenger." My translation takes into account the natural, yet useless and even shame-provoking, tendency to waste time fantasizing about how one would take vengeance upon one's oppressors.

AFFECTIONS

All this happened to us yet . . .

In full consciousness of the degradation of his people, the psalmist turns on their behalf to God. He angrily asserts their innocence and affirms their undeviating loyalty with rhetorical questions and statements. This is the core of his defense of the people, which is, at the same time, a prosecutorial argument against/with God.

> ¹⁸All this happened to us
> yet we did not forget You,
> nor did we betray Your covenant.
>
> ¹⁹Our hearts did not retreat,
> nor did our steps deviate from Your way.
>
> ²⁰Though You crushed us into
>   a desolate place
> and covered us with deep darkness,
> ²¹did we forget the Name of our God
> or spread our hands in prayer to a
>   strange deity?

WORDS

nor . . . betray Your covenant

The word *brit* means "covenant," but it also means "circumcision," the sign of the covenant in the flesh. There are searing stories of courageous women who circumcised their newborn sons before the latter were torn from them and slain or thrown into the fires of the crematoria and burning pits.

into a desolate place

The Hebrew *tannim/tannin* (pl. *tanninim*) has two meanings: "serpents" (Ex. 7:9–12; Jer. 9:11; 10:22; 49:33; Isa. 43:20; Ps. 91:13; etc.) and "sea monsters" (Isa. 27:1; Ezek. 29:3; Ps. 148:7; Job 7:12). The relationship between the two in popular imagination accounts for sea monsters being depicted as gigantic snakelike creatures;

SPARKS

did we forget the Name of our God

Parts of the tradition (Alsheikh, the midrash, and the Talmud) understood this verse as a confession: "Indeed we did forget the name of our God." This, however, could only be envisioned under the most horrible of conditions: "Rabbi Hanina bar Abba said, 'If someone would tell me to give up my life for the sanctification of God's name, I would do it, provided that he kill me instantly. But I could not endure the genera-

tion of the persecution. Then, the enemies took iron balls and heated them until they became white-hot. They placed these balls under the armpits of their pitiable victims and squeezed the life out of them . . .'" (Feuer). How much worse have we seen in our generations. And how sensitive of the tradition to recognize that no one knows for sure if he or she will withstand extreme torture.

CON-VERSES

we are considered sheep to be butchered

History is in the margins. History is of the oppressed, the ignoble — women, prisoners, the insane, soldiers, slaves, patients, homosexuals, refugees. Their suffering is deep; their stories untold; their histories only now being written. The marginal person par excellence is the Jew, rejected and oppressed by western Christian civ-

22Let God Himself investigate this for He knows the hidden recesses of the heart.

23Truly, for Your sake we are killed all day long, we are considered sheep to be butchered.

AFFECTIONS

we are considered sheep to be butchered

"The train full of deportees had crossed the Hungarian frontier and on Polish territory had been taken in charge by the Gestapo. There it had stopped. The Jews had to get out and climb into lorries. The lorries drove toward a forest. The Jews were made to get out. They were made to dig huge graves. And when they had fin-

WORDS

hence "dragons" in the King James English. Assuming, on the other hand, a singular root *tann,* there would be a plural form *tannim* or *tannin* (?and a misformed plural of the plural, *tanninim*). The meaning would be "jackal," hence "a haunt of jackals," drawn from the repeating metaphor in Jeremiah. In the case of either serpent or jackal, a "place of desolation" is meant and I have so translated.

deep darkness
The Hebrew consonants should probably be read *salmut,* meaning "deep darkness," with parallel semitic roots. However, a popular etymology developed which read the consonants *sel-mavet,* "shadow of death" (Kirkpatrick), a meaning enshrined for English readers in the phrase "valley of the shadow of death" in Psalm 23. I have chosen the more scientific etymology. Those who interpret the previous clause to refer to sea monsters understand the darkness here to refer to the depths of the sea.

Our hearts . . . Though . . . did we . . . Let
The lexicography and syntax of these four

sentences (vv. 19–23) allows them to be read in several ways: (1) If one reads *ki* (v. 20) as "though" or "such that" or "when" (with Rashi), then one can link it with "our hearts" (v. 19). Thus King James, JPS, the translations, etc. read: "Our hearts did not retreat . . . even though You crushed us. . . ." Having done this, one must then group vv. 21 and 22, reading *'im* (v. 21) as "if" and linking it with *halo',* "would not" (v. 22). Thus King James, etc. read: "If we had forgotten . . . , God would have [or, would not God have]. . . ." (2) By contrast, I have chosen to group the two middle sentences and to let the first and fourth stand free, because I think this sharpens the challenge to God which is the core of this psalm.

Let God Himself investigate this
Alternately, this can be read as a rhetorical question: "Would God not have discovered this?!" (Feuer). My translation is a challenge flung at God and therefore more in keeping with the tough stance of the psalmist. The clear implication is that the Jewish people is completely innocent and God could check on it in the innermost recesses of human intention.

AFFECTIONS

ished their work, the Gestapo began theirs. Without passion, without haste, they slaughtered their prisoners. Each one had to go up to the hole and present his neck. Babies were thrown into the air and the machine gunners used them as targets . . .

"Not far from us, flames were leaping up from a ditch, gigantic flames. They were burning something. A lorry drew up at the pit and delivered its load—little children. Babies! Yes, I saw it—saw it with my own eyes . . . those children in the flames . . .

"On the last day of our journey a terrible wind arose; it snowed without ceasing. We felt that the end was near— the real end. We could never hold out in this icy wind, in these gusts. . . . Suddenly a cry rose up from the wagon, the cry of a wounded animal. Someone had just died. Others, feeling that they too were about to die, imitated his cry. And their cries seemed to come from beyond the grave. Soon everyone was crying out. Wailing, groaning, cries of distress hurled into the wind and snow. The contagion spread to the other carriages. Hundreds of cries rose up simultaneously. Not knowing against whom we cried. Not knowing why. The death rattle of a whole convoy who felt the end upon them" (Wiesel, *Night*, pp. 4, 30, 97–98).

CON-VERSES

ilization for twenty centuries, exterminated *en masse* in this place and in this time. The final suppressed history is the history of the Jew, the story of the ultimate alien in the midst of western culture. We are the sheep of western history—the disposable element, the demonic element—to be butchered and slaughtered, especially when western civilization is in a moment of crisis.

Who writes the history of the Jews? Who studies it? Who teaches it? But who writes the history of sheep that are to be butchered?

A little bourgeois security has made Jews forget. "The heart of this people is waxed fat, its ears are plugged, its eyes are shaded lest it see with its eyes and hear with its ears and understand in its heart" (Isa. 6:10). . . . The history of the Jew is a fragmented knowledge—a text here, an economic surge there; a bloody pogrom here, a poem there; isolated books, isolated communities. No land, an artificial language, a hostile environment. Can one write Jewish history at all? even in fragments? Yet, can it be ignored? swept under the rug of "civilization"?

A little tolerance has made the western world forget. It finds so many repressed histories to write, yet it represses the history of the Jew in its midst. For the history of the Jew is a

WORDS

for Your sake
Alternately, "because of You," which may even be the stronger reading.

all day long
This is the same phrase as above, "Through

God we praise all day" (v. 9) and "All day, my humiliation confronts me" (v. 16). Its use here marks a bitter irony. The nazi crematoria were known to operate day and night. Note the repetition of the image of slaughtered sheep (v. 12).

CON-VERSES

subjugated knowledge, a repressed story, one which has to fight to surface in the mind. It is repressed not by anti-semites but by the establishment, in the normalized historical assumptions of western historians. For to write the history of western culture is to suppress the story of the Jew in its midst, or else to confront the ugly truth of repression, brutality, fear, jealousy, murder, and mass murder. To confront the fragments of a people considered sheep to be butchered is to confront the butchers.

The event in which the unsaid is said is not yet history. Can that event be grasped, can that history be written, in non-messianic times?

we are considered sheep to be butchered

What blasphemy! The terror was so great who could resist? The violence so brutal, who could fight back? Sheep are not terrorized into going to the slaughter. What person *dares* to say that the Jews went like sheep to the butcher?

If there were people who went passively to the slaughter, they are those whose indifference led them to acquiesce in what they saw going on around them. If there is passive butchery, it is in the banality of evil, which permitted ordinary good folk to witness and to be silent.

It is not the terrorized who were the sheep; it is those who were apathetic.

SPARKS

for Your sake we are killed all day long

Rav Nahman bar Yitzhak said, "[This verse refers to] the student-sages who kill themselves for words of Torah as Rabbi Shimon ben Lakish said, 'The words of Torah are sustained only by one who kills himself for them'" (Talmud, Gittin 57b).

"And you shall love the Lord, your God, with all your heart, with all your soul, and with all your might" (Deut. 6:5). "With all your soul" — even if He takes your soul, as it says, "For Your sake we are killed all day long" (Sifre, ad loc.). Vespasian filled three ships with the leaders of Jerusalem to bring to Rome and to put into houses of ill repute. . . . The first group stood up and recited, "Did we forget the name of our God" and threw themselves into the sea. The second group stood up and recited, "For Your sake we are killed all day long" and threw themselves into the sea. The third group stood up and recited, "Let God Himself investigate this" and threw themselves into the sea (Midrash Rabba to Lam., 1:45; variation with children in Talmud, Gittin 57b).

The faithful shepherd said, "Happy is the holy people who are called 'sheep' for the Holy One, blessed be He, gathers their bones as a sacrifice before Him, as it says, 'For Your sake we are killed all day long, we are considered sheep to be butchered.' Their bones are gathered as sheep when they fast, for the diminution of heart and blood in fasting is considered more than animal sacrifices which diminish blood, fat, and all those innards which are consumed all night" (Zohar, Shemot, 119b).

How can a person be killed more than once? One must resolve to die, on the spot, each time one recites the *Shema'* (Rashba, cited in Feuer).

Each of these four interpretations of this searing verse re-verses, and at the same time expands, the meaning of the text. The simple meaning asserts the innocence of the people and hence the injustice of their being slaughtered indiscriminately. The interpretations give ways in which it is laudable to die for God. This is the intertextuality of text, tradition, and real life at its deepest.

AFFECTIONS

Wake up! Why do You sleep, Lord?!

Finally, in his deepest anguish, the psalmist commands God. It is
an act of protest,
of accusation. No
quarter is given.
Nothing is swept
away in false piety,
in aesthetic im-
agery, or in ele-
gant theological speculation.

²⁴Wake up!
Why do You sleep, Lord?!
Arise!
Do not abandon forever!

The language is very strong: We are
being slaughtered like sheep; God must
save us! God is asleep; He must wake
up! He cannot hide from our suffering!
God is like a drunken soldier Who must
be roused from His stupor to avenge His

CON-VERSES

Wake up! . . . Arise! . . . Get up!

The discourse of transgression. The
interrogation of
the limits. But this
is the interroga-
tion of the moral,
not the epistemo-
logical, limits.
The question is
not, What can we
know? or, Who
determines what we know? or, How do
we know what we know? The question
is: Based on what we know, is it right?
Is it moral?

Truth is knowledge of the limits. The
limit is the moral question that pierces
the heart of the moral structure of the

SPARKS

Wake up! Why do You sleep, Lord?!

Who were "the arousers"? Raḥba said, "Each
and every day that the levites stood on their
platform [to sing psalms], they would recite,
'Wake up! Why do You sleep, Lord?!' He
[Yohanan, the high priest, who abolished this
custom] said to them, 'Can there be sleep in
Heaven? Does it not say, "Indeed, the guardian
of Israel neither slumbers nor sleeps" (Ps.
121:4)?' Rather, [only] when Israel is in time
of trouble and the nations of the world are at
ease does one say, 'Wake up! Why do You sleep,
Lord?!'" (Talmud, Sota 48a; Tosefta, Sota 13:9).

"On that night, the sleep of the king wan-
dered" (Esth. 6:1). The sleep of the King of the
king of kings [wandered], for the Holy One,
blessed be He, saw that Israel was in trouble
[from the plot of Haman]. But can there be
sleep for God, for it says, "Indeed, the guardian
of Israel neither slumbers nor sleeps"? Rather,
when Israel is in trouble and the nations of the
world are at ease (He makes Himself as if He
were asleep [with the commentaries, ad loc.]).
Then, one says, "Wake up! Why do You sleep,

Lord?!" (Midrash Rabba to Esther, 10:1).

"On that night, . . ." But can there be sleep
for Him? Rather, when Israel sins, He makes
Himself as if He were asleep, as it says, "Wake
up! Why do You sleep, Lord?!" and, when Israel
does His will, then "the guardian of Israel
neither slumbers nor sleeps" (unknown
midrash, cited in Cohen).

Again, the tradition modifies the meaning of
the verse through interpretation. The simple
meaning is that the people, when persecuted un-
justifiedly, may call upon God, even in accusa-
tory terms, to vindicate them. The interpretations, however, limit this cry-prayer in three
ways, none of which seems envisioned in the
original text: a case when the Jewish people is
persecuted while the rest of humanity is at ease,
the same case in which God appears asleep ("as
if"), and the case when the Jews have sinned,
at which time God, again, appears as if asleep.
Here, too, intertextuality has responded to tame
the power of the original text, theologically and
religiously.

CON-VERSES

human and of the divine personality. The limit is the demand for engagement, for moral action. To transgress is to ask the question, Where are you? What have you done?—no matter how hurtful. The discourse of transgression is making the moral demand, as strongly as one can—no matter how preposterous, no matter how offensive. Truth is knowing what moral question to ask, and then asking it—no matter how risky the answer.

The discourse of transgression is the opposite of the will to wander, to roam among bodies and pleasures. The interrogation of the moral limits is the opposite of the will to err, to play. The discourse of transgression is the contrary of de-commitment. It is, rather, the angry assertion of commitment, the forceful revendication of engagement, when these have been broken off. The discourse of transgression takes seriously the fragmenting of relatedness and *demands* the restoration of wholeness of relationship rooted in mutuality and morality. To interrogate the limits is to deny withdrawal and to demand integration, to deny the hiding of the face and to demand the light of the face.

The text contains no language of revolution, no talk of revolt. It contains no language of redemptive suffering, no talk of salvific oppression. There is the Word of anger, the Word of anguish, the Word of demand, even of command. There is the speech of relatedness, of justification, of vindication—hard words, hard speech; hard issues . . . no letting go of God and self; no letting Him off the hook.

AFFECTIONS

people (Ps. 78:65). The Hebrew verbs here are in the imperative form. The language is so strong that the levites who chanted this psalm in the temple were called "the arousers," and the rabbis actually repressed the daily recitation of this psalm (see "Sparks").

The emotion of this psalm is rage. It is hurt and anger, magnified. Yet this rage is morally transformed into an affection, into the ongoing emotional attitude of righteous anger. It is not enough to feel rage; it must be channeled into a demand for fairness, into a cry for justice.

The transformation of rage into righteous anger is a function of the theology of covenant. God's proclaimed love for us, and His announced commitment to protect and be fair to us *binds* Him to moral behavior toward us. The covenant holds God in its scope. The rage of disgraceful defeat, then, can be transformed by the covenant into a moral demand. The humiliation of suffering, then, can be transformed through the covenant into a moral claim.

As God is a jealous God demanding loyalty from us in covenant, so we, in our searing humiliation, demand. We transform our anger, through the covenant, into our moral claim against God. As God is angry with us in covenant, so we are angry with Him in covenant. We experience a true anger, which becomes a true moral claim, rooted in our mutual covenantal debt.

Finally, the affection of moral righteousness is a proclamation of love of God, of concern for His honor and His people. Hurt becomes a moral demand, which is really a defense of the Beloved. Anger becomes a moral claim, which is really an expression of love.

CON-VERSES

Redeem us for the sake of Your gracious love

"Help us! Save us! Gore our enemies! Give us victory! Remove our disgrace! Disinherit nations and plant us! Trample those who hate us! Destroy those who tear us to pieces at will! Consume those who devour the sheep! Avenge our blood! Butcher the butchers!"

Fantasy. This is all fantasy. The defeat is real. The suffering is real. The anguish of the blow to the national ego is real. But the appeal to Big Papa to come and gore our enemies is pure fantasy. The plea to Divine Superman to appear out of no-where and no-time and "redeem" us from oppression is an illusion, a projection of our own impotence in the face of ego-destroying power. It is a projection of our frustration at not being able to right the ship of personal shame.

25Why do You hide Your Face?
Why do You forget our persecution and our oppression?!

26For our souls have been pounded into the dirt,
our stomachs are stuck to the ground.

27Get up!
Help us!
Redeem us for the sake of Your gracious love.

Freud was very clear about this—that religion, especially in its cry to super-Power to restore lost human power, is an illusion, a projection. Bruno Bettelheim, in his analysis of fairy tales, is clear that the resort to understanding ego-damagers as the very embodiment of evil and ego-supporters as the very embodiment of good is a necessary stage in the development of a child but that, in an adult, such fantasies are unreal, counterproductive. Rather:

Auto-emancipation. Self-determination. Self-defense. Taking history into our own hands. Armed resistance, not prayer. Liberation, not redemption. Responsible action, not patience. Joshua, not Exodus. The exodus of the Jews from Egypt was the work of God; the Jews just followed, more or less. But the Conquest of the land was the work of Israel—war, blood, spies, strategy; human action. This is the message of

WORDS

hide Your Face . . . forget

Ibn Ezra points out that God has either turned His face away altogether or He has seen our oppression and pushed it out of His mind. The two clauses are, thus, supplementary. Ibn Ezra also points out that "You forget" stands in contrast to "we have not forgotten" (vv. 18, 21). Note, too, that "hide Your Face" stands in contrast to "the light of Your Face" (v. 4). These

subtleties are part of the deep bitter irony with which the psalmist conveys his hurt.

stomachs . . . stuck to the ground

Even animals have feet that keep their stomachs off the ground (Midrash Shemuel, cited in Feuer). But Israel has been reduced to a state that is not only lower than the angels and lower than humanity, but also lower than the animals.

CON-VERSES

Zionism, the movement of Jewish national revival: Do not wait for the messiah; he may never come, if indeed he exists at all. The God Who is supposed to send the messiah also may not exist and, if He does, He has all eternity to make up His mind. We do not have all eternity; we have now. We have the holocaust; we cannot wait, again. Zionism is the arrogation of self-power, the denial of super-Power. This is also the message that underlies Christian liberation theology: human beings must act in their own interest. They may rationalize and believe that God acts through them or that they are doing God's will; but it is humans who determine what to do, when to do it, and how to do it. And it is we humans who *do* it; who act.

The discourse of transgression transgresses. It violates, rapes the traditional theology of providential action. It transgresses, and appropriates action and responsibility. It eschews fantasy. It shuns the appeal to Big Papa. It does not wait patiently, as a good child, for Authority to assert itself. Better to rage authentically than to transubstantiate into fantasy. A curse upon fantasy, for it cripples us, castrates us, and renders us impotent! In the hierarchy of power relations, only transgression through self-determination saves, or at least comforts. Real time, real trouble, real effort, real rage—for better and for worse.

The covenant embodies the hierarchy of power—the national covenant as well as the parent–child covenant. It defines relation. It limits, even as it binds. By sublimation, covenant dis-enrages. By story-fantasy, it dis-humiliates. By appeal to transcendent love and power, it dis-oppresses. By channeling anger, deep anger, covenant castrates; it removes shame and guilt. Breaking the covenant is the only way to assume life. Denying the covenant, personal and national, is the way to auto-emancipation. To be without covenant is to be without the fantasy. It is a hard way, but it is a way free of the web of the story-fantasy which covers the shame of social and personal impotence.

WORDS

gracious love

Hebrew *ḥesed,* variously translated as "grace," "mercy," "faithfulness," "goodness," "kindness," "good will." In my opinion, either "faithfulness" or "gracious love" is correct. The former is God's love within the covenant, that is, His love which we merit. The latter is His love beyond the covenant, that is, His love which we do not deserve. God loves His people with both, and therefore both can be meant. I usually tend toward the latter. Mesudat David seems to agree, reading: "Help us . . ." —if we deserve it; "redeem us . . ." —if we do not deserve it.

SPARKS

our souls have been pounded into the dirt. . . . Redeem us

The character of the Holy One, blessed be He, is not like the character of flesh and blood. For when flesh and blood see a person who is beautiful and rich, they sustain and aid such

SPARKS

a person. And when they see a person who is falling, they push such a person further down. Not so, the Holy One, blessed be He. If He sees a person who has been raised up, He lowers that person, as it says, "You bring low the pride of the people" (Prov. 29:33). And if He sees a person who has fallen as low as possible, He raises that person up, as it says, "for our souls have been pounded into the dirt" and it says right afterwards, "Get up! Help us!" (Midrash Yelamedenu, cited in Cohen).

Israel said before the Holy One, blessed be He, "Master of the universe, when will You redeem us?" He said to them, "When you have sunken to the lowest rung, at that time, I shall redeem you, as it says, 'for our souls . . .' and it says right afterwards, 'Get up! Help us!'" (Midrash to Psalms, cited in Cohen).

Psalm 109

WITH
FOUR
COMMENTARIES

לַמְנַצֵּחַ לְדָוִד
מִזְמוֹר

אֱלֹהֵי תְהִלָּתִי אַל תֶּחֱרַשׁ:

כִּי פִי רָשָׁע וּפִי מִרְמָה
עָלַי פָּתָחוּ
דִּבְּרוּ אִתִּי לְשׁוֹן שָׁקֶר:

וְדִבְרֵי שִׂנְאָה סְבָבוּנִי
וַיִּלָּחֲמוּנִי חִנָּם:

תַּחַת אַהֲבָתִי יִשְׂטְנוּנִי
וַאֲנִי תְפִלָּה:

וַיָּשִׂימוּ עָלַי רָעָה תַּחַת טוֹבָה
וְשִׂנְאָה תַּחַת אַהֲבָתִי:

הַפְקֵד עָלָיו רָשָׁע
וְשָׂטָן יַעֲמֹד עַל יְמִינוֹ:

בְּהִשָּׁפְטוֹ יֵצֵא רָשָׁע
וּתְפִלָּתוֹ תִּהְיֶה לַחֲטָאָה:

A Psalm of Personal Vengeance

*in which the psalmist curses his enemies
and damns those who detest him*

¹From the leader's collection, by David
a psalm

> God Whom I praise, do not be silent.

> ²For the mouths of the wicked and the deceitful
> have been opened against me;
> they speak to me with a lying tongue.

> ³They encircle me with words of hate;
> they fight against me for no reason.

> ⁴Instead of loving me, they detest me
> though I intercede for them.

> ⁵They impose evil upon me in place of good,
> hate in place of my love.

⁶Place a wicked person in command over him;
let a persecutor stand at his right hand.

> ⁶Place a wicked person in command over her;
> let a persecutor stand at her right hand.

⁷When he is tried, let him be convicted;
let intercession for him fail.

> ⁷When she is tried, let her be convicted;
> let intercession for her fail.

יִהְיוּ יָמָיו מְעַטִּים
פְּקֻדָּתוֹ יִקַּח אַחֵר:

יִהְיוּ בָנָיו יְתוֹמִים
וְאִשְׁתּוֹ אַלְמָנָה:

וְנוֹעַ יָנוּעוּ בָנָיו
וְשִׁאֵלוּ
וְדָרְשׁוּ
מֵחָרְבוֹתֵיהֶם:

יְנַקֵּשׁ נוֹשֶׁה לְכָל אֲשֶׁר לוֹ
וְיָבֹזּוּ זָרִים יְגִיעוֹ:

[8]May his days be few in number;
may another take command of his life.

 [8]May her days be few in number;
 may another take command of her life.

[9]May his children be orphans;
may his wife be a widow.

 [9]May her children be orphans;
 may her husband be a widower.

[10]Let his children be
continually on the move, begging;
let them seek alms
from within the decrepit buildings they inhabit.

 [10]Let her children be
 continually on the move, begging;
 let them seek alms
 from within the decrepit buildings they inhabit.

[11]Let the creditor ensnare all that is his;
let aliens pillage that which he produces.

 [11]Let the creditor ensnare all that is hers;
 let aliens pillage that which she produces.

אַל יְהִי לוֹ מֹשֵׁךְ חָסֶד
וְאַל יְהִי חוֹנֵן לִיתוֹמָיו:

יְהִי אַחֲרִיתוֹ לְהַכְרִית
בְּדוֹר אַחֵר
יִמַּח שְׁמָם:

יִזָּכֵר עֲוֹן אֲבֹתָיו
אֶל יְיָ
וְחַטַּאת אִמּוֹ אַל תִּמָּח:

יִהְיוּ נֶגֶד יְיָ תָּמִיד
וְיַכְרֵת מֵאֶרֶץ זִכְרָם:

¹²May no one advocate lovingkindness for him;
may no one be merciful to his orphans.

¹²May no one advocate lovingkindness for her;
may no one be merciful to her orphans.

¹³May his end be to be cut off;
may the family name be blotted out
in the following generation.

¹³May her end be to be cut off;
may the family name be blotted out
in the following generation.

¹⁴Let the transgression of his fathers
be remembered by the Lord;
let the sin of his mother not be blotted out.

¹⁴Let the transgression of her fathers
be remembered by the Lord;
let the sin of her mother not be blotted out.

¹⁵Let them be over against the Lord always;
may God cut off their memory from the earth.

¹⁵Let them be over against the Lord always;
may God cut off their memory from the earth.

יַעַן אֲשֶׁר לֹא זָכַר
עֲשׂוֹת חָסֶד
וַיִּרְדֹּף אִישׁ עָנִי וְאֶבְיוֹן
וְנִכְאֵה לֵבָב לְמוֹתֵת:

וַיֶּאֱהַב קְלָלָה
וַתְּבוֹאֵהוּ
וְלֹא חָפֵץ בִּבְרָכָה
וַתִּרְחַק מִמֶּנּוּ:

וַיִּלְבַּשׁ קְלָלָה כְּמַדּוֹ
וַתָּבֹא כַמַּיִם בְּקִרְבּוֹ
וְכַשֶּׁמֶן בְּעַצְמוֹתָיו:
תְּהִי לוֹ
כְּבֶגֶד יַעְטֶה
וּלְמֵזַח תָּמִיד יַחְגְּרֶהָ:

16Because he did not remember
to act in lovingkindness
but persecuted the suffering poor
to deal the death blow to the crushed in heart.

    16Because she did not remember
    to act in lovingkindness
    but persecuted the suffering poor
    to deal the death blow to the crushed in heart.

17He continues to love cursing—
then let it come upon him;
He continues to not want blessing—
then let it be far from him.

    17She continues to love cursing—
    then let it come upon her;
    She continues to not want blessing—
    then let it be far from her.

18He wears cursing like a uniform;
it penetrates his innards like water
and his bones like rubbing oil.—
19May it be for him like a habit
in which he wraps himself,
like a loincloth which is worn always.

זֹאת פְּעֻלַּת שֹׂטְנַי
מֵאֵת יְיָ
וְהַדֹּבְרִים רָע עַל נַפְשִׁי:

וְאַתָּה יֱהֹוִה אֲדֹנָי
עֲשֵׂה אִתִּי לְמַעַן שְׁמֶךָ
כִּי טוֹב חַסְדְּךָ
הַצִּילֵנִי:

כִּי עָנִי וְאֶבְיוֹן אָנֹכִי
וְלִבִּי חָלַל בְּקִרְבִּי:

כְּצֵל כִּנְטוֹתוֹ
נֶהֱלָכְתִּי
נִנְעַרְתִּי כָּאַרְבֶּה:

בִּרְכַּי כָּשְׁלוּ מִצּוֹם
וּבְשָׂרִי כָּחַשׁ מִשָּׁמֶן:

18She wears cursing like a uniform;
it penetrates her innards like water
and her bones like rubbing oil.—
19May it be for her like a habit
in which she wraps herself,
like a loincloth which is worn always.

20This is the recompense from the Lord
for those who detest me,
for those who speak evil against my very being.

20This is the recompense from the Lord
for those who detest me,
for those who speak evil against my very being.

21You, Lord, are my lord and master
Deal with me for the sake of Your Name.
Because Your lovingkindness is good,
save me.

22For I am suffering and poor.
My heart is hollow within me.

23I am dragged out
as a shadow is lengthened.
I am tossed about like a locust.

24My knees are weak from fasting.
My flesh is thin from lack of fat.

וַאֲנִי הָיִיתִי חֶרְפָּה לָהֶם
יִרְאוּנִי יְנִיעוּן רֹאשָׁם:

עׇזְרֵנִי יְיָ אֱלֹהָי
הוֹשִׁיעֵנִי
כְחַסְדֶּךָ:

וְיֵדְעוּ כִּי יָדְךָ זֹּאת
אַתָּה יְיָ עֲשִׂיתָהּ:

יְקַלְלוּ הֵמָּה וְאַתָּה תְבָרֵךְ
קָמוּ וַיֵּבֹשׁוּ
וְעַבְדְּךָ יִשְׂמָח:

יִלְבְּשׁוּ שׂוֹטְנַי
כְּלִמָּה
וְיַעֲטוּ כַמְעִיל בָּשְׁתָּם:

אוֹדֶה יְיָ מְאֹד בְּפִי
וּבְתוֹךְ רַבִּים אֲהַלְלֶנּוּ:
כִּי יַעֲמֹד לִימִין אֶבְיוֹן
לְהוֹשִׁיעַ
מִשֹּׁפְטֵי נַפְשׁוֹ:

[25]I have become an object of derision for them.
They see me and nod their heads.

[26]Help me, Lord, my God.
Save me
by the standard of Your lovingkindness.

[27]So that they know that such is Your hand;
that You, Lord, have done it.

[28]Let them curse—but You bless.
Let them rise up and be ashamed—
Your servant will rejoice.

[29]Let those who detest me
wear the garment of disgrace.
Let them wrap their shame around them as a robe.

[30]I will openly thank the Lord greatly.
In the presence of multitudes, I will praise Him.
[31]When he stands at the right hand of the suffering,
to save him from those who pass judgment
against his very being.

[31]When he stands at the right hand of the suffering
to save her from those who pass judgment
against her very being.

AFFECTIONS

do not be silent

This is an "imprecatory psalm," that is, a psalm in which the author actually curses his enemies. The commentators have trouble with this because it seems unfitting for the psalmist (King David, according to the superscription and Jewish tradition) to give vent to such violent aggressive feelings. To cover this up, various commentators propose various points of interpretation. Ibn Ezra and Radak say that these are King David's curses against his enemies, not those a normal person might use. Malbim says these are the curses of David's enemies against him, not David's curses against his enemies (Feuer). Rashi reads them as curses against the enemies of the Jewish people (Esau), not personal imprecations. Hacham takes them to be personal (and, it seems, not especially Davidic) but understands the context to be a court trial in which the psalmist has been accused falsely and has been rendered helpless against his accusers. Even then, Hacham says that the psalmist is praying for the destruction of his enemies in petitional prayer, not actually cursing them. Kirkpatrick (pp. 651–654, lxxxviii–xc), in the spirit of Christian piety, points to the "moral difficulty" posed by such psalms and states: "We shall not attempt to justify them. They are the very opposite of the spirit of the Gospel (Matt. 5:43ff.)." He thus ignores completely the imprecatory passages in the New Testament (see,

CON-VERSES

do not be silent

> [1]From the leader's collection, by David
> a psalm
>
> God Whom I praise,
>   do not be silent.

There is disconnectedness here, *décalage,* a gap between language and context: the psalm contains fourteen curses introduced by five verses which set the stage and followed by eleven verses of prayer, at least one of which is also a curse; and there is a sudden shift from plural to singular just at the point where the text moves from context to curse. The verses that set the stage point toward a social or legal confrontation (see "Words" and "Affections"), but the violence of the accusations and the vehemence of the curses point beyond a public or judicial dispute.

Disconnected discourse suggests displacement, a transferring of deep anger from its true cause to some lesser source. A gap between language and context points toward a deeper context. When the punishment does not fit the crime, some more serious crime is alluded to.

The intense language in this psalm shows that social power or legal fencing is not that which is at issue. What is at stake, here, is intimate combat, deeply personal attack and counterattack. The disconnectedness of the discourse points to repressed rage. The vehemence, disproportionate to the context, alludes to a silenced crime. The language here bespeaks abuse—abuse by an intimate or intimates. "Con-verses" will follow this voice, a voice usually silenced in our culture. →

CON-VERSES

To be abused means to be battered, to be beaten, to be assaulted bodily. To be abused means to have the boundary of the skin, the boundary that separates you from the other, violated. Sometimes the suffering is senseless, without purpose or meaning; always it is undeserved. Sometimes to be abused means to be tortured, systematically. To be abused is to have control of your body taken from you, by force.

To be abused also means to be sexually assaulted, physically violated, raped. To be abused means to be bodily penetrated, to be forced open. To be abused is to have your sexuality ripped out of you, perhaps never to be yours again.

To be abused always means to have things done to you against your will, and to be helpless to stop the violence to your person. It makes no difference whether you are male or female. Abuse comes from the outside; it is to your very person, against your body, your mind, and your heart.

To be abused means to be struck in anger, to be punished beyond the seriousness of the deed. To be abused means to be tied up, or shut in a dark closet, or burned with a cigarette, or whipped, or punished in the presence of others. To be abused means to be degraded, physically and in your inner being.

To be abused is also to be threatened into the conspiracy of silence, to be choked until you learn to choke yourself. To be abused is not to tell, lest more violence be perpetrated on you or on others.

To be abused is to live in (hidden) shame and deep fear; to live and not to trust, anyone. →

AFFECTIONS

e.g., Rom. 12:20; 13:2–4; Rev. 3:22–23; 6:10; etc.). Kirkpatrick does, however, acknowledge the personal, and not national, nature of this psalm and points to other passages, all in the "Old Testament," which are equally vindictive (elsewhere in Psalms [especially 55 and 69] and in Jeremiah).

My own interpretation is rooted in four assumptions: (1) The curses invoked here are so intense that only a very serious betrayal could have provoked them. A trial at which the psalmist is falsely accused and cannot establish the plain truth is surely a possibility. But there are many situations in life that might give rise to a deep sense of betrayal and the consequent anger expressed in this psalm. (2) The principle that motivates the psalm is the righteousness of the psalmist's anger. It is not anger as such but the injustice of the betrayal that is the moral core of this psalm. It is not personal sadism but personal integrity and moral truth that are at stake. (3) Personal righteous anger is an affection, an approved ongoing emotional attitude in the psalms, as elsewhere in the Bible. Hence, we have before us a persecuted person who does indeed curse his enemies, among other reactions. Finally (4), given the justification of the anger, the psalm follows biblical psychology and adumbrates the rabbinic principle *midda ke-neged midda*, "measure for measure." As the psalmist has suffered, so should the enemy suffer. This is just; this is fair; and it is legitimate religiously.

Using this approach, this psalm, in all its violence, becomes one upon which one can meditate, with which one can identify, and which one can recite-pray with deep conviction. One

AFFECTIONS

only needs to have true enemies, which we all have sooner or later in life.

The psalm is divided into four parts: the introductory accusations (vv. 1–5), the curses (vv. 6–20), the prayers (vv. 21–29), and the vow to praise God publicly (vv. 30–31).

the mouths of the wicked and the deceitful

"Oh! how I walked in my innocence, in my naïveté" (Ps. 26:1). I didn't think I had enemies. I was always the favorite, the beloved child, the teacher's pet; self-contained, love-assured, unafraid. But, much to my disbelief, they—the enemies—are really there. The wicked open their mouths against me. They really are out to get me, to embarrass me, to disgrace me. And they are wicked, determined, capable of long-range scheming, of subtle innuendo, of dirty social and interpersonal games. Never mind the fact that they are wrong. I never wished them harm, until they showed that they had truly turned against me.

Why? Envy. They envy my security, my success, my happiness, my possessions. Don't they know that I work for it? Success and security don't just happen. Even love has to be won by hard work, cultivation, skill, and dedication. →

²For the mouths of the wicked
      and the deceitful
have been opened against me;
they speak to me with a lying tongue.

CON-VERSES

[*Da capo al fine,* reading "I," "me," and "my" for "you" and "your."]

Abuse can also be emotional, psychologically if not physically violent. To be emotionally abused means to be taken advantage of; to be so in need of affection that you agree to do things you know you shouldn't have to do. It means to be so frightened that you allow things to be done to you that you know are invasive, violent, and wrong.

Unjustified withholding of love, outbreaks of irrational anger, the colossal egocentrism of a parent which does not allow the child space to be, the demand for obedience which leaves no room for freedom . . . yelling, screaming, saying terrible things, personal insults . . . false sweet-talk, seduction . . . drinking, running away, drugs . . . slapping, hitting, smashing things . . . being seduced into the conspiracy of silence—all these are emotional abuse.

Neglect, lack of love, denying achievements, unrealistic expectations, parentalization, judging the other all the time, breaking promises, smothering, comparing children, calling terrible names, the emotional undermining and terrorizing of others—all these are emotional abuse.

Abuse by an intimate does not last a few days or even a year or so; it endures

WORDS

the mouths . . .
   Lit., "For the mouth of the wicked person and the mouth of deceitfulness, they have opened against me," with one concrete and one abstract noun.

CON-VERSES

for a long time, a whole childhood, a whole marriage. Its duration compounds its horror.

Abuse by an intimate is not regular; it is intermittent, alternating with everyday life in an unpredictable pattern. Its capriciousness compounds its terror.

Taking the natural love of a child for its parent, betraying that love by sexual, physical, or emotional abuse, and then telling the child that the abuse is "for its own good" is abuse compounded beyond all measure, for it takes the clear message of abuse and confuses it with love, it takes the clear lesson of deserved distrust and confounds it with traitorous trust. Teaching a child that abuse is "for its own good" fractures the natural bond between parent and child; it inverts the fifth commandment.

There are many forms of abuse: physical, sexual, verbal, and emotional. This psalm is a psalm about abuse, about famili-ar combat, about life and death in the world of the intimate self.

AFFECTIONS

They envy my blessing as they envied Joseph's; not that mine is so great, but they envy it anyway.

Deceit, guile, collusion, connivance, falsification, duplicity, cheating, fraud, dishonesty . . . snares, traps: flytrap, mousetrap, deathtrap, mantrap, womantrap, firetrap . . . ambush . . . masquerade, camouflage, dissemblance, pretext, mockery . . . craftiness, maneuvering, intrigue, knife in the back, machinations, subterfuge, deception— who knew these things existed?

I ask a question and I get clever evasions, or a shrewd question in return. They ask questions—not to know, to feel, and to share but to trap, to ensnare, to score a point. "Aha! I've got you on that!" "I got a piece of information out of you. You should have been clever enough to conceal it." I have to watch what I say. Everything I say will be used against me; even if I tell the truth, it will be distorted in the reporting; it will be tattle-taled back to hostile sources; it will be woven into the conspiracy against me.

with a lying tongue

They lie!! They don't tell the truth! Either they distort the truth so that it comes out against me, or they outright make things up. How can a person purposely say something that he or she knows is false, and do it for the purpose of maligning another who has done them no wrong?! People, distorted by jealousy, do the damnedest things.

To tell the truth about someone when it will hurt that person is *leshon ha-ra*', "speaking evil of someone." To tell a complete falsehood about someone is *moṣi' shem ra*' "to give someone a bad

AFFECTIONS

CON-VERSES

name." The latter is punishable by
leprosy, as Miriam was punished (Numbers 12). "Tale-bearing," *rekhilut*, is one
of the sins for
which it is almost
impossible to re-
pent, because
once one has
begun a rumor,
one does not know where it may end
(Maimonides, *Mishne Torah*, "Laws of
Repentance," 3:14 and 4:5).

words of hate

I have seen the face of hatred—distorted in anger, twisted in jealousy,
warped by the intent to harm, to hurt.
I have also heard the words of hate—
vicious, ugly, boundless, tearing the
other to shreds.

Such words are an encirclement, a
siege, a battle, a war; no quarter given,
none expected; a war of extermination,
annihilation. The other must vanish to
satisfy the hating self.

Why? Why do people hate? not dis-
like, not envy; but hate. From deep in
one's being, it wells up. From milk not
forthcoming, from love given to another,
from fear—deep fear—that the other
will desert us; from joy taken away,
from identity robbed, from years of
frustration, from decades of lack of success, from wanting what one cannot
have even if one is entitled to it; from

words of hate

In a highly attentuated sense, every
person, in the nor-
mal process of so-
cialization, is
"abused," that is,
forced to suppress
his or her rebel-
lion and anger in favor of getting along
in the world. We are all trained to
repress our anger, especially our rage,
even if it is justified, for the sake of some
greater good. This is called "being
respectful" or "being good." However,
sometimes we learn this in ways that are
more violent or more seductive than
others; sometimes the lesson of sociali-
zation is embedded in words of hate.
"'Such disobedience amounts to a
declaration of war against you. Your
son is trying to usurp your authority,
and you are justified in answering force
with force in order to insure his respect,
without which you will be unable to
train him. The blows you administer
should not be merely playful ones but
should convince him that you are his
master. Therefore, you must not desist
until he does what he previously refused
out of wickedness to do. If you do not
pay heed to this, you will have engaged
him in a battle that will cause his wicked
heart to swell with triumph and him to
make the firm resolve to continue dis-
regarding your blows so that he need

*3They encircle me with words of hate;
they fight against me for no reason.*

WORDS

encircle
  Or, "besiege," paralleling "they fight against."

they fight . . . for no reason
  Hebrew *va-yillahamuni hinnam*. Note the

overlapping sounds (Hacham), an expression
of the unconscious realization that all war is in
vain.

CON-VERSES

not submit to his parents' domination. If, however, he has seen that he is vanquished the first time and has been obliged to humble himself before you, this will rob him of his courage to rebel anew.' . . . For parents' motives are the same today as they were then: in beating their children, they are struggling to regain the power they once lost to their own parents. . . . Although parents *always* mistreat their children for psychological reasons, i.e., because of their own needs, there is a basic assumption in our society that this treatment is good for children. . . . Beatings, which are only one form of mistreatment, are *always* degrading, because the child not only is unable to defend himor herself but is also supposed to show gratitude and respect to the parents in return" (Miller, *For Your Own Good,* citing Kroger and responding, pp. 15–17).

"'Only humiliation can be of help here. . . . Someone who is unduly proud of his accomplishments should be assigned tasks far beyond his abilities and should not be dissuaded if he attempts to take on more than he can handle; halfhearted measures and superficiality should not be tolerated in these attempts. . . . Hold up to a talented lad the examples of living or historical figures who possess far more splendid talent than his.' . . . The conscious use of humiliation (whose function is to satisfy the *parents'* needs) destroys the child's self-confidence, making him or her insecure and inhibited; nevertheless, this approach is considered beneficial" (Miller, *For Your Own Good,* citing Villaume and responding, pp. 21–22).

AFFECTIONS

parents too enwrapped in their own lives and selves to care; from colleagues out to build a career at one's expense; from the fear of death and the envy of youth; from sheer inner meanness of character; from the desire that can never be satiated to control the other; from a need, which can never be satisfied, for more love; from unknown and unspoken fears and angers that surge up from the depths to spill out and over the other.

for no reason

There really is no reason. I did not do anything. I live my life cleanly. I even go out of my way to be understanding. I'm the only one left with some sympathy for my enemy. My friends cannot understand why I haven't fought back, why I haven't lashed out. But I haven't. Nor did I do anything to begin with. I'll even settle for the enemy just going away, for leaving me alone. But no; that's not good enough. It must be war, war to the end. Where will this lead? Where can it lead, except to more ugliness, more hatred, more connivery, more lies?

It's not that I am holy, innocent. I'd be glad to accept the blame but I don't see any good in that. How can I be responsible for someone else's subconscious?! for someone else's inner life theater in which I happen to be only a player, and not by my choice?!

The reasons they do give are all lies, subterfuges; an attempt to avoid confronting the ugly truth of ugly deeds and ugly thoughts, of ugly roots and ugly fruits.

Everyone has muck in them; why can't my enemies admit that, and then

AFFECTIONS

go on?! Do they think I deny my own muck? Do they think I will tolerate their willful blindness to theirs? Even if I played along with the assertion of my guilt, would they admit theirs? I may be innocent but I'm not saintly, nor do I wish to be; just fair.

Do my enemies expect me to roll over and get kicked again? to turn the other cheek? What for? so that they can hit me again? even though there is no reason for it? I'd even do that if I thought it would bring peace. But it won't. Hatred cannot be appeased; jealousy cannot be pacified. Even if I admitted my guilt and not theirs, would that help? Certainly not. Annihilation is a thirst that is unquenchable.

Instead of loving me, they detest me

Once, he loved me. I was child/companion/colleague/lover/parent. But he turned away from me, turned on me, turned against me. He betrayed his love for me, and my love for him. He repudiated the trust others placed in him, in me, in us. And now, he detests me, despises me, rejects me, spurns me, hates me. . . . The pain of it all.

[*Da capo al fine,* reading "she" and "her" for "he" and "him".]

> 4Instead of loving me, they detest me though I intercede for them.

CON-VERSES

Instead of loving me, they detest me

"The voices begin again. Wicked voices from the outside, devaluing my importance and presence. Telling me girl children have to sit in the back seat. That fat girls will never find dates. My nightmare from age eight to age eleven was that I would go through high school without one date. Voices asking me why I was using lip gloss as no one would ever want to kiss me. . . . 'Sugar and spice and everything nice; that's what little girls are made of.'

"Those wicked outside voices have a worse function. They wake up the wicked inside voices. Those are the kind that do not go away. Suicidal thoughts emerge, even at the age of ten or so. How to end a wretched life that seems to matter so little: Suffocation, simple suffocation. Suffocation, that's the name of the game. First you take a plastic bag, then you take a rubber band, over the head. And that's the end; suffocation.

"Those inside voices will not go away, echoing and magnifying the outside voices. And they do lie. They speak of things unimaginable . . . guilt, guilt, guilt. All your fault your little sister is an unhappy young woman. All your

WORDS

loving me

Most read, "in place of my loving [them]" or "in spite of my loving [them]," which is the usual usage of a noun with possessive suffix and which also fits well with the next verse, where the same phrase occurs. I have tried to nuance this, however, following the usage in Hos. 9:15,

where the same noun is used with an objective suffix. Rashi renders, "Because I have loved [You]. . . ."

I intercede for them

Hebrew *va-'ani tefillah,* "and I am prayer." The syntax parallels "and I am peace" (Ps. 120:7) →

CON-VERSES

fault your parents never have any money. All your fault love relationships fail.

"They lie to fit the occasion. You are way too fat. You are way too weak. See how unhappy you are . . . and it's all your own fault.

"Those voices speak against me . . . tearing at my self until I scream in pain. But in the end there appears but one possible judgement . . . Guilty" (Amy).

AFFECTIONS

though I intercede for them

How often have I intervened in family councils and professional meetings to defend them? to explain the difficulties of their position? to sympathize with the bind they find themselves in? to call for tolerance and understanding?

What is love, if it is not the effort made to understand the other when he or she detests you, when she or he is

WORDS

or "and his hands were faith" (Ex. 17:12), meaning respectively: "though I speak peace," "his hands were firm/faithful."

The Hebrew root *palal* has two meanings: "to enter into a court action" or "to judge" and, in the reflexive form, "to pray" or "to intercede" (see "Affections" and "Con-verses"). Four meanings are, therefore, possible: (1) "Although they detest me, I give myself over to continuous prayer to You" (Rashi; King James). (2) "Although they detest me, I pray, or intercede, for them" (Ibn Ezra and others). (3) "Although they

detest me, I am what they pray(ed) for." And (4) "although they detest me, I intercede for them in court." The last meaning fits with vv. 7 and 31, where a court proceeding is alluded to. Some take this to be the key to the situation behind the psalm, that is, that the psalmist is on trial against persons who have sworn false testimony against him. While this last suggestion is possible, the intensity of the imprecations indicates, in my opinion, something stronger (see "Affections"). My rendering can be read with either meaning (2) or (4).

SPARKS

Instead of loving me, they detest me

The Holy One, blessed be He, said: "Were it not for Israel, no blessing would come to the entire world, as it says, 'God will command blessing with [because of] you' (Deut. 28:8); and, were it not for Israel, the heavenly bodies would not give light, as it says, 'Were it not for My covenant [with you] day and night' (Jer. 33:25); and, the rain would not fall, as it says, 'God will open for [because of] you His good treasure' (Deut. 28:12)." [Hearing this,] the Jews asked the nations of the world, "God does all these things for you because of us and yet you hate us, as it says, 'Instead of loving me, they detest me' (Ps. 109:4)?!"

[And Israel said to the nations of the world:] "We offer up seventy bulls on the holiday [of

Sukkot] corresponding to the seventy nations of the world. And we pray that rain fall for them. And yet, 'Instead of loving me, they detest me' (Ps. 109:4)." "Shall good be repaid with evil" (Jer. 18:20)? Indeed: "They impose evil upon me in place of good" (Ps. 109:5; Midrash Rabba).

though I intercede for them

The Rebbe of Pshiskhe [reading, "and I am prayer"; see "Words"] said: "This can be compared to a decent poor man who came to see a rich man but he dressed himself in the clothes of a merchant such that the rich man did not recognize that he was poor and in dire straits. The poor man, thus, had to present his case and explain his terrible need. But, had the poor man

AFFECTIONS

CON-VERSES

hostile? What is love, if it is not the dogged energy expended to sympathize with the other when she or he is caught in a web of passions beyond her or his control, when he or she is out on an emotional limb from which retreat seems impossible?

> 5They impose evil upon me in place of good,
> hate in place of my love.

Palal means "to judge." In the reflexive form, it means "to pray." To pray is to judge oneself, as one would wish to be judged. Prayer is a reflexive exercise of moral judgment. Therefore, one must be careful about that for which one prays.

Prayer is also a reflecting upon oneself as one approaches the Holy One. It is dialogic: a reflection upon oneself in light of one's world and one's self; and a reflecting upon oneself in the presence of the Self; and a reflection upon the Self in the presence of the self. A mutual judgment, a reciprocal affirmation of rectitude, a commensuration of creature and Creator.

They impose evil upon me

They not only ignore my attempts at kindness, rectitude, and sympathy, but they detest me, they hate me, they talk about me behind my back, they scheme against me, they try to turn the older generation and colleagues and friends against me. →

They impose evil upon me

"I have never felt really loved all my life. When the baby was born, I thought he would love me; but when he cried all the time, it meant he didn't love me, so I hit him" (an abusing mother).

Generally, children do not complain when punishment is deserved and fair; they protest only if punishment is unjust. In this, children are human, like the rest of us, for when we are treated justly, we accept punishment but, when we are treated unjustly, we experience anger, righteous anger. It is righteous because we know we have done no wrong; we know we are right and the other is wrong.

The abused person, however, is the object of a hate she or he cannot understand. Abusive behavior surges up from the unconscious of the abuser; it fits no framework of justice or fairness. Abusive behavior wells up from the depths of the abuser; it has no justification, no reason or purpose. Abuse is only cruel, hate-ful. It preempts the innocence of the victim. An abused person, therefore, does not experience righteous anger at what fate has meted out to her. Rather, he experiences silenced rage, passive anger.

When an abused person reencounters abuse from an intimate in later life, she

SPARKS

come before the rich man beaten, in torn clothes, and crippled, he would not have had to speak at all, for the rich man would have seen for himself the poor man's lowly and dire state.

This, then, is what Kind David, may he rest in peace, wanted to say, 'I am so broken and crushed by my suffering that my very presence is a prayer'" (Imrot Tehorot).

CON-VERSES

is again helpless, precisely because she realizes that she did no wrong and hence did not deserve the abuse. On the contrary, he knows that, actually, he deserved reward, for he was a "good" child or a "good" friend or a "good" spouse or a "good" parent. She knows that she did what was expected of her. He knows that he fulfilled his part of the conspiracy of violence and silence. She knows that she was loyal to God, to country, to authority, to parents, to ideals, even to sociocultural and administrative fiat. He knows that he was obedient.

Yet the abused person also knows that he or she was a real object of real abuse. She felt the blows on her body; he felt the humiliation on his face. Furthermore, the abused person could not respond in kind; that was impossible because of size and strength, and it was strictly forbidden by all social rules.—Helplessness multiplied by helplessness, and then multiplied again, magnified by the black wall of silence.—Slowly, ever so slowly, the abused person may come to experience genuine rage, the justified moral outrage and righteous anger that the rest of us know: "It *really* is *they* who are wrong. It *really* is *they* who abuse, who 'impose evil upon me in place of good, hate in place of my love.'"

AFFECTIONS

They also impose their own narrow, hateful vision of me upon me. They look at me but do not see me; they listen but do not hear. "I am for peace but, when I speak, they are for war" (Ps. 120:7).

They force me into their language, into their modes of relatedness, into their assumptions about reality. They compel me to lower my own standards of human decency. For I, too, rant and rave. I am tossed about like a locust (v. 23) by the anger of being hated, by the passion of revenge, by the frustration and the uselessness of it all, by the waste of my time and my energy, by the creeping moral corruption of my self. Against my will, I am drawn into speaking war, into hatred. Their hatred transforms my lovingness into hatred, my goodness into evil. Violence is seductive, compelling, compulsive.

AFFECTIONS   CON-VERSES

Place

The curses begin here; they embody
the psalmist's rage.
This commentary
follows that rage.

6Place a wicked person in command
over him/her;
let a persecutor stand at his/her
right hand.

a wicked person in
command

7When she/he is tried, let her/him be
convicted;
let intercession for her/him fail.

A concentration
camp guard, sense-
less beatings, end-
less roll calls,
forced marches,
Sisyphus tasks, the steps of Mauthausen.
No free will. Less than a slave. Willful,
capricious commands of an all-powerful
authority that cannot be avoided and from
which there is no escape.

persecutor

A continuous accusation, a taunting
derision, a contemptuous temptation.
Food left in the open to be eaten on Yom
Kippur while one is starving in the

Place

The curses begin here. The abused
person who is
walled in by
silence will turn
the rage inward;
this commentary
follows that voice.
The abused per-
son who has mov-
ed toward righ-
teous anger and
moral outrage will
turn the rage out-
ward; "Affections" follows that voice.

a wicked person in command

"And now for the sentence. I cannot
stand on my own. Place a judgmental
fool over me who will constantly remind
me of my unworthiness, who will be
uninterested in me and my ideas. Let me
love him with all my heart, but have him
despise me and remind me daily of my
subservient place" (Amy).

WORDS

Place
The curses begin here, and the rhythm of the
Hebrew changes to short, choppy phrases.

him . . . her
The psalmist here switches into the singular.
There are several ways to take this: (1) as a
collective noun for the enemies; (2) as directed
at the "leader of the gang" (Kirkpatrick); or
(3) to view this part of the psalm as the important part and the plural of the preceding verses
as a polite form, adumbrating the strong personal attack of this second part. I prefer the last
interpretation.
The person against whom the following im-

precations are directed need not be a man,
although, given the patriarchal milieu of the
psalms, it is likely that a male was meant. To
get closer to the violent feelings of the psalm
and to shift the burden of evildoing from men
alone, I have chosen to do a complete double
reading. I have tried to achieve this effect in the
full translation by parallel verses and, here, by
the use of him/her and her/him in alternating
verses. To get the full effect, one should read
this section out loud using pronouns of one
gender and then return to the beginning and
read it out loud again using the pronouns of
the other gender, as in the full translation. It is
a very powerful reading when done this way. →

AFFECTIONS

camps. A lie carefully placed in the ear of someone powerful that one is a traitor. Let him or her be able to trust no one because anyone might betray her or him.

be convicted

And imprisoned; hanged, executed! A formal, public acknowledgment of duplicity and treachery.

intercession . . . fail

No "influence" in the trial. No "interference" in the sentencing. No mitigating circumstances. No mother to soften the sentence. No spouse to mediate and console. No daughter to proffer peace and comfort. No son to bargain and palliate. No friends to negotiate and moderate. No parole. No grace.

WORDS

This, however, does not change the male, indeed patriarchal, character of the substance of the imprecations themselves.

a persecutor

Hebrew *satan,* with Hebrew *yistenuni,* "they detest me" (v. 4). This yields: "May the enemy have someone who detests him/her as s/he has detested me. . . ." On *satan* as a prosecutor, cf. Zech. 3:1. From this, Kirkpatrick deduces that it was a custom in ancient courts to have the prosecutor stand on the right hand of the accused. "Satan," in the sense of the Tempter or the Devil, is a later meaning.

be convicted

Lit., "come out wicked"; the wicked person is acknowledged publicly as wicked, that is, convicted. Rashi assumes that the trial is in heaven; Radak assumes that an earthly trial is meant.

intercession . . . fail

Again, the Hebrew is *tefillah,* and it bears the

ambiguity of court action, prayer, and intercession. To complicate matters, the Hebrew *la-hata'ah* can mean to "miss the mark" (Judg. 20:16) or "be considered as sin."

Taking *tefillah* as "prayer," the following meanings are possible: (1) "May his prayer that I die [Rashi] miss the mark"; (2) "May his prayer for himself [Mesudat David] miss the mark"; and (3) "May his prayer [any kind] be considered as a sin and not as a prayer." Kirkpatrick points out that the prayer of the wicked is often not considered true prayer (Isa. 1:15; Prov. 1:28; 28:9; Ps. 66:18) because such a person is really praying for himself or herself, attempting to draw God into the fray on her or his side.

The alternative is to preserve the ambiguity of "intercession," in which case it must "miss the mark" or "fail." The verse, then, would mean: "Let the intercession which I have exercised in prayer and/or in court on behalf of the wicked in spite of his or her detesting me [v. 4] fail." I have followed the more open translation because it allows the greatest number of possible meanings.

AFFECTIONS

days be few

And full of suffering, pain. And aggravation, heartbreak, and sorrow.

take command of . . . life

Have life and death control over him or her. Rob her of her husband; deprive him of his wife. Seize her fortune. Chop off his future.

orphans . . . widow[er]

Not just his or her own death but loneliness, depression, and oppression for the children. Cheated of their inheritance; deprived of whatever minimal parental love they received; not even a gravesite to return to.

Not just his or her punishment but the spouse locked in; no embrace; only widow(er)'s gossip, vicious games. Turned in upon oneself; growing old, weak, sick, and alone.

"'I shall be angry with you and I shall kill you with the sword, and your wives shall be widows and your children orphans' (Ex. 22:23)—From the fact

8May his/her days be few in number; may another take command of his/her life.

9May her/his children be orphans; may her husband/his wife be a widower/widow.

CON-VERSES

take command of . . . life

"That man will control me as I need to be controlled. May I eventually die of a broken heart. Please have pity and allow that to happen" (Amy).

WORDS

May . . . Let

The Hebrew verbs are in the future (imperfect) but can be read in the jussive. Hebrew does not distinguish between "may" and "let." I have chosen to alternate for reasons of English style.

command

Hebrew *pequdato*, with *hafqed* (v. 6). Many meanings are possible: "take charge (or command) of" –"the days of her life" (Targum); "his greatness" (Rashi); "her fortune" (Mesudat David); "her soul" or "his wife" [or, her husband] (Ibn Ezra); and "his task" or "her mission" (with Acts 1:20). I prefer the linkage with v. 6, that is, with the idea that the wicked person should lose control over her or his life.

CON-VERSES

AFFECTIONS

creditor ensnare . . . aliens pillage

"I have taken and taken all my life. My expensive education. My expensive car and clothes. I don't deserve what I have. Take it from me. That which I produce is useless; it deserves to be criticized by outsiders. I will offer it up myself in order to get cut down faster" (Amy).

¹⁰Let his/her children be continually on the move, begging; let them seek alms from within the decrepit buildings they inhabit.

¹¹Let the creditor ensnare all that is hers/his; let aliens pillage that which she/he produces.

that it says 'I will kill you,' would I not know that 'your wives shall be widows and your children orphans'? [Why is the last clause inserted into the verse if it is self-evident?] Rather [this teaches us] that this is a separate curse: that your wives will be bound as living widows because there will be no witnesses to the death of their husbands and they will be forbidden forever to remarry. And the children will always be orphans because the court will not allow them to inherit the goods of their fathers, for it will not be known if the fathers are dead or alive" (Rashi, cited in Feuer).

on the move, begging . . . decrepit buildings

Let the children be homeless persons, sleeping and living on the streets. Wanderers, no place to put down their heads, no home; no refuge from reality, from the cold, from the heat. Strange beds, in strange places, among strangers,

WORDS

let them seek alms

Kirkpatrick notes that the Septuagint reads "and let them be driven out of their ruined homes." This would imply a Hebrew text of *ve-gorshu*, which is not far from *ve-darshu*. Perhaps this is related to the medieval debate about whether to read: *ve-darshu* or *ve-dorshu* (see Hacham).

ensnare

Most of the commentators take this from the root *yqsh*, meaning "trap." Rashi notes, however, that the form is wrong and suggests: "May the creditor enthusiastically pursue . . ." or, working with a root I do not know: "May the creditor have a lien against. . . ." For the depredations of the creditor, see 2 Kings 4:1; Neh. 5:1–7; etc.

AFFECTIONS

in shelters run by strangers. Dragging in tow sisters, brothers, or children. Food on the dole, dished out by aliens who cannot un- derstand. No privacy. Decrepit buildings, rats, dead people, gar- bage, no water, no heat. Danger—of drugs, of rape, of theft, of disease. Only to be evicted each morning, to a useless life in an in- different world.

creditor ensnare . . . aliens pillage

The relentless claim of money. No getting ahead of the game, even for the employed. Price gouging, usury, loan sharks, enforcers, eviction, auction blocks. Get it all, little as it is, for a steal. Thugs, hoodlums, hired hands wrecking whatever the creditor does not claim, sometimes even before the creditor arrives. Looting, despoiling, pillaging; taking, ruining the rest, destroying one's "castle," one's domain, one's home.

[12]May no one advocate lovingkindness for him/her;
may no one be merciful to his/her orphans.

no one advocate lovingkindness

No one to speak a kind word. No one to do a kind deed. No one to urge others to kindness. No one to speak kindly on one's behalf. No one to draw out one's own inner kindness.

No one to hold true to the covenant. No one to demand fairness and justice, if not kindness.

no one be merciful to . . . orphans

Young or old; urchins or adults. Let the natural cruelty of society be their lot, not the protective apparatus of family, friends, and professional advo- cates.

WORDS

advocate
Hacham and Kirkpatrick understand "some- one who will continue lovingkindness into the next generation." The French reads: "Que nul ne conserve pour lui de l'affection."

CON-VERSES   AFFECTIONS

to be cut off . . . family name be blotted out

to be cut off . . . family name be blotted out

"This has been my curse from the moment of conception. A female fetus with no right to the family name . . . worthless. She is too weak even to carry that name to future generations. For this, sons are born. For this reason my father scoffs at my desire to keep my name even after marriage" (Amy).

¹³May her/his end be to be cut off; may the family name be blotted out in the following generation.

¹⁴Let the transgression of his/her fathers be remembered by the Lord; let the sin of his/her mother not be blotted out.

No continuation. No name. No history. . . . Cut off. Wiped off the books. Erased. Eradicated. . . . No memory.

WORDS

her/his end

Most commentators understand Hebrew *'aḥarit* to refer to that which one leaves behind, that is, one's descendants, especially one's son (with Ps. 37:38). The meaning, then, would be: "May his/her son die childless [so that] the family name be blotted out in the next generation." My own rendering is less precise, just in case it takes more than two generations for the wicked to be completely cut off. The French, "que ses descendants soient exterminés," sounds too strong after the holocaust, even for this psalm.

transgression . . . sin

There are two moments in the Jewish understanding of things in which the fate of the whole world hung in the balance. The first was after the sin of the golden calf: Moses went up on Mount Sinai to seek forgiveness, and God came down and taught him the proper prayer to say (the original "Lord's Prayer," so to speak). The text reads as follows: "God came down in a cloud. H/he stood with H/him there. H/he called in the Name of the Lord. The Lord passed before him and H/he called out: 'Lord, Lord—

God, Who loves compassionately and cherishes, Who is patient and overflows with lovingkindness and truth. He stores up lovingkindness for the thousands of generations. He forgives *'avon, pesha', ve-ḥata'ah*. He cleanses'" (Ex. 34:5–7).

The second moment was during the annual atoning for the sins of the people and the sanctuary. On the Day of Atonement, the high priest went into the sanctuary, performed the daily sacrifices and then, over specially designated animals, he recited the confession of sins three times, once for himself and his household, once for the priests, and once for the people of Israel. The blood of two of these sacrificial animals was used to purify the sanctuary, while the third animal, the goat upon whose head the sins of the people had been confessed, was sent to the desert and killed (the original "scapegoat"; Leviticus 16). The text of the high priest's confessions is not given in the Bible, but a disagreement about it is recorded in the Talmud (Yoma 36b) as follows:

"How did he confess? [He said], *'aviti, pasha'ti, ve-ḥata'ti* [over his animal and] over the scapegoat, as it says, 'He shall confess over it all the *'avonot* of the Israelites and all their

WORDS

pesha'im, even unto all their *hata'ot'* (Lev. 16:21). Similarly, Moses prayed, 'He forgives *'avon, pesha', ve-hata'ah* (Ex. 34:7). This is the opinion of Rabbi Me'ir. But the sages say: *'avonot* are purposeful sins as it says . . . ; *pesha'im* are rebellious sins as it says . . . ; and *hata'ot* are inadvertent sins as it says . . . [They add:] Since the high priest confessed [first] the purposeful and rebellious sins, how can he then confess the inadvertent sins [the latter, being much less serious, belong logically first]? Rather, thus would the high priest recite confession: *'hata'ti, 'aviti, pasha'ti,* I/we have committed inadvertent sins, I/we have committed purposeful sins, and I/we have committed rebellious sins.'"

Two issues are at stake here: the meaning of the three terms, and the conflict between a scriptural and a logical sequence for the sins within the actual text of the confession. On the matter of the sequence, Scripture favors *'avon, pesha', hata'ah* (Ex. 34:7 and Lev. 16:21) while the rabbis favor the logical sequence, *hata'ah, 'avon, pesha',* based on a typology of sin. The Talmud resolves this question in favor of logic, not Scripture, and it is that usage that was incorporated into the liturgy of the sacrificial service on Yom Kippur and which is still present in the conceptual substratum of one of the two recurring public confessions recited every Yom Kippur. On the matter of the meaning of the terms, the typology of the rabbis prevailed, the respective meanings being: *'avon*=intentional sin, *pesha'*=rebellious sin, and *hata'ah* (alternate form, *hata't*)=inadvertent sin.

Using these rabbinic categories on the text of Psalms here, we obtain the following meaning: "Let the purposeful sin (*'avon*) of his or her fathers be remembered by God; let the inadvertent sin (*hata't*) of her or his mother not be blotted out." (Similarly in Ps. 51:7 [see below]: "Truly, I was formed in a dance of purposeful sin (*'avon*) and, in the heat of inadvertent sin (*het'* [*hata't*]), my mother became pregnant with me.") Because, however, I am not certain that the words *'avon* and *hata'ah* bore the same connotations for the psalmist as for the rabbis, I have chosen to preserve the difference, but without nuancing, by translating *'avon* as

"transgression" and *hata'ah* as "sin."

The full range of meaning here, however, can probably be understood as: "Let the deep, secret sins (the sexual sins); the inadvertent, purposeful, and rebellious sins; the transgressions of the conscious, the subconscious, and the unconscious—even in the preceding generations—be counted against the wicked."

be remembered . . . not blotted out

Hacham points to the subtle contrasts between this verse and the preceding one: "be cut off . . . be blotted out" contrasts with "be remembered . . . not be blotted out." Similarly, "fathers . . . mother" contrasts with "his/her end [i.e., the son or the descendants] . . . the family name." Hacham takes "fathers" with "descendants" and "mother" with "name" because of the singular and plural forms. Because of the patrilineal nature of biblical society, I prefer to take "fathers" with "name" and "mother" with "end" (or "posterity").

The commentators, following the Targum to Ex. 20:5 (end) and the early rabbinic sources, say that God "remembers the sins of the fathers" only if the children continue the sins of their parents. This, while morally more coherent, does not express the reality that patterns of sinfulness and rebellion, some more subtle than others, are indeed passed down by training and psychological identification from generation to generation. Nor does it express the view that some sins are so serious that only multigenerational punishment seems adequate; or the idea that an innocent person can be so victimized that he or she feels deeply the need to invoke punishment beyond the immediate wicked person. (Matt. 23:32–36, pointed to by Kirkpatrick, also seems to use this concept in a different way.)

transgression . . . sin

The psalmist does not list the sins here but the echo of Ps. 51:7 is too loud not to deserve a moment of attention. There the same two forms of sin (see above) are mentioned, and "sin" is associated with the mother. The text there, on first glance, reads: "Truly, I was formed in transgression, and my mother conceived me

CON-VERSES

not remember . . . persecuted . . . deal
the death blow

"I am a bad per-
son with evil
thoughts and little
value. I forget to
be nice. I am so
impatient and
compulsive. I am
scared" (Amy).

15Let them be over against the Lord
    always;
may God cut off their memory from the
    earth.

16Because she/he did not remember
to act in lovingkindness
but persecuted the suffering poor
to deal the death blow to the crushed
    in heart.

AFFECTIONS

over against the Lord always

Let them always be fighting with
God — aggravating
Him, irritating
Him, exasperating
Him, provoking
Him. And let God
always be fighting
with them — rebuk-
ing, arguing, scold-
ing, reproving,
reprimanding,
chiding, censor-
ing, and correct-
ing them.

cut off their memory from the earth

Their personal memory but not their
memory as a symbol. May they become
a sign and a symbol for evil: Amalek,
Pharaoh, Nebuchadnezzar, Haman,
Esau, Edom, Vespasian, Titus, the
Crusaders, the Inquisition, Ishmael,
Chmielnitsky, Hitler.

WORDS

in sin." Understanding *ḥolalti* as also related to
the root for "to dance" and *yeḥematni* as also
related to the root for "to be hot," one might
read more imaginatively: "Truly, I was formed
in a dance of transgression and, in the heat of
sin, my mother became pregnant with me." The
psalmist here may be invoking the most primitive and basic of transgression-sins, sexuality
(perhaps even the fantasy of incest), as a sin to
be remembered by God and invoked against the
enemy.

them be over against

I take this to refer to the whole family. Rashi,
Ibn Ezra, and others take it to refer to the transgressions and read: "Let them be before God

always so that God cut off their [the family's]
memory. . . ." The German reads: "Der Herr
müsse sie nimmer aus den Augen lassen." For
a parallel, see Ps. 34:17.

did not remember

Because he or she did not remember, her or
his memory will be cut off. Because she or he
did not act in lovingkindness, he or she will have
no advocate of lovingkindness (v. 12).

the suffering poor

Hebrew *'ani ve-'evyon* is a hendiadys,
pointing to physical, psychological, and
monetary deprivation (Hacham). The commentators take the suffering poor person to be the

AFFECTIONS

not remember . . . persecuted . . . deal the death blow

One leads to the other, a spiral of increasing sinfulness. Evil turns in upon itself; it feeds itself; it expands its own appetite. Evil impregnates itself and gives birth to demons, to compulsions. Evil grows, like any natural thing, but it can grow wild, out of control, destroying and killing.

The victim, too, spirals downward— from the neglected one to the suffering poor to the crushed in heart. *La danse macabre.*

continues . . . then let . . .

The enemy wants only to hurt others; then let hurt come upon him or her. The enemy denies justice and love and kindness and human decency; then let injustice, hatred, betrayal, and meanness come upon her or him.

wears cursing like a uniform . . . like a habit

For some people, picking fights is a way of life. To lie, to provoke, to

17He/She continues to love cursing— then let it come upon him/her; He/She continues to not want blessing— then let it be far from him/her.

18She/He wears cursing like a uniform; it penetrates her/his innards like water and her/his bones like rubbing oil.—

19May it be for him/her like a habit in which he/she wraps him/herself, like a loincloth which is worn always.

besmirch, to degrade the other is a habit so deep that it is "natural." Crushing others is an instinct. Degrading others is a reflex. Crush first, think later; demean first, reconsider later; lash out first, apologize later. Some people are mean by character. Such people wear physical and verbal abuse naturally, like clothing.

For others, physical and verbal molestation is an art form. They cultivate the art of the demeaning rejoinder. They carefully hone the skills of physical and verbal exploitation. They practice being mean, and they become good at it. They are the artists of moral and physical rape. Such people wear malevolence like a uniform, which calls forth a sense of task, of goals, of purpose.

Let such a person be swept up in his or her abusiveness. Let her or him receive it back in full measure. Let him or her get caught in his or her own meanness. Let violence turn back upon the perpetrator. Let viciousness turn back upon the self. Let rottenness overwhelm. She or he deserves to be raped. Let such a person rape him self or her self.

WORDS

psalmist (with v. 22), but the wicked person described here would persecute anyone, even someone who is not a psalmist.

S/he continues to . . . then let

On this jussive form, which makes much more sense than the past tense, see Hacham and

CON-VERSES

This is the recompense

The rule is: the abuser is always an abused. "Those who are intimidated will be intimidating, those who are humiliated will impose humiliation" (Miller, *For Your Own Good*, p. 232). To curse is to respond to abuse with abuse; it is to fight back, measure for measure, id for id.

The psalmist grapples with his helplessness: He invokes command over his enemy. He urges the conviction of his opponent. He curses his adversary with homelessness. He calls orphanhood upon the children of the perpetrator and isolation upon the spouse. He demands

> [20]This is the recompense from the Lord for those who detest me,
> for those who speak evil against my very being.

AFFECTIONS

This is the recompense from the Lord

How can a person get so angry ("rage" is the word)? The normal human instinct is to flinch from the rage. The usual reflex is to deny it, to tone it down — even when reading it. But, there it is, in the Psalms: rage. An affection, an emotional attitude, an approved feeling — and in a context of personal assault, not national disaster.

Yes, there are mean people in the world — in one's family, among one's colleagues, among strangers — people driven by hatred, jealousy, greed, and fear; and yes, it is all right to feel vindictive, vengeful, reciprocally cruel. →

WORDS

A. E. Cowley, *Gesenius' Hebrew Grammar*, 2nd ed., III:I:A:111u–w (p. 329, bottom), contra Kirkpatrick.

uniform . . . habit

A uniform for work (Hacham), meaning that the wicked person has made cursing others a profession and a habit. Note the play in my rendering of the next sentence, the point being that the wicked person who has become a full-time curser of others should be cursed with cursing and not be able to extricate himself or herself from it.

my very being

Hebrew *nafshi* with v. 31 (*nafsho*). King James follows the later meaning and renders "soul." The German reads: "meine Seele . . . sein Leben." Kirkpatrick follows King James but

understands v. 31 as: "condemn to death." Chouraqui renders imaginatively: "mon/son être."

The sense of the text and the accumulated tradition press me to search for something more than just the personal pronoun, though that is problematic. On the one hand, the psalmist may not have had an abstract conception of personhood. On the other hand, his use of *nefesh* in the closing verses of two sections of the psalm must have some meaning. I have, therefore, chosen "very being" to convey the emphatic sense of self that I believe the psalmist intended, without tangling the text up in a later theology of soul and body.

Da capo al fine, for the imprecatory verses as a whole, with the pronoun of the other gender. For the full effect, see the full translation preceding the commentaries.

AFFECTIONS   CON-VERSES

But there is no sexually provocative sadism. No long drawn-out torturing of the victim, as was common in the dungeons and at public executions during the middle ages. Vindictiveness yes, but no gory detail. Vengeance yes, but no pornographic violence.

Instead, there is the art of imprecation; the tailored, almost restrained, language of execration; the carefully considered malediction. Not the ladylike demur or gentlemanly protest, but the well-placed curse. A lost art in our day.

A curse is performative speech, speaking is doing; it is not expressive language, verbal catharsis. To curse is to call down supernatural vengeance; it is not to vent one's deepest feelings. To curse is to call down violence on the oppressor, to invoke abuse on the abuser.

And yet a curse is not performative action; it is not accomplishing one's rage in social deed. The text acknowledges the power of the curse but shies away from it—perhaps in modesty, perhaps for ethical reasons. The psalmist now turns to this.

the social and economic collapse of his foe and even prays that his enemy be eradicated physically and wiped off the slate of memory. He returns curse with a curse. [*Da capo al fine,* reading "she" and "her" for "he" and "his."]

The cycle of abuse . . . *La danse macabre.*

The cycle of abuse is not ethical, even though it is natural. Given everything Eichmann did to us, it is natural to wish evil not only upon him but also upon his wife and children, even if it is not ethical to do so. Given the violence of the perpetrator, it is natural, when the rage turns outward, to invoke a deep curse upon him or her and upon her or his loved ones.

The rule also is: not all abused persons become abusers. Some victims avoid the re-victimization of the cycle of violence. Some survivors live to see a better, fuller day. The psalmist makes a suggestion in this direction; the victim may well reject it.

CON-VERSES

AFFECTIONS

You, Lord, are my lord and master

You, Lord, are my lord and master

"Affirm the vision of true compassionate justice, and ask God to act on behalf of our joint cause. Acknowledge God's justice and power, and invoke His power on behalf of our joint mission."

21 You, Lord, are my lord and master
Deal with me for the sake of Your Name.
Because Your lovingkindness is good,
save me.

Fantasy. Sublimation. To acquire, at the moment of powerlessness, the power of the father; by fantasy.

"God is King." — "And, therefore, set fear of You, oh Lord our God, over all that You have made, and dread of You over all You have created so that all that You have made will fear You and all the creatures will bow down before You; so that they will all form one unit to do Your will, with a whole heart, for we know, oh Lord our God, that dominion radiates forth from You, that strength is in Your hand and power in Your right hand, and that Your Name is awesome above all You have created. . . . Rule, You Lord, alone, over all that You have made. . . . 'The Lord of hosts is raised in justness, and the holy God is made holy in righteousness.' Blessed are You, oh Lord, the holy King" (High Holiday liturgy, citing Isa. 5:16).

Fantasy. Projection. Sublimation, at best. Sublimation is not healing.

Rage is an exhausting emotion. It drains the inner core of the self. It feeds itself, consumes the self, flares up, is snuffed out, flares up again, consumes again. Depression is rage-in-waiting, smoldering anger.

The psalmist resolves this rage by putting the self in the context of God's power. As Ibn Ezra comments: "After he has cursed the wicked and all those who detest him, he returns to plead before God that he not be destroyed with those who vilify him because [he realizes that] he does not have the strength to resist them" (Feuer). The psalmist accomplishes this in two dialectical steps, setting the goal for the reader at the same time.

First, we recognize that all our rage, justified though it is, is powerless in itself to effect change in the real world. Rage alone does not right a wrong. We acknowledge that we are overwhelmed, helpless; that the working of justice does not ultimately come from us. We affirm the vision of true compassionate justice, but we also admit that it is not we who effect it. We are the suffering poor.

Second, we place our rage within the

WORDS

You, Lord, are my lord and master
Hacham takes this as a nominative sentence, contrasting the lonely "against my very being" of the previous verse with the comforting "Lord

. . . lord and master" of this verse.
The first term is the Tetragrammaton. The exact pronunciation of this Name is not known. Unpronounced, the consonants are YHVH,

AFFECTIONS

power of the Source of justice. This step is the dialectic within the dialectic, for we do this by acknowledging God's justice and His power; and by asking God to act for us. We pray that our cause, because it is just, be His cause and that His cause be our cause; and that He act against evil on behalf of our joint mission. We call upon God's lovingkindness and His goodness because, through them, God will recognize and acknowledge us as the loyal servants we have been; and we ask that this lovingkindness lead to action by God on our behalf.

At the same time, we do not conceal our continuing anger; we do not hide our rage; nor do we simply spew it forth from us. Rather, we incorporate our rage into our prayer. We place ourselves within God's power, and we petition for action on God's part. We submit to God, and we evoke His righteous rage on our behalf.

In this section, the psalmist lives this dialectic. Verse 21 is prayer, while vv. 22–25 evince repressed anger. Verse 26 is prayer while vv. 27–29 are a reversion to cursing. The transition from personal rage to God's just power is very difficult.

Deal with me . . . save me

"You, Sister/Self, are in control here. You must awaken and begin the saving process. I will remain in the pits of self-pity timelessly if You, Sister, do not reveal your Self as a new source of spiritual energy. Recovery is possible, and I have hope in You" (Amy).

for the sake of Your Name

A name. What is in a name? There are two kinds of name/noun. There is the noun that names by classifying. "This is a dog; that is good. This is a concept; that is unjust." And there is the

WORDS

usually reconstructed by Bible scholars as "Yahveh" (or "Yahweh"), the fourth conjugation imperfect tense of the verb "to be," which would mean "he who causes to be," that is, "he who creates and sustains." Not a bad guess. In Jewish tradition, one sees the consonants YHVH and usually reads "Adonai," "[my] Lord." My translation follows this custom.

There is another term for God: "Elohim," usually rendered "God." From the existence of these two terms for God, one a proper noun or name and the other a generic noun, biblical scholars turned to Exodus chaps. 3 and 6 (and other key texts) and deduced that there are several main "documents" in the Bible. There are those that use YHVH; there are those that use Elohim; and there are those that use the compound form "YHVH Elohim," "Lord God." Scholars then divided up the Bible into these

(and other) documents. This is known as the "Documentary Hypothesis," and much literature is available on the arguments for and against this literary analysis.

There are hundreds of times where the text shows, "Adonay YHVH." Originally, one probably read, "Adonay Yahveh," "[my] Lord, Yahveh." However, once the tradition of reading the Tetragammaton itself as "Adonay" developed—probably rooted in those verses where YHVH and Adonay are used in parallel fashion (Ex. 4:10; 5:22; 15:17; Isa. 49:14; etc.)—one would have to read that phrase, "Adonay, Adonay." This, however, engendered two problems. First, two words that are spelled completely differently would be read alike. And, second, the only place in the Bible where the Tetragrammaton occurs twice in successive words (Ex. 34:6) is in the prayer that God

AFFECTIONS

noun that names as an ideogram; it labels that which is unique: "David," "Jane," "Pop," "Bip," "America," "YHVH." The latter type, known in English as a "proper noun," tells us nothing and everything. It tells us nothing about the class to which the named belongs, but it encompasses everything we know about the named, and all that we do not know about it.

God's "Name" (YHVH) is a proper noun. It tells us nothing conceptual about God. But it identifies all we know about Him; it crystallizes His being for us. He is His Name, and His Name is He; which is true of each of us too: I am my name and my name is I. "I/i am who I/i am."

What do we know about God? That He is a person; that, as a person, He is fair, just, loving, and kind but also demanding, strict; that He rejoices and is angry and filled with sorrow; that He chooses and has His faithful from whom He demands loyalty; that He is addressable as I, You, He; that He is powerful though He does not always act in ways that justly display that power; and that He is holy, transcendent, not quite within our grasp. Scripture teaches us this; tradition and experience confirm it.

No one knows how to pronounce God's Name. Jewish tradition forbids pronouncing even its substitutes. But the heart of the people cannot do without a name for God, so we call Him "*Hashem,*" literally, "the Name," but in reality, a name, like yours or mine; or "God." We also call Him "*Rebono shel olam*/Master of the universe" or "*Avinu*/our Father," but these are also nouns of classification which place Him in the class of deity and set Him in relation with us. "*Hashem*/God" is God's Name.

For God to act "for the sake of His Name" is for Him to act to defend His Person, to act so as to be consistent with that which we know about Him from Scripture, tradition, and experience. For God to act "for the sake of His Name" is for Him to respond to our faith in Him. His being allows us the privilege of calling upon Him; our faith justifies and grounds our right to call upon Him. He must be faithful, as we are faithful. He must act "for the sake of His Name" because we have acted "for the sake of His Name."

To pray for God to act "for the sake of His Name" incorporates both dialectical moments of the process of resolving one's anger. Saying rage that is

WORDS

teaches to Moses for use in exceptional moments (see above, at v. 14). In that context, one would see "YHVH YHVH" and say, "Adonay Adonay," "Lord Lord." In all other places where one sees, "Adonay YHVH" and would want to read "Adonay Adonay," the tradition actually reads, "Adonay Elohim," "Lord God."

In six places, the text shows "YHVH Adonay": Hab. 3:19; Pss. 16:2; 68:21; here; 140:8; and 141:8, with parallels in Ps. 8:2, 10 and Neh. 10:30. Originally read "Yahveh Adonay," "Yahveh [my] Lord," it too, after the shift in pronunciation should have been read "Adonay Adonay." However, for the same reasons, this phrase too was changed and is read "Elohim Adonay," "God Lord."

Here, given the text "*'ata* YHVH Adonay" and understanding it as a nominative sentence most parallel to Ps. 16:2, there are two ways

AFFECTIONS

rooted in righteous anger is an "acting for the sake of His Name" and we call upon God to act in response. Speaking anger because He has not already acted is rooted in what we know about Him, in what He / His Name means to us; it is an "acting for the sake of His Name." We do not hide this anger; we rise to it and ask that He "deal with me for the sake of Your Name." In asking God to respond "for the sake of His Name," we affirm the vision of justice and place ourselves in His power. At the same time, we acknowledge our helplessness and say, "My enemies have acted for their own interest . . . but I, who pray to You, do not ask for You to act because of my merit; rather, I ask You to act for the sake of Your Name, [Your Glory, Your Reputation, Your Own Standards]" (Hacham; see also Muffs).

WORDS

to read this verse: (1) "You, YHVH/Lord, are my master/lord" — following the consonantal text, or (2) "You, God [Elohim], are my master/lord" — following the vocalized text. One can also read these two terms as appositives and not as a nominative sentence, yielding: "'ata, YHVH, Adonai (You, Lord, Master)" or "'ata, Elohim, Adonai (You, God, Lord / You, God, Master)." I have chosen to follow the consonantal text and to read this as a nominative sentence (with Hacham). At the same time, I have tried to capture (with an English hendiadys) the sense that the Lord is more than just a master. Hence: "You, Lord, are my lord and master."

Chouraqui follows an old rabbinic distinction that YHVH represents God's gracious mercy and Elohim represents God's firm judgment. Since God is always present to creation in both aspects, Chouraqui always renders the Tetragrammaton with the term Elohim written inside the Tetragrammaton, that is, with both names of God appearing simultaneously. (This also follows the kabbalistic interpretation that Malkhut and Tiferet are united in one divine Name.) He thus renders: "Et, Toi, IHVH-Elohim, Adonai."

because Your lovingkindness is good
An echo of the recurring phrase "Give praise unto God for He is good; His lovingkindness endures forever" (Pss. 118:1; 136:1; etc.; Hacham).

CON-VERSES

AFFECTIONS

For I am suffering and poor

my heart is hollow within me

"I am so sad. My face doesn't smile anymore. All of my love and emotion has been stolen by my persecutor/self. Will I ever recover it? Is it possible to rise above?" (Amy).

> 22For I am suffering and poor.
> My heart is hollow within me.

There is a void in my heart, a painful emptiness. A person can die of this void, if it grows to the point where the heart breaks.

The curses turn against the self — guilt at expressing violence, especially against the intimate, loved, powerful one(s). Hide me from myself. *Kol Nidre* (with Reik, pp. 167–221).

It is said that self-abasement is a virtue borrowed from Christian culture; but here it is in Psalms. Still, living among those who preach (even if they

WORDS

suffering and poor
The same phrase as in v. 16. While this phrase is a hendiadys, its terms can also occur separately as in Ps. 35:10: "He saves the poor from him who is stronger than he, and the suffering poor from him who exploits him" (Hacham).

hollow
From the root *halal*. If from the root *hul*, the meaning would be "trembles within me" (see "Sparks").

SPARKS

my heart is hollow within me
The rabbinic tradition reads the Hebrew *halal* as "a slain person," thus engendering the meaning: "My heart is slain within me."

The evil inclination had no dominion over three persons and these are they: Abraham, Isaac, and Jacob, as it is written. . . . Some say that David too [was among those over whom the evil inclination had no power], as it says, "My heart was hollow / is slain within me" (Ps. 109:22) [with Rashi: The evil inclination is dead within me]. What, then, does the first authority

[who does not list David in this group] say [of the verse from Psalms? He replies:] "David was simply describing his pain" (Talmud, Bava Batra 17a).

Rabbi Yose of the Galilee says, "The righteous are judged by their good inclination [only], as it says, 'My heart is slain within me.'" To this, the Lubavitcher Rebbe commented: "The righteous person has no evil inclination for he has killed it with fasting" (Tanya, chap. 1, probably alluding to v. 24).

CON-VERSES

do not always practice) sacrificial love reinforces the tendency to self-abasement. It is also said that self-abasement is a virtue of the exile; but here it is in Psalms. Still, living in a society where it is better to swallow one's pride and avoid confrontation reinforces the instinct toward self-abasement.

The positive roots of self-abasement, however, go much deeper. They surge up from the deep fear of violence — in oneself. "If adolescents were to show their true feelings openly, they would run the risk of being sent to prison as dangerous terrorists or put in mental institutions for the insane" (Miller, *For Your Own Good,* p. 107). And not just adolescents; each one of us.

How far can violence go? It has actually gone very far already: "'We had the moral right, we had the duty to our own people, to kill this people that wanted to kill us. . . . By and large, however, we can say, that we have performed this most difficult task out of love for our people. And we have suffered no harm from it in our inner self, in our soul, in our character.' . . . In order to make the struggle against these humane impulses easier, the citizens of the Third Reich were offered an object to serve as the bearer of all these qualities that were abhorred because they had been forbidden and dangerous in their childhood — this object was the Jewish people . . . everything they had feared in themselves since childhood could be attributed to the Jews. . . . [They] led a million children, whom they regarded as the bearers of the feared portions of their own psyche, into the gas chambers. One can even imagine that by shouting at them, beating them, or photographing them, they were finally able to release the hatred going back to early childhood. From the start, it had been the aim of their upbringing to stifle their childish, playful, and life-affirming side. The cruelty inflicted on them, the psychic murder of the child they once were, had to be passed on in the same way: each time they sent another Jewish child to the gas ovens, they were in essence murdering the child within themselves" (Miller, *For Your Own Good,* citing Himmler and responding, pp. 79–80, 86–87).

We fear our inner selves. The fabric of civilization is tissue paper. Self-abasement is not the answer.

AFFECTIONS

I am dragged out . . . tossed about

²³I am dragged out
as a shadow is lengthened.
I am tossed about like a locust.

²⁴My knees are weak from fasting.
My flesh is thin from lack of fat.

²⁵I have become an object of derision
for them.
They see me and nod their heads.

I am exhausted by the actual, and by the inner, struggle. I fight and make no progress, externally or internally. I resist, but the resistance consumes me. I have no more strength of my own.

WORDS

I am dragged out as a shadow is lengthened
This is a very complex metaphor. The lengthening of a shadow suggests two things: a long slow movement and a movement that will blend and fade away into the darkness. The verb in this stich means "to go, to walk." But it occurs (only this once in the Bible) in a conjugation that suggests either duration or passivity.

Using the durative sense and the long slow meaning, Hacham renders: "I move now, slowly, as a shadow. . . ." Using the passive sense and the fade-away meaning, JPS renders: "I fade away like . . . ," and Rashi and Feuer render: "I am about to disappear as. . . ."

The possible parallel with the second stich suggests a movement that is compelled, which is against the will of the psalmist. Hence: "I move against my will as a shadow is lengthened" (Mesudat David), which is not quite a coherent metaphor. Kirkpatrick combines both: "I am made to depart [against my will] as a shadow. . . ." I have tried to capture the greatest ambiguity.

like a locust
A locust has no nest and therefore is moved about (Rashi; Ibn Ezra). It is also lightweight and tossed about by the wind (Hacham).

fasting
The psalmist has been fasting in prayer, either for himself or for his enemies. The latter arouses their derision (Hacham).

thin from lack of fat
Kirkpatrick renders: "is shrunken for want of oil," pointing to the fact that abstaining from oil was a sign of mourning (2 Sam. 14:2).

object of derision
This is a source of psychological and moral pain, over and above the physical pain of the previous verse (Hacham).

nod their heads
To "nod" one's head is to move it vertically in a sign of affirmation as if to say, "He deserves

SPARKS

I am dragged out as a shadow is lengthened
It is well known that before a person dies his shadow leaves him and, because of this, he must die (Zera' Ya'akov).

AFFECTIONS

Help me . . . save me

"Dear Sister, come into me and resurrect my soul from the depths of manic depression. Cure my ills. Show me love and peace. Prove that harmony is possible and not beyond the reach of one who tries" (Amy).

26Help me, Lord, my God.
Save me
by the standard of Your lovingkindness.

by the standard of Your lovingkindness

Hebrew, *ke-ḥasdekha*. The biblical Hebrew *ḥesed* has two meanings, both of which are intended here. It means, first, God's love for us insofar as that love is totally unmerited, totally independent of our observance, our study, our faith, our loyalty, and our feelings. *Ḥesed,* in this sense, is God's unconditional love for us, God's grace. The psalmist's prayer, here, then is: "Since my strength has not been sufficient to make justice prevail in the outside world and since it has not succeeded in making faith triumph over anger in the inner world, I cast myself on Your mercy, God, and ask that You act out of Your unconditional love, out of Your grace. I abandon my self and ask that You act, not in response to me, but out of Your gracious Self."

Second, *ḥesed* means God's love for us that is rooted in His contract with creation. God did not have to create the world; He did not have to give us free will and judgment; and He did not have to reveal Himself and His standards and expectations. But God did and, having done so, God is obligated to abide by the agreement to be our God and to protect us when we do His will, just as we, by accepting God as our God, are obligated to ponder His will and to act according to our best understanding of it. *Ḥesed,* in this sense, is God's covenantal love for us, God's compassionate dealing with us, God's faithfulness. The psalmist's prayer, here, then is: "Since I have tried and failed to win the inner and the outer battles which are mine because of my covenantal love for You, I now respectfully but forcefully call upon You to assume Your share of the responsibility in this fight because You, too, are bound to our covenant."

I have tried to capture both meanings of *ḥesed* with the term "lovingkindness" but I am afraid that I have not succeeded. The other terms [see "Words"] are not better.

WORDS

it." To "shake" one's head is to move it horizontally in a sign of sympathy as if to say, "What a pity." The French translates "secouer" (to nod) and Chouraqui translates "hocher" (to shake). In Hebrew the predominant root is *no'a* (six occurrences: here; Ps. 22:8; Lam. 2:15; Job 16:4; 2 Kings 19:21; Isa. 37:22), though the root *nud* also occurs (twice: Jer. 18:16 and Ps. 44:15). I cannot tell which motion is meant nor whether

affirming the deservedness of the disaster or expressing sympathy is intended (assuming that the head motions conveyed these same feelings in biblical antiquity). Since "shaking" one's head in contemporary English has other connotations, I have chosen "nod."

lovingkindness

Mercy (King James), kindness (Feuer), faith-

AFFECTIONS

Your servant will rejoice

A resurgence from the depths of the psalmist's rage. A fully legitimate response; irrepressible yet not satisfying, concretely or spiritually.

openly . . . multitudes

It is not enough to thank God silently; one must testify publicly to God's help. To many modern Jews, this seems strange; "testify-

27So that they know that such is Your hand;
that You, Lord, have done it.

28Let them curse—but You bless.
Let them rise up and be ashamed—
Your servant will rejoice.

29Let those who detest me
wear the garment of disgrace.
Let them wrap their shame around them
as a robe.

30I will openly thank the Lord greatly.
In the presence of multitudes, I will
praise Him.

ing" is not a common Jewish procedure. But the psalmist is very clear: one must acknowledge what God has done publicly. If standing up in a group is not one's style, one is required at least to admit God's saving action to persons who ask. One may not speak of a saving act casually, or take credit for it personally.

Note that "thank" and "praise" contrast with the speech of the wicked (v. 2; Hacham).

WORDS

fulness (JPS), Gnade (German), bonté (French), and chérissement (Chouraqui). See "Affections" for a discussion of the range of meanings of this word.

Your hand
This was not an accident (Mesudat David) or the result of personal effort.

bless . . . rejoice
This is an expression of confidence as well as a prayer (Hacham). Mesudat David puts it clearly: "and I will rejoice at their downfall." For the same feeling, see Isa. 65:13.

rise up and be ashamed
Let them rise up against me (Ibn Ezra). Their

shame will come from two sources: first, their evildoing will be exposed, and, second, they will feel pain, anger, and frustration that they did not succeed (Hacham).

servant
This is linked with "You are my lord and master" (v. 21; Hacham).

disgrace . . . shame; wear . . . wrap
The same set of words as above (vv. 18–19). Note that in biblical idiom the subject "puts on" his or her disgrace or shame. It is an act of enwrapping, of clothing oneself. The subject, thus, is seen to deserve that which she or he suffers.

SPARKS

Let them curse—but You bless
As you did with Balaam (Numbers 22–24; Zera' Ya'akov).

CON-VERSES

When He stands at the right hand of the suffering

And when He does *not* stand at the right hand of the suffering to save her or him from those who pass judgment against his or her very being? And when He is *silent?*

> [31]When he stands at the right hand of the suffering,
> to save her/him from those who pass judgment
> against her/his very being.

. . . even after I have been "good"? even after I have expressed my rage but not forgotten to place it within the framework of His power and His justice? even after I have admitted my helplessness and have cast myself upon His ultimate saving grace?

Psalm 109 enables us to re-read Psalm 44: "God, with our own ears we heard how You did mighty deeds . . . You are my king, God, command the victory of Jacob . . . But now, You desert and shame us, You sell Your people for nothing . . . All this happened to us yet we did not forget You . . . Truly, for Your sake we are killed all day long, we are considered sheep to be butchered . . . Wake up! Why do You sleep, Lord! Arise! Do not abandon forever! Why do You hide Your Face?! Why do You forget our persecution and our oppression?!" National disaster. Holocaust. Not standing at the right hand of the suffering.

". . . and it *was* so." There *was* a holocaust. Where should my/our rage turn? Who is the abused? And who is the abuser?

If I am / we are the abused, who is the abuser? The answer is self-evident: the abused is always abused by an abuser. "Those who are intimidated are always intimidated by one who intimidates; those who are humiliated are always humiliated by one who humiliates."

Who said, "I shall wipe out humankind which I have created from upon the face of the earth—humanity, the animals, the creeping things, and the birds of the sky—for I regret that I made them" (Gen. 6:7)?

Who threatened, "And if you do not listen to Me in this and you go rebelliously with Me, I shall go in the rage of rebellion with you, punishing you sevenfold for your sins . . . You shall eat the flesh of your boys and consume the bodies of your girls. . . . As He rejoiced over you to show goodness to you and to multiply you, so will He rejoice over you to destroy you and to annihilate you. . . . In the morning you will say, 'Would that it were evening' and in the evening you will say, 'Would that it were morning' because of the fear which you

WORDS

When . . .
Indeed (Hacham), When (Mesudat David), For (King James). I prefer the conditional, as the psalmist is still praying.

at the right hand
Contrasting with v. 6, where it is the prosecutor who stands at the right hand of the accused.

CON-VERSES

will feel in your heart and the sights which you will see with your eyes" (Lev. 26:27, 29; Deut. 28:63, 67)?

Who terrified Job, saying, "Who is it who darkens counsel with [mere] words, without having knowledge? Gird your loins like a man so that I can cross-examine you and you can let me know! Where were you . . . Would you contradict My justice? convict Me so that you can be acquitted? Do you have an arm like God? or a voice that can thunder like His" (Job 38:2–4; 40:8–9)?

Who casts His fear and dread over His dominion and is thereby made "holy" in His justice?

Who let a million children be cast into the fires?! Who let no woman survive Treblinka . . . ?! . . . ?! . . . ?!

And who deprives me of my rage? Who requires our accepting self-abasement? Who demands that rage be "civilized," halakhically proper, theologically acceptable? Who instantiates His authority in those who would crush me/us for my/our truth?

If I am abused, then He is the Abuser. If I am violated, then He is the Perpetrator. If I must do intimate battle, then He is the Adversary. If I must engage in life-and-death combat in the innermost world of the self, then He is the One Who Threatens. God is the Abuser, and we are the abused.

We live and re-live God's abusiveness. We tell the stories, we recall the history, and we do not even know what we are saying. Our bodies mirror His acts, our minds and hearts echo His deeds, and still we have not learned. From generation to generation, oblivion threatens; therefore, it must be told. "Truth is the seal of the Holy One, blessed be He;" it is also the truth of humanity.

And if I have become the abuser, the one who curses, it is because I really have been abused. If my anger has turned to rage, it is because His anger has been irrational. ". . . it is Yahweh himself who darkens his own counsel. . . . He turns the tables on Job and blames him for what he himself does: man is not permitted to have an opinion about him. . . . For seventy-one verses he proclaims his world-creating power to his miserable victim, who sits in ashes and scratches his sores with potsherds, and who by now has had enough of superhuman violence" (Jung, p. 16).

Who abused the Abuser such that He abuses? Did we, humanity, do that, as it says, "I raised children and exalted them but they betrayed Me . . . evil seed, destructive children; they desert the Lord, they provoke the Holy One of Israel, they turn their backs" (Isa. 1:2, 4)? Can a child terrorize a parent, or is this blaming the victim? Are we really guilty, or do we simply not want to know that abusiveness is a quality of God, a structure of Being and, hence, of being? We have turned guilt inward so as not to know that irrational unjust violence is an attribute of God and, therefore, of His creation. We do not want to recognize that "God does not want to be just; he merely flaunts might over right" (Jung, p. 16), so we hold ourselves responsible, we wrongly blame the victim(s).

Can one even say such things? It is easier to say that the Abuser is a projection of the abuser, as Father is of father. As son, I live the abuse of F/father; as father, I re-live the abuse of F/father; the Abuser is only an idolatrous conflation of text and psyche. Answers that are too easy. Rather, the incestuous ugly truth is hidden under layers of denial and piety, concealed in

CON-VERSES

story and praise. The innermost comba-
tive truth is obscured by layer upon layer
of authority and tradition. As to the
truth, "Were it not written in Scripture,
it would be impossible to say it" (Talmud, Sanhedrin 95b; Hulin 91b; Eruvin
22a; etc.).

to save him/her

Is there really salvation? Can the
broken pieces of abused relatedness really
be put back together? Is there *tikkun?*
W/who will save w/Whom? The question remains in con-vers[e]-ation.

Psalm 27

WITH
FOUR
COMMENTARIES

לְדָוִד

יְיָ אוֹרִי וְיִשְׁעִי
מִמִּי אִירָא
יְיָ מָעוֹז חַיַּי
מִמִּי אֶפְחָד:

בִּקְרֹב עָלַי מְרֵעִים
לֶאֱכֹל אֶת בְּשָׂרִי
צָרַי וְאֹיְבַי לִי
הֵמָּה כָשְׁלוּ וְנָפָלוּ:
אִם תַּחֲנֶה עָלַי מַחֲנֶה
לֹא יִירָא לִבִּי
אִם תָּקוּם עָלַי מִלְחָמָה
בְּזֹאת אֲנִי בוֹטֵחַ:

אַחַת שָׁאַלְתִּי מֵאֵת יְיָ
אוֹתָהּ אֲבַקֵּשׁ
שִׁבְתִּי בְּבֵית יְיָ
כָּל יְמֵי חַיַּי
לַחֲזוֹת בְּנֹעַם יְיָ
וּלְבַקֵּר בְּהֵיכָלוֹ:

A Psalm of Healing

*in which the psalmist reaches out to God
for comfort and closeness*

[1]By David

The Lord is my light and my deliverance
of whom am I afraid?
The Lord is the fortress of my life
whom do I fear?

[2]When evildoers draw near to me in war
to gorge on my flesh,
my tormentors and my foes become mine;
it is they who stumble and fall.
[3]If an army encamps against me,
my heart will not be afraid;
if it rises up in war against me,
in this do I trust.

[4]I have asked but one thing of the Lord,
that do I seek—
that I dwell in the house of the Lord
all the days of my life,
to have visions of the sweet bliss of the Lord
and to ponder in His sanctuary.

כִּי יִצְפְּנֵנִי בְּסֻכֹּה
בְּיוֹם רָעָה
יַסְתִּרֵנִי בְּסֵתֶר אָהֳלוֹ
בְּצוּר יְרוֹמְמֵנִי:

וְעַתָּה
יָרוּם רֹאשִׁי עַל אֹיְבַי
סְבִיבוֹתַי
וְאֶזְבְּחָה בְאָהֳלוֹ
זִבְחֵי תְרוּעָה
אָשִׁירָה וַאֲזַמְּרָה לַיְיָ:

שְׁמַע יְיָ קוֹלִי
אֶקְרָא
וְחָנֵּנִי וַעֲנֵנִי:

לְךָ אָמַר לִבִּי בַּקְּשׁוּ פָנָי
אֶת פָּנֶיךָ יְיָ אֲבַקֵּשׁ:
אַל תַּסְתֵּר פָּנֶיךָ מִמֶּנִּי
אַל תַּט בְּאַף עַבְדֶּךָ
עֶזְרָתִי הָיִיתָ
אַל תִּטְּשֵׁנִי וְאַל תַּעַזְבֵנִי
אֱלֹהֵי יִשְׁעִי:

כִּי אָבִי וְאִמִּי עֲזָבוּנִי
וַיְיָ יַאַסְפֵנִי:

⁵That he conceal me in His sukka
on the day of evil,
that He hide me in the hidden places of His tent—
that He raise me up high on a rock.

⁶And now,
let my head be raised up high above my enemies
    all around me
then, I shall offer in His sanctuary
sacrifices with trumpeting;
I shall sing and chant to the Lord.

    ⁷Hear my voice, O Lord.
    I call.
    Be gracious unto me and answer me.

    ⁸My heart echoed You saying, "Seek My Face."
    I do seek Your Face, Lord.
    ⁹Hide not Your Face from me.
    Do not push away Your servant in anger.
    You have been my help.
    Do not forsake me and do not abandon me,
    God of my deliverance.

¹⁰Alas, my father and my mother have forsaken me
but the Lord will gather me in.

הוֹרֵנִי יְיָ דַּרְכֶּךָ
וּנְחֵנִי בְּאֹרַח מִישׁוֹר
לְמַעַן שׁוֹרְרָי:

אַל תִּתְּנֵנִי
בְּנֶפֶשׁ צָרָי
כִּי קָמוּ בִי עֵדֵי שֶׁקֶר
וִיפֵחַ חָמָס:

לוּלֵא הֶאֱמַנְתִּי
לִרְאוֹת בְּטוּב יְיָ
בְּאֶרֶץ חַיִּים:

קַוֵּה אֶל יְיָ
חֲזַק
וְיַאֲמֵץ לִבֶּךָ
וְקַוֵּה אֶל יְיָ:

¹¹Show me the way to You.
Lead me on a level path
for the sake of my watchful enemies.

¹²Do not give me over to the will of my
        tormentors.
Indeed, false witnesses have risen against me
and people who breathe violence.

¹³Were it not for the fact that I have been certain
that I would see the goodness of the Lord
in the land of life, [. . .]

¹⁴Have confidence in the Lord.
Be strong,
and He will give courage to your heart;
then, have confidence in the Lord.

AFFECTIONS

The Lord is my light

Danger frightens us; stress makes us angry. All humans face moments of danger and of stress. The psalmist, here as elsewhere, is frightened and perhaps angry, yet he will not allow us to compartmentalize our anger and fear into an inner space devoid of God's presence. Rather, the psalmist teaches that we must bring fear and anger into dialogue/confrontation with God. The result of this dialogue/confrontation is a reaffirmation of the vision of relatedness between humanity and God that is the core of biblical theology, even when that relatedness seems fractured, unjustified. For this reason, this is a psalm of religious healing, an exposition of the affections of spiritual healing. It is to be read together with Psalms 44 and 109. The psalm begins by placing anger and fear within four series of images of comfort (vv. 1–8), continues with a prayer for God's

¹by David

The Lord is my light and my deliverance of whom am I afraid?
The Lord is the fortress of my life whom do I fear?

CON-VERSES

The Lord is my light

Reading against Psalm 128 allowed us to question traditional blessing and to develop another form of blessing. Converse-ing with Psalm 44 permitted us to question the traditional understanding of providence, covenant, and redemption and to walk an alternate path to truth and national empowerment. Reading against Psalm 109 surfaced the abused person with her and his attendant rage. It also led us to see ourselves as abused children of God and to contemplate God as an abusing parent. What will con-verse-ing with Psalm 27, the psalm of healing, yield?

There are two types of healing: personal and religious. The former brings us to fuller humanity in the interpersonal context; the latter, in the context of our relationship to God. Both go beyond rage.

There are also two modes of healing: the traditional and the psychothera-

WORDS

deliverance

The Hebrew *yish'i* means "a saving from concrete trouble" and not "a spiritual saving." Hence, I do not use "salvation," which in English conveys the latter.

fortress

As Ben Iehouda notes, the Hebrew *ma'oz* is from the Arabic root *'adha* (noun *ma'adh*), which means "fortress" or "refuge." It is easily confused grammatically and conceptually with

the similar Hebrew root *'azza* (noun *ma'uzz*), "strong," "strength." Both roots occur interchangeably in Psalms, e.g., 28:8; 31:3, 5; 43:2; etc. (see "Affections").

afraid . . . fear

The Malbim says that "being afraid" (Hebrew *yir'ah*) is felt in the presence of an identifiable danger, while "fear" (Hebrew, *pahad*) is felt in the face of an unknown threat (Feuer).

CON-VERSES

peutic. "Affections" will follow the traditional mode of spiritual healing through the powerful imagery and affections of the psalm. "Con-verses" will follow the psychotherapeutic mode of healing through the personal and then the religious types of healing. The question here will be whether religious healing can learn something from personal healing as developed by competent and sensitive therapists. The problem here will be to find a new way to spiritual wholeness by walking against the traditional path.

of whom am I afraid

I am afraid precisely of the f/Father who raped me, who allowed my enemies to humiliate and torture me. I fear precisely the F/father who violated the covenant between parent and child, the God Who allowed the holocaust. If God is God and I am innocent yet violated, it is He of Whom I am afraid. If F/father can, but does not, protect me, it is H/he whom I fear. "And Isaac said, 'Who will save me from the hand of my f(/F)ather?'" (see "Sparks" to v. 10).

This question—the question of Job, the question of the suffering righteous, the question of the good and loving and just God Who allows suffering—is the Achilles' heel of monotheistic faith and patriarchal psychology.

The traditional answers are known: (1) I am not innocent but sinful, in thought or intent if not in deed;

AFFECTIONS

presence (vv. 7–9, 11–12), wavers briefly (vv. 10, 13), and finishes on a note of confidence (v. 14).

deliverance . . . fortress

The first cluster of images is military. God is "a deliverance and a fortress" (here). He is also called "a rock, a fortress, a citadel, a boulder" (Ps. 31:3), "a shield and a help" (33:20), "a shelter and stronghold" (46:2), "a rock, a deliverance, and a haven" (62:3), "a sun and a shield" (84:12), "a shield and a king" (89:19). The most explicit list of appellatives is in Ps. 18:3, "O Lord, my rock, my fortress, my rescuer, my God, my shelter in Whom I seek refuge, my shield, my mighty champion, my haven." The clearest call to God to act in a military manner is in Ps. 35:1–3, "Lord! Do battle with my enemies! Make war on those who war against me! Grab shield and buckler, and rise to my defense! Ready the spear, and close in on my pursuers! Tell me, 'I am your deliverance.'" In Christian culture attuned to the teaching of turning the other cheek, such imagery may feel strange. But in biblical religion, the enemy is acknowledged as a real enemy, his or her enmity is felt as a war (vv. 2–3 and elsewhere), and God is the powerful protector Who is not above waging bloody war on behalf of His chosen, His righteous ones. "The Lord is a God of warring; His Name is Lord" (Ex. 15:3) has a strong echo in Jewish history and religion.

SPARKS

my light and my deliverance

"My light" on Mount Sinai and "my deliverance" after the sin of the golden calf. "My light" on Shabbat and "my deliverance" on the week-

days (Sefat Emet). "My light" at night [in times of trouble] and "my deliverance" by day [in times of plenty]. "My light" in matters pertaining to the soul and "my deliverance" in matters

CON-VERSES

therefore, I deserve punishment; God is good and just. (2) God's ways are just but unknowable; therefore, I must bear my suffering and know that it has ultimate meaning. (3) God is testing or purifying me, for my own benefit; He is just and good. (4) God is good and just, but He cannot force humans to be good and just to one another because that would deprive us of free will; therefore, evil is our fault, not God's. (5) God, too, has an irrational, passional dimension which, in tandem with my behavior, can act in ways that are unjust; but then it is my fault for initiating the cycle of wrong behavior into which He would not fall on His own because of His goodness and justice (Zohar).

These answers are a reassertion of the traditional hierarchy of reality. They are a reinstantiation of the Father. They cover our fear by affirming order. The traditional answers teach that the God Who violated me, or Who allowed me to be violated, is my light, my deliver-

ance, my fortress, and my hope. They teach that, because of His Presence, I am not afraid. Thinking and saying these things are a reaffirmation of sovereign, cosmic, transpersonal order.

To affirm the traditional answers to injustice, however, is also to reverse reality. To say that He Who did not protect me earlier will protect me now is to invert common sense. To say that those who have done evil to me will be vanquished by the God Who did not shield me previously is to overturn experience; it is to trust the untrustworthy. To say that the abuser has turned guardian is wrong, and dangerous. Traditional healing is an assertion which is a denial, a sublimation which is a repression, a contra-vers(e)ing of the plain vers(e)ion of experience.

This is not the way. Rather, one must say the truth as it is: I/we am innocent. F/father has failed me. I feel anger toward H/him, and it is justified.

SPARKS

pertaining to the body (Ibn Ezra).

"My light" on Rosh ha-Shana [when God opens the book of judgment and shows us the way of repentance] and "my deliverance" on Yom Kippur [when God seals our judgment] (Vayyikra Rabba 21). On the basis of this midrash, it is customary to begin reciting this psalm a month before Rosh ha-Shana, when the penitential season begins, and to continue reciting it until the seventh day of Sukkot (Hosha'na Rabba) when the judgment is completed. "And I have heard that [another] reason one recites this psalm during the penitential season is that it contains the Tetragrammaton

thirteen times, corresponding to the thirteen attributes of God which radiate light during this period" (cited in Imrot Tehorot). The recitation of this psalm twice daily is a source of great comfort as one confronts the breadth and depth of one's sinfulness.

"My light and my deliverance: When a person has contemplated the light above and when the Holy One, blessed be He, has illumined that person, such a one has no fear of the upper beings or of the lower beings, as it says: 'Arise and be light, for your light has come and the glory of God has shone upon you' (Isa. 60:1)" (Zohar).

CON-VERSES   AFFECTIONS

in this do I trust   **be afraid . . . trust**

Invoking trust is not enough; re-creating it through incantation will not work. Hope is not enough; dreaming success does not create it. Rather:

²When evildoers draw near to me in war to gorge on my flesh, my tormentors and my foes become mine; it is they who stumble and fall.

Anxiety is the opposite of trust. We experience anxiety—a feeling that ranges from gnawing fear to hysteria—when we have done, or are about to do, some-thing we know is

"Therapists who work with adults abused as children have one overrid-ing goal. That is to repair the

³If an army encamps against me, my heart will not be afraid; if it rises up in war against me, in this do I trust.

wrong. Anxiety, thus, is different from excitement, or fear of the un-known, or a ra-

client's self-image. . . . [T]he therapist enables the client to experience a healthy human interaction. . . . . [T]he therapist must teach the client to recognize and express their [sic] own feelings, to communicate, to take con-trolled risks, to solve problems, to iden-tify and negotiate personal needs . . . to combat the client's sense of entrapment, despair, helplessness, isolation, and self-blame. . . . The trauma of adult sur-vivors is resolved when they cease to feel victimized and instead feel self-fulfilled and whole" (Gil, pp. 59–61).

Therapy for an adult who was an abused child has six main steps: (1) de-veloping trust by empowering the client

tional fear of risk or harm. Anxiety is a moral fear, a more or less intense trepidation connected to our sense of self, and of right and wrong.

The rabbis recognized this connec-tion between anxiety and morality, between fear and sin. "The Talmud (Berakhot 60a) tells of the student who walked in the street shaking with fear. His teacher called out to him, 'You are surely a sinner, for it is written, "The sinners were frightened in Zion, tremb-ling seized the insincere" (Is. 33:14).' Similarly we read, 'And Jacob was very fearful and sorely distressed' (Gen. 32:7). How does fear differ from dis-tress? Fear gripped Jacob as he prepared

WORDS

draw near . . . encamps . . . rise up in war
For the root *qarav* in the sense of "to make war," cf. Deut. 20:2, 10; Pss. 78:9; 144:1; Zech. 14:3; etc. Note the three stages of war men-tioned here (Hacham).

become mine
Alternately, "it is they, my tormentors and my foes, who stumble and fall." My translation

yields greater contrast between *li*, "become mine" and *hema*, "it is they."

in this
According to some, the referent is the con-fession of faith in v. 1; according to others, the referent is in the following verses. I tend toward the latter. An alternate might be: "in spite of everything, I trust" (Hacham).

AFFECTIONS

to encounter his hostile brother, Esau. Jacob felt that this excessive fear was proof of his own guilt and therefore he became 'sorely distressed'" (Feuer).

Here and elsewhere the psalmist expresses a lack of fear. The rabbis understood this to be a lack of anxiety, that is, a lack of a sense of sin or guilt. And this is true, for when we have not done (or are not about to do) something wrong, we have a clean conscience. In that situation, we may be afraid of a real threat but we do not feel guilt or anxiety. Rather, we feel trust, which is a being free of guilt and anxiety. Hence, the confidence and trust of the psalmist.

CON-VERSES

to make decisions and exercise choices, and by empathy and understanding; (2) helping the client to confront her or his helplessness, to acknowledge its reality; (3) helping the client to feel the rage, to express it, and then to break the terrible silence by talking about the trauma, by speaking the truth; (4) guiding the client to mourn the past, to care for himself or herself while allowing the past to remain in its irreducibility and facticity as past; (5) helping the client to develop an ability to manage the resurgence of memory and the recurrence of destructive behavior; and (6) empowering the client further to ex-

SPARKS

if it rises up in war

"By war itself, one knows that one possesses that in which one can have trust: The Torah has exempted one who is afraid because of one's sins from engaging in war (Deut. 20:8). Therefore, as long as one is at war, one must [logically] still have strength with which to fight" (Sefat Emet). The author means to say that, since one who is afraid because of one's sins is exempt from war, the very fact that one is at war implies that one must also have good deeds and faith, which are the strength needed to wage physical and spiritual war.

in this do I trust

In zoharic usage, *zo't* ("this") refers to the lowest of the sefirot, Malkhut/Shekhina, which is the aspect of God that is closest to us and, hence, the portal or conduit by which we address our prayers to the more inner aspects of God (e.g., Tif'eret, the King). The Zohar, then, teaches that the psalmist here has no fear because he trusts in Malkhut/Shekhina. The author of the Tikkunei Zohar (6:24–26) artfully strings together various passages using *zo't*

("this"), giving each this new spiritual meaning as follows:

"Whoever wishes to have knowledge of the King does not have permission to do so except through the Shekhina, as it is written, 'Let not the wise person boast in his or her knowledge, nor the brave person boast in his or her courage, nor the rich person boast in his or her wealth. Rather in "this" shall a person boast: in understanding and having knowledge of Me . . .'" (Jer. 9:22–23).

"When Aaron [the high priest] went into holy of holies on Yom Kippur, he went in with the Shekhina, as it is written, 'With "this" shall Aaron come into the sanctuary'" (Lev. 17:3).

"Moses taught that the world is sustained by Malkhut, as it is written, 'And "this" is the blessing'" (Deut. 33:1).

"Jacob, because he knew that the entire desire of the King is for her, commanded his children not to approach the King except through Malkhut, that all their requests, prayers, and petitions to the King should be through her, as it is written, 'And "this" is what their father said to them'" (Gen. 49:28). →

CON-VERSES

ercise current options in a constructive
way and to develop collateral supportive relationships that will sustain her or
him. Through this
process, the sur-
vivor of child
abuse comes to a
sense of positive
self-esteem, to a
realistic evalua-
tion of her or his
successes, to inter-
relatedness with
others, and to a
sense of control
over his or her life
(Gil, pp. 63–134).

**4I have asked but one thing of the Lord,
that do I seek—
that I dwell in the house of the Lord
all the days of my life,
to have visions of the sweet bliss of the
    Lord
and to ponder in His sanctuary.**

This is trust—trust in the other and
trust in the self. It cannot be achieved
through asserting the denial, or subli-
mating the repressed, or contra-verting
the plain version of experience. This is
the alternate way, the other healing.

I have asked but one thing

For the Jew living in the shadow of
the holocaust, the issue is confronta-

AFFECTIONS

to have visions . . . to ponder . . .

The Hebrew word *no'am* (adj. *na'im;*
noun *ne'ima* and
Na'omi) means
"something good,
pleasant, sweet,
pleasing," and it is
used of music, of
wise words, or of
a lover or friend.
No'am/na'im is
the quality of hav-
ing, and radiating,
sweetness that
borders on bliss. It
is used here and in Ps. 90:17 of God and
refers to the human experience of the
presence of God as sweet bliss, as well
as to the presence of that quality in
God. (Hacham's rendering of "beauty,
grandeur, radiance" is, thus, incorrect,
though such an experience is well
attested elsewhere in the psalms.)

The medievals, recognizing the religious experiential nature of the word,
understood "the *no'am* of God" to refer

WORDS

asked . . . seek
    The Malbim points out that "to ask" is to
express verbally while "to seek" is to yearn in
one's heart. The psalmist's request, then, has
been both his inner and his expressed desire.

The parallel is to Esth. 5:7: "My verbal request,
which is indeed my heart's true desire . . ."
(Feuer).
    Alternately, "the request is that that which I
have asked be always that which I seek" (Feuer).

SPARKS

"And David, because he knew that all the
King's desire, power, and strength come from
her, said, 'If an army encamps against me . . . in
"this" do I trust' (Ps. 27:4). . . . And he added
concerning one who is not attentive to this, 'and
a fool does not understand "this"'" (Ps. 92:7).

I have asked but one thing
    "It is the nature of people that that for which
they pray changes. Sometimes one prays for
food; sometimes for wealth; and sometimes for
health. All these prayers are for material things.
It is not so, however, when one prays for

AFFECTIONS

to mystical experience, parallel to the Arabic *ni'ma* and the Hebrew *devequt,* "clinging to God" (Deut. 4:4; 10:20; 11:22; 30:20). For some, this was an ecstatic experience; for others, an intellectual experience (see, e.g., Maimonides, "Hilkhot Teshuva" 8:4, cited in Feuer and Maimonides, *Guide of the Perplexed,* III:51); and for yet others, a theurgical experience. To capture this special mystical meaning, one should retain the translation "sweet bliss," but one might replace "ponder" with "meditate" or "abide in."

The second cluster of images of strength and comfort, then, is cultic: the house of God and His sanctuary. There one can bring one's anxiety, anger, and fear. There one can be healed by having visions of the sweet bliss of God. The intense re-experiencing of the presence of God does not do away with danger or injustice; rather, it gives strength and comfort, it puts into perspective, it re-establishes contact, connectedness. As long as we are connected to God, as long as we are in His pres-

CON-VERSES

tion, trauma resolution. We cannot be loving children of the abusing God, nor can we worship Him, without confronting Him, without some resolution to His treatment of us in our common history. As Jews, as theologians, as co-victims, we must speak, we must seek a new relatedness — bearing in mind the inadequacy of earlier answers while acknowledging the desire and the obligation to be what we are: children of our Father.

to have visions . . . to ponder . . .

Justice is not an adequate concept for three reasons: (1) Justice implies that the wrong committed can be righted, that evil can be compensated. But true evil cannot be redressed; it is indelible, enduring. (2) Justice emphasizes accountability and, in so doing, does not pay sufficient attention to mourning and living with the pain of evil. (3) Justice is restitutive, but it is concerned with restoring God's honor, not that of the victims. What concept, then, speaks for the victims? (Keshgegian).

WORDS

dwell . . . have visions . . . ponder
    "To dwell" does not mean "to live in"; rather, it means "to have regular access to." It may also

mean "to come for a sojourn or retreat" as in 2 Sam. 7:18, "And King David came and dwelled in the presence of God." →

SPARKS

spiritual things, as King David, peace be upon him, said, 'I have asked but one thing of the Lord.' When I was a shepherd and, now that I am a king, 'that do I seek.' And what is it that he seeks? 'that I dwell in the house of the Lord all the days of my life' in this world and, afterwards, that I 'have visions of the sweet bliss of the Lord and abide in His sanctuary'" (cited in Imrot Tehorot).

"All the requests of a person are one — to arouse the spiritual quality of Shabbat always, as it will be in the world-to-come which is 'a day which is all Shabbat.' Nonetheless, [even in life-after-death,] there will be a difference between Shabbat and workdays. 'To have visions of the sweet bliss of the Lord' is Shabbat; 'to abide in His sanctuary' is workday; [meaning,] that there will be a need for work [even in the

CON-VERSES

house . . . bliss . . . sukka . . . tent

The traditional answers are a reinsertion into hierarchy. They are a retreat into the male womb: into the house of the Lord, into His sukka. They are a re-pen(e/is)-tration into the hidden folds and lips of His tent. The reversed image is the shadow that sheds light on the reversed reality.

This is not the way. Rather, one must acknowledge the real hurt, the pain of immediate history. And one must acknowledge the history of the pain, the archaeology of the hurt: I/we am hurt, hurting. I/we have been hurt before, years/centuries of pain. The hidden truth is the Truth. Ultimately, this Truth must be confronted; it must be admitted.

> 5That he conceal me in His sukka
> on the day of evil,
> that He hide me in the hidden places of
>   His tent—
> that He raise me up high on a rock.

AFFECTIONS

ence / see His Face, we can cope with the troubles of existence. God's Face is the "safe place" of religious healing. As one of the rebbes of the holocaust said, "Were it not for the fire of the Divine, I could not have withstood the fires of men."

sukka, tent . . . rock

The third cluster of images for God's strength and comfort is composed of womb images: sukka (a protective booth), hidden places, tent. With this, the psalmist reaches into the deepest levels of the human psyche, where the troubled person is embraced, en-wrapped, enfolded into secure space. From it, however, he re-turns, quickly, to the battle imagery of the rock and imminent victory, and he makes a vow.

WORDS

The Hebrew *ḥaza* always means "to have visions," though it is related to the Aramaic root "to see."

The Hebrew *levaqqer* has disputed meanings. Some take it from the root for "morning" and render, "to come every morning, to frequent." This parallels "to dwell." Others take it from "to investigate" (Lev. 13:36; 19:20; 27:33) and render, "to study, to inquire." As Feuer points out, the later rabbinic usage *levaqqer ḥolim*, "to

visit the sick," does not mean simply "to visit" but "to see to the needs of the sick." From it, the modern usage of "to visit socially" is derived.

The psalmist, thus, maintains that his truest desire has always been to have regular access to the sanctuary so that he may have visions there and be able to study (with the priests) there. For the religious experiences intended, see "Affections."

SPARKS

world-to-come], like the work before the fall of Adam, as it says, 'And the Lord, God, took Adam and put him in the garden of Eden to work it and to preserve it' (Gen. 2:15)" (Sefat

Emet). This is a very profound comment because the author teaches that even bliss has levels, that even the garden of eden and the world-to-come are based on work.

CON-VERSES

And then the Truth must be mourn-
ed. "Mourning is the opposite of feeling guilt; it is an expressio of pain that

things happened as they did and that
there is no way to change the past. . . .
[I must] acknowledge and hate my per-

WORDS

sukka . . . hidden places . . . tent . . . rock

The *sukka* was a lean-to used in the fields
for shelter from the burning sun. Such structures are still visible in the Middle East. It
became, too, the booth, the temporary dwelling in which Jews live during the holiday of
Sukkot. By extension, sukka came to designate
the sanctuary (e.g., Ps. 76:3; Lam. 2:6; etc.) and
finally to represent the messianic kingdom
("May the All-merciful rebuild for us the sukka
of David which has fallen" [Grace After Meals]).
I retain the original Hebrew so as to catch all
the overtones. For the irregular grammatical

form, see Hacham.

Seter is "a hidden place" and can be used of
God's tent (here), Face (Ps. 31:21), and wings
(Ps. 61:5), or without an additional noun (Ps.
32:7; 91:1; etc.). Tent and rock, too, can designate God's sanctuary (Ps. 15:1; Isa. 30:29). The
sudden shift of imagery is characteristic of
Psalms.

on the day of evil

This can be read with the previous, or the
following, phrase.

CON-VERSES

secutor for what he or she has done, only then will the way to forgiveness be open to me" (Miller, *For Your Own Good*, pp. 250, 248).

We must re-experience our helplessness before God, mourn that it was and is so, and grieve that it cannot be changed. We must re-open the wounds of the spirit, mourn the loss of our ideal Father, and grieve over our lack of love. We must confront the Truth directly, mourn the loss of an unreal God, and grieve over our loneliness and His. Tears and lamentations save from denial, from D/death.

**6And now,
let my head be raised up high above my
    enemies all around me
then, I shall offer in His sanctuary
sacrifices with trumpeting;
I shall sing and chant to the Lord.**

that He hide me

"A person who can understand and integrate [her or] his anger as part of himself [or herself] will not become violent. [Such a person] has the need to strike out at others only if [she or] he is thoroughly unable to understand his [or her] rage . . . was never able to experience it as part of himself [or herself] because such a thing was totally unthinkable in [her or] his surroundings" (Miller, *For Your Own Good*, pp. 42, 65).

At the root of our being, each of us has a deep need to be recognized as self, and this need is very rarely filled, even in our earliest years. It is this inner void and the pain that it causes us, personally and as a people, that we must face and then mourn: ". . . loneliness in the parental home is later followed by isolation within the self . . . enjoys success and recognition, but these things cannot . . . fill the old gap. . . . [O]nly the mourning for what he [or she] has missed, missed at the crucial time, can lead to real healing . . . no longer be forced to earn love. . . . When finally the narcissistic wound itself can be felt, there is no more necessity for all the distortions" (Miller, *Drama*, pp. 14, 43, 57, 89).

be raised up high above my enemies . . . sing and chant

Denial. Omnipotence fantasies.
Omnipotence is a veil for omni-impotence; omniscience a screen for omniignorance; omniloving is a shield for omniloved; and omnipresence a cover for omniabsence. →

WORDS

let my head . . . then,

This verse is a both a declaration of trust in the outcome and an oath or a cultic promise (Hacham, Mesudat David). Note the repetition of "raise up high," the play on *'ohel* as "tent" in the preceding verse and as "sanctuary" here, and the rendering of the *vav* of *ve-'ezbeha* as

"then," which preserves the declarative as well as the cultic nature of the verse.

sacrifices with trumpeting

Or: "sacrifices with shouting." Hacham points out that shouting, singing, and chanting designate sounds that accompanied the sacrifices.

AFFECTIONS   CON-VERSES

Hear my voice

The tone changes here, but it is not that "David seems to have lost the tremendous confidence of the preceding lines" (Feuer) nor that "God seems to be on the point of hiding His face" (Kirkpatrick). Rather, when one is in real trouble, one's emotions swing, sometimes rather wildly. One feels confidence and panic, hope and hurt. One calls to mind the good times, evokes the covenant, pleads, boasts, makes vows, ponders one's enemies, confronts one's own helplessness, fantasizes about victory over the enemies, worries about one's moral

> 7Hear my voice, O Lord.
> I call.
> Be gracious unto me and answer me.

This is not the way. Rather, the way is between the omnis. Between omnipotence and omniimpotence is partial, limited power; between omniscience and omniignorance is partial, limited knowledge; between omniloving and omniloved is partial love; between omnipresence and omniabsence is P/presence that is not fully present and A/absence that is not totally absent.

Polarity is not the way; no one can have it all, not even God. To think that, to want it, is denial. Rather, ambiguity is the reality of human and divine existence. Ambiguity is fullness. Partialness is the *imago Dei,* the essential attribute of God and humanity.

WORDS

I call

The syntax is ambiguous.

be gracious unto me

The Hebrew root *ḥnn* has connotations that depend more on the reader than on the texts. Some render "have pity"; others, "have mercy"; and still others, "favor me." I understand the basic meaning to be "to act in grace," that is, to act in a way that shows love and concern above and beyond that which is commensurate with the relationship invoked. Thus: "For God has been gracious unto me and I have everything" (Gen. 33:11); "I shall be gracious unto

those unto whom I am gracious and I shall be merciful unto those to whom I am merciful" (Ex. 33:19); "Lord, Lord, God, merciful and gracious" (Ex. 34:6); "If I have found favor in your eyes [i.e., if you feel graciousness toward me]" (recurrent phrase); "May the Lord cause His Face to shine upon you and be gracious unto you" (Num. 6:25); etc. This is not the same as "have pity" or "have mercy," both of which imply a much more dependent relationship. This latter experience also exists but is, I think, better embodied in the root *rḥm,* which means both "to have pity/mercy" and "to be compassionate."

AFFECTIONS

integrity, and contemplates the future and the ultimacy of the stakes. The psalmist shifts voice rapidly, as we have seen, and here he turns to pray to God.

I call . . . answer me

Having moved back and forth, rapidly, between the images of the military and victory and the images of the cult and embracing womb-space, the psalmist's vulnerability is suddenly plain. In the space between v. 6 and v. 7, the psalmist painfully realizes the truth. In the silence of the shift of voice, the psalmist sees into the depths.

The psalmist realizes that he really cannot help himself; that all his anger against his enemies—even though it is fully justified—has the effect of creating dis-continuity between him and God; that all his righteous indignation has actually de-solidarized him with God's Torah and God's people; that all his expressions of confidence, all his metaphors of victory and comfort, are hollow. Suddenly, the psalmist is alone and helpless. His anger has expressed his inner anguish, his confidence has expressed his faith, but somehow this has not helped him to reintegrate himself into God's Presence; this has not helped him to reach beyond himself to the tasks of a life with God.

And yet the psalmist clearly wants to be a servant of God, a child of the Father. He does not reject God or deny the mutual relatedness between him and God. "My soul has clung to following You, while Your right hand has supported me" (Ps. 63:9); "I am always with You, while You have held my hand" (Ps. 73:23).

Pondering this truth, the psalmist cries out in prayer for help from beyond himself, and then he turns to face God.

AFFECTIONS

"Seek My Face"

A suckling infant stares at its mother's face; a senile person follows a face as it moves through the field of vision. Face is the first thing we see; it is also the last act of full recognition that we experience. Face is the basic template of personhood. Face is presence, and presence is face.

The Face of God is God's Presence; God's Presence is present in God's Face—which is why Face is capitalized.

We seek the Face of God; we look for it; we search for it; we long for it: "As a deer yearns for a stream of water, so my inner being yearns for You, God. My innermost self thirsts for the living God; when shall I come and see / be seen by Your Face" (Ps. 42:2–3).

We study God's Face; we look at it; we ponder it; we question it: "Study the Lord and His mightiness; seek His Face in all times and places" (Ps. 105:4).

CON-VERSES

Seek . . . Hide

8My heart echoed You saying,
"Seek My Face."
I do seek Your Face, Lord.

". . . a new model for early experiences of emotional intensity and exchange which emphasizes reciprocity as opposed to gratification or separation. Already at three to four months, the infant has the capacity to interact in sophisticated facial play whose main motive is social interest. At this age the baby can already initiate play. She can elicit parental response by laughing and smiling; she can transform a diaper change into a play session. In this play, the reciprocity that two subjects can create, or subvert, is crucial. . . . The child enjoys a dose of otherness . . . [which leads] to a recognition that is based on mutuality. . . . The mother addresses the baby . . . the infant responds . . . in which the partners are so attuned that they move together in unison. This early experience of unison is probably the first emotional basis for later feelings of oneness. . . . Play

WORDS

my heart echoed You

There are two grammatical problems in this verse: the pronoun *lekha* and the plural of the command verb. Ignoring the second problem, one could render: "About you, my heart said" (Saadia); "Unto you, my heart said" (Kirkpatrick; Chouraqui). However, if the plural be recognized, the command is to the people, not the psalmist. In that case, the meaning is: "On your behalf, my heart says [to the people], 'Seek My Face'" (Feuer; Rashi; French; Ibn Ezra). But then how can the psalmist's heart "say" anything to the people? The solution is that the psalmist's heart remembers and echoes the general com-

mand of God to the people to seek His Presence/Face (Deut. 4:29; Jer. 29:13; Ps. 105:3, 4; and elsewhere). Hence, my rendering: "My heart echoed You saying, 'Seek My Face.'" Having recalled from the depths of his being the general command to seek God in times of trouble, the psalmist confesses that he does indeed seek God's Face.

A more farfetched solution is that, for God's sake, King David's heart commands the people to seek his (David's) face as a symbol and mimesis of seeking God's Face: "For You, my heart said [to the people], 'Seek my face'" (Meiri, cited in Feuer; Etz Hada'at Tov in Sefat Emet).

CON-VERSES

interaction can be as primary a source of the feeling of oneness as nursing or being held. . . .

"In the interaction situation, when stimulation becomes too intense, the infant regulates her own arousal by turning her head away. . . . The mother who jiggles, pokes, looms, and shouts 'look at me' to her unresponsive baby creates a negative cycle of recognition out of her own despair at not being recognized . . . how the search for recognition can become a power struggle: how assertion becomes aggression. . . .

"But at seven to nine months . . . [w]hen mother and child play 'peekaboo' . . . a sense that inner experience can be joined, that two minds can cooperate in one intention. This conception of emerging intersubjectivity emphasizes how the awareness of the separate other enhances the felt connection with him: this other mind can share my feeling. . . . The baby who looks back as he crawls off toward the toys in the corner is not merely refueling or checking to see that mother is still there, but is wondering whether mother is sharing the feeling of his adventure—the fear, the excitement, or that ambiguous 'scarey-wonderful' feeling" (Benjamin, pp. 26–31).

"A person comes to feel that 'I am the doer who does, I am the author of my acts,' by being with another person who recognizes her acts, her feelings, her intentions, her existence, her independence. Recognition is the essential response" (Benjamin, p. 21).

Recognition is the way. Real-izing mutual P/presence is the way. Reclaiming the pre-oedipal, reappropriating the inter-narcissistic, reawakening connectivity, rap-proche-ment—this is the way. Healing is in the interstices of being; being is in the intersubjectivity of interpersonal relatedness.

AFFECTIONS

What kind of Face does God have? What does it communicate? What do we read when we read God's Face, His Facial expression?

We rejoice to see God's Face; it is a light for us and we are jubilant: "May the Lord cause His Face to shine upon you, and be gracious unto you" (Num. 6:25); it shines upon us and we are saved: "God, bring us back; cause Your Face to shine upon us and we will be saved" (Ps. 80:4, 8).

We also fear God's Face; we flee Him: "Where can I go away from Your spirit and where can I flee from Your Face" (Ps. 139:7). We hide our face from God: "Moses hid his face because he was afraid to look upon God" (Ex. 3:6). Jonah.

God hides His Face from us and we are left existentially alone, isolated, without Presence. This undermines our presence, our orientedness; it constricts our face: "You hid Your Face; I was terrified" (Ps. 30:8; 104:29). And we yearn even more deeply to see God's Face again, to be seen by God's Face again, to return to His Presence: "I have sought out Your Face with all (my) heart; be gracious unto me according to Your Word" (Ps. 119:58); "when shall I come and see / be seen by Your Face" (Ps. 42:3).

A face, God's Face, has many facets: anger, joy, shame, pain, light, severity, humor, doubt, kindness, waiting, expectation. There are as many facets to F/face as there are modes of relatedness.

F/face has ten special expressions: inexpressibility, wisdom, understanding, grace, power, judgment, timelessness, beauty, fundamentality, and majesty (Zohar).

F/face is the meeting point of the inner self and the outer world. F/face is the welling forth of inexpressibility and inner depths into the stream of manifest

AFFECTIONS

consciousness. It is the majestic portal of expression of, and access to, grace, power, judgment, and beyond. F/face is the veil that renders the invisible visible. It is the gateway to the S/soul, the allusion to P/presence (Zohar).

F/face is the fourth image cluster of this psalm.

> 9Hide not Your Face from me.
> Do not push away Your servant in anger.
> You have been my help.
> Do not forsake me and do not
>   abandon me,
> God of my deliverance.

I will look to Him, but I shall argue my ways to His Face" (Job 13:3, 15). The Rebbe of Kotzsk, millennia later, put it perhaps more strongly: "Send us our Messiah, for we have no more strength to suffer. Show me a sign, O God. Otherwise I rebel against You. If You do not keep Your covenant, then neither will I keep the promise, and it is all over: we are through with being Your Chosen People, Your unique treasure" (Laytner, p. 189). But a theology of protest is not enough, religiously; again, Job: "Oh you, who spit your soul out in anger, shall the earth be abandoned for you? shall the rock be uprooted from its place?" (Job 18:4). Even placing one's anger within the Source of justice is not enough. One must seek spiritual reintegration with God, renewed relatedness and presence. The psalmist now addresses the spiritual steps and religious affections that are necessary to reconstitute and heal a relationship to God that has been shaken.

Hide not Your Face . . . in anger

Psalms 44 and 109 have already established for us the long tradition of the "theology of protest." The religious person is bound, obligated — for him or herself as well as for the good of the relationship with God — to state injustice, fully, forcefully, and clearly. The religious person, confronted with God's unjust action is not only justified but required to speak up to God, to express moral outrage and righteous anger; that is the meaning of covenant. Job, speaking in the book that bears his name, puts it well: "Rather, I will speak to the Power-ful God; I need to argue with God. . . . Indeed, He would slay me;

WORDS

Hide not . . . do not push away

The Malbim points out that this is two requests: first, that God not hide His Face so that one not feel abandoned and, second, that God not treat one so harshly that one be tempted to lose one's faith (Feuer; see also Ps. 125:3).

"Hide not" occurs elsewhere: Pss. 69:18; 102:3; 119:19; 143:7; and as a rhetorical question in Pss. 13:2; 44:25; 88:15; 104:29; Job 13:24. The obverse, God's threat to hide His Face, occurs most prominently in Deut. 31:17–18; 32:20; Ezek. 39:23–24; and His promise not to hide His Face anymore in Ezek. 39:29.

CON-VERSES

Alas . . . have forsaken me

Whether the helplessness comes from real external enemies (as vv. 2–6
suggest), or from
the death of one
or both of one's
parents and the
recognition of the
narcissistic void at
the core of all personal development (as
this verse, together with Miller, suggests), personal healing lies in intersubjectivity.

Personal healing is in intersubjectivity
with real father-and-mother: not with
the mother-and-father who didn't do
this or that, nor with the father-and-
mother who should have done this or
that; rather, with the real mother-and-
father who did do as they did and didn't
do as they didn't, for human reasons.

Personal healing is also in intersubjectivity with real others: with spouse,
with children, with friends, with asso-
ciates: not with our projections of them
but with them as they are and as they are
not, which includes our reasonable expectations of them in relation to us.

Personal healing is also in intersubjectivity with the self: ". . . one becomes
more and different by taking in more of
what is different. . . . Interconnection
and individuality seem to coexist with-

> [10] Alas, my father and my mother
> have forsaken me
> but the Lord will gather me in.

AFFECTIONS

You have been my help, do not . . .

Reading Psalm 27 with the other
psalms explored
here, one can say
that the process of
religious healing
includes: (1) the
strongest possible
statement of one's
fear, of one's
anger, and of one's sense of betrayal;
(2) a recalling of moments of connectedness, of the abidingness of covenant,
and of the history of P/presence and
help; (3) a reassertion of God's saving
power; (4) a reaffirmation of the way of
connectedness as the way of deliverance
and a stubborn insistence on re-turning
to that way; and (5) an actual call for
help.

Religious healing, then, after stating
one's pain, consists in acknowledging
that one is lost, looking at the compass,
and setting out again on the correct
heading. Religious healing is the re-
sumption of the pursuit of spiritual
relatedness. Religious healing is the
serious seeking which follows serious
hiding.

Alas . . . gather me in

This is an exclamation of despair;
hence, "alas" and not "indeed / when

WORDS

forsake . . . abandon
Hebrew *natash . . . 'azav.* Mesudat Zion
understands these as synonymns. Alsheikh
understands the former as a partial estrangement and the latter as complete abandonment

(Feuer). Note that the latter is used in Ps. 22:2
and is cited in the Gospels. Note, too, that this
is the obverse of v. 1, the other voice of the
psalmist, while still echoing its address to God
as "my deliverance."

AFFECTIONS

/ since / although." The despair at realizing that one's parents, despite their good intentions, have not reached into one and sustained one's very inner being, is one of the most heartbreaking moments in a person's life. Sometimes this realization comes after a parent dies; sometimes it comes while parents are still living. It is the realization of forsakenness, not the moment of physical death, that constitutes the experience of abandonment.

Religious healing comes with the realization that acceptance, gathered-inness, comes from God. God sees into the heart (1 Sam. 16:7), into the inward recesses of one's consciousness, into all our confusion, and into the sin and guilt that that confusion of heart brings. God sees our helplessness. He may not like what He sees, but He accepts. God gathers us in; He affirms our goodness, our strengths. And when even these fail or elude us, God affirms our intentions, our desire to be good. God meditates on the light of the candle that burns and flickers within us (Prov. 20:27). When we know this, we are gathered-in, embraced, personally P/presence-d.

CON-VERSES

out contradiction, indeed to enhance each other. The more diversity I take in, the more I feelingly connect — and the roomier is my individual character . . . composite selfhood . . . many-selved integrity . . . polymorphic integrity" (Keller, pp. 136, 186, 163, 226). Not unity of the self with the S/self; nor pulling oneself together and returning to the dominating conquest of reality. But openness — to the otherness within the self and of others, to the void within and without, and to the presence of the self to the self and to the other; "healthy narcissism" (Miller, *Drama,* pp. 32–34).

None of these precedes the other; rather, one focuses *seriatim*, as a boat heading into the wind tacks to one direction and then to the other. What, then, is religious healing? How does one relate interconnectivity to religious healing?

but the Lord . . .

Religious healing must also be in intersubjectivity — with the transcendent Father Who is also Mother (Isa. 66:13): not with the omnipotent Father who is

WORDS

Alas . . . gather me in

Many meanings are possible here: that the psalmist's parents have died, or will die; that they have abandoned him; or that they cannot help him further (see "Affections" and "Sparks").

Hacham points out that, in rabbinic Hebrew, a child who has been abandoned and taken in is called an *'asufi,* "one who has been gathered in," perhaps on the basis of this text or the text dealing with a lost animal (Deut. 22:2). Note, too, the reverse echo of "and he was gathered in to his people" (recurrent phrase) as an indication of someone's death.

SPARKS

my father and my mother have forsaken me

"'Have forsaken me' — In the act of intercourse, they were concerned only with their own pleasure. When they finished their pleasure, he turned his face away and she turned her face away. 'But the Lord gathers me in' — The

CON-VERSES

a projection of our psychological and real helplessness and an artifact of our patriarchal culture, which demands a heroic male self image; nor with the omniloving Mother who is a projection of our narcissistic need and an artifact of our patriarchal culture, which demands a threatening yet loving female figure. Rather, spiritual healing is to be found in intersubjectivity with the Father/Mother Who anguishes yet

> [11]Show me the way to You.
> Lead me on a level path
> for the sake of my watchful enemies.

cares, Who is concerned yet not controlling, Who feels pain and joy in interaction with us—just as real parents feel concern, joy, and pain in working out the destiny of their children together with them.

Show me the way to You

How does one achieve openness on a personal level? How does one reclaim recognition, connectivity, and intersub-

WORDS

the way to You . . . watchful enemies

Alternately, "Your way"; my rendering catches the mood of the psalm better. Also, a "level path" is better than a rocky or mountainous one; alternately, "the path of integrity" (Feuer).

Note that the language of Ps. 25:4–5 is parallel to some of the phrasing here: "Make

known to me Your ways, Lord; teach me Your paths. Direct me in Your truth, and teach me that You are the God of my deliverance; I have had confidence in You all day long."

The Hebrew *shorerai* ("watchful enemies") occurs only in Psalms and only in the plural (5:9; 54:7; 56:3; 59:11; 92:12, variant). It is

SPARKS

Holy One, blessed be He, watched over the drop and formed the fetus" (Rashi, ad loc).

"Isaac said to Abraham, 'Here is the fire and the wood? But where is the sheep for the offering?' (Gen. 22:7). Abraham replied, 'You are the offering, my son.' At that moment, Abraham's face was changed and he said, 'I am old and he is young; perhaps he will run away and then what will become of me?' Isaac said, 'Father, do not fear. May it be the will of the Omnipresent that one quarter of a *log* of my blood be accepted willingly [as a sacrifice]. However, bind me well that I not tremble. And, when you go to my mother, Sarah, do not tell her [what has happened] suddenly lest she injure herself —lest she be on the roof and die

in a fall, or be by the well and throw herself into it, or have a knife in her hand and kill herself with it.'

"In that moment, Isaac agreed to [being sacrificed] verbally but in his heart he said, 'Who will save me from the hand of my father? I have no help other than the Holy One, blessed be He, as it says, "My help is from the Lord, the Maker of heaven and earth" (Ps. 121:2).'

"[Seeing this] the angels of service said, 'Come and see two righteous men: the father slaughters and the son is prepared to be slaughtered, and neither inhibits the other'" (manuscript of *'Avot de-Rabbi Nathan*, cited in M. Kasher, *Torah Shelemah*, "Vayera," ad loc. [vol. 3b, page 882]).

CON-VERSES

jectivity for one's personal existence? It is not as simple as willing it to be.

First, personal healing requires the "never-ending work of mourning [which] can help us not to lapse into this illusion. A mother such as we once urgently needed—empathic and open, understanding and understandable, available and usable, transparent, clear, without unintelligible contradictions—such a mother was never ours, indeed she could not exist" (Miller, *Drama,* 28). Mourning is admitting the recurrent patterns of humiliating behavior and acknowledging the rage of unfulfilled narcissistic expectations. Mourning is not "to turn that [vengeance] over to God which leaves Israel free to hope for the new Jerusalem. . . . [S]uch rage is not only brought into Yahweh's presence. It is submitted to Yahweh and relinquished to him. . . . The submission to Yahweh is real and irreversible" (Brueggemann, pp. 77, 85–86). Rather, mourning is confronting the hurt, engaging the emotional pain which radiates from the void, and recognizing that the paths of distortion are just that—distortions: distractions from the pain that is real and veils for fears that are unfounded. As the hurt is legitimized and the unfoundedness of the fears uncovered, "the workers of iniquity are scattered" (Ps. 92:10) by themselves; the veil is lifted, the distractions no longer attract.

All this is the work of mourning, whether one mourns the loss of a loved one or the loss of a part of one's self: acknowledging the pain, recognizing the distortions which the desire to hold on to a lost past impose, acknowledging the pain ever anew, and then the release of inner energy for engagement in other tasks. The work of mourning does not finish on a specific date. Like life itself, it circles back to engage us again and again. So we mourn again and then we live again. We mourn others, and we mourn our selves. We struggle to identify the overlay of past experience on the present, to re-call and then to re-member.

Second, personal healing requires the slow work of engaging in new tasks, of using the newly released energy in ways that express and embody the new relatedness. This is a trial-and-error process. One tries a pattern, a relationship; one attempts a task. It succeeds and fails to different degrees. So one modifies the task and tries again. One also circles back to confront the distortive currents that well up to the surface, deals with them, and then continues on the new path. Slowly, one grows in strength, and experience. Slowly, the new replaces the old, more and more of the time.

How does one also achieve openness with God? How does one reclaim recognition, connectivity, and intersubjectivity in one's religious existence? It, too, is not as simple as willing it to be.

The process of reconstructing relatedness to God is the same as it is for

WORDS

assumed to come from the root *shur,* "to see" (Hacham on Ps. 5:9). The point is that the enemies are keeping a close eye on the righteous, just waiting for him or her to stumble and fall (the obverse of v. 2).

CON-VERSES

reclaiming personal relatedness. First, there is the work of mourning: recognizing that God has in fact failed me/us and admitting the great pain that that recognition causes; then realizing that some of our expectations of God are, to put it plainly, childish reenactments of narcissistic needs; then admitting that experiencing those needs is itself a projection of unfulfilled narcissistic needs stemming from our relationships with our real parents; then mourning those real and projected losses. This projection of expectations onto God is, in religious terms, idolatry. Transference is always distortive even, and perhaps most significantly, in our relationship to God. It is not possible to completely rid ourselves of our transference to God, but it is possible to continually examine what we expect of God in that light and to try to separate, again and again, the way we read God from the way God is known in the texts, tradition, and history.

Second, there is the work of strengthening the ego to face God, of developing skill and experience in meeting God face-to-Face. Relatedness grows, connectivity creates helpful bonds — even with God. Not that things are always psychologically smooth or piously peaceful; but that one is intersubjective, interpersonal, in mutual recognition, in rap-proche-ment. This is not reentry into the male womb, or re-pent-ance, or reassertion of heirarchy, or in-breaking of grace, or mystical at-one-ment, or supernatural intervention. Rather, this is a path one walks, a way one follows, "the way to You."

Lead me on a level path

We are the abused children of God.

What is our therapy? What is our "level path"?

First, we must empower ourselves to make decisions and exercise options, especially in matters concerning our security. We cannot hide behind pious faith in providence; we must help ourselves as intelligently as possible.

Second, we must confront our helplessness. We must acknowledge, as difficult as that is, that we were victims, at the beck and call of our persecutors, subject to their every whim and cruelty. This is very hard.

Third, we must feel the rage of betrayal. We must express that rage. We must break the terrible silence and say out loud, "God did it. God allowed it. And it is not the first time, but part of a pattern of abandonment and betrayal."

Fourth, we must mourn that past of betrayal. We must mourn the facts as they were, and the relationship as it was and is. We may not deny it; we must mourn it. We must care for ourselves intelligently, cry and grieve.

Fifth, we must learn to cope with the memories as they surface, sometimes in context and sometimes out of nowhere. The horror comes back: at night, in crisis, or for no reason at all. We must learn to confront it, again and again; to mourn it, again and again. And we must learn to avoid further victimization, to release ourselves from the paralysis of rage when it comes.

Sixth, we must empower ourselves ever again by exercising the options of life intelligently and by building the relationships and strengthening the bonds of human kinship and relatedness.

And, in the end, we must seek God's Face. We must engage resolution. We must reenter intersubjectivity with God.

AFFECTIONS

Were it not . . .

This verse is a fragment; it is truncated speech. It also begins with a negative conditional clause; hence, it contains unspoken thoughts, implied speech.

There is something wistful, threatening, and defiantly faithful about this congery of statement and allusion. It is a fragmented mixture of anger, regret, and loyalty.

The meaning is as follows: I wish things were different—were it not for the fact that I have been, and remain, certain that You will vindicate me, I would

¹²Do not give me over to the will of my tormentors.
Indeed, false witnesses have risen against me
and people who breathe violence.

¹³Were it not for the fact that I have been certain
that I would see the goodness of the Lord
in the land of life, [. . .]

CON-VERSES

Were it not . . .

A wound is an injury; it is pain and suffering that comes from without. A wound or injury is not one's fault. It is also given to healing, when cared for. Wound is a better image than suffering.

As it heals, a wound forms a scar. A scar evidences healing. A scar also remains, always, as a witness to suffering and pain, and evil. Scar is a better image than complete healing.

A wound can be healed into a scar by the agency of the wounded and by the

WORDS

will . . . breathe violence
The Hebrew *nefesh* ("soul") sometimes has the meaning of "will" as in Gen. 23:8 (Mesudat Zion). The French catches the capricious, willful sense well: "Ne me livre pas au bon plaisir de mes adversaires."

The root *yafe-ah* has the meaning of "a (false) witness" in Ugaritic and elsewhere in Scripture

(Hacham). But I, like most of us, have known people who breathed violence, and so cling to that translation.

Were it not . . .
There is no word in this sentence without its problem: What is the strange form *lulei*, and why does it have dots above some letters and

SPARKS

Were it not
Exodus 12:42 — "It is a night of vigilance for the Lord, to take them out of the land of Egypt." The Ramban comments on this (ad loc.): "He [God] was vigilant in the matter for them, from the time that He decreed exile for them—that He would take them out on this night, when the end would come, immediately, [as it is

written] 'In its time, I will hasten it' [Isa. 60:22]." On this, the Hever Maamarim (cited in Hebrew of Chavel, ad loc.), comments: "From this, we learn an important rule about the characteristics of God, may He be blessed—that, even when He holds fast to the rule of judgement, He is also full of mercy except that sin is causative and prevents [Him from acting]. Thus, He, may

CON-VERSES

loving care of those who surround and support the wounded (Keshgegian).

goodness . . . in the land of the living

Can there really be reconciliation between us? Does the abused child ever *love* his or her f/Father, again?

"I *can* become functional again, without You: I can hold down a job. I *can* be a reasonably good parent and spouse. I can think, and relate, and build. I can be happy; I can even rejoice—without You. Who needs the pain of confrontation? Why must resolution be engaged? Empowerment can come by excluding, by deciding that I need not reenter intersubjectivity with You."

Is there really a "goodness . . . in the land of life"? Or is that itself an illusion? a false hope?

"I *have* survived. I have done what was necessary to keep myself together, physically and psychologically. It wasn't always nice, but I did it. I have built a life for myself and for those around me. →

AFFECTIONS

not be able to remain true to You and to our life together.

Three thoughts are thus hidden here: First, the psalmist, although he has turned away from his anger against his enemies, still recognizes the justice of his claim against them and the injustice of God not having vindicated him. Here he reasserts his claim, indirectly, in the negative conditional clause. Here the psalmist reaffirms his theology of protest, even though he has recognized that the way of protest has limits within the life of the religious person.

Second, the psalmist, because he is rooted in the interconnectedness of the human and the divine expresses, and does not express, the fragility of that interconnectedness. The psalmist, because he understands relatedness to be the primary category of human existence, says, in the unwritten ellipsis, that every relationship is contingent on trust, on knowing that one can count on the other and that, in this group of psalms, God's acting in a way that has not cultivated trust has undermined the

WORDS

below others? What is the connotation of the root 'mn, usually translated as "believe"? How can one "see" the goodness of God? What is the "goodness" of God? And what is "the land of life," this world, the next, or something else? The sentence as a whole is difficult also because it is not a sentence but a phrase. What did the psalmist mean to say?

Lulei' means "were it not" in the present tense

and "had not" in the past tense. It is a negative subjunctive. The dots above and below the letters, here as elsewhere in Scripture, indicate either passages of grammatical difficulty or passages with an unusual allusion. As S. Lieberman pointed out (*Hellenism in Jewish Palestine* [New York: Jewish Theological Seminary, 1950] 38–46), using dots in this way was standard practice among the Alexandrian gram-

SPARKS

He be blessed, was as if He were sitting all the time and calculating the end, counting each

minute and second, [anticipating] the time when He could redeem them."

AFFECTIONS

relationship between Him and him. The psalmist wants God to know this, even if it is only alluded to in a fragmentary way. The fragmentedness of the speech be-speaks the fragmentedness of the interrelationship.

Third, together with his anger-protest and his regret-threat, the psalmist asserts, by implication, that he has, does, and will continue to believe, to be certain, that God will vindicate him — in this world (and, for the rabbinic reader, in the next). This is faith in defiance of the facts; it is contrary-to-fact loyalty to P/presence.

This verse, then, is an echo of the emotion of earlier verses, and other psalms. And yet the psalmist lets it stand, clearly, amidst verses of healing and integration. He juxtaposes fragmentedness to wholeness, anger to prayer, protest to praise, and dark doubts to the new and re-new-ed confidence of the next verse.

CON-VERSES

I have engaged myself and others in constructive living. It has not been easy, but I have done it. And I have done it myself, out of my own resources. Who needs You? especially since You didn't help, when I needed it most?

"At most, You can be my remote Father, my limited King; but You cannot be my Judge. You may be my Creator, though I resent Your claiming credit for my existence; but You cannot be my Friend, my trusted Guide. I must be my own judge, friend, and guide. I must be my own father, king, and creator. I have assumed life, and I must assume life further. Yes, say it: I have been my own god, and I must be my own god further."

Angry doubts, very angry doubts; in an unfinished sentence.

WORDS

marians. Hence, here the dots may signal the syntactic irregularity of a phrase marked as a verse, or the interpretive opportunity of the content of the verse.

The root 'mn means "to be firm" ("[Moses'] hands were firm until the setting of the sun" [Ex. 17:12]). From this it comes to mean "to have firm trust, or belief in a non-doctrinal sense, in people" ("[Jacob's] heart was faint because he did not believe/trust them" [Gen. 45:26]). And then, "to have firm trust, or belief in a non-doctrinal sense, in God" ("[Abraham] believed/ trusted in God" [Gen. 15:6]; "[the Israelites] trusted/believed in God and in Moses, His servant" [Ex. 14:31]). Here I have chosen to use "be certain" to convey the firmness of the psalmist's trust/belief and "have been" to capture the ongoing and present nature of that sense.

"To see the goodness of the Lord" means "to enjoy the blessing of God" or "to be under God's protection" (Hacham).

"The land of life," in its scriptural context, refers to this world (Hacham, Mesudat Zion; cf. Isa. 53:8; Ps. 52:7; etc.). Nonetheless, the Talmud (Berakhot 4a), Saadia (ad loc), and Maimonides ("Hilkhot Teshuva" 8:7) understood this as referring to the place of true life, that is, the world-to-come.

"[. . .]" is used to present the fragmentary nature of this verse. The psalmist, in his meditation on danger, sin, and healing, leaves the thought unfinished and each reader must complete it: ". . . I would have been destroyed/I would not have survived physically and spiritually/I would not have the strength to go on, to turn yet again to You/ . . ."

CON-VERSES

Have confidence . . . have confidence

Doubt. The return of the repressed. Failed relation. Defeated rap- proche-ment. . . . The difficulty of surrendering fan- tasied omnipo- tence; the pain of giving up the comfort of narcissistic dependence.

Yet some success. Measured, but measurable. Don't deny it, even though asserting it is anxiety provoking.

Courage. Back to work. . . .

". . . the patient . . . is freer to change because he or she is not as encumbered by the distortions of trans- ference. . . [S]he or he chooses to change in a specific way because it is the most viable and valuable alternative

AFFECTIONS

confidence . . . strong . . . give courage . . . confidence

The psalmist is talking to himself, and indirectly to the reader.

There are four steps to religious healing set forth here: First, "have confidence in the Lord." There are moments when we feel that God has deserted us nationally (Ps. 44:10–15) and personally (Pss. 109:22–25; 27:9), even that God has broken His covenant with us (Ps. 89:40). But there are also moments when we know God is near to us, present in our personal and national lives (Pss. 44:6–9; 109:21, 30–31; 27:1–3). And there are the moments of remembering God's promise not to

> 14Have confidence in the Lord.
> Be strong,
> and He will give courage to your heart;
> then, have confidence in the Lord.

WORDS

confidence . . . courage

"Confidence" is much better than "hope/look to/wait patiently on" because it conveys a more active sense (see "Affections").

The words "give courage to your heart" can be understood as an impersonal imperative and taken together with the recurrent phrase "be

strong and of good courage" (Deut. 31:6, 7, 23; Josh. 1:6, 7, 9, 18; Hacham). But it can also be taken with the implied subject as God. I have chosen the latter, following the heuristic ten- dency of the Talmud (Berakhot 32b, cited in Feuer; see "Affections").

SPARKS

Have confidence . . . have confidence

"Rabbi Hama bar Hanina said, 'If one sees a person [even oneself] who has prayed and has not been answered, that person should pray yet again, as it says, "Have confidence . . . and have confidence"'" (Talmud, Berakhot 32b).

"The sages taught: 'Four things require being strong: Torah study, good deeds, prayer, and a livelihood . . .'" (ibid.).

"[Concerning] the teaching of the Talmud 'he should pray yet again,' the meaning is that, after partial deliverance has come from God, blessed be His Name, one needs to be even stronger in prayer because the evil impulse incites one [to think] that one does not need to pray further. The truth is that, after deliverance, one needs prayer more than before. . . . This is the pur- pose of the first and final three blessings of the

AFFECTIONS

desert us even in the depths of our sinfulness and in the agony of our suffering (Lev. 26:42, 44–45; Deut. 30:1–10; Ps. 89:34–35). Remembering the good moments and calling to mind the promise gives us a sense of, and a reason for, confidence.

Second, "be strong." Having confidence is no simple matter, even if it has reasons and roots in experience and tradition. Those moments of affirmation must be affirmed, again and again. And they must be acted upon, incorporated into deed. Being strong means affirming and reaffirming the positive. It also means resuming one's social and moral responsibilities with re-new-ed vigor, reentering the world of action with that confidence. Finally, being strong means reentering one's relationship with God, being strong and reconfronting God, going in again to His Presence.

Third, "have courage." If one has confidence based on experience and tradition, and if one gathers strength and reenters life and God-relatedness, God will give courage to one's heart. The tradition teaches: "If one comes to be purified, he or she is to be helped" (Talmud, Shabbat 104a; etc.). Or, as the popular adage has it: God helps those who help themselves.

CON-VERSES

before him or her. By narrowing the range of competing options, he or she obtains greater freedom to experience"—in an incomplete and imperfect world (Wolstein, 208 [egalitarian language added]).

in the Lord

"The soul [is] that essential being of a person that is more than the psychological self. . . . The healing that comes in time (and healing *will* come) touches us, filling us with a sense of solemn wonder, with a sense of purpose and meaning. . . . I have life, I have meaning. I know pain, and I know healing. For now, life is good. I am grateful. I am full . . . a moment pregnant with the possibilities of love and creativity (spontaneity). It is for this that we live. . . . Stay connected to that Goodness with all your being, however it manifests itself to you. Acquaint yourself with the shadows that lie deep within you. And then, open yourself, all that is you, to the Light. Give freely. Take in abundantly. . . . Embrace your world, this world that holds you safely now. Grasp the small tender mercies of the moment. Let you be loved. Let you love. The shattered soul will heal" (Steele, "Sitting," pp. 19–25).

SPARKS

silent devotion [which are words of praise]: First, one orders one's praise of the Omnipresent, [then one prays,] and then one orders one's praise again so that one be ready for further prayer. . . .

"The rule is that all one's worship is to draw down the share in the holy Torah that belongs to each soul in Israel; this is the root of that soul. In proportion to one's worship and prayer,

one is given [access to] the root of one's soul. To be sure, when one receives any enlightenment from the root of one's soul, one needs to be more on one's guard than before when that root was guarded on high, as it says, 'May the Lord bless you and guard you' (Num. 6:24)— that, after blessing, one needs even more to be guarded" (Sefat Emet).

AFFECTIONS

Fourth, have re-new-ed confidence — confidence rooted this time not just in personal memory and sacred tradition but also in action, in the success of renewed relatedness to people, to Torah, and to God.

The way to the Lord is not straight; it has ups and downs, twists and turns. Perseverance is the method. Re-turning (Hebrew *teshuva*) is not a triumphal march. Like any real therapy, if one works hard at it, healing moves forward by circling backward; repentance is a backstitch.

Religious healing requires initial memory and recall; then confidence; then strong reaffirmation and action; and then renewed confidence.

Re-sponse

CHAPTER 11

Prelude

INTER-TEXTING is the weaving of already woven texts into the evolving fabric of a life. It is a reading-together of life and text, a reading that is already an inter-pretation. W-rite-ing is the ritual of committing the new inter-text to in-scribed form. It is an attempt to display the new fabric to others. To re-spond is to pledge back, to reciprocate. It is to give in return toward that which one has received. To co(r)-re-spond is to pledge back and forth, to reciprocate *seriatim*.

A book is not a monologue; it is read by readers. Sometimes an author hears from his or her readers; occasionally an author invites readers to make themselves heard. Especially, a book on theology and psychology must involve readers, as well as the author, because psychology and theology are shared realms of thought and feeling. A theology of image, conceived anthropo-pathically, must be human in its formation, not only in its conceptuality. Accordingly, I invited two friends and colleagues to read and correspond with me as this book evolved. One, Diane, is a professor; she is also an adult survivor of child abuse. The other, Wendy, is also a professor; she is a systematic theologian. The original correspondence seemed too personal and too diffuse to reproduce. The dialogues that follow are, therefore, edited versions, organized by topic to highlight important points. The dialogue is co(r)-re-sponsive, a pledging back and forth. It is, however, incomplete; I return in the closing chapters of this book to some of the points raised. The reader who reads co(r)-re-spondence is also part of the discussion; such a reader is invited to re-spond—to me or to some other. As the circle widens, knowledge and connectivity are established.

A book on theology and psychology can also be taught; it can be studied. Then the students must re-spond. Accordingly, I invited the young people who studied this material to contribute. Several of their comments have already been incorporated into the commentaries. One inter-pretation stood out in its fullness and power. "Beth's Psalm" is presented here as a witness, as a re-sponse.

The psalms chosen for this book are not the only psalms on the subject of anger and healing; there are many more. It seemed appropriate, therefore, to set forth several more psalms, without commentary; they are included in "Addressing the Abusing God." Re-turning to psalms is also a way of con-templating.

*Dialogue
with an Adult Survivor
of Child Abuse*

The Voice of the Abused

June 7, 1989

Dear David,

Your abused voice is the voice of one who had a good childhood and first encountered abuse as an adult (fortunate you). You have missed what abuse from the beginning does to the soul. Miller [*For Your Own Good*] cannot help you because Miller has intellectual outrage only. She does not convey the feeling-state of abuse.

Diane

November 26, 1989

Dear Diane,

I cannot tell you how deeply your letter and your autobiographical manuscript affected me. I know this book of psalms contains passages that are very tough, even heretical. I feel confident that I can stand up to the theological criticism. However, your comment that I do not really know what I am talking about when I write about abuse cut me down to size in a very healthy way.

You are right. I, unlike you, did not grow up in a physically abusive environment. My home was a typical Jewish middle-class home, that is, one with the usual dose of emotional and verbal abuse (if I can use that word at all in the context of your experience), mixed with love and an emphasis on achievement. Perhaps, because the abuse I experienced was not severe, and thanks to years of psychoanalysis and therapy, I can and do feel anger, indeed rage, at the mistreatment I experienced. I know this anger to be justified, righteous anger. What I received was not my "fault"; it was the product of the distorted personal needs of those around me.

In preparing to do this work on abuse, I have had, too, to confront incidents in my own childhood that had long since been buried. I have had to realize that I have no real analogy in myself for what I have heard. I have had to confront my helplessness at the extent of the damage that I have seen done. And I have had to realize that my hopes to "cure" people are fantasies, compensations for impotence by a weak person. I am not the messiah, not even a healer. Sympathy alone is not enough. All this is true of my work with the holocaust as well.

My response to your manuscript is one of horror bordering on disbelief. I know one is not supposed to express disbelief to adult survivors of child abuse but I confess that, if I did not know you personally, I would be more inclined than I already am to block this material and deny it. How can someone throw a child off a bridge into a river? How can someone beat a small child? How can someone rape a three-year-old? How can a father have oral intercourse with his daughter and know she is choking, gasping for air? How can a mother watch her husband rape her child? It happens, because you (and others) say it happens, but I have no analogy in myself by which to comprehend. The analogies I do have—and there are some—pale in intensity. But then, I say the same thing about holocaust survivor accounts.

Shalom, David

December 11, 1989

Dear David,

The person abused as a child does not feel righteous anger, either at the time or later. It may be that righteous anger eventually appears when all has been recalled and processed. I can't speak to that. There is anger, of course, but the anger is diffuse, non-focussed, in part directed at the self. You seem to be far too strongly influenced by Miller. She understands the process of transmission of anger but does not understand the physically and sexually abused child who has grown to be an adult.

December 29, 1989

I did not feel righteous anger as a child. I feel it now, in reflecting upon what I experienced in the past. "Now," however, is after four years of therapy. As a child I was too busy feeling other things to have time and energy for anger.

January 17, 1990

Okay, I am beginning to get in touch with anger that I felt as a child, but it is not righteous anger. It is ice-cold rage. So, you are half right, maybe.

Diane

On God and Jewish Identity

June 7, 1989
Dear David,

I am beginning to see why I try to be [religiously] observant but have not *davened* [prayed intimately] for two years except to say, "Please be patient with me." For now, I have nothing to say to God because, like all abused as children, I expect no response that will help. I view my silence as temporary, as a time of self-healing. Just as I have deliberately simplified my world for two years by interacting emotionally with very few people, so too have I withdrawn from God. He offers no comfort, only stress and complication. Stress and complication are not my needs right now. I am a Jew who fully, without doubt, believes in God because I have felt Him; I do my best to observe [the rituals], but I do not speak to Him.

Anger? Possibly, but I do not feel it. I was trained early to have no expectations of comfort and protection from those with power over me, and I have never had those expectations of God. Troubles, pain, hurt—they are mine to deal with, alone, without help from anyone, especially anyone with power over me. And that, my friend, is classic abused child. There's no such emotion as righteous anger for such as me when it comes to "Father" (as opposed to boss, or the courts, or any institution encountered first as an adult). People, in my experience, ordinary people with no power are much more just than "Father." For the ordinary person I can have righteous anger, but not for "Father." Having experienced justice from ordinary people, I have expectations; having not experienced it from "Father," I have none. Righteous anger requires expectations.

Why observe religiously? It is my (voluntarily assumed) obligation. It is not love. I do not think that I love God. Do I resent the obligation? At times, but I had a choice that you did not [when I chose to become Jewish], so my resentment is very low. Do I feel guilty when I fail to observe? No, I feel as if I have failed to be who I am. Do I feel anxiety when I fail? No. Do I feel fear when I fail? Yes, and no. Yes, because failure can take me farther from God. No, because I trust that He understands that my failure is not rebellion. Am I sometimes rebellious in my failure? Yes. But I do not fear then, either, because I trust that He sees behind the rebellion.

Why all this trust? There is no basis for it except, perhaps, the hope that God is an ideal parent (idolatry). But the ideal parent protects and comforts, while I do not have that expectation from God. I am not trying to be logical about all this; I am reporting emotional states.

I respect God enough to be willing to accept His judgment, even when He is wrong. If He is wrong, I will tell Him. The God I know makes terrible mistakes at times. He acts, and does not act, wrongly. Maybe He is so busy keeping His eyes on all those sparrows that He does not have enough time for all those people who need His help and don't get it. Sometimes, He looks away; then, when He looks back, He does not understand what is occurring and so He acts wrongly. He's only human, after all.

Ultimately, do I fear God? Yes. He can wipe me out in a time of indifference or a time of irrational anger. I cannot control that, however. I do what I can with Him. I tell Him when He is wrong, I discuss, I argue, I praise when appropriate, and I hope that we can work things out. He is like an emotionally not very sensitive spouse. . . . That is pure idolatry; all of this is pure projection.

Diane,

November 16, 1989

Dear Diane,

I am a theologian, and that means that I must be able to speak for God to my people, and for my people to God. In this sense, I reflect upon our collective experience of the holocaust (I never capitalize that word) and I search for an analogy with which to better understand us and God. My rule is: *If it is good psychology, it is good theology; and if it is bad psychology, it is bad theology.* This is, I believe, the way of the Bible, of the midrash, of the liturgy, of hasidism, and of the commonsense theology of the people. I trust this language (though I know and have been trained in the systematic conceptual language of the philosophers). My own path, therefore, has been from the holocaust as a subject of inquiry, to individual survivors, to my own experience, and then to the psychology of the abused. The quest, however, aims for long range understanding; it is theological/psychological, or psychological/theological.

Shalom, David

December 11, 1989

Dear David,

For me, the practice of Judaism is the mechanism whereby I sometimes, unfortunately rarely, meet God.

If God is an abuser, the adult non-sick response should be to turn away permanently from Him. Why stick around and be hurt more? *Or, if . . . ,* then the adult response should be to reach a resolution which includes a clear understanding by both of us of what He has done and its effects. He should come seeking forgiveness from each of us.

December 13, 1989

As I re-read "Con-verses" [to Psalm 109], a part of me kept hoping that you would provide a way to avoid the obvious conclusions that you were approaching. Surely somewhere in the Talmud these same questions had been considered and rejected. Surely somewhere there was a traditional resolution of these problems which I could hide behind. Then I recalled the very unsatisfactory discussions of Job that I have read, and I knew that the tradition was not going to provide an emotional escape for me.

Perhaps, despite my doubts, I am more predisposed to accept what you write because of my own experiences as an abused child. Authority, to me, is by definition non-benevolent. For years I have resisted the concept of an omnipotent God because I knew that omnipotence carried with it abuse and that I would be the abused. By denying omnipotence, I was denying the potential for further abuse. I was also denying that I held God at least in part responsible for what happened to me as a child.

If projection is idolatry, then I was and still am committing idolatry. I do not trust omnipotent God *not* to abuse His power. I do not trust omnipotent God to care for me. I much prefer omnipotent God to stay away than to be involved intimately in my life. These are my emotional responses.

Yet and still, in my two recognized meetings with God, there was no abuse. There was fear, once, and comfort, the other time.

To avoid the pain of the emotional truths that you write, I intellectualize. Yes, God is abusive, but that was in the past, before He essentially withdrew from His world. Also, no trait describes the entire person, and no attribute describes all of God; you are simplifying and exaggerating out of proportion. Finally, there is a major difference in degree between the abuse that parents wreak on their children's lives and the abuse that you attribute to God. And then I hit a stone wall because I recognize my intellectualizations for what they are.

Any family therapist, and I am one, would recognize immediately the pattern of pathology that God established in His family. God was directly responsible for what happened between Cain and Abel. He showed extreme, irrational preferences and provoked the child-Cain to a rage that culminated in the death of his brother. God told Abraham to banish Ishmael and, later, to sacrifice Isaac. God, as role model, was responsible for the divisive choosing between Isaac and Esau. Again, as role model, He was responsible for the preferential treatment of Joseph and for his brothers' jealousy. When God chose us, the Jewish people, He unleashed a jealousy that has yet to calm down. God is truly a jealous God, and His children learned their jealousy at His knees. What does the tradition say about each of these events? It rationalizes.

Judaism rationalizes; Christianity flees. Neither approach is a solution to the problem. The problem, as you have so clearly stated, is that our God, the traditional God of Judaism, has shown by word and deed that He is an abusive Father to His children.

When I attempted as an adult to reach a resolution with my own abusive father, I first tried to establish a dialogue. He denied all that he had done to me. He stated that I had fantasized the events that I so clearly recalled. Eventually, I gave up trying to talk to the man, and put him out of my life. What should I do about God as the abuser?

Tradition states that He should come *to me* to seek *my* forgiveness; that I should help Him to reach a clear understanding of the consequences of His acts; that we should talk until I am convinced of *His* repentance. Then, and only then, would He be deserving of my forgiveness. That will never happen. Should I turn my back on Him as I did to my father? What is it that I owe to God?

One of God's commandments is to honor one's parents. I have had a hard time with that commandment, because it told me that I should honor the father who raped me and the mother who watched without interfering. Several years ago, I concluded that the commandment meant that I should behave in such a way as to bring honor on my parents for *my* sake, not theirs. To behave dishonorably would hurt me far more than it would hurt them. If that is correct, the same holds with my relationship to God/Father. I shall behave in such a way as to bring honor to God and, perhaps, He will be shamed by my behavior and seek forgiveness for His.

Diane

January 26, 1990

Dear Diane,

You do not trust omnipotent God to care for you; you would rather omnipotent God remain at a distance. It hurts to read that, personally and in its larger sense, for if the Jewish people after the holocaust is an abused child—and it surely is, with all the symptoms of silence, denial, patterns of active abuse, even dissociation and multiple personality disorder symptoms—then we, too, do not trust omnipotent God to care for us, and we would rather omnipotent God remain at a distance from us. And that is *healthy,* a sign of sanity.

As I see it, the thoroughgoing ethnopolitical orientation of Jewish identity in the modern world is a sign of a deep mistrust of the God Who was our

Father for so long. Further, the resurgence of neo-orthodoxy, with its "trust in the sages" and total devotion to God, is a sublimation, a form of denial, of the same realization. Finally, the dark side of the repression of the Palestinian revolt is a sign of abuse turned to abusiveness. These are unhealthy, spiritually and therapeutically, because they do not confront the issue directly. But what would be healthy, spiritually and therapeutically? How would one express relation, yet distance? desire for trust, yet justified wariness of it? and do it directly?

You write, Diane, about your efforts to reach resolution with your real father. He denied what he did. You know that this is standard behavior by the abuser. For this reason, clients are urged not to try resolution unless they are fully aware that there is a good chance the abuser will deny it and, hence, that the client will be abused one more time. One must not go into resolution with expectations of confirmation, much less of reconciliation. One undertakes such a confrontation, I think, only because of the need to speak—independent of how the hearer will hear. Do we need to do that with God? to protest, steadfastly, independent of whether He hears or not? independent of whether He reacts or not? My answer is yes. We, like the psalmist, must protest. He must answer and, if He does not, we continue to protest—in this world and in the next. If necessary, Judgment Day will be a confrontation, and maybe not the final one either.

The other alternative is to do as you suggest: to *interpret*, to understand honor of p/Parent as reflected honor. If I am honored by my own behavior, p/Parent is honored; and the converse. Theologically, one might say that p/Parent is honored when the deeper i/Image is honored.

The question of projection/idolatry that you have raised several times is very complex. When in doubt, follow the rule *If it is good psychology, it is good theology*. This leads me to observe that one is never rid of projection and transference in human relations; one only learns to recognize the situations and patterns of their occurrence and to reframe one's behavior from unstudied psychological reflexes to conscious consideration of other options. My father is always with me; how could it be otherwise? I have learned, however, to better (but not always) recognize when he is present and how that presence distorts some of my behavior. Then I consider my other options and I act as coherently as I can, with as much self-responsibility as I can.

The same is true of our projections of God. Of course, we want God to be the ideal Father and we personally shape Him into this rather incoherent image, which is a mirror-image of our un-ideal fathers. And, of course, the tradition, too, shapes God into its ideal Father/God, which is a mirror-image of the un-ideal God of historical reality. But all we need to know is that such a process exists, that it can be identified, and that we need not be bound by such imagery. We need to know what our options are—personally and nationally, intellectually, morally, and spiritually—and then we need to think and to act as responsibly as we can, knowing all the time that we cannot be completely free of the language and imagery we use, which is indeed the language of projection/idolatry.

Shalom, David

January 29, 1990

Dear David,

Let's take a look at your idea of the Jewish people as an abused child after the holocaust. There is a difference between being abused by a parent and being abused by someone other than a parent. Unless you are saying, and I cannot believe that you are, that God directly caused the holocaust, then the analogy is to a child being abused by someone other than a parent. Either the parent, God, was negligent so that the abuse occurred, or the parent was powerless to prevent the abuse. True, God set the stage by choosing us over the others, but He was not the one who built the camps; people did that.

A good case could be made for negligence based upon past performance. A charitable view would be that He was simply unaware of what was transpiring, but I do not accept that. I prefer the view that non-omnipotent God was powerless to protect. He could comfort afterwards but He was powerless to intervene between Joseph and his brothers, so to speak. Or, if He was not powerless, He made a mistake in judgment, thinking that His children could not possibly go to the ends that they did. *Non-omnipotent or mistaken God* can comfort and heal. Neo-orthodoxy, then, can be seen not as sublimation and denial but as children clinging for comfort.

Perhaps, though, the above is yet another expression of my fear of omnipotence and a denial of God's true role in what occurred. If I assume for a moment that God is omnipotent, then He could have intervened but chose not to do so. At worst God was negligent and uncaring, for He had to have known what was happening to His children if He is omnipotent. I will not accept that our God is capable of being so uncaring that He simply allowed the holocaust to occur with full knowledge and full ability to intervene. If He in fact is that way, then He has lost the right to any claims on the Jewish people until He fully atones for what He did.

About fifteen years ago, I began the process of rejoining my extended family, from whom I had cut myself off out of anger as a young teenager. It turned out that most of them had been unaware of what had been happening in my house; all of them expressed sorrow at not knowing and at not having intervened. They have been a source of comfort to me ever since. Those who had been aware would not talk with me, out of guilt I assume. Perhaps we can use those two responses of my extended family to assess God's awareness of the holocaust. *Has He talked with us since and expressed His sorrow, or has He turned His back on us? Is He comforting now, or is He rejecting?*

We need to remember that what is going on between the abused Jewish people and God is not simply controlled by God. I feel, but have no proof, that non-omnipotent or mistaken God is attempting to comfort now but that the Jewish people are acting out their anger, much like the abused teenager steals, joins violent gangs, runs away, and in general is antisocial. We, as a group, are flailing out at all those who knew, who did nothing, who [did not] feel guilty at not having acted, and so deny our reality. We are not yet ready for the comfort that is offered by those who did not know, or by those who did know but were powerless to intervene. We are hyperalert and hypervigilant, as all who were abused as children are. We over-react to new threats because of the flashbacks they trigger.

The Palestinian revolt and our response to it must be looked at from the viewpoint of a flashback. During a flashback the individual is literally in other time, just as we as a people perceive one stone-throwing teenage Palestinian as the Nazis coming to destroy us again. Of course we over-react. We can do nothing but that, until we are comforted and healed. The problem that I see is that I am not convinced that healing from the trauma of abuse can fully occur, either for the individual or for the Jewish people.

The abused individual has had a shattering of basic trust. I do not feel that basic trust can be reestablished once it is broken, although I would love to be proven wrong. Dissociation is also a very common outcome of abuse. Although you will find many psychologists and psychiatrists use the word "dissociation," very few actually understand the concept. Those that do are the ones who, since approximately 1980, have been trying to understand multiple personality disorder.

As I now understand dissociation, the process is as follows: A stimulus from the environment triggers a flashback. The flashback is then repressed through the mechanism of dissociation (loss of emotional components), or the individual enters the flashback and experiences an abreaction, during which time she or he is also dissociated (loss of intellectual processing and controls). As a third alternative, the individual goes into what I have termed "total dissociation." Total dissociation is a loss of both emotions and intellect. The individual is impervious to pain and other strong stimuli, very much including emotional stimuli such as comforting.

Flashbacks, along with the other symptoms of post-traumatic stress disorder, are regarded as a physiological process by many people. They can be suppressed by drugs (also by neo-orthodoxy). Various psychodynamic therapies have been devised to treat the symptoms, with varying degrees of success. The most effective involve abreaction, but abreaction has a fairly substantial rate of failure. The reason for the failure, in my opinion, is that nothing changes for the individual during the abreaction. A new experience, such as being comforted during the time of extreme fear, needs to be added to the "scene" in order for the abreaction to be successful.

As I understand Israeli interaction with the Palestinians, flashbacks are triggered by the Palestinian throwing stones. Sometimes in response to these flashbacks, we brutally beat and shoot Palestinians, who are really the Nazis at that point. However, this abreaction does not change anything because neither God nor the rest of the world comforts us during these times of extreme fear. I do not know why God fails to comfort; it may be that He does comfort and we are not yet ready to accept His comforting. I certainly can understand why the rest of the world does not comfort us at such times. At other times in response to these flashbacks, we lose all emotion. We repress that which would allow us to see the humanity in the other and instead come up with brutal policies for handling the Palestinians. At times, we enter total dissociation, in which we experience a complete paralysis of both emotion and intellect. Those are times of extreme danger for everyone involved. It's all very sad, and the only way out that I see is that God will have to continue comforting, if He has in fact begun, and we will have to express enough rage and fear so that we are at the point of being able to accept His comforting.

Looked at in this way, the Jewish people is still in the early stages of repair and healing. We are at the angry, acting-out stage. We need someone to hold us firmly and gently so that we can flail without hurting others. Only God can do that; only God can change the re-experiencing of our abreactions so that we are comforted during our extreme fear. We eventually will be able to accept that from a non-omnipotent or a mistaken God. We will not be able to accept comfort if God is omnipotent, if He perceived what would happen and simply did not care enough to intervene. Besides, if that is the case, He will be incapable of true comfort because His guilt, which He will have to feel forever, will make that impossible.

Your view seems to be that God is omnipotent, that He knew the outcome, and that our task is to protest until such time that He atones for His uncaring negligence. I guess that then we, the Jewish people, will be in a position to accept His comforting so that the abreactions will be changed and healing can begin. I have serious doubts about that. I wonder if that is good psychology.

Let's assume that my father had responded, that he had truly understood the damage he had done to me, that he was truly sorry, that he truly offered comfort, and that I was capable of perceiving all this truth. Would I have been able to accept his comfort? I do not know for sure, but I doubt it. If I could have accepted his comfort, could I trust him as I did when a child? Absolutely not, because (1) I am not a child and (2), having broken trust once, he could not be trusted not to break it again. The problem is that no comfort can take place in the absence of trust. In other words, had my father done all that is stated above, all that would have been accomplished would have been that

I had spoken my truth and it was heard. No comforting could have taken place because basic trust cannot be restored.

This leaves the Jewish people with only one hope for true healing. We have to hope that the God of our tradition is *not* the omnipotent God that we thought He was. Otherwise, there will be no healing because He is our only hope of comfort and healing.

All of the above presupposes that what has been done to me was so extreme that complete forgiveness is impossible under any circumstances or conditions whatever. I am, in fact, angered by the word "forgiveness." I want no part of that. I get furious whenever I read of therapists who advocate forgiveness as the route to healing. Interestingly, almost all of those therapists are Christians, usually of the born-again variety.

It seems to me that forgiveness of what was done to me would be to deny at some level not the experiences themselves, but the reverberations of those experiences through my life at all levels. True healing for me, if it ever occurs, will remove the flashbacks and other symptoms of post-traumatic stress disorder: I will no longer dissociate, I will no longer feel like a threatened child when I first awake in the morning, I may even approximate basic trust. But true healing cannot do anything about the losses that have occurred to me during all of the years when I have suffered because of my past. It cannot magically restore me to the time and place where it was once possible to love and I ran, because the man who offered that love has gone on without me. It cannot restore me to the academic potential that I had and did not meet, because the jobs that were open are long since occupied by others. It cannot, and this is the worst part, make my adult children infants again and give me another chance at parenting them. They have been damaged by the damage that was done to me. To set the record straight, I did not abuse them in any way that I, my therapist, or they can detect. I simply passed on to them many of the symptoms of post-traumatic stress disorder such as an untrusting approach to life. Their children also will be damaged to a degree, as will their grandchildren, etc. A style of relating to the world came out of my experiences, and that style will reverberate in all those who come from me.

The same is true of the Jewish people. We have been changed for all time as a result of the holocaust. What might have been will never be. Mistaken God or non-omnipotent God or negligent God cannot change that, no matter what He does from this point forward.

January 30, 1990

God, omnipotent and uncaring, is someone whom I would never wish to encounter again. I would stay as far away from Him as possible, forever. He would not be deserving of my company, comfort, praise, and love. Furthermore, I could not force myself to give anything to Him *because fear, once felt, can never be forgotten.* When first encountered, it immediately weaves itself into the fabric of being. Maybe this is why I think that changes in behavior do not constitute healing. Perhaps ultimate healing cannot exist.

Diane

On Healing

November 29, 1989

Dear David,

The opening section [of my autobiographical novel] — being thrown off the bridge as a child — occurred as a flashback some five years after I quit therapy, and I handled it by myself on a very lonely Sunday. Then I drove to your house without calling ahead because I had a desperate need to see a good father–child interaction. You invited me in, were yourself with your boys, and I got what I needed in the watching. Do not, my friend, sell your healing capabilities short. Sometimes we teachers are privileged to see the effect we have on our students; most often we do not know when and upon whom we have the greatest impact. We sow seeds in the wind, and sometimes they take root. Healing resembles teaching in that respect. Last year a student told me at the end of my course that, because I openly state that I have dyslexia and joke about it when it shows up during lecturing, I gave him the self-confidence and hope to consider the possibility that he was not stupid because of his dyslexia. I healed in passing because of who I am, and you do that also.

If the above does not convince you, consider this: You are one of three people to whom I have shown my manuscript. You are one of at most five friends who know about the sexual abuse. Why? I trust you to understand. My trust does not come easily, and there is something in you that evokes it. So, please, do not berate yourself on any level for what you perceive that you can and cannot do. You mostly are unaware of your effect on people, just as all of us are.

January 29, 1990

It is reassuring to have someone who has not been abused be concerned about the issue. It says to me, and I assume to others that some, among the greater society, do care. Those of us who were abused were physically alone. We thought that we were emotionally alone, but your concern says clearly that we were *not* alone. Concern expressed by the non-abused offers a way back into the community of human beings, from which I, at least, felt alienated for many years.

When, on the horrible day two years ago that the first memory of sexual abuse came to me during physical therapy, I had a series of responses, some of which were very Jewish. All occurred when I was very much in a state of shock. My first was to search almost frantically through the refrigerator of my therapist's office for something to eat. I found an apple, cut it into three parts, and insisted that she and her assistant, both of whom were recovering from the stress of living through the memory with me, join me in eating. I said to them: "Eat, that is what people who are alive do." In other words, I was rejecting the death-aspect of the experience and I was requiring them to join me in a life-affirming ritual. It would not have been sufficient for me to eat alone; I needed community. Both of them are Jewish and later said that, for the first time, they understood why funerals are followed by meals.

My second response was to declare quite formally that all relationships, all promises, all commitments, all statements made by me no longer held, including those made to God. The only exception was to my children, and even there I would have to review some decisions. Each commitment had been made under a set of assumptions by me that had turned out not to be true, and therefore I could not be bound by decisions that had been made with incomplete knowledge. Even at the time, I was vaguely aware of the parallel with *Kol Nidre.*

My third response, which was in contradiction to my first response, was to declare myself a member no longer of the human race. That was not a Jewish response, but it expressed quite clearly my disgust, revulsion at what I had just re-experienced and of the evil that humans are capable of committing. So, although I needed community to affirm a life stance, I was simultaneously rejecting all ties with people. At the time, I was aware of overgeneralizing my rejection, but I simply did not care if some people were hurt by that. Finally, I said something to the effect that he, my father, invaded and defiled my body but he did not reach and make unclean the essence or core of who I am. I still feel that way.

January 30, 1990

Your quotes from Gil in "Con-verses" [to Psalm 109] bother me. The therapeutic goals outlined there are just fine, but they do not solve the problem of having been abused. I recognize and express my feelings, I communicate, I take controlled risks, I solve problems, I identify personal needs, etc. I have a sense of personal power, I do not self-blame, I am not isolated, I do not feel victimized, and I do feel self-fulfilled. The only stated goal that I am unsure of for myself is the feeling of wholeness, and that is because I am not quite sure what the author means. Perhaps that is indicative of a lack of wholeness. Nevertheless, the goals, when achieved, do not solve the problem of having been abused. To say that they do is to enter once again into the realm of denial. The therapist who wants to believe that she helps people who have been traumatized has a basic need to be successful, even if it means that the patient's reality is denied.

The steps of therapy that you cite later in the commentary likewise bother me, and for the same reason. Trust, and its breaking, is simply not understood by the therapists you quote. I know that you think Gil has written an excellent book; I have ordered but not yet received it. However, there is a difference between being trustworthy to the patient, that is, helping the patient go through all the steps that are outlined, and restoring trust that has been broken. I certainly have people in my life whom I trust to be gentle with me, to care about me, to take my needs into consideration, and to protect themselves from me when necessary. Nevertheless, I do not have a trust that generalizes from these people.

The real issue that I have with the quotations revolves around what constitutes healing. The therapist is changing behavior, which is necessary, *but I am not at all convinced that changed behavior results in healing*. Changes are necessary for healing to occur, and perhaps they are indications of a degree of healing, but they must not be mistaken for the state of having been healed. To confuse the two is to deny the patient's reality.

I am who I am because of what I have experienced, and to eliminate the basic fear that is a part of me is to eliminate who I now am. Does that last sentence, David, say that I cling to my fear and resist undefined ultimate healing because the fear is a part of me and I fear losing it? Perhaps. Or perhaps it says that I value all parts of me, even those parts that come from terrible experiences. Certainly I value the strength that I have seen in myself, the understanding of the human condition that I have gained, the joy I have learned to feel, the sense that in therapy I have successfully dismantled who I was, looked at the pieces, and then put them back together in a new way, becoming the architect of myself. All these are sources of pride to me.

You write [in "Con-verses" to Psalm 109], "Personal healing is in the intersubjectivity with real father-and-mother. . . ." The problem here is that real fathers and mothers who abuse are incapable of intersubjectivity, for the most part. Had they been capable, they would not have abused. Or, having abused during moments of a lack of intersubjectivity, they would have later come to the child and comforted, not abused more. Also, having abused once and destroyed trust, it would still have been too late.

Ultimately, I guess that I am unforgiving in my stance towards abuse. It is one of those acts that crosses over the line of the unthinkable, the undoable. Having been done, the person loses for all time the right to rejoin the community of humans as far as I am concerned. Nothing can atone for such an act. Yes, I realize that my anger is strong, undiluted with pity, with the recognition of the humanness of the abuser, and with the recognition that the abuser, as child, may have been abused. None of that is an excuse for the abuse. There is righteous war, I realize, and hurting and killing may occur within the context of righteous war, but there is no such thing as righteous war against infants and small children. Furthermore, if God is the abuser, healing will not come from intersubjectivity with Him, either.

It occurs to me that I am being quite dogmatic in my stance. Another, who perhaps experienced less extreme events than I, may not hold my views. What I have been saying is angry and unforgiving. I have studied my parents as they were as children and young adults, and I have very strong sympathy for them as they were. I think that I understand them well. I know at least some of the forces that shaped them. I believe that I understand how they felt in most respects. Yet, none of what they experienced excuses what they did. My mother used to say to me, "Do not be angry at your father, he is sick." I accepted that as a child and swallowed my rage and fear. I did not ask as a child why she did not protect me from him. As an adult, I now feel my rage, feel it to be justified, and ask what was missing in them both that made them behave as less than animals. The woman who made excuses for the man cannot be excused, just as the man who acted cannot be excused.

Diane

February 28, 1990

Dear Diane,

I think you expect too much from the word "healing." No one ever is healed wholly, at least not in matters of the heart. Psychological healing is not like medical healing; it is always partial. Life gets better; it never reaches the garden of eden. To put it another way: Mickey and Minnie do not go off into the sunset holding hands.

On further reflection, how could it be otherwise? Life contains ups and downs, some of them very severe. We cope, sometimes better and sometimes worse. We are lucky if we have a spouse, or friend, or therapist who can help through the down times.

You have put it well yourself: control, not absence of pain, is the goal. That's the best I can do; perhaps the best anyone can do.

Shalom, David

*Dialogue
with a Systematic
Theologian*

On Covenant

September 18, 1988

David,

I find your analyses of these psalms wonderful, horrifying, fascinating; I'm very glad you shared them with me. This strange format you are using permits wildly different readings of the text to exist side by side, complementing and contradicting each other — in this way getting at the immense depth and richness of the psalms in a way that I have never seen before. For example, you can describe the significance of the covenant as undergirding even the terrible anger and anguish of Psalm 44, transforming what would be despair into a part of faith, a demand for justice, and a continuing relationship. But you can also make radical attacks on the idea of covenant. This may move close to a defiance of the logic of noncontradiction (maybe that is part of deconstructionist thinking), but it also permits an enormous range of emotional and theological engagement with the psalms.

At several points, especially in "Con-verses" to Psalm 44, you deal with the subject of covenant in the context of radical suffering. I would like to comment to this: I agree that radical suffering, injustice, and evil do challenge seriously a theology of providence, but I do not see that the call for unyielding self-determination necessarily follows from that critique. You appear to have made an equation between providence, covenant, and fantasy, reading covenant through a "logic of sovereignty" and equating it with a neurotic attempt to deny the reality of pain and humiliation. This neurotic illusion, then, you understand to serve to deepen the humiliation because one must protect oneself from it by way of a childlike dependence on a fantasy figure. According to this view, one's human dignity is assaulted first by the victimization and second by the theological interpretation of it. Hence, the solution is to emancipate oneself from God, from the covenant, and from faith since liberation from these is liberation from illusion.

You seem, however, to be locked into the "logic-of-sovereignty" reading of covenant (especially by way of a Freudian rendering of it) and are, therefore, trapped into an either/or—faith or fantasy, a theology of providence or violent self-determination. Any theology confined to this logic will indeed have to choose between these two alternatives, but I am unconvinced that either theology or faith is best served by remaining within that logic and by being confined to those two choices. It is not clear to me that covenant necessarily implies either hierarchy or a parent–child model of relationship. Of course, that may be how it has typically functioned, but if that is the case, then the critique would be not necessarily toward covenant but toward a simplistic or self-destructive interpretation thereof. Without meaning to be polemical, I suggest that *the critique might be directed against a patriarchal rendering of the meaning of covenant.*

The patriarchalism of Freud and of theologies of providence prevents any other positive reality of covenant even from being investigated as a creative alternative both to atheistic "auto-emancipation" and to self-effacing, self-destructive docility in the face of evil and suffering. I would think that theologically the idea of covenant would be intrinsically *anti*-hierarchical—a category implying mutuality rather than dominance and subordination. I would also think that it would imply a "creative fidelity" not only *toward one another* but also *together* in the face of all the dangers, distractions, and violations of history. Such fidelity and mutuality would presuppose freedom and responsibility on both sides but would also presuppose a freedom and danger in history itself. If world history outside the covenant relationship is also at least partially autonomous, suffering could not be strictly reducible to the fault of either God or Israel. To augment the sin–punishment pattern (which quickly degenerates in the face of historical injustice into the abusive father pattern, as you argue), a sense of the real contingency of nature and history is needed.

Because the concept of covenant presupposes the freedom of Israel and, at least by implication, the freedom of creation in general, I would not think it would be necessary to assume that, if the Assyrians or the Nazis try to wipe out the Jewish people, it is because God is using an alien army to hammer Israel because of some real or imagined sinfulness. *This is the result of interpreting covenant through a "logic of sovereignty," and through an excessively penal mentality which seems to be a concomitant of sovereignty and patriarchy, but it doesn't seem to me to be a necessary way of understanding covenant.* I would think that there would be resources in a reconstructed theology of covenant that could be used to critique the idea of "Big Papa" who abuses human beings as a corrupt and dehumanizing form of religious faith. That is, Freud offers only a rather narrow and ultimately not very profound criticism of religion, but the idea of covenant is enormously rich and could be used to make a much stronger attack on the patriarchal, masochistic, "logic-of-sovereignty" forms of theology and faith, precisely from within the context of radical suffering and not as extrinsic to it.

On another subject: You have made the claim, in "Con-verses" to Psalm 44, that the Jew is the "marginal person par excellence." This is an idea I keep running into when I read feminist, or Jewish, or black, or third world material—the claim that one's own group is the supreme sufferer. Such a claim does serve to awaken one to the intensity and specificity of that group's oppression, suffering, and marginalization in a way that universal claims about the human condition don't. But the way the claim is made also functions to imply that the suffering of these other people, in a certain way, doesn't matter, or doesn't matter as much. A feminist, for example, might quickly, spontaneously acknowledge that, of course, the Jews suffered and were marginalized through history, that the enslavement of the black race was a terrible thing etc., but what really matters, what really counts is *our* suffering. *Attentiveness to one's own suffering, a recovery of one's own tradition, making central what was marginal to us does not necessarily nurture one in compassion toward others.* It does not necessarily help one to shape an ethic or a theology that is sensitive to the infinite permutations of evil, and to the infinite demand of obligation. One's own suffering can become an excuse or a device for nourishing indifference toward others. I can't help wondering if there isn't a way to preserve the power of your specificity and passion which would not contain this tacit trivialization of other sufferings and oppressions.

Wendy

Ethical, Spiritual, and Theological Nihilism

April 6, 1989

David,

I think you are right to try to retain the intensity of Psalm 109 and to illustrate the curses with contemporary examples. But there are three levels of your analysis to which I would like to respond: the ethical, the spiritual or dispositional, and the theological. My general concern is that, at all three levels, your analysis is nihilistic. In "Intimations," you suggest that the direction toward nihilism or amorality which deconstruction can take is one rejected by yourself, but this piece of writing looks to me as nihilistic as anything I have read—in its own way, even more so than *Erring*.[1] I bring this up partly because I myself

---

[1] Mark C. Taylor, *Erring: A Postmodern A/theology* (Chicago: University of Chicago Press, 1984; reviewed by me, "But Rabbi David Says," *Cross Currents* 38 [Winter 1988–89], 468–74).

don't like nihilism, but mostly because I understood you to reject it as well, and so am curious about the implications.

(1) *Ethical.* The psalm itself is very strong in its cursing, extending the curse beyond the enemy to the enemy's mother, wife, and children. I don't intend to enter into "dueling exegesis," so my response will be only to the implications of your argument and not to whether or not the text tends to justify your reading. You use two examples to illustrate the consequences of the curse: a concentration camp and homelessness. The implication is that the enemy and those near and dear to the enemy should be subjected to the absolute extremities of physical, emotional, spiritual, and social degradation and destruction; that is, that revenge, or punishment, or destruction of evil is not enough. The only thing that will satisfy this rage is what Simone Weil calls "affliction," the spiritual destruction of the other.[2]

Further, this "affliction" must be extended not only to the enemy, but to the enemy's loved ones. The use of torture, rape, imprisonment of family members of the enemy is a very common practice around the world—What could hurt someone more than watching one's wife being brutally raped? What could hurt a parent more than watching and listening as electric shocks or whips or fire are applied to the body of one's three-year-old daughter?—In reducing the enemy to an object deserving punishment, the inclusion of the family is important, since this inclusion assaults the enemy in a way that even fairly extreme sorts of individual punishment cannot.

There are two aspects of this interpretation of the curse that look ethically nihilistic to me. The first involves the desire that the enemy experience *unlimited suffering.* The desire for "affliction," rather than punishment or even suffering, seems to go beyond a vision of justice. Any view that cannot restrain the suffering and humiliation which might constitute "just deserts" or revenge seems to me to be chaotic rather than ethical. The inability to see that, for example, concentration camps are *intrinsically* wrong, and not only wrong when I (or my family or my people) are their victims, amounts to a fundamental inability to tell right from wrong, good from evil, and is therefore a kind of ethical nihilism. Such a view seems to suggest that there is no real difference between good and evil, right and wrong, other than whether or not I am experiencing it. You seem to be saying that the camps are wrong when I suffer in them, but their wrongness comes from the fact that I am suffering and not from the fact that "affliction" and the desire to "afflict" others is in itself wrong and evil.

The second aspect of the analysis that looks ethically nihilistic is the *inclusion of the family* in the (unlimited) suffering one desires for the enemy. It would seem that the inability to distinguish evildoers from non-evildoers, or

2 Simone Weil, "Love of God and Affliction," *Simone Weil Reader,* ed. G. Panichas (Mt. Kisco, N.Y.: Moyer Bell Limited, 1977).

the guilty from the innocent, would again indicate a fundamental ethical nihilism. I would think that any self-respecting ethical system would have to be able to tell the difference between the punishment of wrongdoers and the gratuitous infliction of suffering and humiliation—hunger, torture, homelessness—upon children. In other words, you are describing a situation in which the distinctions between right and wrong, good and evil, and innocence and guilt have no role to play; they are meaningless. The only good is the (sadistic) good of the "affliction" of the enemy and the enemy's family. This looks like ethical nihilism to me.

(2) *Spiritual.* The second step of the argument is to reject the possibility that the psalm is an emotion, a feeling of rage that, like all feelings, passes; that, like all emotions, is accompanied or modified by other emotions; and that, also like all emotions, can become irrational, or excessive, or out of balance. The desire for the enemy's unlimited suffering is not just a temporary aberration or a dark side of human consciousness; it is a religious *disposition,* in your interpretation. I do not know exactly how you mean this, but I am familiar with the literature on religious dispositions. Disposition is distinguished from feeling, doing, and knowing as a fundamental orientation for the whole person. Through this enduring disposition, the person encounters, and interprets, and responds to the world. Disposition integrates disparate feelings, ideas, actions, obligations, and experiences into a cohesive world of meaning. A religious disposition occurs when this interior, enduring orientation is ordered toward God and so reflects, however partially, the effects of redemption and liberation. Edwards, for instance, described the central religious affection as love, as consent to being, as true virtue, etc.

Your argument is that rage in the sense of an unrestrained desire for innocent and guilty suffering is *not* a passing emotion, *nor* a pathology human beings are capable of, but a fundamental orientation of the religious person toward the world. The organizing principle of such a self is not only anger or a bad temper, not a consuming desire for justice or revenge, not even a localized racism or sexism or an excessive tendency toward violence. The organizing principle of such a self is self-righteous sadism. The self, having itself been the victim of unjust suffering, now is ordered toward the world on the basis of this principle. Unjust suffering is the only reality, first because the person suffered unjustly, and second (and consequently) as the unlimited right of the victim. This does not look to me like a religious disposition; it looks like either pathology or evil.

That a victim of unjust suffering would (and should) be angry, even enraged, is understandable; that such a victim would organize his or her world around the experience of such suffering in one way or another is also a common enough occurrence—and perfectly understandable; that victims of brutality and betrayal would want revenge is not nihilistic, but an aspect of psychological health and even justice. It may be that this enraged and unrestrained desire for a kind of justice is what the psalm is about. But that is not what you seem to be describing. You seem to be disclosing a transition from innocent or unjust suffering and betrayal to rage and a (healthy) desire for justice and, then, to a pathological disruption of the self in which no reality other than an endless repetition of the cycle of violence and affliction can exist. Healthy anger and desire for justice are transformed into a situation in which the human being becomes incapable of anything but suffering and inflicting suffering; that is, into a world which has no reality beyond this cycle of unjust suffering and unlimited sadistic venting of the pain and rage that betrayal caused. This becomes the world, reality. Because rage in this sense is the way the world is constituted—and not something passing or partial—you describe it as a disposition rather than an emotion or catharsis.

You say over and over again that the abuser is the abused and that the abused is the abuser. This is certainly the case when one looks at patterns of family violence. That you are describing a real psychological and empirical situation can hardly be denied. You seem to be describing the broken and pathological world of a victim of abuse who has not found redemption or healing. The self is experienced as the one betrayed and hurt; the other is experienced as the object of rage, the one deserving punishment and affliction. Maybe it is still the brokenness of pathology rather than sin or evil, but in either case the nightmare world of a person broken in this way is not the same thing as a religious disposition. The inability to distinguish between a religious disposition and the pathological cycle of abuse appears to me to be a form of spiritual nihilism.

(3) *Theological.* In one sense you are right in saying that the portrayal of God as an abusive father is a reading across the text. Psalm 109 itself understands God as the power who will justify the betrayed and suffering victim. God is the one place or power to turn to in a world in which neither love nor hope, nor justice, has any efficacy. In the psalm, this mitigates the excessiveness of the rage. However extreme the suffering and the rage of the psalmist, a power remains that is understood to be just, to be characterized by steadfast love—and therefore there is a reality that stands over against the victim's experience. This power calls into question the world of betrayal, violence, and helplessness. These are not the final words for the psalmist, and so rage is not the final word, destruction is not the final word. While you have described a world in which there is no other reality even to appeal to, for the psalmist the nightmare of brokenness is not absolute. In this sense, you are reading across the text, and introducing a picture of the world very different from the picture presented by the text.

In another sense, you are not so much reading across the text as you are projecting onto that other reality the rage and violence which the psalmist feels. The effect of this is that the nihilism of the ethical realm and the nihilism of the spiritual realm come to absorb also the theological realm. Not only are unjust suffering, betrayal, and violence the dialectic of the person's own experience; they are the ultimate principles of reality. The pattern of abused and abuser, of being the victim of unjust suffering and then the perpetrator of unjust suffering, is a microcosm of the divine reality, of reality itself.

Any way of talking about God will, of course, be inadequate to its subject matter. I agree with you that a simple moralism projected onto God is not rich enough and that compassion is not an adequate cipher or paradigm of God.[3] There is a good deal of plurality in the religious traditions in their attempts to evoke something of the divine reality—kings, judges, lovers, unmoved movers, being itself, beyond being and nonbeing, the *Urgrund,* the Master of the Universe, and so on. All inadequate. But you are doing something different from adding to this plethora of images or concepts, or from denying the adequacy of ethical attributes. Just as in ethics you describe not a different form of ethics but an anti-ethics, and just as you describe not a different form of spirituality but the antithesis to religious dispositions, so here you do not describe a different idea of God but an un-God. Your ultimate power or reality is not ineffable, "my thoughts are not your thoughts." This power is not mysterious at all; it is perfectly clear what sort of power this is. It is the power of the sadist and the traitor. The nightmare of the abused child is not a bad dream, not even an aberration caused by a sick or wicked parent; it is the proper and true expression of divine power and reality.

One wakes from the nightmare to unjust suffering, violence, and betrayal and finds no one to pray to: "but thou, O God my Lord, deal on my behalf for thy name's sake; because thy steadfast love is good, deliver me!" Awakening, one finds that the hope, the other reality, the power of deliverance—the one to hold one and protect one from the nightmare—this one is the Abuser. One looks outside the nightmare world, the un-world of the concentration camps, betrayal, and abuse for something which might say no to it all, to provide an ethic other than violence and more violence, a disposition other than rage and sadism. But the nightmare is the only reality. There is no vindication; there is at best participation in ultimate reality, viz., the desire for suffering, abuse, degradation, etc. Nothing else exists—sadism and betrayal are the principles of the universe. This is the ultimate nightmare. One dreams of being hurt and pursued, and in terror, one wakes up and turns to the person next to one in bed for comfort and sees that it is the one who was tormenting you in the dream. This looks to me like the ultimate form of nihilism, because it projects the emptiness of despair and the cruelty of sadism onto God, and makes them the ultimate principles of reality.

Perhaps I am pushing this to logical conclusions that you may or may not intend. It seems, though, that what you have written is not just provocative

---

[3] [See Professor W. Farley's book, *Tragic Vision and Divine Compassion: A Contemporary Theodicy* (Louisville, Ky.: Westminster/John Knox Press, 1990).]

or conflictual, but is a serious prayer for an un-world in which one prays to God who is the un-God, the deification and justification of the lust for humiliation and torment.

Wendy

April 13, 1989

Dear Wendy,

Yes, this is more challenging and even more "nihilistic" than *Erring,* partly (to me as a Jew) because of its form as a commentary on Psalms and partly because of its ethics, spirituality, and theology.

On ethical nihilism: Your assumption is that ethics is the process of reasoned regulation of human interchange and that, therefore, that which is unreasoned and unregulated, like rage, is not ethical. I wonder about the scriptural and psychological basis for that. Scripturally, God does choose and does avenge God's chosen. Psychologically, people outside western culture do choose and avenge their own blood. Even westerners, in the depths of their psyches, do the same, if Freud is right.

What, then, is ethics where it is *not* reasoned regulation of human affairs? That is the question that puzzles and haunts me. Speaking from out of Scripture and depth psychology, I say that ethics is a function of blood loyalty, of tribal kinship, of fierce attachments. Hence, right and wrong are defined by blood loyalty. I know that westerners think that this is "primitive" and needs to be transcended by reasoned regulation. I know that Christians think that Christianity transcends this by self-sacrificing love (discounting the passages for punishing the wicked and the doctrines of eternal damnation, etc.). But I wonder whether these sublimations of tribal rightness-wrongness, these purifications of blood loyalty, are correct. I wonder whether the converse is not true: that the original definitions are what God revealed to us as God's will, because they are truer to our deepest natures.

I do not want to say that *only* blood loyalty can serve as a basis for ethics (nor does Scripture) but I do not wish to deny, transcend, or sublimate it either. *That* is what I am trying to do in Psalm 109, and why I won't do a prophetic (as understood by the west) critique. Just what *do* the passages calling for vengeance mean, if they *are* within the will of God?

On spiritual nihilism: Your assumption is that a disposition must be salvational, that is, good, redemptive; otherwise, the experience must be transitory. That is, in my mind, an error in the literature, and that is what I am trying to correct. The scholars you derive this from simply did not take the dark side of personhood as seriously as they did the good side. If I am right, what would be a *dark disposition?* I think you have identified it correctly, following the psalmist, as self-righteous sadism, a spiritual world that is without redemption. The dark night of the mystics is not a phase of experience; it is an aspect of being. So is rage.

Violence is an inherent part of religious anthropology. As further evidence, I adduce Pss. 58:7–12; 59:11; 69:23–29; 74:22; and 79:6–12; and the liturgy for vengeance; and the closing lines of holocaust responsa which call for vengeance. With all this evidence, I cannot but believe that a curse is performative language — that is, that it is fully done, fully prayed, and fully intended to bring about fully real results. It is not expressive, cathartic; though it is not physical action either. It is part of the heart-to-Heart, depth-to-Depth, face-to-Face dialogue we have with God; just as God's irrational anger with us is part of that dialogue. We cope; God copes; together, without severing the bond.

Other cultures recognize this too. Our colleague, Thee Smith, has provided me with a parallel quotation:

> Thar's a day a-comin'! Thar's a day a-comin'! . . . Oh Lor'! gib me de pleasure ob livin' till dat day, when I shall see white folks shot down like de wolves when dey come hongry out o' de woods.[4]

And a student provided me with the following from the holocaust literature written by a woman survivor, Sonja Milner:

> The [Russian] soldiers fell upon the Germans and began to rape the young girls, the women and the children. Some ten or twenty fell upon a little girl and raped her. . . . We watched and beamed with satisfaction. We were finally being avenged. . . . We were entitled to that satisfaction. It was a legitimate reaction, a natural all-too-human response on our part.[5]

I agree that there is something cruel about this "justice," but I do not want to deny it as a culturally and religiously sanctioned emotional attitude, as an "affection," though not one we live with (or would want to live with) all the time.

On theological nihilism: Yes, the counter-reading is that in the post-holocaust world, there is un-world and un-God. And yes, this is deconstruction and it is nihilistic. *But:* (1) Don't we all share that nightmare? Doesn't that nihilism hover around the consciousness of each of us, even the most doggedly optimistic? It does for me, as well as for many others. (2) It is not "un-world" and "un-God"; it *is* world and it *is* God. The concentration camps are not un-world, but world. "Deliver me" is a call for revenge, not for freedom from revenge. "Save me" is a call for "affliction," not for freedom from fantasy. Ultimately, I think Brueggemann is wrong on the *sensus literalis*.[6] The psalmist does not hand over or submit his vengeance to God knowing that God won't

---

[4] A. Raboteau, *Slave Religion* (Oxford: Oxford University Press, 1978), p. 3.

[5] A. Roiphe, *A Season for Healing: Reflections on the Holocaust* (New York: Summit Books, 1988), pp. 25–26.

[6] W. Brueggemann, *The Message of Psalms* (Minneapolis: Augsburg Publishing House, 1984).

act. He asks for, indeed demands, vengeful action in the name of blood loyalty
and loyal devotion and merit. I don't think I am "projecting," as you suggest,
but simply reading. This is all to say that, while for most western readers,
I appear in "Con-verses" to be cross-reading the text, I am really reading it
straight when I say that un-God is God.

God *is* a sadist / abusing parent in Jewish and Christian tradition—God does
stand by while God's son is whipped and crucified, even though God is
empowered! See also Leviticus 26 and Deuteronomy 28. And we, too, are
sadists / abusers, because God and we are in one image. *But* neither God nor
we are like that *always,* which is why God and we have not destroyed one
another (yet). We always have each other to react with, against: "Wipe me,
then, from Your book." This is also the way it is in real life: We restrain one
another, as well as support one another; we forge a common existence. Left
on God's own, God would have destroyed the Jewish people; left on his own,
so would Abraham. Left on God's own, God would have destroyed the whole
world at the flood. But we are not alone (Heschel), and neither is God.
Fortunately, in all marriages, it is very rare that both partners are "down," are
en-raged, at the same time. Granted then, that there are healing processes
(which I explicate in Psalm 27), Psalm 109 deals with the terror of rage in
a non-western—but scriptural and depth-psychological—ethical, spiritual, and
theological context.

Shalom, David

May 26, 1989

David,

One of the principles of deconstruction and of pluralism is that the truth
is elusive; it can be sought but never possessed. No single insight or perspective is final or complete. I have serious criticism of the relativistic turn this
argument can take, but the claim itself seems important. It is like Kierkegaard
(following Schelling) humbly choosing the left hand, that is, the pursuit of
truth rather than truth itself. I agree that theology is oriented toward the truth
and it is important to have the courage to say what we see. I like the confidence and vitality of, say, Thomas Aquinas, who is not afraid to ask anything.
This is in contrast to fundamentalists who have heart failure at the prospect
of subjecting ideas and texts to real criticism and reflection. Still, I find your
insistence that it is, in some literal and unambiguous way, *true* that God is
an abusive father rather disturbing on two grounds.

First, theologically, *how is it that any attribute is univocally applied to God?*
Even to apply a category like time is problematic. But to say that God *is* an
abusive male looks to me like the crudest form of anthropomorphism, which
projects a very limited and localized experience onto divine being. It is an

unsophisticated form of idolatry to take some small portion of human experience and absolutize it, grant it divine status—and to do so unambiguously, literally. Why do abusive men have divine status? Why should this claim be any more persuasive than to say that God is a black, or that God is white, or that God is a lesbian, or that God is a lion, or a bad tempered sensualist that lives on top of Mount Olympus? How is it that this kind of claim avoids violating the second commandment?

Second and more important, *religiously, I can't imagine worshiping an abusive father.* Psychologically, it is neurotic and ethically it is immoral. What happens, psychologically, to someone who is not only victimized and abused, but somehow must love the one who tortures her or him? I recently read an essay from the 1950s by Levinas, who lost his entire family to the Nazis. He describes the power of tyranny as a power which can not only make people obey orders or can kill people, but can create a servile soul. "Tyranny," he writes,

> can exterminate in the tyrannized soul even the very capacity to be struck, that is, even the ability to obey on command. True heteronomy begins when obedience ceases to be obedient consciousness and becomes an inclination. The supreme violence is that supreme gentleness. To have a servile soul is to be incapable of being jarred. . . . The love for the master fills the soul to such an extent that the soul no longer takes its distances. Fear fills the soul to such an extent that one no longer sees it, but sees from its perspective. That one can create a servile soul is not only the most painful experience of modern man [*sic*], but perhaps the very refutation of human freedom.[7]

You seem to be describing precisely this phenomenon, when the soul is tyrannized by an utterly cruel power and becomes servile in its neurotic love for what abuses it. If it were true that God were an abusive father, the only psychologically, religiously, and morally adequate response would be rebellion *à la* "Prometheus Bound," *The Plague,* and "Rebellion" in *The Brothers Karamazov.* The worship of evil is antithetical to both religion and ethics. To worship one's abuser is psychologically self-destructive. I think that it is also very dangerous to try to claim religious justification for the worship of violence, injustice, and irrational cruelty. How would it be possible to be critical of *any* cruelty, or injustice, or persecution if it is a divine principle? What right does the psalmist have to complain about unjust treatment, if such injustice is sanctioned by God? How can one respond even to the holocaust as an *ethical* problem, if it too is sanctioned by God? You are describing a completely chaotic worldview which resembles not the heretics as much as the superorthodoxy of Khomeiny.

You are like someone counseling the abused wife to be a good, obedient wife and to take her beatings passively. You are defending the abusing parent,

---

[7] E. Levinas, *Collected Philosophical Papers,* trans. A. Lingis (Dordrecht: Martinus Nijhoff, 1987), p. 16.

or husband, and forcing the victim to love the person who degrades and tortures him or her. This does not look to me like very good cathartic psychotherapy, and therefore it is a violation of your principle of identity between good (or bad) psychology and theology. It looks like a radicalization of the problem.

To put it differently: It is possible that the victim can become so destroyed by suffering that the capacity to resist, even psychologically or spiritually, is crippled. It is possible for victims to become the tyrant's accomplice in their own destruction.

> Another effect of affliction is, little by little, to make the soul its accomplice, by injecting a poison of inertia into it. . . . This complicity impedes all the efforts he [*sic*] might make to improve his lot; it goes so far as to prevent him from seeking a way of deliverance, sometimes to the point of preventing him from wishing for deliverance. . . . It is as though affliction had established itself in him like a parasite and were directing him to suit its own purposes. . . .[8]

Worship of the abusive father god looks to me like just this kind of servility or complicity. It is a refusal to resist evil or destruction. It is the refusal even to want something other than evil, humiliation, injustice, and cruelty. It is a kind of neurosis, in which one seeks out and clings to the very thing that tortures and destroys oneself. I think it is important to try to resist the temptation of confusing neurosis with prophetic theology.

Wendy

June 2–4, 1989

Dear Wendy,

On the matter of the attributes of God: Attributes of God are language we—theologians, exegetes, poets, liturgists—use about God. They are rooted in the tradition of how God speaks of Godself and in the accumulated vocabulary of later thinkers. All such words are used ambiguously (equivocally); that is, we use them of God in the usual meaning in human speech but with the reservation that they do not apply to God fully because God is beyond description. You know the medieval history of this problem as well as I do. The alternatives of complete univocity or no language at all are unacceptable to me.

Working within the ambiguity of the language of such texts as Psalms 44 and 109, plus zoharic mysticism and a theology of image rooted in psychology, I accept that we can use even ethically immoral language and use it as an attribute of God. That is rather heretical, but not incoherent, and not neurotic or idolatrous. To put it another way, if one can attribute goodness to God, there is no grammatical reason for not attributing abusiveness to God.

---

[8] Weil, "Love of God and Affliction," p. 443.

On the matter of worshiping an abusive God: It is not quite fair of me to speak of how one deals with an abusive parent (father or mother, and there are abusive mothers) because I am not a physically or sexually abused child; nor do I know the literature well enough to claim professional competence. Further, I cannot speak about abusing spouses of either sex, for lack of experience and expertise. Nonetheless, having broached the possibility, I need to respond to it. And there is a sense in which each of us is "abused," that is, improperly or inadequately loved, even verbally or psychologically abused. Here, unfortunately, I can talk with some competence, both as an abused child and as an abusing parent.

My basic position is as follows: In all cases of abuse, there must be a stance of protest / rebellion. However, *except in cases where the victim is in danger of life and limb*, parent–child abuse (unlike spouse abuse) should be open to a tolerance on the part of the victim. I say this because respecting parents is both a psychological and an ethical value not to be broken lightly although fully justified when real self-defense requires it. The vertical bond of blood is not like other relationships, as we know and as the tradition teaches. I say this too because I do not believe that one can ever really heal such a broken relationship. One learns to cope, to live with, a parent's faults, perhaps even with a parent's evils. (I have no such compunctions about spousal relationships, which start as voluntary and should always remain such.)

God, as Parent, is subject to the same rules. We recognize that God's action is sometimes evil. We protest that vigorously. But we do not sever the relationship. I agree that we could not worship an evil or an abusive God, but God, in a theology of image rooted in personalist language, like real people including ourselves, is not always abusive. Therefore, we protest *and* worship God, as indeed we resist *and* respect our parents even if they are psychologically and verbally abusive because they are not only abusive. I think that this is what P/parenting, chosenness, and covenant mean. I admit, though, that this is a far cry from the holocaust and from the physically and sexually abusive parent, and I need to give this more thought.

In any case, I am not *forcing* the victim to worship an abusive God or to respect an abusive parent. I am only saying that, if one rejects severing the relationship, one must cope with parent and with God. And indeed one *must* not do either of these things: one can ignore or repress the problem, or one can go into a state of permanent anger/protest. I suspect you favor the last since it is more prophetic/social gospel, but even prophetic critics make a certain peace with society and its ambiguities. The psalmists of 44 and 109 (and there are many others) continue to worship, even when they put the blame squarely on the shoulders of God. Jesus, too, made peace with the Father who was about to crucify him.

Shalom, David

June 10, 1989

David,

I know some abused children and know of abused children. My mother directed a residence for abused adolescent girls for about ten years, and my sister has worked on behalf of abused and neglected children and volunteers at a shelter for battered women. The damage and deep, terrible pain that abusive relationships cause strikes me as one of the most terrible kinds of suffering that can assault a human being. If it is bad enough, it can cripple and destroy a child (or adult). The self-hatred and guilt which a criminal should feel, but usually doesn't, is taken into the abused child's own soul and poisons her or him throughout his or her whole life. The natural desire to love and be loved is often twisted and becomes a self-destructive drive. Battered children often seek out relationships that will continue to hurt and humiliate them—and are unable to get out of this cycle. It is awful to see the damage that abuse does to a person and to see how difficult it is for such a person to find real healing—in their own person, let alone by being reconciled with the person who has hurt them. The metaphor of abuse strikes a very deep chord in me, since I have had the occasion to see it in people around me and to listen to the battle stories of my mother and sister. It's very hard for me to translate these experiences into the divine life.

Wendy

On Healing

May 26, 1989

David,

Your psalm of healing doesn't really take on the angry psalms, let alone the abusive father. It seems to me to be a mild reconciliation of moderate evil. There is healing because you do not acknowledge the brokenness. You do not take seriously your own claims about God, about anger, abuse, etc. You just lay them side by side: "I am unfairly and cruelly abused by history, by my enemy, and by my father-God" lies quietly next to "be confident in God, remember the promises, strengthen the relationship, etc." How or why would one be confident in an abusive father? Your multivalency—perhaps, esotericism—has become an excuse for not taking your work seriously.

I think that part of the power of this book is the unflinching way it takes on the seriousness of the problem of evil, suffering, and victimization. It does what few religious reflections do, and that is to place anger at the heart of the response to evil. But the ideas become incoherent at some points, especially in the claim that God is an abusive father. I think this incoherence undermines rather than strengthens or radicalizes your reflections. I understand that you don't want to give that idea up, but I wonder if the reflections on healing could take on the seriousness of Psalms 44 and 109 more thoroughly?

Wendy

June 2–4, 1989

Dear Wendy,

You are correct that "I am abused by my Father-God" lies quietly next to "be confident in God." I am disturbed by that fact; it was your first criticism many months ago. I too wonder whether this is not a compartmentalization or a psychological (and therefore, theological) evasion. You are right that I need to engage the anger of Psalms 44 and 109 more directly.

Upon reflection, I do not think my taking this side-by-side position is lack of courage or intellect; I have proved myself in many situations in these matters. It may be because, deep down, I am not sure we can do better, psychologically and hence, theologically. Coping means living with contradictions. It means alternating between moral outrage and piety. The path of life is not a "righteous path"; it is a meandering, erratic movement toward a vision of how things ought to be. Hence, it can be true that I am abused, that I am enraged, that I protest—and that I nonetheless love the *non*-abusing dimensions of my p/Parent, that I act piously, in respect and in love, toward that p/Parent. I don't think I know any other way to be—as a person, as a child, and as a parent looking to children. I don't think all this is neurotic, or more so than any other "solution" to the human condition, though I admit it is rooted in an understanding of abuse that is not fully horrible.

Shalom, David

Beth's Psalm

Psalm 27

*as understood by a Christian woman, age twenty-one,
who was raped at sixteen
and who has struggled to heal*[1]

the Lord is my light and my deliverance

"The Lord is my light" — the burning ball of fire that lifts me; the vision and the joy, the shimmering that I see in the distance; and I smile because I know it is there for me.

"The Lord is also my deliverance" — "Our Father who art in heaven hallowed be thy name . . . deliver us from evil." Take me away, surround me with light and love; protect me as I do your will.

"The Lord is my light and my deliverance" — This is the old text. When they broke in, stripped me of my clothes and my power, and said, "Do you want to fuck, white bitch," the text burned right before my eyes.

of whom am I afraid

that's easy.

I am afraid of the men with guns,

of the men who hate and destroy

---

[1] This interpretation of Psalm 27 contains language that may seem offensive. It is my strong feeling that those of us in the helping professions, particularly those of us who represent religious life, owe it to the victims of violence to allow survivors to speak in their own sometimes very anguished terms; we must listen and hear, even when their anger is offensive; and we must affirm the language of their pain. Accordingly, I have left this text largely untouched. [Ed. note]

because they have nothing better to do on a Saturday night.

What a stupid question to ask.

the Lord is the fortress of my life

The strong structure, the shell. I fill in the inside and I am safe there. But the walls fall down around me and I scream in horror, "Wait! Where are you going? Why did you fall?"

God, the world looks different now. I am just standing here, there is nothing to lean on, there is nothing around me. . . . Why did you leave me, God? Why did you let them do it? I was not doing anything wrong, I was being good. I was just a little girl.

whom do I fear

anyone, I have no walls, no protection, no structure. I am just standing amidst rubble. What do you mean, "Whom do I fear?" Everyone.

when evildoers draw near to me in war, to gorge my flesh . . . my heart will not be afraid

"My heart will not be afraid" — this does not make any sense. Evildoers are going to *gorge my flesh;* they are going to rip, tear, eat, puncture, burn my tender flesh with knives, guns, with violent words — and my heart is *not* going to be afraid? If it beats, it fears. Even shock does not totally numb.

Evildoers *did* gorge my flesh. And my heart, my soul, my mind, my body, my spirit all were afraid. All trembled, shook, and looked straight into the eyes of two men who promised to "fuckin' kill me" if I didn't do what they said.

Only people who have never seen, who don't know, can listen to the text as it is because, if you *know,* you know it is not true.

I have asked but one thing of the Lord . . . that He conceal me in his sukka on the day of evil

"I have asked but one thing of the Lord" — that he keep his promises! If you say you are my protector, then protect me. If you cannot protect me, at least tell me so. Don't pretend you can conceal me, protect me, or shield me. Don't pretend to be a rock or a shepherd. Don't pretend to have a sukka.

"I have asked but one thing of the Lord" — please heal me, and please don't let that ever happen to anyone else again. On the day of evil, I was not concealed in a sukka, whatever that is. . . . I was an open target. I was a lamb, and the shepherd was asleep.

Hey Lord, remember the Psalm, I think it is 23, "The Lord is Your Shepherd, You Shall Not Want?"

Well your lamb was mutilated.
And I did / do want.
I screamed
If you are real, God,
come now
and get these monsters off of me.
I did want, I prayed
I want you here
I want to live
I want to die and I want you to hold
me in your loving presence
I want you to deliver me from
this horror and violence.
I want you to be the shepherd.
Wake the hell up
and see me!

I am crumbled by the side of the bed, can you see me?
I have been stripped of my clothes

my innocence, my virginity.
Weren't / aren't you watching??

I shall sing and chant to the Lord
Hear my voice, O Lord.
I call.
Be gracious unto me and answer me.

Where were you???
Where were you???
Where were you!!!

This will be my chant,
where were you when I needed you?
They said they wanted money, a television, and me;
all they got was me.
Where were you?

I sure was calling. Either you heard my voice and did not / could not answer, or you cannot even hear me. Either way, I was betrayed and left alone, unprotected.

I do seek your Face . . . hide not Your Face from me

It is *my* choice now, whether or not to seek your face.

NOW I CAN SEE YOUR FACE. IT IS BRUISED AND SCARRED.

YOU ARE NOT SMILING.

Your face is battered!

Maybe the help you can give is limited. That is not your fault.

But it is the nun's fault for teaching me wrong.

do not forsake me and do not abandon me

These are your words to *me*. Now I understand.

You know that you let me down and now you are saying: don't leave me, give me another chance, stick with me. Should I?

Can you play a part in the healing of something that you let happen? Should I even let you?

Goddamn, after all the hell I have been through on this earth that you created and after all of the broken promises and the bullshit about tents and rocks and shepherds . . . after all of that, I am supposed to yearn for / turn to you?

do not give me over to the will of my tormentors

You already did.

> maybe you cried too . . .

Were it not for the Face[2] I would be certain that I would see the goodness of the Lord in the land of life . . .

I have seen your battered and bruised face.

I know what the world is like.

But will this prevent me from seeing the goodness in the land of life? That is the constant struggle.

That is, I think, what healing is about.

---

[2] Lit., "fact." [Ed. note]

Healing

An interesting word. Over the years I have found out that it is hard to do. It takes work. Healing is work and patience. After I was raped, I decided to "put it behind me." I did that for three years and I discovered that healing is not ignoring. You can't forget a rape. As I began therapy I learned that you also can't make sense of it, or resolve it, or forgive it, and you definitely can't "make the best of it." God, I hate that one. What you can do is heal from it, whatever that means.

For years I hurt deep inside and I thought there was no way to fix the hurt. My world had been crushed. Whenever I saw little girls, I wondered what asshole would come along and ruin them. I felt emotionally ruined. I knew. I knew what horror and hate were. The transition from basketball and cheerleading to horror and hate happened in one split second. When I turned the corner and I saw them and they said, "Oh, look what we found . . . ," I grew up. And I have resented it ever since.

Healing does not mean forgetting that it happened, or ever thinking that it was / is all right. I think that healing means looking deep into it, right into its face, and then moving through it to the other side.

I think now that I am on the road to healing because I finally know that I will be ok. For years I would have told you that I was going to be ok, but that would have been my head talking and not my heart. I never stopped functioning, but I stopped believing it was worth it. The humor and the joy in life were clouded by the sadness. I could not really love because I hurt so much. What a wonderful thing those men took from me . . . the ability to love innocently, with the knowledge and belief that I was protected. The gift of childhood — everyone must lose it, but I lost it violently: through pain and tears and shock and loneliness. And I do not understand why.

I had been taught that God had a "plan" for everyone; well, if this was part of the plan, then I hated and resented God. I stopped going to church because I knew that the Bible was a lie. God had been put to the test and he had failed miserably. Also, I started to really hate the whole idea of Jesus. I really resent Jesus because I think he should have said, "Hell no! I am not going to hang bloody on that cross. What good will that do? That is the stupidest idea I have ever heard of." But instead he said, "Why me, Lord?" and then, "Ok, Lord, I will do it." He said, "Ok, I will suffer and it will be good." Yuk!

Once I called my preacher and I asked, "How exactly did Jesus' suffering save us from sin?" His answer, of course, was, "Faith tells us so." The idea that God would ask someone he loved to suffer revolted me, and no one could give me an acceptable reason for why it had to happen. Well, I don't think suffering is good. I don't see that it does any good. And I hate the idea of a sacrificial lamb. Was that what happened to me? Was I sacrificed for some reason?

I don't think that the rape of a child, the rape of me, is good — in any sense of the word; and I resent like hell the people who imply that, in some way, it will be good. People at the church have said, "Well, at least it will make her stronger." That infuriates me. Suffering was *not* good.

Though the suffering Jesus revolts me (I cannot even take communion anymore because the idea of Jesus giving his flesh for us to eat makes me sick), I cannot throw out my religion completely either. Spirituality has always been a part of my life and I want it to be part of my life again. But I can't accept the things I used to believe in wholeheartedly. I am going to have to rework my image of God, of the world, and of God's involvement in the world.

I cannot forget or forgive what it felt like to be abandoned by my shepherd. I think I now need to heal spiritually. And I am not sure I know what that means. So I read Wiesel and I try to understand how he still loves and trusts God after the holocaust. I think, in some ways, we are on the same journey.

Beth's Healing Psalm

abandonment.
I am cold. I am alone. I am hurt.
Why??
If Jesus wants to be the sacrificial lamb
FINE
but I don't want it.
I want to be left whole
and right now I am being ripped and torn . . .
I do not understand and I am mad as hell.
anger. confusion. betrayal.
my trust is stripped and crushed.

And yet, the deep dark green of the trees
And yet, the running mountain water
And yet, the bliss of trusting again, of running through sprinklers
on a summer day, laughing and kissing and feeling complete.
A tear.
A promise.
Yes, Lord, I will still participate in
the PROCESS.

                                                                    Beth
                                                                July 1990

CON-TEMPLATION

CHAPTER 15

Prologue

To con-template is to go into the temple together, to divine, to ponder collectively. The richness of the psalms and re-sponses requires that we go into the divine Presence together to ponder the meaning of what we have learned. The multivalent reading of the psalms and re-sponses obligates us to consider what we have read and to reflect on what we have felt and thought, and then to look upon the Face of God together.

Theo-logy is a speaking about God; it is a con-templative act; it brings us into the Presence of God. The question, then, becomes: In view of the facts of historical and personal abuse, how can one live in faithfulness to God? How can adult survivors of child abuse have faith in God? How can Jews who have survived the holocaust have faith in God? And how can those of us who identify with and share the anguish of survivors have faith in God? How, indeed, can one have faith in God in a post-holocaust, abuse-sensitive world? Facing God, without flinching, is the task of theology. In this time, in this place, these questions are of the essence.

After considering the texts, there is a need to bring together some of the thoughts engaged in this book, to weave the threads into a fabric, even if the fabric is motley.

In "The Abusing God," I begin by setting forth the rules of interpretation I use; I then cite some of the scriptural texts that clearly portray God as an abusing person; and I close by addressing forthrightly abusiveness as an attribute of God.

In "Facing the Abusing God," I appeal to the tradition of the theology of protest and suggest distrust and challenge as appropriate religious affections; I then offer a new form of religious healing rooted in psychotherapeutic healing; and I close by addressing several psychological and theological problems that this study has generated.

Finally, in "Addressing the Abusing God," I reformulate the theological stance before the abusing God; I then present five psalms; and I close by offering several prayers. Some of these prayers suggest changes in the traditional Jewish liturgy, because liturgy is of the essence of traditional Jewish relatedness to God; some are new. All attempt to em-body the theology of protest.

CHAPTER 16

The Abusing God

Standing In-Between

THE INTERPRETER (Latin *interpres*) is one who stands between the offers and negotiates the price (Latin *inter+pretium*), or one who mediates between the parties (Latin *inter+partes*). The interpreter is an intermediary, an agent; hence, a spokesperson, ambassador, or one who expounds a text, dream, law, or omen.

Doing theology is an act of inter-pretation, of standing between the text-tradition, God, and the reader or believer. In the period after the holocaust and at a time when we are increasingly aware of child abuse, inter-pretation is critical; it is the ineluctable task of the theologian. For me, there are several rules that guide inter-pretation:

First, in discourse with one another and before God, we must always speak the truth, as best as we know it and can express it. Sometimes the truth is awesome; sometimes it is awful. But we owe it to one another, to the tradition, and to God to speak the truth and to let the truth stand, unmitigated by our anxiety or our dreams — even if the truth is heretical by community standards.

What we perceive as truth changes as we change intellectually, emotionally, and spiritually. The inner resonance by which we judge something to be true is tuned differently at different moments in our lives. Sometimes it is distorted by rage or by joy, by ideas or by fear. "Truth has legs"[1] but "the seal of the Holy One, blessed be God, is truth" (Talmud, Shabbat, 55a) and so we must speak it — even if it is critical and offensive.

---

[1] Aleph-Bet of Rabbi Akiva, second version, *Batei Midrashot*, ed. A. J. Wertheimer (Jerusalem: Ktab Wasepher, 1968), 2:404. See also Maimonides, *Mishne Torah*, "Hilkhot Teshuva," 4:3.

Second, there are ways of disposing of those parts of the tradition with which one does not agree. One can label them a product of their historical period and, therefore, outmoded, primitive, old-fashioned. This is a very seductive method, which allows us freedom to select from the tradition that which we find appealing and to exclude that which we find offensive. But it contains two assumptions. The first is that of historicism — that, when we have identified the conditions in which something was created, we can classify it as belonging to those conditions and not engage it existentially. For example, the patriarchalism of biblical and rabbinic tradition can be contextualized and then existentially dismissed as archaic. The second assumption is that of moral evolution — that the modern period is morally more sophisticated than earlier periods; hence, we can disregard the moral imperatives of earlier times. For example, the eye-for-an-eye teaching can be contextualized and then discarded as morally primitive compared to today's more advanced ethical standards. Both these assumptions are very naïve. Establishing historical situatedness does not absolve us from existential engagement, and the century of Auschwitz and Hiroshima cannot boast of its moral excellence. Both historicism and moral evolutionism are motifs of modern culture that can be wrong and misleading.

By contrast, I choose to engage seriously the texts as we have received them. The tradition expresses this by saying that the book of Psalms was written with the holy spirit and that the inter-pretive tradition embodies the presence of the Shekhina. There is, thus, for me, a certain sacredness to the tradition, *prima facie,* and I try to work within it. For this reason, I reject attempts to "clean up" the psalms, to interpret away the rage, to make them more "pious." The book of Psalms is, for the most part, not prophetic in character, and, hence, the psalmist does not usually exercise a prophetic critique. Rather, the psalmist seeks to bring all of life into the presence of God, in God's fullness and in ours. The book of Psalms, perhaps more than the rest of Scripture-tradition, also deals with the dark side of the human psyche. Human nature has not changed since the biblical period, and the inter-preter must face that fact and deal with the texts which deal with it.

Third, in accepting the tradition as the home within which one does theology, I accept also the rule that one cannot reject God. This is a rule inherent in the inter-pretive process, for to inter-pret is to stand between God and the people, to mediate, to negotiate; not to deny God. In addition, my own personal religious experience forces itself upon me. I suppose that, if I had no awareness at all of the holy and personal presence of God, I would be free to deny God. But, having experienced that Presence, I cannot deny that it exists, nor can I deny that it engages me and that I engage it. The analogy is to psychology: one can be angry with, accuse, repress, or even curse one's father or mother; but one cannot deny her or his existence.

This leads to a paradox. By not denying God and, at the same time, by trying to speak the truth, one is easily drawn into heresy (from the Greek, "to take to oneself"). Herr-esy is the arrogation of critical judgment to oneself, the assertion of the right to dissent. But dissent is always from something, from some order. To make a heretical claim is to dissent from the text, that is, from the community which inter-prets the text, from the tradition which mediates the text. Some of what I say is heretical. But I choose to stay within the tradition, to assert my questions within the language and text of the community, to put forward my critique to God Godself. To do otherwise is to reject God, the tradition, the community, and the integrated self. To do otherwise is to fail at inter-pretation.

Fourth, inter-pretation is the interaction of the personalities of God, the writers of the sacred texts, the readers, and the teachers; hence, inter-pretation is always plurivocal. The reader changes, the inter-preter changes, God too responds to God's creatures. Time adds to the number of those who read and inter-pret.[2] In the end, the text has more than one meaning, the reader reads on more than one level, and the teacher teaches more than one meaning. Text and life itself are multifaceted; inter-pretation is multidimensional. Plurivocity is normal; not hierarchy, not the single authoritative teaching. Creation is an English garden, not a French park. To write theology is to resist the temptation to make authoritative declarations of doctrine, textual interpretation, and religious practice. Rather, to do theology is to preserve the many-sidedness of R/reality. Plurivocity is, thus, not only normal; it is normative, it is what the norm should be.

Because the tradition is, and because we are, plurivocal; because life itself is multifaceted though sequential; the text can only be read *seriatim*, that is, one unit after another. At one moment, we/the text speak of rage; at another, of healing. At one moment, we/the text inter-pret holiness; at another, we inter-pret beauty; at still another, we inter-pret righteous indignation. The Hebrew word for truth, *'emet*, is composed of the first, the middle, and the last letter of the alphabet; it embraces all. Truth does not harmonize or homogenize all; it embraces all, one after the other, *seriatim*. We, seekers of truth, must follow this seal of God if we are to be true to truth, if we are to be real within reality.

These rules guide my standing in-between, my relation, my inter-pretation, my inter-mediacy of the text-tradition. They keep me in touch with my constituencies, who are God, the text, the tradition, the reader, life, and my self. These rules create the rooms in the home within which I think, write, act, and do theology.

---

[2] See H. Fisch, *Poetry with a Purpose: Biblical Poetics and Interpretation* (Bloomington, Ind.: Indiana University Press, 1988; reviewed by me in *Midstream* [August–September 1992], 41–43), pp. 109–115: in reading biblical poetry, the I immediately invokes the I–Thou, which, in turn, immediately invokes the we–Thou.

Abusiveness: The Scriptural Texts

In a remarkable little book entitled *Batter My Heart,* Gracia Fay Ellwood has gathered together most of the violent and abusive passages in the Hebrew and Christian Scriptures.[3] I thought I had read them all but Ellwood showed me some new ones, as well as some old ones in a new light.

God is the abusive husband, who goes through the well-known fight–beat–reconcile cycle.[4] God wounds, heals, and wounds again.

I have crushed, and I shall heal; there is no escape from My hand. (Deut. 32:39)

Who gave Jacob for a spoil and Israel to the robbers? Was it not the Lord, the One against Whom we sinned [in] not wishing to go in His ways and [in] not listening to His Torah? Therefore, God poured His wrath and the fury of battle on him, setting him on fire all around. . . . Now, thus says the Lord, your Creator, Jacob; the One that formed you, Israel: "Do not be afraid for I have redeemed you. When you go through water, I am with you and the rivers will not sweep you away; when you go in the midst of fire, you will not be burned and the flame will not consume you. . . . Since you are precious in my sight and honored, I love you." (Isa. 42:24–43:4)

Awake! Awake! Arise Jerusalem, which has drunk of the cup of the Lord's anger from His hand; you have drunk to the dregs the beaker-cup of poison. . . . Two things have happened to you, who will bemoan your fate?—desolation and destruction, famine and sword—who can comfort you? Your sons have fainted and lie on the streetcorners like antelopes in a net, full of the wrath of the Lord and of the rebuke of God. . . . Thus says your lord and God, the Lord, Who will fight the battle of His people: "Behold, I have taken the cup of poison from your hand, the beaker-cup of My wrath; you shall drink of it no more. I shall put it into the hands of those that afflict you. . . ." (Isa. 51:17–23)

God is also the humiliator of the oppressed woman, the one who strips the unfaithful wife naked and encourages gang rape.

"This is your fate, the portion measured out to you by Me," says the Lord, "because you have forgotten Me and put your trust in that which is false. I shall surely cover your face with your skirts and your personal parts will be seen." (Jer. 13:25–26)

The Lord said: "Since the daughters of Zion have grown haughty, walking with stretched-forth necks and roving eyes, provocative in their steps and wiggling their

---

[3] Gracia Fay Ellwood, *Batter My Heart* (Wallingford, Penn.: Pendle Hill Pamphlets, 1988). The title is taken from John Donne's "Holy Sonnet 14": "Batter my heart, three person'd God; for you / As yet but knock, breathe, shine, and seek to mend. / Take me to you, imprison me, for I / Except you enthrall me shall never be free, / Nor ever chaste, except you ravish me."

[4] This seems not to be the pattern of contemporary abusing Jewish husbands. See M. Scarf, *Battered Jewish Wives: Case Studies in the Response to Rage* (Lewiston, N.Y.: Edwin Mellen Press, 1988; reviewed by me in *Conservative Judaism* 43:3 [Summer 1991], 88–89), chap. 6.

feet, the Lord will smite the head of the daughters of Zion with scabs and will expose their personal parts." (Isa. 3:16–17)

In two searing passages, God sexually abuses Israel, and then takes her back in love.

Now I shall expose her nakedness before the eyes of her lovers; no man can save her from Me. . . . I shall betroth you to Me forever; I shall betroth you to Me with justice and fairness, with grace and love; and I shall betroth you to Me in faithfulness and, then, you will know the Lord. (Hos. 2:12, 21–22)

And I passed by and saw you rolling in your blood and I said: "In your very bloodiness, live! In your very bloodiness, live!" . . . "I spread My garment over you, I covered your nakedness; and I swore a covenant to you," said the Lord, "and you became Mine." . . . Thus says the Lord: "Since your lewdness has been poured forth and you have revealed your personal parts in your carryings-on with your lovers . . . therefore, I shall gather all your lovers to whom you pledged yourself, those whom you loved together with those whom you hated, I shall gather them all against you round about, and I shall expose your private parts to them and they shall see your nakedness. . . . I shall give you over to their power and they shall break your back and shatter your proud points; they shall strip you of your clothes and take your valuable things, and leave you nude and naked. . . . Then I shall have satisfied My wrath against you and My jealousy shall pass from you; I shall be calm, and I will be angry no longer." (Ezek. 16:6–8, 36–42)[5]

And then there are the passages where God curses the people:

"And if you do not listen to Me in this and you go rebelliously with Me, I shall go in the rage of rebellion with you, punishing you sevenfold for your sins. . . . You shall eat the flesh of your boys and consume the bodies of your girls. . . ." As He rejoiced over you to show goodness to you and to multiply you, so will He rejoice over you to destroy you and to annihilate you. . . . "In the morning you will say, 'Would that it were evening' and in the evening you will say, 'Would that it were morning' because of the fear which you will feel in your heart and the sights which you will see with your eyes." (Lev. 26:27, 29; Deut. 28:63, 67)

"Were it not written, it would not be possible to speak thus."[6]

God, Ellwood points out in these passages, is the "nurturing betrayer" or the "betraying nurturer." The picture is not better in the Christian Scriptures.[7]

---

[5] See Fisch, 44, where this passage is referred to as a "romantic tale of the foundling girl who becomes the beautiful bride of her foster father" [sic] (Poetry, p. 44).

[6] Talmud, Sanhedrin 95b, Hulin 91b, Eruvin 22a, etc. Cf. also Gen. 6:7; Job 38:2–4 and 40:8–9 with "Con-verses" at the end of Psalm 109 (p. 156 above).

[7] Ellwood, Batter My Heart, pp. 16, 20–23 (with special attention to Revelation 17–19). Feminist scholarship has been very active in bringing these passages to light. In addition to the works of P. Trible and M. Bal, see now The Women's Bible Commentary, ed. C. Newsom and S. Ringe (Louisville, Ky.: Westminster/John Knox Press, 1992), especially the essay on Jeremiah by K. O'Connor (pp. 169–77) and the naming of the Hebrew word for abuse— 'inna, used to designate

And then there are the historical and personal texts, the searing stories of the abuse of children and women.[8] These are the life texts through which the scriptural texts are read; they are the inter-texts. These inter-texts rupture our ability to read Scripture; they fragment the sanity and the wholeness of our discourse. The effect is devastating, as Sharon Ringe has commented:

> Both the silence of women and their silencing—the contempt in which they are held and the violence with which they are treated—in the Bible mirror the realities of many women's lives. For them, the Bible is experienced as giving the divine stamp of approval to their suffering. Far from bringing healing of the hurt or empowerment toward freedom from oppression, the Bible seems to bless the harm and abuse with which women live and sometimes die.[9]

And then there are the historical and personal texts of the holocaust. They too are life inter-texts, and they too rupture our reading of Scripture and our discourse.[10]

What shall we do with scriptural passages like those cited above? How shall we read them in their twentieth-century context of the holocaust, family abuse, and, God forbid, the destruction of the State of Israel?[11] We must begin, under the seal of truth, by admitting that Scripture does indeed portray God as an abusing person; that God, as agent in our sacred texts, does indeed act abusively; that God, as described in the Bible, acts like an abusing male: husband, father, and lord. Further, we must begin by admitting that, read inter-textually with the lives of abused persons, the impact of such scriptural texts is devastating. Reading parts of the Bible, if one is abused, is traumatic; it is re-victimization. All this is hard to hear; it is difficult to absorb. Our deepest psychological and theological instincts move us to denial; our deepest spiritual sense rebels against this idea: It cannot be so, God cannot be an abusing parent,

---

rape and to characterize Sarah's treatment of Hagar—by T. Frymer-Kensky (p. 55). Feminist scholars have also pointed to the "rhetoric of blame" in the use of women as symbols of wickedness and as metaphors for unacceptable behavior (pp. 162, 170, 179). Van Dijk-Hemmes has put it well, "Why is Israel represented in the image of a faithless wife or harlot rather than in the image of a rapist" (cited in N. Graetz, "The Haftarah Tradition and the Metaphoric Battering of Hosea's Wife," *Conservative Judaism* 45:1 [Fall 1992], 29–42, at n. 24).

[8] The literature on this grows daily. See S. Fraser, *My Father's House: A Memoir of Incest and Healing* (New York: Ticknor & Fields, 1988) for a very powerful literary rendering; and L. J. "Tess" Tessier, "Women Sexually Abused as Children: The Spiritual Consequences," *Second Opinion* 17:3 (January 1992), 11–23, for a good analytic study.

[9] *Women's Bible Commentary,* 4.

[10] Here too the literature is enormous. See the works of Wiesel, Des Pres, and others. See pp. 8–9 above for the rupture that this literature creates.

[11] The most unspoken of the horrors of contemporary Jewish existence is the possibility of the destruction of the State of Israel. This event would evoke unbearable guilt in contemporary Jewry and would provoke an unparalleled loss of faith in God among Jews. For this reason, defense of the State of Israel, not defense of Jewish religion, is the litmus test of loyalty for Jews everywhere.

God cannot be an abusing spouse. Can one not, somehow, put these passages under erasure? Can one not, somehow, inter-pret these passages away?

There are several ways to set about the task of erasure. The traditional way is to speak of our sin and, hence, render God's actions not abusive but justified.[12] I cannot accept, however, that throwing one million children on burning pyres was justified. I cannot accept that, even though the Jewish people was sinful, the holocaust was fitting punishment for the sin. Nor can I accept that years of physical and/or sexual abuse is punishment for the wrongdoing of any child.

Ellwood has another way of erasure. She assembled these passages as an act of piety, for, although she is an academic, she is also a Quaker and admits that, "[b]ecause the final authority for the Friends is not the written page but the Light within and because of their commitment to nonviolence and equality, they find it comparatively easy to learn from the Bible's wealth without struggling with 'difficult' passages that affirm violence."[13] One way to deal with God's abusiveness, then, is to say, on spiritual grounds, that those passages cannot represent actions of the "true" God; they are not "Scripture." This approach seems to me to be spiritually, as well as theologically and textually, unsophisticated precisely because it suppresses the "difficult" side of human and divine being, precisely because it denies the "dark dispositions" of the personalist image which is the bond between God and humanity.

Others use contextualism and historicism to read such passages into a "primitive" human past which contrasts with our more "advanced" ethical consciousness. This approach, too, appears to me to be intellectually, theologically, and ethically unjustified precisely because, as I stated at the beginning of this chapter, this thinking embodies the historical fallacy and the wholly unwarranted assumption of human moral progress. To claim, too, that these texts reflect only patriarchal contexts and processes which distort theology, and therefore to leave God untouched by such texts, also seems to me to relieve the inter-pretive tradition of its theological responsibility and to undermine precisely the serious religiosity of such "texts of terror."

Walter Brueggemann, in *The Message of Psalms,* makes what seems to me the most serious scholarly and theological effort to deal with the dark side of human being.[14] In his chapter entitled "Psalms of Disorientation" (pp. 51–121, but especially pp. 51–88 and 115–121), Brueggemann, extending the work of C. Westermann, recognizes that these texts are serious calls for vengeance,

[12] See pp. 165–166 above where I have listed the usual arguments (Psalm 27, "Con-verses," beginning).

[13] Ellwood, *Batter My Heart,* p. 3.

[14] W. Brueggemann, *The Message of the Psalms* (Minneapolis: Augsburg Publishing House, 1984). This is not the place to address Brueggemann's unfair treatment of Zionism in the pages under discussion.

that they are imprecations, but that "[t]he stunning fact is that Israel does not purge this unguardedness but regards it as genuinely faithful communication" (p. 55). Of Psalm 79, he says, "Appeal is made to the partisan holiness of God . . . there is no attempt to protect Yahweh from how it really is . . . we would not think to pray that way very often, but it is thoroughly biblical" (pp. 71–72). Of Psalm 88, he writes, "The psalms also hold God's feet to the fire. . . . The failure of God to respond does not lead to atheism or doubt in God or rejection of God. It leads to more intense address" (pp. 78–79). Of Psalm 109, he says, "It is rather a raw undisciplined [sic] song of hate and wish for vengeance . . . a free, unrestrained speech of rage seeking vengeance. . . . [H]atred is one mode of access to the God who cares for his majesty" (pp. 83, 85, 87).

In spite of his honesty in recognizing the psalm of rage as a legitimate literary and theological form, Brueggemann does not recognize it as ethically legitimate. Hence, he writes, "Thus the motivation runs the gamut from conventional covenantal concerns to a less 'honorable' appeal to Yahweh's self-interest. . . . Perhaps the most regressive element is the imprecation . . . ignoble and unworthy . . ." (p. 55). "The speech is not reasoned" (p. 59). "[T]he prayer-life of the speaker is filled with anger and rawness" (p. 66). "No doubt this prayer is self-serving" (p. 72). "[T]he venomous wish . . ." (p. 73). "[A] yearning for retaliation and vengeance of the sort we do not expect to find in the 'edifying' parts of the Bible" (p. 82). The feelings of Psalm 109 are "not focused by Yahweh, not shaped by the covenant" (p. 85). "[B]ut I suggest it reflects someone who is only half living" (p. 87). These are psalms of "*dis*-orientation."

Brueggeman also cannot tolerate the great tradition of the lawcourt form of address, of confrontation and bargaining with God, which Anson Laytner has documented so thoroughly as a basic form of address to God—perhaps *the* most fundamental response of human beings to God's injustice.[15] Thus, Brueggemann writes, "At times the motivation comes peculiarly close to bargaining, bribing or intimidating . . ." (p. 55). "This . . . sounds like bargaining or threatening, like dangling a carrot in front of Yahweh" (p. 65). And he points disparagingly to the "triangling" of God, that is, "lining up Yahweh with him two against one, against the enemy" (p. 67).

Brueggemann, thus, admits the reality of the call for personal and national vengeance, but he rejects it, on ethical grounds.[16] Perhaps this is why Brueggemann calls these "laments" and not "psalms of rage."

---

[15] A. Laytner, *Arguing With God: A Jewish Tradition* (Northvale, N.J.: Aronson, 1990; reviewed by me in *Modern Judaism* 12:1 [Feb. 1992], 105–110). See pp. 249–257 for a full discussion of this tradition.

[16] Brueggemann refers frequently to the "uncivilized" nature of this language. I cannot believe, however, that a scholar of Brueggemann's depth can see the "civilities" of civilization as sufficient ground for theological propositions. On this subject, see J. M. Cuddihy, *The Ordeal of Civility* (Boston: Beacon Press, 1974).

The same critique has been raised by Wendy Farley in "Dialogue with a Systematic Theologian";[17] namely, that the call for personal and national vengeance does not distinguish between right and wrong, allowing evil if it is not directed against me but against the enemy. Nor does it distinguish between the guilty and the innocent, between the one who committed injustice and his or her spouse and children. Such a worldview also cultivates rage as a religious disposition, which is not possible because religious dispositions must be ethical, good, and generative of spiritual wholeness. The vengeful view of the psalms is, therefore, ethically, spiritually, and theologically nihilistic.

Because Brueggemann cannot accept the dark side of humanity as a permanent and equally valid moment in human existence, he proposes that the solution to rage in the book of Psalms is not to repress anger and rage but to state it clearly and forcefully to God, to "speak it honestly to the throne" (p. 77). The solution is to "submit" rage to God, to "relinquish" it to God. It is to ask God to take vengeance, but not to act oneself. It is to reject forgiveness as a mode of coming to terms too easily while speaking the rage and yet leaving the vengeance itself to God (pp. 76–77, 85–86).

I disagree with the view represented by Farley and Brueggemann, as I have partially indicated in my response to Farley. Human beings do have a dark side; they do have "dark dispositions"; and this aspect of humanness runs very deep, perhaps deeper than goodness. Sixty years of experience with psychoanalysis and psychotherapy, fifty years of study of the holocaust, and a decade of contact with survivors of child abuse have surely taught us to take into account more fully the dark side of humanity. Anthropologically, ethical censorship of our view of humankind is false, and dangerous.[18] Theologically, the ethical censorship of sacred texts and traditions deprives us of knowledge of a basic part of God's personality. We cannot understand God (or ourselves) if we censor out what we do not like, or what we would like not to see. The texts on God's abusiveness are there. To censor them out because they are not "ethical" is to limit our understanding of the complexity of human and divine existence. It is to underrate and undermine the theology of image. It is to deprive ourselves and God of the fullness of self-understanding and interrelatedness. One cannot just cast aside the "bad" passages and concentrate on the "positive" sources—for example, the Song of Songs, long seen as a love dialogue between God and the people—and the references to humans as the friends and lovers of God (Isa. 41:8; etc.). One cannot just cast aside the "bad" in favor of the "good/prophetic." Rather, accept what you do not want to know

---

[17] See pp. 213–224 above.

[18] Brueggemann's and Farley's views may be rooted in their Christian stance that the dark side of human nature results from the Fall and, hence, represents a distorted image of "true" humanity, the latter being better represented by prophetic ethics. In our unredeemed world, such a view would seem religiously unrealistic.

and, "with the tender strength that comes from an openness to your own deepest wounding,"[19] turn to address God.

Abusiveness as an Attribute of God

In the middle ages, thinkers debated the question of whether God has any qualities that are crucial to our understanding of God, that are part of God's very essence. Maimonides taught: God is so unlike anything we can think that God cannot have any attributes at all. At our most coherent, therefore, we can only say that God is not a member of the class of beings that possess any given trait or its contrary. This is the *via negativa,* "negative theology."[20] Saadia Gaon taught: God must have some attributes. That is the evidence of the Scripture and tradition; it is also the result of logic, for without words we cannot talk of God at all. Hence, according to Saadia, there are some qualities which are of God's essence. There are others, too; however they are just words we use to relate to God. The former are called "essential attributes"; the latter are called "accidental attributes."[21]

As I see it, God has two essential attributes of which we are aware by virtue of the sacred texts of the tradition and by virtue of our own personal experience of God; they are holiness and personality.[22] "Holiness" is that quality that conveys the sense of the sacred. It is an awareness *sui generis;* it is not an extension of the aesthetic, the moral, or a psychological projection. Holiness, sometimes called "wholly otherness," is a quality we sense in moments, in people, in texts, and in places. It is our cue to the presence of God in that context. "Personality" is that quality that conveys the person-ness of the subject who engages us. It is that congery of emotion, intellect, moral judgment, and personal presence that identifies each of us to ourselves and to others. God, too, has personality. We know this from the texts and traditions, and from our own experience of God's Presence. A trans-personal God, as in some eastern traditions or in certain philosophical understandings of Judaism, is,

[19] K. Steele, "Sitting With the Shattered Soul," *Pilgrimage: Journal of Personal Exploration and Psychotherapy* 15:6 (1989), p. 24.

[20] Maimonides, *Guide of the Perplexed,* trans. S. Pines (Chicago: University of Chicago Press, 1963), I:50–58.

[21] Saadia Gaon, *The Book of Beliefs and Opinions,* trans. S. Rosenblatt (New Haven, Conn.: Yale University Press, 1948), II:1–4, 13. For a more complete exposition of these two schools of thought, see H. A. Wolfson, "Crescas on the Problem of Divine Attributes," *Jewish Quarterly Review* 7:1 (1916), 1–44; 7:2 (1916), 175–221, reprinted in *Harry A. Wolfson: Studies in the History of Philosophy and Religion,* ed. I. Twersky and G. Williams (Cambridge, Mass.: Harvard University Press, 1977), vol. 2, pp. 247–337; and, less technically, D. Blumenthal, "Croyance et attributs essentiels dans la théologie médiévale et moderne," forthcoming.

[22] For a fuller discussion of this, see pp. 6–8, 11–31 above.

in my opinion, an incorrect reading of the texts of God's Presence.[23] It contradicts the tradition, as well as common Jewish experience.

Holiness and personality are the *imago Dei,* the *selem 'Elohim,* the image of God in which humanity is created (Gen. 1:26–27). It is what God and we have in common. It is that which enables us to talk about, and with, God. Holiness and personality are attributes; they are relation and relatedness. This is the theology of image. To do theology faith-fully is to speak those attributes, to work from and with the holiness and personal-ness of God, of the text, of the reader, and of the inter-preter.

My "solution" to the problem of the conflict between vengeance and ethical behavior, in life as in sacred text, is composed of three moments. First, we recognize the call for vengeance as performative speech, that is, that saying is doing in the fullest sense of the word. Second, we recognize that vengeance is within the ethical; that is, that there is an ethics of blood loyalty, of em-bodied covenant, which embraces both loyalty beyond morality *and* morality that questions loyalty. Thus, the prophets do not propose the abrogation of the em-bodied covenant or the annulling of the bond of blood loyalty that exists between God and the people; rather, they raise probing moral questions about the moral content of that relationship. Ethical consciousness, then, alter-nates between loyalty beyond morality and morality beyond loyalty, but it encompasses both, *seriatim.* And third, we recognize that we experience the vengeful dispositions *and* the ethical dispositions *seriatim,* that we use the performative language of the imprecation alternately with the piercing ethical language of moral discourse. I think too that, following the logic of the theology of image, God does the same thing. Sometimes God speaks and acts in vengeance, and sometimes God speaks and acts in a moral consciousness which privileges the oppressed over the chosen.[24] In any case, closing off either set of dispositions or either usage of language censors an aspect of the image. Stifling "bad" character or action represses a truth of our common being.

Is abusiveness, then, an attribute of God? Is abusiveness a quality without which we cannot understand the ultimate reality that we call God? Yes; and to the six personalist attributes listed in "Personality," I must now add a seventh: *God is abusive, but not always.* God, as portrayed in our holy sources and as experienced by humans throughout the ages, acts, from time to time, in a manner that is so unjust that it can only be characterized by the term "abusive." In this mode, God allows the innocent to suffer greatly. In this mode, God "caused" the holocaust, or allowed it to happen.

---

[23] See the works of A. J. Heschel and M. Kadushin cited above, p. 12.

[24] See the commentaries on Psalms 44 and 109, where I have suggested these ideas in another form. On em-bodied covenant, see Michael Wyschogrod, *The Body of Faith: Judaism as Corporeal Election* (New York: Seabury Press, 1983; reviewed by me in *Association for Jewish Studies Review* 11 [1986], 116–121).

Moments of abuse are characterized not only by deep human suffering but, most importantly, by the innocence of the victim. When a perpetrator acts abusively, the victim is innocent; when an abuser abuses, what happens to the victim is not in any way her or his fault. The victim usually has not wronged the perpetrator at all; however, even if the victim has wronged the abuser, the abuser's reaction is out of all proportion to the wrong committed. *The innocence of the victim, not the depth of the suffering or the cruelty of the perpetrator, is what makes abusive behavior "abusive."* For this reason, we reject victimization of the victim.

Furthermore, since the behavior of the victim has not justly provoked the abuser's action, we may not know why the perpetrator is abusive. This makes no difference. Intentionality is not an issue; the motives of the abuser are not relevant. *Abusive behavior is abusive; it is inexcusable, in all circumstances.*

What is true of abusive behavior by humans is true of abusive behavior by God. When God acts abusively, we are the victims, we are innocent. When God acts abusively, we are the hurt party and we are not responsible for God's abuse. Our sins—and we are always sinful—are in no proportion whatsoever to the punishment meted out to us. Furthermore, the reasons for God's actions are irrelevant, God's motives are not the issue. Abuse is unjustified, in God as well as in human beings.

But God is not always abusive. God is often loving and fair, even kind and merciful. We know, from our own experience or from that of others as well as from the Scripture and tradition, that God is, indeed, good too, even if our being abused inhibits us from clearly seeing and feeling God's love and fairness, from experiencing God's kindness and mercy. Our gratitude for God's fairness, love, kindness, and mercy, however, does not stop us from acknowledging God's abusiveness.

To have faith in a post-holocaust, abuse-sensitive world is, first, to know—to recognize and to admit—that God is an abusing God, but not always.

*Facing
the Abusing God*

THE FIRST STEP in reconstructing a post-holocaust, abuse-sensitive faith
is to face up to the truth, resistant as we are to admitting it. We must break
the conspiracy of silence and tell the truth—to ourselves, and to God; it is
the seal of God's being, and ours. The second step is to develop a theological
stance and religious affections that can guide us in living this new-found faith
which, in turn, will enable us to face God. Both must be rooted in the tradition, as well as in our experience; theology and religious affection must be
inter-texts, woven from the fabric of the past, the present, and the future.

Protest and Challenge, Distrust and Suspicion
as a Post-Holocaust, Abuse-Sensitive Stance

In *Night,* Elie Wiesel tells the story, but he also speaks his rage.[1] The most
searing passage, in my opinion, is:

> Never shall I forget that night, the first night in the camp, which has turned my
> life into one long night, seven times cursed and seven times sealed. Never shall I
> forget the little faces of the children, whose bodies I saw turned into wreaths of
> smoke beneath a silent blue sky.
> Never shall I forget those flames which consumed my faith forever.
> Never shall I forget that nocturnal silence which deprived me, for all eternity,
> of the desire to live. Never shall I forget those moments which murdered my God
> and my soul and turned my dreams to dust. Never shall I forget these things, even
> if I am condemned to live as long as God Himself. Never.

---

[1] Elie Wiesel, *Night,* trans. S. Rodway (New York: Bantam Books, 1960; repr. 1982), p. 32,
also quoted in "Con-verses" to Psalm 44.

Wiesel confronts God again, later in his own life, in *Ani Maamin*, a little-known oratorio, the title of which means "I Believe."[2] The oratorio, which is a modern re-reading of a midrash on Lamentations, ends with the patriarchs reproaching God and God crying. Significantly, the book is dedicated to Wiesel's son.

Although Wiesel takes up the theme of the holocaust in all of his books, he approaches the issue of God's responsibility yet again in *The Trial of God*.[3] This play, which is a modern re-reading of the Book of Job, is set in the midst of the Chmielnitsky (Cossack) massacres of the Jews in 1348–1349. God is put on trial by an innkeeper named Berish, three wandering Jews, and a defending attorney called Sam, abbreviated from Samael, one of the names of Satan. The victims recount the horrors they have seen even as the threat against them grows. The substance of the play is the vivid debate among the wanderers, Berish, Sam, and the other characters concerning God's culpability in the pogrom. At the end, the three itinerants are completely taken in by Satan, that is, they accept the usual defenses of God.[4]

The hero of *The Trial of God* is, as I see it, Berish, who, although resistant in the beginning to the idea of a trial of God, insists to the very end that he will hold God responsible and yet stay loyal to his Jewish identity *and* to God:

> If He insists upon going on with His methods, let Him — but I won't say Amen. Let Him crush me, I won't say Kaddish. Let Him kill me, let Him kill us all, I shall shout and shout that it's His fault. I'll use my last energy to make my protest known. Whether I live or die, I submit to Him no longer. . . . And they kept quiet? Too bad — then I'll speak for them. For them, too, I'll demand justice. . . . To you, judges, I'll shout, "Tell Him what He should not have done; tell Him to stop the bloodshed now. . . ." I lived as a Jew, and it is as a Jew that I die — and it is as a Jew that, with my last breath, I shall shout my protest to God! And because the end is near, I shall shout louder! Because the end is near, I'll tell Him that He's more guilty than ever![5]

With this play, probably Wiesel's most powerful confrontation with God and the holocaust, Wiesel has explicitly adopted the way of the "theology of protest." As the paradigmatic survivor of the holocaust, Wiesel has let it be known that he, and hence we, cannot forgive God; nor can he, and hence we, be silent. He must let his voice ring out, he must protest; so must we.[6] The theology of protest goes back to the Bible and is present most force-

---

[2] Elie Wiesel, *Ani Maamin*, trans. M. Wiesel (New York: Random House, 1973).

[3] Elie Wiesel, *The Trial of God*, trans. M. Wiesel (New York: Schocken Books, 1979).

[4] In his portrayal of Berish and the friends, Wiesel echoes the Book of Job. However, in casting Satan as the only defender of God and in the ending of the play, in which the pogrom recurs and the remnant victims are probably exterminated, Wiesel departs from the biblical and rabbinic understanding of the texts.

[5] Wiesel, *Trial of God*, pp. 133–134, 156.

[6] Wiesel makes a similar point in *Messengers of God: Biblical Portraits and Legends* (New York: Summit Books, 1976), when he writes that Cain should have protested against God's efforts to make him shed the blood of his brother (pp. 63–64).

fully in the Book of Job. The central figure in that text, Job, never questions God's existence, nor God's power to do what God is doing. Rather, Job questions God's justification, God's morality, God's justice. Throughout, Job rejects the moral panaceas and theological rationalizations of his friends, as does God in the end. No pat answers; rather, the repeated assertion of his innocence and the recurrent questioning of God's justice. No easy resolutions; rather, the repeated assertion of loyalty to God and the recurrent accusation of injustice:

> And Job answered [the friends] saying: "How long will you aggravate me and oppress me with words? Ten times you have humiliated me; are you not ashamed that you have dealt harshly with me? . . . Know now that it is God Who has twisted me, Who has cast His net upon me. I shout 'Violence' but I am not answered. I cry out but there is no fairness. He has blocked my way; I cannot pass. . . . My skin and flesh cling to my bones, and I am left with [only] my skull. . . . For I know that my R/redeemer is alive and, though H/he be the last being in the universe, when the period of my abuse is at an end, [all] this shall be struck away and then, from my [reconstituted] body, I shall see God, Whom I once envisioned, Whom my eyes once saw, and Who was [then] not strange to me. . . ." (chap. 19)[7]

Between the Book of Job and Elie Wiesel, there is a long tradition of the theology of protest. It has been very well documented by Anson Laytner in *Arguing With God: A Jewish Tradition*.[8] In the introduction and overview, Laytner identifies the basic form he will discuss, the lawcourt pattern of address to God, in which complaints and charges against God are allowable. Laytner, then, begins with the evidence from the Bible (chapter 1): Abraham arguing for Sodom (Genesis 18) and Moses' spirited defense of the people (Exodus 5 and 32; Numbers 14), showing the emergence, in these earliest strata of the tradition, of three basic themes: questioning of God over the issue of justice; the appeal to God to act for the merit of the ancestors, the covenant, and the sake of God's Name; and confession of guilt.[9] Laytner then moves to Jeremiah and Psalms, where he shows the national and the personal lament as a form.[10]

Having cited the biblical evidence, Laytner deals with the evidence from the rabbinic sources: interpretations of biblical passages and motifs (chapters 2 and 3); special prayers (chapters 4 and 5); and the statutory liturgy and

---

[7] The King James translation renders: "My bone cleaveth to my skin and to my flesh, and I am escaped with the skin of my teeth. . . . For I know that my redeemer liveth, and that he shall stand at the latter day upon the earth. And though after my skin worms destroy this body, yet in my flesh shall I see God. Whom I shall see for myself, and mine eyes shall behold, and not another; though my reins be consumed within me." For my translation, see D. Blumenthal, "A Play on Words in the Nineteenth Chapter of Job," *Vetus Testamentum* 16:4 (1966), 497–501.

[8] A. Laytner, *Arguing With God: A Jewish Tradition* (Northvale, N.J.: Jason Aronson, 1990; reviewed by me in *Modern Judaism* 12:1 [Feb. 1992], 105–110).

[9] Ibid., pp. 7–12.

[10] See also Yochanan Muffs, *Love and Joy: Law, Language, and Religion in Ancient Israel* (New York: Jewish Theological Seminary, 1992), esp. chap. 1, "A Study of Prophetic Intercession."

religious poetry (chapters 6 and 7). Laytner's analysis of these rabbinic materials leads him to four important conclusions. First, the rabbis emphasized and deepened the anthropopathism of the biblical sources.[11] As a result, the rabbis made the protest argument more explicit than it is in the biblical texts. Second, the rabbis recognized the tradition of explicit protest prayer only when the prayer was executed by especially saintly rabbis and only under restricted circumstances. They also recognized the value of protest in the midrash. Third, by contrast, in the statutory liturgy, the rabbis, under the leadership of Akiva, suppressed protest and adopted the submissive-penitent form of prayer as the official stance. Fourth, the tension between protest prayer and submissive prayer, however, could not be fully repressed, and protest prayer surfaced again in medieval religious poems, many of which were adopted into the liturgy.

The high point of Laytner's book may be in chapter 8. In it, Laytner deals with the modern materials. He begins with the hasidic traditions, including the protest-threat of the Kotzker rebbe:

> Send us our Messiah, for we have no more strength to suffer. Show me a sign, O God. Otherwise I rebel against You. If You do not keep Your covenant, then neither will I keep the promise, and it is all over: we are through with being Your Chosen People, Your unique treasure.[12]

Although echoed in the early rabbinic materials, this statement (and there are others like it) is audacious to the point of being almost heretical. Following this, Laytner, with D. Roskies and A. Mintz, moves to the popular and secular literature of protest, including Bialik's poem in which God calls us to rebel against God.[13]

Moving into the holocaust and post-holocaust literature, Laytner cites from contemporary Jewish poets: Glatstein, Greenberg, Zeitlin, Segal, Moldowsky, Katzenelson, and others. This material is very bitter:

> You watched. . . . There is no God in you, false, empty heavens.

> We shall remember, Lord God, that in these years, You settled with Your eternal people every old score.

> O God of Mercy
> For the time being
> Choose another people.

---

[11] "Anthropopathic" means having human feelings, as opposed to the usual "anthropomorphic," which means having human form.

[12] Laytner, *Arguing With God,* p. 189 (also cited in "Con-verses" to Psalm 44).

[13] Ibid., pp. 192–193.

We are tired of death, tired of corpses,
We have no more prayers. . . .
Grant us one more blessing—
Take back the gift of our separateness.[14]

In this vein, Laytner also cites the *din Torah,* the rabbinic "trial-of-God" tradition that grew up in the camps:

Creator of the worlds, You are mighty and terrible beyond all doubt. But from the circle of true lovers of Israel, we Galicians, forever shut You out![15]

As part of his discussion of the holocaust and post-holocaust material, Laytner presents, too, an extended analysis of Wiesel, in the course of which he sets forth two principles that characterize Wiesel's position. First, there is Wiesel's "faithful defiance," embodied in Berish's position, and, second, there is Wiesel's "defiant activism," rooted in the words of a character from another work: "Maybe God is dead, but man [*sic*] is alive. . . . Suffering is given to the living . . . it is man's [*sic*] duty to make it cease."[16]

In summarizing his examination of the modern sources, Laytner identifies five characteristics of the modern protest forms: the "for-our-sins" mentality is rejected; the material is created by poets and authors and not by rabbis, with the result that there is a transition from liturgy to folk forms; the texts are addressed to the people, though God is often present in the background; the forms embrace many differing attitudes and experiences, foregrounding none in particular; and the lawcourt pattern is conspicuously absent, except in the *din Torah* form.[17]

Laytner's work in bringing before us the long tradition of the theology of protest, even in its secularized modern forms, is very important. The depth and breadth of this tradition lead me to suggest that, in the post-holocaust era, challenge is a proper religious affection. Given our post-holocaust setting and given the continued insecurity of the Jewish people in the modern world, protest is a religiously proper faith stance toward God. Furthermore, in an era when we are also becoming familiar with the depth and breadth of child abuse, we must assert again that challenge is a proper religious affection. Given what we know of sexual, physical, and emotional abuse of children and its effects on later adult life, protest is a religiously proper faith stance toward God. Stated generally: *Given Jewish history and family violence as our*

---

[14] Ibid., pp. 203, 206, 207–208.
[15] Ibid., p. 206, with n. 50 for other incidents of such "trials of God."
[16] Ibid., pp. 214–227; quotation from pp. 221–225.
[17] Ibid., pp. 196–197.

generations have experienced them, unrelenting challenge is a proper religious affection, and a theology of protest is a proper theology for us to have.[18]

Further reflection on the ending of the book of Job and on the ending of *The Trial of God* is very disquieting. In the ending according to the poetic section of the book of Job (40:1–42:6), God overwhelms and threatens Job, who in turn responds:

> The Lord answered Job, saying, "Shall he who argues with the Mighty One condemn Him?! Let him who rebukes God answer for that!"
>
> And Job answered the Lord saying, "Behold, I am nothing; what shall I say to You in return? I put my hand to my mouth. I have spoken once, I shall not respond; even twice, I shall not continue."

There follow fifty-two verses, most of them in the form of rhetorical questions, all of which are intended to show God's might and Job's insignificance. The tone is set at the beginning:

> The Lord answered Job from the storm saying, "Gird your loins like a man! I will interrogate you! Give me your answers! Would you void My judgment?! Would you declare Me guilty, so that you be innocent?!" (40:6–8)

At the end of this tirade, Job responds in the most enigmatic of texts:[19]

> And Job answered the Lord, saying, "I know that You can do everything, that no scheme is impossible for You.
>
> Who is it who 'unknowingly hides counsel'? Indeed, I have related—even though I do not understand—things which are hidden from me and that which I do not know.
>
> Listen, I pray, and I will speak. 'I will interrogate You. Give me Your answers.'
>
> I had heard of You through the hearing of the ear, but now my eyes have seen You.
>
> Therefore, I am as nothing and I am remorseful, being [only] dust and ashes." (42:1–6)[20]

What kind of God reacts this way to a suffering loyal servant? What kind of personality does such a God have? Jung comments bitterly on this:

> [I]t is Yahweh himself who darkens his own counsel. . . . He turns the tables on Job and blames him for what he himself does: man is not permitted to have an opinion

---

[18] José Faur, in discussing the work of René Girard, puts this in a clear, if overstated, way: "The difference between the Jewish people and all other victims is that they alone refused to collaborate with the persecutor and efface their own perspective. Unlike countless victims that remained voiceless, the Jewish people expressed and transmitted their history from their own perspective. It is solely by virtue of breaking the silence that the persecutor is barred from invading the self of the persecuted. In crying out the persecuted confirm their own selfhood, thus meriting salvation" ("Jewish and Western Historiographies," *Modern Judaism* 12 [1992], p. 26).

[19] The phrases in single quotation marks are a reprise of God's words in a very pointed repartee. Note, too, that each verse is a thought unto itself; for that reason, I have set each one off in a separate paragraph. This is typical fragmented, lapidary biblical style.

[20] Alternate for the last phrase: "Therefore, I renounce and am comforted, being. . . ." Any twofold combination of the four verbs seems to me to be justified. Therein lies the difficulty.

about him. . . . For seventy-one verses he proclaims his world-creating power to his miserable victim, who sits in ashes and scratches his sores with potsherds, and who by now has had enough of superhuman violence.[21]

While I disagree with Jung's christological resolution to this problem, I agree that the ending of the book of Job according to the poetic section reveals a God Who is an abuser. What became of the relationship of Job and God after this tirade? Did Job trust and worship God again? Does the enigmatic last sentence mean that Job was so terrified that he repressed his question completely? Or does it mean that Job had a religious, or mystical, experience which transformed his question and his spiritual being to a higher plane?[22] Does the ending signify that Job was somehow satisfied with having attracted God's direct attention and that that was enough?[23] Do these closing verses indicate that Job resolved his suffering by ultimately accepting his inferior status and hence God's judgment?[24]

The prose ending to the book of Job (42:7–17) is no easier to understand: Job's happiness is returned to him in greater measure than before; he is reinstated in this world, better off than he was. But did Job simply take up his relationship with God again, with no after-effects? Did Job accept his second blessing without question? Did he resume his pious life without reservation?[25]

The ending of The Trial of God is even more disturbing: the remaining Jews are killed in the recurrence of the pogrom; the last Jews of Europe are

---

[21] C. Jung, Answer to Job, trans. F. C. Hull (Princeton, N.J.: Princeton University Press, 1958), p. 16.

[22] This is the view of Rudolph Otto in The Idea of the Holy (New York: Oxford University Press, 1958), pp. 77ff.; and André Neher, The Exile of the Word (Philadelphia: Jewish Publication Society, 1981), p. 205, though Neher goes on, citing Wiesel, to say that the proper modern stance is one of "silence and perhaps" (pp. 227–239).

[23] This is a recurring biblical theme: that our suffering is mitigated when we have been "seen," noticed, or acknowledged by God. Thus, for example, the four framing chapters of the book of Lamentations, written after the destruction of Jerusalem and its great temple, have three main themes: mourning over the terrible losses (1:1–11, 16; 2:9–16, 18–19; 4:1–5, 7–10, 14–19, 17–20, 22; 5:2–6, 8–18); an admission that God is responsible for the destruction wreaked on the people (1:12–15, 17, 21; 2:1–8, 17–21; 4:11, 16); and a prayer for direct attention from God, a call for God to "see" the suffering of the people (1:9, 11, 20; 2:20; 5:1, 19–22). Note, too, the themes of anger and revenge (1:22; 4:21; 5:7) and the sinfulness of the people (1:18; 4:6, 13). H. Fisch says that, while God does not answer Job's questions directly, God does make two points: first, that God can be summoned and will appear; and, second, that survival, choosing life, is the primary response (Poetry with a Purpose: Biblical Poetics and Interpretation [Bloomington, Ind.: Indiana University Press, 1988], pp. 30–32, 37–41).

[24] This is the view of Robert Gordis in The Book of God and Man (Chicago: University of Chicago Press, 1956), chaps. 10–11. See also Carol Newsom, "Job," in The Women's Bible Commentary, ed. C. Newsom and S. Ringe (Louisville, Ky.: Westminster/John Knox Press, 1992), pp. 130–136.

[25] Wiesel says that Job, as a survivor, should not have agreed to a tranquil life but should have protested further; that, in effect, God "forced Job to welcome happiness" (Messengers, p. 234).

exterminated; a final solution. There is no repression and getting on with life; no compensating religious experience; no satisfaction of having been addressed by God; no accepting of one's inferiority and, hence, of God's judgment. There is also no return of happiness, no second blessing, no resumed relationship with God, no reinstated life of piety. The ending of *The Trial of God* seems to preclude life after suffering.

The book of Job and *The Trial of God,* then, are silent on the religious nature of life after suffering. In both works, abuse has traumatized the text into a deep silence. But what *would* constitute a proper religious response to abuse in a life lived while healing from abuse? What would be an appropriate spiritual response to abuse within a life which is recovering from suffering?

First, there is the response of protest, for, as noted above, Berish is the hero of the play and it is Berish's "faithful defiance" that is its main motif.[26] Second, also noted above, there is "defiant activism" embodied in the life of Wiesel himself, who has survived and has gone on to a distinguished, constructive post-holocaust life. Still, is there nothing else? no other religious affection? no other theology?

There are several effective ways to deal with abuse, depending on the nature of the abused: One can repress the abuse and go on living one's life as well as one can. Many survivors of child abuse and the holocaust do this: they try not to think of it; and they go on with the daily tasks of living, as best as they can. One can also subsume the abuse into some greater experience or cause. Many survivors of child abuse and the holocaust do this: they dedicate themselves to God, or to the Jewish people, or to caring service to others; and they go on with the practical tasks of a life devoted to the cause they have adopted. And one can also live with the dark shadows of the past, allowing them to haunt one, to disorient one toward life and the world, even as one goes on with life. Many survivors of child abuse and the holocaust do this: they remain consciously and unconsciously haunted by the abuse, they remain distrustful and wary of others, they stay hypervigilant against impending abuse; and they go on with the daily tasks of living, as best they can, in a world that is potentially hostile, indeed dangerous.

I understand those who suppress, as well as those who lift up, the terror of their past; I have deep empathy for both these responses to abuse, and I honor them both. However, I also understand and empathize with those who live in the continuous shadow of the holocaust, who remain hypervigilant and yet persevere through life. I think, therefore, that in the post-holocaust era we can say that distrust is also a proper religious affection. Given our post-holocaust setting and given the continued insecurity of the Jewish people in the modern world, sustained suspicion is a religiously proper faith stance toward God. Furthermore, in an era when we are also becoming familiar with

---

[26] I understand, then, Berish's protest—and not the ending—to be the message of *The Trial of God.*

the depth and breadth of child abuse, we must assert again that distrust is a proper religious affection. Given what we know of sexual, physical, and emotional abuse of children and its effects on later adult life, sustained suspicion is a religiously proper faith stance toward God. As Diane has commented in "Dialogue with an Adult Survivor of Child Abuse," the appropriate non-sick response to abuse is turning away, a necessarily unforgiving stance, and maintaining the question whether, given the intensity of the abuse, one even *ought* to accept comfort from the F/father. Stated generally: *Given Jewish history and family violence as our generations have experienced them, distrust is a proper religious affection, and a theology of sustained suspicion is a proper theology to have.*

A Re-new-ed Form of Religious Healing

"Affections" to Psalm 27 presented the traditional mode of religious healing. It comprises seven steps: (1) recognize and state one's fear, anger, and even one's rage (as in Psalms 44 and 109); (2) recall moments of connectedness and closeness to God (fortress, the house of God, having visions of sweet bliss, the sukka of God, the rock of God); (3) reaffirm God's saving power and one's desire for it; (4) acknowledge one's helplessness and vulnerability; (5) actively call on God for help; (6) acknowledge one's doubt; and (7) resume spiritual relatedness with God. This process of religious healing is a reinsertion into the heirarchy of divine authority, a re-accepting of God's overwhelming authority to decide for us, an agreeing to be again a child in God's home.[27]

For some, indeed for many, this is true healing; it is finding a "safe place" and living in it. But for others, agreeing again to be a child in God's home is not healing for, if F/father was an abuser, one cannot, and should not, readily agree to return to that place. If one has been abused in family or in history, God's home is not a "safe place."

"Con-verses" to Psalm 27 presented a psychotherapeutic mode of healing. It too comprises seven steps: (1) avoid recreating the situation of abuse; (2) state the truth: "I am the victim, I am innocent, you are wrong"; (3) feel justified rage; (4) grieve for the loss of relatedness in the past, mourn the loss of relatedness in the present, and cry for the loss of relatedness in the future; (5) learn to accept and manage painful memories; (6) develop new concepts of partial love, partial power, partial resolution, intersubjectivity, and connectedness; and (7) empower oneself by acknowleging fully, "I have survived"; empower oneself by setting and accomplishing new realistic tasks and building confidence in one's ability to cope. This process of healing is a confrontation with a real but terrifying past, set in the context of acquiring the skills necessary

[27] See above, pp. 179–180 and 187–189.

to deal with daily life as well as with that past. It is a slow and painful program of building a fragmented self.[28]

Toward the end of "Con-verses" to Psalm 27, I suggested that a re-new-ed form of *religious* healing might embody some of the same processes as psychotherapeutic healing but in relation to God: (1) state the truth: "I am/we are the victim(s), I am/we are innocent, You are wrong"; (2) feel and express to God justified rage (as the psalmist does); (3) grieve for the loss of relatedness to God in the past, mourn the loss of relatedness to God in the present, and cry for the loss of relatedness to God in the future; (4) learn to accept and manage painful memories; (5) develop new concepts for understanding God: partial love, partial power, partial resolution, intersubjectivity, and connectedness; (6) empower oneself by acknowledging fully, "I have survived"; empower oneself by setting and accomplishing new realistic spiritual and religious tasks; build confidence in one's ability to cope spiritually;[29] and finally (7), turn to address God, personally, in prayer; open oneself to God's presence, turn one's face to the Face of God. This form of religious healing is not a re-insertion into the heirarchy of divine authority, a re-accepting of God's overwhelming authority to decide for us, or an agreeing to be again a child in God's home. Rather, it is a confrontation with a real but terrifying past, set in the context of acquiring the spiritual and religious skills necessary to deal with God as well as with that past. It is a slow and painful program of building a fragmented self into a relationship with God.[30]

Religious psychotherapeutic healing, like personal psychotherapeutic healing, requires an openness to the good side of the O/other, to the love of the o/Other. This is so difficult, precisely because the victim of personal or historical abuse has no reason at all to trust the O/other. On the contrary, the victim of family abuse or the holocaust has every reason to expect, realistically or transferentially, more abuse, as Diane has noted in "Dialogue with an Adult Survivor of Child Abuse." But I think that there can be no religious healing without some openness to the love of God—tentative, hesitating, even suspicious and distrustful; but present. The call of the psalmist must be at least an echo if the spiritual life is to grow.

Religious psychotherapeutic healing, like personal psychotherapeutic heal-

---

[28] An important part of this process would be analyzing transference distortion, the process by which we inter-text current and past reality; for instance, when one understands a normally tough authority figure to be abusive because one is expecting such a figure to act abusively, one is reading the present through the emotional eyes of the past. See above, pp. 167–170, 171–173, and 179–180.

[29] A very important part of this process would include activating oneself in social justice causes, particularly in the protection and helping of fellow victims and survivors of abuse and/or in the protection and helping of fellow Jews. This would be Wiesel's "defiant activism." Another important part of this process would be acquiring the Jewish skills of study, mitsvot, and prayer, which allow entry into the world of spiritual healing.

[30] See above, pp. 180–183.

ing, is not a "straight path." It is, rather, a backstitch, a moving forward which proceeds by circling backward; it is tacking into the wind; it is *seriatim*. For this reason, one tacks toward truth and protest;[31] then one tacks toward healing and love;[32] one repeats the process, many times. Slowly, one advances into the wind of life, even as one is plagued by doubts, as the psalmist says, "Were it not for . . ."

In sum: *In the post-holocaust era, it is not enough to push abuse out of our minds and hearts. In the era of increasing knowledge of child abuse, it is not enough to accept reality for what it was and go on with life. To have faith in God in a post-holocaust, abuse-sensitive world, we must: (1) acknowledge the awful truth of God's abusing behavior; (2) adopt a theology of protest and sustained suspicion; (3) develop the religious affections of distrust and unrelenting challenge; (4) engage the process of re-new-ed spiritual healing with all that entails of confrontation, mourning, and empowerment; (5) resist all evil mightily, supporting resistance to abuse wherever it is found; (6) open ourselves to the good side of God, painful thought that is; and (7) we must turn to address God, face to Face, presence to Presence.*

Some Theological and Psychological Considerations

There are many forms of child abuse: cult-related abuse, which is really a form of torture; sexual abuse, which is rape and other forms of forced entry into the body of the victim; physical abuse, which is beating and other forms of nonsexual aggression against the body of the victim; sexual abuse by seduction, which is emotionally if not physically violent; abuse by a parent or intimate adult, as opposed to abuse by a spouse or a stranger; emotional and psychological abuse, verbal or behavioral; physical or emotional neglect; and physical or emotional indifference. And then there are combinations of these forms of abuse. There is also abuse by identification; that is, when one sees or hears any of these forms of abuse, one identifies with the victim and participates in the survivor's pain.

There are also many forms of holocaust abuse: having been in a death camp for a long period of time; having been in a death camp for a short period of time; having been in a labor camp for longer or shorter periods of time; having been in hiding for longer or shorter periods of time; and having been the object of "special treatment" in any of these settings. And then there are combinations of these forms of abuse. There is also trauma by identification; that is, when one sees or hears any of these forms of holocaust abuse, one identifies with the victim and participates in the survivor's pain. For Jews, there is also abuse by collective identification, by knowing and feeling in one's bones

---

[31] This is the tack toward Gevura.
[32] This is the tack toward Hesed.

that the victims were abused because they were Jewish, for no other reason, and knowing that I, too, am Jewish and subject to the same abuse.

There are other forms of abuse, too, which are not child or holocaust abuse but are moments of deep hurt, events that produce profound rage and require serious healing. There is one-time abuse: rape, kidnapping, torture, assault, the sudden death of a loved one. There is also ongoing abuse not due to a human cause: disease, disability, especially the disabling disease of a child. And there are also spouse abuse, elder abuse, and socioeconomic abuse. These forms of abuse differ from child and holocaust abuse in many ways, yet they are rooted in the injustice of the event, provoke rage, and require sensitive treatment. All these forms, too, also evoke identification in those who listen sympathetically and hear.

Child and holocaust abuse are similar in some ways:[33] Both are rooted in real historical events, both really happened; this is not true for fantasied abuse, which may have deep psychic roots but did not actually happen. Both deal with moments of utter victimization, of dehumanization. Both contain trauma that is massive in scope, penetrating over a long period of time into the psyche of the victim. Both entail a deep sense of abandonment by those who should have helped. Both evoke psychic numbing, depression, suspiciousness, rage, isolation, and a conspiracy of silence. Therapy for both runs the great risk of re-victimization.

Yet child and holocaust abuse are dissimilar in significant ways. For the holocaust survivor, the pain is not only personal; it is historical and national. The degradation and extermination were intended for all Jews. It was also part of a pattern of Jew-hatred that had existed for centuries and is perceived to continue to exist. For the survivor of family abuse, there was the lack of any support, utter aloneness. There was no underground, no resistance, no other prisoners; no fellow Jews. The non-abusing parent was part of the conspiracy; sometimes so were the siblings. For the holocaust survivor, there was real death: emaciated corpses, healthy corpses, mutilated corpses, screaming infants cast onto pyres, excremental attack, the walking dead. And it was large in scale, all around, all the time. For the survivor of family abuse, the suffering lasted longer, sometimes for more than a decade. Family abuse was also interwoven with normal daily living; it was not isolated in a hell-place and a hell-time; it took place at home, not in a prison or camp. For the survivor of family abuse, abuse also came from those who loved, or claimed they did, even as they abused. And it came from those one is supposed to love, from those who love and are loved in other peoples' homes. Holocaust abuse came from the enemy, who was the real sub-human, who could be hated. For the

---

[33] I first broached this topic in "A Genesis of Faith," which is an extended book review, in *Religious Studies Review* 18:3 (July 1992), 209–11. A thorough study of this comparison needs to be done.

holocaust survivor, recovery was sustained by the Jewish people and embodied by the State of Israel.[34] Family abuse survivors were lucky to find a spouse who would be tolerant, and even luckier to find a therapist who would listen.[35]

To speak of "child" or "family abuse" and to write about "holocaust abuse" as homogeneous constructs and to compare them are, in view of this diversity, misleading. Looked at from the point of view of the intensity of the rage of the victim, all the forms of abuse may be the same, though the protocols for treating the survivors will be different. However, grouping the more severe forms of abuse together has an advantage: it enables us to compare the experience and healing process of two forms of deeply traumatized human experience. This, in turn, enables us to gain insights from one area which may be useful in the other. Accordingly, I have made the analogy between holocaust and child abuse, but I do it hesitantly and with reservations that are motivated as much by methodological questions as by modesty and embarrassment.

Theologically, insisting that God is present and active in the holocaust and, hence, designating God as abusive re-creates the classical problem of free will versus providence: if God is active in our personal and collective lives, how can we be said to be free agents, and, conversely if we are free agents, how can God be said to be active in our lives? When in doubt, Judaism always opts for human free will, asserting that we are completely responsible for what we do. This enables God's judgment and activates the whole theology of reward and punishment rooted in deeds which is central to Jewish religious self-understanding. Notwithstanding this approach, Judaism also asserts that God is active, that providence is a real force in our lives. This does generate a contradiction, but Judaism lives with it.[36]

In connection with the holocaust, our deepest theological instincts are to bracket God's action and to assert that only human beings were responsible

[34] When we, at Emory University in the 1980s, began interviewing American GI's who had liberated the concentration camps, one of the first things we discovered is that they had never talked about the liberation experience, even though they had talked about the war. There was no one to talk to. Jews who had survived or liberated camps, on the other hand, had a community that at first did not want to listen but, by the late 1960s, was beginning to support this kind of sharing. In addition, Jews haunted by the holocaust could, and did, channel their rage and fear into working for the protection of the surviving remnant of the holocaust by establishing and maintaining the security of the State of Israel.

[35] There are some clinical phenomena which seem to exist only among holocaust survivors: "transposition" (the tendency of children to live out the persecution of their parents), "enmeshment" (the tendency of parents to see children as leading the lives they did not lead, and of children to heroize or victimize the parents), and "mission" (developing a positive Jewish communal identity, speaking publicly about the holocaust, assuming the social role of "holocaust survivor," attending public commemorations, being active in human rights issues). This last pattern might actually prove useful as a conscious therapeutic technique for child and spouse abuse therapy.

[36] See, e.g., Maimonides, *Mishne Torah,* "Hilkhot Teshuva," chaps. 5–6; and *Guide of the Perplexed,* trans. S. Pines (Chicago: University of Chicago Press, 1963), III:10–20.

for what happened. However, Judaism demands that we take the doctrine of providence seriously; hence, I have chosen to assert God's action in the holocaust and to draw the conclusions to which that assertion drives us. To be sure, I do not wish to indicate, nor have I done so, that humankind is not responsible. On the contrary, human beings did perpetrate the holocaust and human beings must resist abuse everywhere. But God was involved, too; God was co-responsible. God's co-responsibility does not in any way absolve human beings of their responsibility. However, by considering abuse from the point of view of God's providential action, we can articulate a deeper religious understanding of the role of God in these events and a more profound response on our part to God's action in history.

In "Dialogue with a Systematic Theologian," in "Con-verses" to Psalm 27, and in "Standing In-Between," I have suggested that one cannot reject God. One can question God, one can even accuse God; but one cannot reject God. This position is grounded in several arguments: First, there is the irreducibility of one's parents: one can question them, one can accuse them, one can even exclude them from one's active life. But one cannot deny the presence of one's parents in one's life; they are always there, consciously and unconsciously. Parents are generators, creators of life. There is a vertical bond of blood that is stronger than any other association. One cannot deny one's rootedness in the being of one's parents; one cannot disallow one's connectedness to them. For this reason, maintaining connectedness with one's parents is different from relating to other people. One need not honor one's parents if they do not deserve it; one need not even respect one's parents if they do not deserve it. Rather, one learns to cope as best one can, to live with the presence of one's parents. Theologically, this is expressed in the doctrine of creation and covenant: God is our creator, and God is in a covenant with us that cannot be nullified. God's presence is irreducible and we are in a relationship with God that cannot be nullified. God may act in ways that cause us to lose our ability to honor and respect God, but the liaison, the contact, is inalienable. For this reason, we do not reject God; rather, we learn to cope with God and God's actions.

Second, there is the appeal to personal spiritual experience: there are experiences of the holy and of the personal presence of God. For some, these are direct personal experiences; for others, these are mediated through the communication of others. But experience of God, in God's goodness and holiness, does exist and one cannot deny that experience any more than one can deny the experience of abuse. To be true to our own selves and our own experience of non-abusing God, we do not reject; rather, we maintain contact.

Third, to do theology is to accept a religious tradition as a home, and to do that is to accept that God, for better and for worse, is part of one's universe of discourse. Accordingly, we do not reject; we inter-pret.

There is one caveat: *In cases where the victim is in danger of life and limb, the victim must distance himself or herself from the perpetrator.* There can be no compromise on this issue. But where relatedness can be held in tension without severance, it should be attempted.

Transition into the Presence

In the inner reaches of Jewish religious reflection, the question is asked whether God can make a mistake, whether God can sin. The biblical evidence is that God *can* make a mistake: God changes God's mind in the case of Noah and in the desert regarding the rebellious people.[37] In the Rosh ha-Shana liturgy, God prays that God's mercy overcome God's anger, implying, if not stating clearly, that God can be overwhelmed by factors in Godself.[38] And, in the zoharic strain of Jewish mystical thinking, God's inner stability can be destroyed, provoking great destruction.[39] In a personalist theology, then, God can sin.

But how does God repent? How does God do *teshuva*? If the echoes of the book of Lamentations and the book of Job are heard seriously, God repents by talking to us, by seeing us, by taking notice of us, by acknowledging us in some concrete way. For some Jews, the creation and continued existence of the State of Israel are such an acknowledgment. For others, that is insufficient on three grounds: First, the trauma has simply been too great, the loss too severe. Second, the very historicism that allows us to rationalize away certain texts also forces us to see history for what it really was; we can no longer paradigmatize history and count this suffering in with all the others. The holocaust is abuse, and there is no excuse for it. Finally, we know from a study of repentance in Jewish tradition and from an examination of the therapy of healing from abuse that acknowledgment of the abused by the abuser is simply

[37] Gen. 6:6 and Ex. 32:14. See also 1 Sam. 15:11, 35; 2 Sam. 24:16; Joel 2:13-14; Amos 7:3, 6; Jonah 3:9, 10; 4:2; Jer. 26:13, 19; Ps. 106:45; 1 Chron. 21:15. See also p. 16.

[38] "Our God and God of our ancestors, call up a memory of us before You, a good memory, and take note of us in the most ancient heavens, a noting of deliverance and mercy. Remember for us, O Lord our God, the covenant, the grace, and the oath you took to Abraham, our father, on Mt. Moriah. May the binding which Abraham, our father, bound Isaac, his son, on the altar in which he suppressed his mercy to do Your will with a whole heart appear before You. So, too, may Your mercy suppress Your anger from upon us and, in Your great goodness, may Your wrath turn away from Your people, Your city, and Your portion" (Rosh ha-Shana liturgy, "Remembrances"; *The Authorized Daily Prayerbook,* ed. J. Hertz [New York: Bloch Publishing, 1960], pp. 880–882). See also pp. 28 and 290.

[39] See D. Blumenthal, *Understanding Jewish Mysticism* (New York: KTAV Publishing House, 1978), vol. 1, part 2; and I. Tishby, *The Wisdom of the Zohar,* trans. D. Goldstein, Littman Library (London: Oxford University Press, 1989), parts 2, 4, and 5.

not enough.[40] Both Jewish teaching and proper therapy require much more: they require knowledge by the abuser of the grounds and causes of the abusing behaviors; and a commitment, acceptable to the abused, never to abuse again. They require self-empowerment of the abused and reestablished intersubjectivity and interrelatedness between the abused and the abuser. With God, this has not happened, and, while reconciliation may not be possible in cases of abuse, it is nonetheless the goal and the ideal in both psychotherapeutic and religious healing.

To re-connect, one must address; it is to this that we now turn.

[40] See, e.g., Maimonides, *Mishne Torah,* "Laws on Repentance," especially chap. 2. See also E. Gil, *Treatment of Adult Survivors of Child Abuse* (Walnut Creek, Calif.: Launch Press, 1988; reviewed by me in *Religious Studies Review* 18:3 [July 1992], 209–11).

*Addressing
the Abusing God*

Taking a Stance

IN PART 1, "Beginning Somewhere," we, readers of this book including myself, worked through some first premises; in part 2, "Text-ing," we studied Psalms 128, 44, 109, and 27; in part 3, "Re-sponses," we read the dialogues and "Beth's Psalm"; and in part 4, "Con-templation," we wrestled with abusiveness as an attribute of God, we pondered a theology of protest as well as sustained suspicion as a proper theology and unrelenting challenge as well as distrust as proper religious affections in a post-holocaust, abuse-sensitive world, and we considered a re-new-ed form of religious healing.

In the course of our work, we have had to confront ugly facts in ourselves: We have felt wrath and rage against those who perpetrate abuse, personally and nationally. We have seen that, "unproductive" as it may be, we human beings do yearn for revenge against our enemies and that we expect our God to take that revenge for us when we are helpless to do it. While struggling with this material, we have had to realize that there is an abused child in each of us, and, worse, we have had to confront the ugly fact that there is an abuser in each of us. That is part of the reason why this study has evoked in us the intense response that it has.

In the course of our work, we have also had to confront strange and even ugly texts, traditions, and ideas about God: In a theology of image, there is a fragile moment in God, a vulnerable side to God. This idea is rooted in God's creatorship, for, as Jon Levenson has shown, the biblical view of creation implies that God can create the world but cannot completely control it, either nature or humankind.[1] Similarly, in medieval philosophy, God cannot violate

---

[1] Jon D. Levenson, *Creation and the Persistence of Evil: The Jewish Drama of Divine Omnipotence* (San Francisco: Harper & Row, 1988; reviewed by me in *Modern Judaism* 10 [1990], 105–110), passim, especially pp. 127, 139.

humankind's free will, nor can God do the impossible,[2] while in the zoharic stream of Jewish mysticism, God actually needs the effort of humankind to achieve stability in Godself and in the cosmos.[3] Insofar, then, as God has a fragile dimension, we relate to God in a supportive manner, tending to God's garden and caring for it (Gen. 2:15). This is not new in the history of Jewish religious thought. It is also not germane to the survivor of abuse, for, to the victim, the perpetrator's problems are irrelevant; safety is the issue, and intelligently defensive behavior is what is called for.

In a theology of image, there is also in God, as we have unwillingly seen, an ugly moment: an abuser, a perpetrator. That, too, is part of the reason why these texts exert upon us a powerful attraction, and repulsion. This abusiveness in God is witnessed, first, by the texts we have read and studied. It is witnessed, second, by our experience in Jewish history and in family violence. And finally, it is witnessed by the logic of the theology of image that posits the essential attributes of holiness and personality, in all their complexity and depth, in God and in humanity. How does one deal with this testimony? How does one speak to God the Perpetrator? How does one address God the Abuser?

First, we must make it clear to ourselves, as noted above, that we have been the victims, victims of abuse; that we have been objects of unjustified punishment and suffering. Furthermore, we must make it clear to ourselves that we are not guilty, that we will not accept the blame for what has happened. We have suffered, and we have suffered unjustly; and we will not, nor will we allow others, even God, to blame the victims. There was no possible reason or justification for what was done to us; none! Our suffering is the result of abuse, by the Perpetrator; it is the Perpetrator Who must answer, not we. We are innocent, existentially and spiritually, in what was done to us; God alone is responsible.

Second, in our hurt and in our good common sense, we will distance ourselves from the Perpetrator. We will think twice about whether we can, or even should, approach God. We will be very wary, and we will not be apologetic about that, for to trust the untrustworthy is itself immoral and sick. We will guard our distance—theologically and spiritually, in worship and in study.

Third, we will point the finger, we will identify the Abuser, we will tell this ugly truth. We will not keep silent, neither out of fear nor out of love. We will not be drawn into the conspiracy of silence, or into the cabal of rationalization. We will cling tenaciously to our rage, and we will speak. And, in our

    [2] See Maimonides, *Mishne Torah*, "Laws of Repentance," chaps. 5–6 and *Guide of the Perplexed*, III:15.
    [3] See D. Blumenthal, *Understanding Jewish Mysticism* (New York: KTAV Publishing House, 1978), vol. 1, part 2; and I. Tishby, *The Wisdom of the Zohar*, trans. D. Goldstein, Littman Library (London: Oxford University Press, 1989), part 5.

speaking, we will accuse, we will place the blame where it belongs. We will say, "The fault was not ours. You are the Abuser. The fault was yours. You repent. You return to us."

Fourth, we will empower ourselves by acknowledging fully our survival, by building human relationships, by participating in worthy causes, and by working and accomplishing our daily and social tasks.

Fifth, we will not deny our own spirituality; rather, we will affirm it. We will affirm the miracle of healing and the wonder of life. We will affirm the grace of human contact and the sublimeness of the experience of the transcendent. And we will affirm the reality of God's presence, God's power, and even God's love—insofar as we have experienced these, or respect others who have. Ours will not be a self-effacing affirmation, nor a self-denying love; those days are gone. Rather, ours will be an acknowledgment of the Other Who is present to us in fear *and* in kinship, in terror *and* in presence. As a people, too, we will affirm that the State of Israel is as real as the holocaust; we will affirm the God Who has worked wondrously through us, just as we acknowledge the God Who worked aw(e)fully against us.[4]

One cannot forgive an abusing f/Father. This is the classical position of religious thinkers in our tradition from Job to Elie Wiesel. It is also one of the lessons we learn from psychotherapy with adult survivors of child abuse and the holocaust. Rather, we will try to accept God as God is; we will protest our innocence, as our ancestors and greatest thinkers have done. And we will accuse God of acting unjustly, as fully and as directly as we can, as our greatest poets and sages have done. We cannot forgive God and concentrate on God's goodness. Rather, we will try to accept God—the bad along with the good—*and* we will speak our lament. We will mourn the bad, and we will regret that things were, and are, not different than they are. This face-to-face alone will enable us to maintain our integrity, even though it leaves an unreconciled gap between us and God. These steps alone will enable us to have faith in God in a post-holocaust, abuse-sensitive world. Unity and reconciliation are no longer the goal; rather, we seek a dialogue that affirms our difference and our justness, together with our relatedness to God.[5]

---

[4] These lessons seem to be confirmed by studying the religious attitudes of holocaust survivors: They are unwilling to judge God, and, hence, they accept various theodicies available through the tradition. They also believe that actions are more important than faith, and so they continue to be active in Jewish causes and even to be religiously observant. However, they never fully recover their belief; they serve God, but not in love. See P. Marcus and A. Rosenberg, *Healing Their Wounds: Psychotherapy with Holocaust Survivors and Their Families* (New York: Praeger Publishers, 1989; reviewed by me in *Religious Studies Review* 18:3 [July 1992], 209–211), pp. 227–256 with summary, pp. 234–239.

[5] Many serious Christians do not agree with this approach. See, e.g., James Leehan, *Pastoral Care for Survivors of Family Abuse* (Louisville, Ky.: Westminster/John Knox Press, 1989; reviewed by me in *Religious Studies Review* 18:3 [July 1992] 209–211); and idem, *Defiant Hope: Spirituality for Survivors of Family Abuse* (Louisville, Ky.: Westminster/John Knox Press, 1993).

Psalms for an Angry Generation

In seeking dialogue with God, we turn first to psalms.

PSALM 38

מִזְמוֹר לְדָוִד לְהַזְכִּיר:

יְיָ אַל בְּקֶצְפְּךָ תוֹכִיחֵנִי
וּבַחֲמָתְךָ תְיַסְּרֵנִי:

כִּי חִצֶּיךָ נִחֲתוּ בִי
וַתִּנְחַת עָלַי יָדֶךָ:

אֵין מְתֹם בִּבְשָׂרִי מִפְּנֵי זַעְמֶךָ
אֵין שָׁלוֹם בַּעֲצָמַי מִפְּנֵי חַטָּאתִי:

כִּי עֲוֹנֹתַי עָבְרוּ רֹאשִׁי
כְּמַשָּׂא כָבֵד יִכְבְּדוּ מִמֶּנִּי:

הִבְאִישׁוּ נָמַקּוּ חַבּוּרֹתָי
מִפְּנֵי אִוַּלְתִּי:

נַעֲוֵיתִי
שַׁחוֹתִי עַד מְאֹד
כָּל הַיּוֹם קֹדֵר הִלָּכְתִּי:

כִּי כְסָלַי מָלְאוּ נִקְלֶה
וְאֵין מְתֹם בִּבְשָׂרִי:

נְפוּגֹתִי
וְנִדְכֵּיתִי עַד מְאֹד
שָׁאַגְתִּי מִנַּהֲמַת לִבִּי:

אֲדֹנָי נֶגְדְּךָ כָל תַּאֲוָתִי
וְאַנְחָתִי מִמְּךָ לֹא נִסְתָּרָה:

לִבִּי סְחַרְחַר
עֲזָבַנִי כֹחִי
וְאוֹר עֵינַי גַּם הֵם אֵין אִתִּי:

A Psalm of Confusion

[1]A psalm of David, as a reminder.

> [2]Lord, do not yell at me in Your wrath.
> Do not discipline me in Your anger.

> [3]Truly, Your arrows have struck me.
> Your hand has struck out against me.

[4]There is no wholeness in my body because of Your fury.
There is no peace in my bones because of my sin.

[5]I am surely over my head in transgressions.
They are as a heavy burden, too heavy for me.

[6]My wounds smell, they fester,
because of my stupidity.

[7]I am deformed.
I have been bent to the limit.
I walk around morose, all day long.

[8]Inside, I am truly filled with shame.
There is no wholeness in me.

[9]I am out of energy.
I am depressed, to the limit.
I roar at the hurt in my heart.

> [10]Lord, all my lust is exposed to You.
> My sighing is not hidden from You.

[11]My heart is dizzy.
My strength has left me.
The light in my eyes—even that is no more a part of me.

אֹהֲבַי וְרֵעַי מִנֶּגֶד נִגְעִי יַעֲמֹדוּ
וּקְרוֹבַי מֵרָחֹק עָמָדוּ:

וַיְנַקְשׁוּ מְבַקְשֵׁי נַפְשִׁי
וְדֹרְשֵׁי רָעָתִי דִּבְּרוּ הַוּוֹת
וּמִרְמוֹת כָּל הַיּוֹם יֶהְגּוּ:

וַאֲנִי
כְחֵרֵשׁ לֹא אֶשְׁמָע
וּכְאִלֵּם לֹא יִפְתַּח פִּיו:

וָאֱהִי כְּאִישׁ אֲשֶׁר לֹא שֹׁמֵעַ
וְאֵין בְּפִיו תּוֹכָחוֹת:

כִּי לְךָ יְיָ הוֹחָלְתִּי
אַתָּה תַעֲנֶה אֲדֹנָי אֱלֹהָי:

כִּי אָמַרְתִּי פֶּן יִשְׂמְחוּ לִי
בְּמוֹט רַגְלִי עָלַי הִגְדִּילוּ:

כִּי אֲנִי לְצֶלַע נָכוֹן
וּמַכְאוֹבִי נֶגְדִּי תָמִיד:

כִּי עֲוֹנִי אַגִּיד
אֶדְאַג מֵחַטָּאתִי:

וְאֹיְבַי חַיִּים עָצֵמוּ
וְרַבּוּ שֹׂנְאַי שָׁקֶר:

וּמְשַׁלְּמֵי רָעָה תַּחַת טוֹבָה
יִשְׂטְנוּנִי תַּחַת רָדְפִי טוֹב:

אַל תַּעַזְבֵנִי יְיָ אֱלֹהָי
אַל תִּרְחַק מִמֶּנִּי:

חוּשָׁה לְעֶזְרָתִי
אֲדֹנָי תְּשׁוּעָתִי:

¹²My lover and my friends keep away from my misery.
My near relations too keep their distance.

¹³Those who are out after me set traps.
Those who wish me evil speak aloud their evil desires,
they construct plots all day long.

¹⁴And I,
I am like a deaf person, I cannot hear;
I am like a dumb person, who cannot open his mouth.

¹⁵I have become like a person who does not listen,
who has no rebuttal in his mouth.

¹⁶Truly, I look to You, Lord.
You, my Liege and my God, will respond.

¹⁷Truly, I have said, "Lest they rejoice over me;
when my step fails, they will lord it over me."

¹⁸Truly, I am destined to misfortune.
My pain confronts me always.

¹⁹Truly, I tell of my transgression.
I am anxious because of my sin.

²⁰But my enemies teem with life.
Those who hate me multiply lies.

²¹Those who pay evil for good
detest me because I pursue good.

²²Do not ever desert me, Lord.
Don't You go away from me, my God.

²³Hurry to my aid.
My Lord is my salvation.

PSALM 88

שִׁיר מִזְמוֹר לִבְנֵי קֹרַח
לַמְנַצֵּחַ עַל מָחֲלַת
לְעַנּוֹת
מַשְׂכִּיל לְהֵימָן הָאֶזְרָחִי:

יְיָ אֱלֹהֵי יְשׁוּעָתִי
יוֹם צָעַקְתִּי
בַלַּיְלָה נֶגְדֶּךָ:

תָּבוֹא לְפָנֶיךָ תְּפִלָּתִי
הַטֵּה אָזְנְךָ לְרִנָּתִי:
כִּי שָׂבְעָה בְרָעוֹת נַפְשִׁי
וְחַיַּי לִשְׁאוֹל הִגִּיעוּ:

נֶחְשַׁבְתִּי עִם יוֹרְדֵי בוֹר
הָיִיתִי כְּגֶבֶר אֵין אֱיָל:

בַּמֵּתִים חָפְשִׁי
כְּמוֹ חֲלָלִים שֹׁכְבֵי קֶבֶר
אֲשֶׁר לֹא זְכַרְתָּם עוֹד
וְהֵמָּה מִיָּדְךָ נִגְזָרוּ:

שַׁתַּנִי בְּבוֹר תַּחְתִּיּוֹת
בְּמַחֲשַׁכִּים בִּמְצֹלוֹת:

עָלַי סָמְכָה חֲמָתֶךָ
וְכָל מִשְׁבָּרֶיךָ עִנִּיתָ סֶּלָה:

הִרְחַקְתָּ מְיֻדָּעַי מִמֶּנִּי
שַׁתַּנִי תוֹעֵבוֹת לָמוֹ
כָּלֻא וְלֹא אֵצֵא:

עֵינִי דָאֲבָה מִנִּי עֹנִי
קְרָאתִיךָ יְיָ בְּכָל יוֹם
שִׁטַּחְתִּי אֵלֶיךָ כַפָּי:

A Psalm of Unrelieved Depression

¹A song-psalm, by the Koraḥ family,
from the collection of the leader of the *maḥalat,*
for chanting,
a meditation by Heyman, the Ezraḥite.

²Oh Lord, the God of my salvation,
I cried out during the day;
at night, I was against You.

³Let my prayer come before You.
Bend Your ear to my murmuring.
⁴For I am filled to the brim with evils.
My life has reached down to the netherworld.

⁵I am considered as one who has gone down to hell.
I am like a person completely without power.

>⁶Among the dead, one is free
>like the slain who rest in the grave
>whom You call to mind no longer—
>but they are cut off from Your guidance.

⁷You have put me in the lowest of pits,
in the darkness, in the depths.

⁸Your anger has leaned upon me.
You have pressed all Your waves down upon me. Selah.

⁹You have alienated my acquaintances from me.
You have made me repulsive to them.
I am shut in and I do not go out.

¹⁰My eyes hurt from oppression.
I have called out to You, Lord, every day.
I have spread out my hands to You.

הֲלַמֵּתִים תַּעֲשֶׂה פֶּלֶא
אִם רְפָאִים יָקוּמוּ יוֹדוּךָ סֶּלָה:

הַיְסֻפַּר בַּקֶּבֶר חַסְדֶּךָ
אֱמוּנָתְךָ בָּאֲבַדּוֹן:

הֲיִוָּדַע בַּחֹשֶׁךְ פִּלְאֶךָ
וְצִדְקָתְךָ בְּאֶרֶץ נְשִׁיָּה:

וַאֲנִי אֵלֶיךָ יְיָ שִׁוַּעְתִּי
וּבַבֹּקֶר תְּפִלָּתִי תְקַדְּמֶךָּ:

לָמָה יְיָ תִּזְנַח נַפְשִׁי
תַּסְתִּיר פָּנֶיךָ מִמֶּנִּי:

עָנִי אֲנִי וְגוֵֹעַ מִנֹּעַר
נָשָׂאתִי אֵמֶיךָ אָפוּנָה:

עָלַי עָבְרוּ חֲרוֹנֶיךָ
בִּעוּתֶיךָ צִמְּתֻתוּנִי:

סַבּוּנִי כַמַּיִם כָּל הַיּוֹם
הִקִּיפוּ עָלַי יָחַד:

הִרְחַקְתָּ מִמֶּנִּי אֹהֵב וָרֵעַ
מְיֻדָּעַי מַחְשָׁךְ:

[11]Will You do miracles for the dead?
Will the deceased rise and acknowledge You? Selah.

[12]Will Your faithful grace be spoken of in the grave?
Your trustworthiness in the world of nothing?

[13]Will Your wonders be made known in the darkness?
Your righteousness in the land of no memory?

[14]Yet still I cry out to You, Lord.
In the morning, my prayer is waiting for You.

[15]Why do You ignore me, Lord,
and hide Your Face from me?

[16]I am depressed, dying of youthfulness.
I have born Your terrors and I am empty.

[17]Your angry moments have passed over me.
Fears of You are always with me.

[18]They encompass me as water, all day long.
They gang up against me, all together.

[19]You have alienated lover and friend from me.
My acquaintances are darkness.

PSALM 94

אֵל נְקָמוֹת יְיָ
אֵל נְקָמוֹת הוֹפִיעַ:

הִנָּשֵׂא שֹׁפֵט הָאָרֶץ
הָשֵׁב גְּמוּל עַל גֵּאִים:

עַד מָתַי רְשָׁעִים יְיָ
עַד מָתַי רְשָׁעִים יַעֲלֹזוּ:
יַבִּיעוּ יְדַבְּרוּ עָתָק
יִתְאַמְּרוּ כָּל פֹּעֲלֵי אָוֶן:

עַמְּךָ יְיָ יְדַכְּאוּ
וְנַחֲלָתְךָ יְעַנּוּ:
אַלְמָנָה וְגֵר יַהֲרֹגוּ
וִיתוֹמִים יְרַצֵּחוּ:
וַיֹּאמְרוּ לֹא יִרְאֶה יָּהּ
וְלֹא יָבִין אֱלֹהֵי יַעֲקֹב:

בִּינוּ בֹּעֲרִים בָּעָם
וּכְסִילִים מָתַי תַּשְׂכִּילוּ:

הֲנֹטַע אֹזֶן הֲלֹא יִשְׁמָע
אִם יֹצֵר עַיִן הֲלֹא יַבִּיט:
הֲיֹסֵר גּוֹיִם הֲלֹא יוֹכִיחַ
הַמְלַמֵּד אָדָם דָּעַת:

יְיָ יֹדֵעַ מַחְשְׁבוֹת אָדָם
כִּי הֵמָּה הָבֶל:

אַשְׁרֵי הַגֶּבֶר אֲשֶׁר תְּיַסְּרֶנּוּ יָּהּ
וּמִתּוֹרָתְךָ תְלַמְּדֶנּוּ:
לְהַשְׁקִיט לוֹ מִימֵי רָע
עַד יִכָּרֶה לָרָשָׁע שָׁחַת:

כִּי לֹא יִטֹּשׁ יְיָ עַמּוֹ
וְנַחֲלָתוֹ לֹא יַעֲזֹב:

כִּי עַד צֶדֶק יָשׁוּב מִשְׁפָּט
וְאַחֲרָיו כָּל יִשְׁרֵי לֵב:

A Psalm of Righteous Anger

¹The Lord has been a God of vengeance.
God of vengeance, appear!

²Prevail, Judge of the world!
Return just measure to the haughty!

> ³For how long, Lord, will the wicked—
> for how long will the wicked be joyful?
> ⁴spout words? speak arrogantly?
> all those who do evil talk insolently?

> ⁵They crush Your nation, Lord.
> They persecute Your bloodline.
> ⁶They kill the widow and the stranger.
> They murder the orphan.
> ⁷They say, "The Lord will not see.
> The God of Jacob will not figure it out."

⁸Figure it out yourselves, stupid ones among the people!
Fools, when will you become smart?

⁹Does not He Who shapes the ear hear?
Does not He Who forms the eye look?
¹⁰Does not He Who disciplines the nation rebuke?—
He teaches people what they know.

¹¹The Lord knows a person's thoughts;
truly they are futile.

> ¹²Happy is the person whom the Lord disciplines,
> whom He teaches from His Torah,
> ¹³giving one tranquility in days of evil
> until a grave has been dug for the wicked.

> ¹⁴Truly, the Lord will not desert His people.
> He will not abandon His bloodline.

> ¹⁵Truly, He will return the law to justice
> and all the upright of heart to Him.

מִי יָקוּם לִי עִם מְרֵעִים
מִי יִתְיַצֵּב לִי עִם פֹּעֲלֵי אָוֶן:

לוּלֵי יְיָ עֶזְרָתָה לִי
כִּמְעַט שָׁכְנָה דוּמָה נַפְשִׁי:

אִם אָמַרְתִּי מָטָה רַגְלִי
חַסְדְּךָ יְיָ יִסְעָדֵנִי:

בְּרֹב שַׂרְעַפַּי בְּקִרְבִּי
תַּנְחוּמֶיךָ יְשַׁעַשְׁעוּ נַפְשִׁי:

הַיְחָבְרְךָ כִּסֵּא הַוּוֹת
יֹצֵר עָמָל עֲלֵי חֹק:

יָגוֹדּוּ עַל נֶפֶשׁ צַדִּיק
וְדָם נָקִי יַרְשִׁיעוּ:

וַיְהִי יְיָ לִי לְמִשְׂגָּב
וֵאלֹהַי לְצוּר מַחְסִי:

וַיָּשֶׁב עֲלֵיהֶם אֶת אוֹנָם
וּבְרָעָתָם יַצְמִיתֵם
יַצְמִיתֵם יְיָ אֱלֹהֵינוּ:

[16]Who rose up with me against the wicked?
Who stood with me against the evildoers?

[17]Had not the Lord been a help to me,
I would surely have sunk into the realm of silence.

[18]When I said, "My foot has slipped,"
Your gracious love, Lord, sustained me.

[19]When my confusions were greatest within me,
Your words and acts of comfort engaged and soothed me.

[20]Can the reign of terror have anything in common with You?
Or he who generates oppression through the law?

[21]They gang up against the righteous
and sentence the innocent to death.

[22]The Lord has been a tower of refuge for me;
my God, my sheltering rock.

[23]He has turned their wickedness against them.
In their evil, He will annihilate them.
May the Lord, our God, annihilate them.

Psalm 121

שִׁיר לַמַּעֲלוֹת

אֶשָּׂא עֵינַי אֶל הֶהָרִים
מֵאַיִן יָבֹא עֶזְרִי:

עֶזְרִי מֵעִם יְיָ
עֹשֵׂה שָׁמַיִם וָאָרֶץ:

אַל יִתֵּן לַמּוֹט רַגְלֶךָ
אַל יָנוּם שֹׁמְרֶךָ:

הִנֵּה לֹא יָנוּם וְלֹא יִישָׁן
שׁוֹמֵר יִשְׂרָאֵל:

יְיָ שֹׁמְרֶךָ
יְיָ צִלְּךָ
עַל יַד יְמִינֶךָ:
יוֹמָם הַשֶּׁמֶשׁ לֹא יַכֶּכָּה
וְיָרֵחַ בַּלָּיְלָה:

יְיָ יִשְׁמָרְךָ מִכָּל רָע
יִשְׁמֹר אֶת נַפְשֶׁךָ:

יְיָ יִשְׁמָר צֵאתְךָ וּבוֹאֶךָ
מֵעַתָּה וְעַד עוֹלָם:

A Psalm of Comfort

¹A song for the steps.

I lift my eyes to the mountain range
from where will my help come?

²My help will come from the Lord
Who makes heaven and earth.

> ³May He not let your foot stumble.
> May your guardian not nod off.

⁴Certainly, the guardian of Israel
neither nods off nor sleeps.

> ⁵May the Lord be your guardian.
> May the Lord be your covering shadow.
> May He be strong at your right hand.
> ⁶Then the brazen forces will not strike you during the day,
> nor the sinister forces at night.

> ⁷May the Lord guard you from all evil.
> May He guard your very being.

> ⁸May the Lord guard your going out from this world
> and your coming in unto the next.

PSALM 124

שִׁיר הַמַּעֲלוֹת לְדָוִד

לוּלֵי יְיָ שֶׁהָיָה לָנוּ
יֹאמַר נָא יִשְׂרָאֵל:

לוּלֵי יְיָ שֶׁהָיָה לָנוּ
בְּקוּם עָלֵינוּ אָדָם:

אֲזַי חַיִּים בְּלָעוּנוּ
בַּחֲרוֹת אַפָּם בָּנוּ:

אֲזַי הַמַּיִם שְׁטָפוּנוּ
נַחְלָה עָבַר עַל נַפְשֵׁנוּ:

אֲזַי עָבַר עַל נַפְשֵׁנוּ הַמַּיִם הַזֵּידוֹנִים:

בָּרוּךְ יְיָ שֶׁלֹּא נְתָנָנוּ
טֶרֶף לְשִׁנֵּיהֶם:

נַפְשֵׁנוּ כְּצִפּוֹר נִמְלְטָה מִפַּח יוֹקְשִׁים
הַפַּח נִשְׁבָּר וַאֲנַחְנוּ נִמְלָטְנוּ:

עֶזְרֵנוּ בְּשֵׁם יְיָ
עֹשֵׂה שָׁמַיִם וָאָרֶץ:

A Psalm for Survivors

[1]A song to be sung on the steps, by David.

Were it not for God Who was with us—
Israel can say it now—

[2]were it not for God Who was with us
when people rose up against us,

[3]surely, they would have swallowed us alive
in the burning of their anger against us;

[4]surely, the waters would have swept us away
a torrent would have overcome our very being;

[5]surely, the raging waters would have overcome our very being.

> [6]Blessed is God Who did not allow us all
> to be prey to their teeth!

> [7]We the survivors escaped as a bird from the fowler's trap.
> The trap was shattered, and we escaped.

> [8]Our help is in God Godself,
> the Creator of heaven and earth.

Closing Prayers to the Abusing God

Theology is not real unless one can pray it. A theologian must be able to bring his or her reflections into the presence of the living God. Accordingly, I end this difficult meditation on God and abuse with prayer.

A cautionary word: Traditional Jewish prayer is liturgical; it is rooted in words of long and hallowed custom. One does not tamper lightly with the liturgy. Usually, when one wants to invest the traditional words with inner intent, or to stretch their meaning to new dimensions, one controls one's thoughts and one guides one's consciousness, while reciting the already-formed phrases. This process of directing intent or consciousness is called *kavvana*.[6] The situation of having to address an abusing God, however, requires more than just new *kavvana;* hence, I have expanded the liturgy itself. As a result, the prayers here interweave passages from the traditional service with new material. I translated the ancient texts and, for the new prayers, I composed the Hebrew before the English because Hebrew is the language of traditional Jewish prayer.

When composing prayers for insertion into the liturgy, I have retained gendered language. The reasons for this are many, though not all will agree:[7] I composed these words in Hebrew, which has no nongendered form; given the personalist trope I have chosen, gendered language is required; as a male, I relate more easily to male-gendered language; and, finally, the traditional liturgical context would seem to demand male-gendered forms of expression. I have, however, tried to provide alternate inclusive renderings of those prayers which are not inserts into the already established liturgy, and I encourage colleagues who feel more at home with female-gendered or with inclusive language to inter-pret and to w-rite appropriate prayers and liturgies.

A further cautionary word: Addressing the abusing God is not easy. Addressing the abusing God in the language of the tradition is even more difficult. One cannot simply recite these words; one cannot pick them up and pray them. Prayer of this type requires preparation. One must have a deep commitment to God, a deep desire to want to be with God, to want to have a relationship with God. It must be important, indeed a matter of spiritual life and death, to be able to address God. One must have, too, deep and abiding faith in the covenant, in our ability to address God no matter what the circumstances and no matter how severe our prayer may be; and in God's desire

---

[6] See pp. 25–27 above, for a discussion of this.

[7] See pp. 40–41 and 75–79 above, where I have discussed this. Arthur Green has commented that parental, royal, and pastoral metaphors are all out of place in the modern world. He therefore favors lover-spouse over father-king or male–female language (*Seek My Face, Speak My Name* [Northvale, N.J.: Jason Aronson, 1992; reviewed by me in *Modern Theology* 9:2 (April 1993), 223–225], pp. 15, 39–42).

to hear us and to help us address God. One must also have a sense of proportion about our relationship to God. We are creatures, not Creator. We are innocent, as victims of abuse; but we are sinners, in many other matters. We are accusers, yet we are children. This creates a tension in our images of ourselves, of God, and of the proper relationship between us; yet we must live, think, and pray within this tension. Finally, one must have courage — the courage that comes from having examined a problem and from knowing that one's solution is true and just, the strength that comes from experienced faith. And we must have the courage to address God with the truth, and the strength to use ideas that are strange to the heart and words that are alien to an ear sensitized to the traditional liturgy. It takes conviction, and time, to pray these texts.

A Prayer and a Greeting[8]

May God, Who is our Parent and our Sovereign,
    Who injures, destroys, and harms beyond reason,
    Who also loves graciously, and is compassionate, and cares —
May God turn God's Face to you so that you can see God.
May God's Face smile upon you, and may you know that.
May God share with you God's anguish and God's shame at God's own
        hateful actions.
May God bless you, and may you receive God's blessing.
Amen.

May God, Who is our Father and our King,
    Who injures, destroys, and harms beyond reason,
    Who also loves graciously, and is compassionate, and cares —
May God turn His Face to you so that you can see Him.
May His Face smile upon you, and may you know that.
May God share with you His anguish and His shame at His own hateful
        actions.
May God bless you, and may you receive His blessing.
Amen.

---

[8] A universal, nontraditional prayer to be used as a greeting and/or parting blessing for our friends who have suffered abuse.

For Yom Kippur[9]

אַתָּה בְחַרְתָּנוּ מִכָּל הָעַמִּים.
אָהַבְתָּ אוֹתָנוּ וְרָצִיתָ בָּנוּ,
וְרוֹמַמְתָּנוּ מִכָּל הַלְּשׁוֹנוֹת.
וְקִדַּשְׁתָּנוּ בְּמִצְוֹתֶיךָ,
וְקֵרַבְתָּנוּ מַלְכֵּנוּ לַעֲבוֹדָתֶךָ.
וְשִׁמְךָ הַגָּדוֹל וְהַקָּדוֹשׁ עָלֵינוּ קָרָאתָ. . . .

אֱלֹהֵינוּ וֵאלֹהֵי אֲבוֹתֵינוּ,
מְחַל לַעֲוֹנוֹתֵינוּ בְּיוֹם הַכִּפּוּרִים הַזֶּה;
מְחֵה וְהַעֲבֵר פְּשָׁעֵינוּ וְחַטֹּאתֵינוּ
מִנֶּגֶד עֵינֶיךָ.
כָּאָמוּר: אָנֹכִי אָנֹכִי הוּא מוֹחֶה פְשָׁעֶיךָ
לְמַעֲנִי
וְחַטֹּאתֶיךָ לֹא אֶזְכֹּר.
וְנֶאֱמַר: מָחִיתִי כָעָב פְּשָׁעֶיךָ
וְכֶעָנָן חַטֹּאתֶיךָ
שׁוּבָה אֵלַי כִּי גְאַלְתִּיךָ.
וְנֶאֱמַר: כִּי בַיּוֹם הַזֶּה יְכַפֵּר עֲלֵיכֶם
לְטַהֵר אֶתְכֶם מִכָּל חַטֹּאתֵיכֶם
לִפְנֵי יְיָ תִּטְהָרוּ.

אֱלֹהֵינוּ וֵאלֹהֵי אֲבוֹתֵינוּ
בַּקֵּשׁ מְחִילָה לַעֲוֹנוֹתֶיךָ בְּיוֹם הַכִּפּוּרִים הַזֶּה;
מְחֵה וְהַעֲבֵר פְּשָׁעֶיךָ וְחַטֹּאתֶיךָ מִנֶּגֶד עֵינֵינוּ

---

[9] See *The Authorized Daily Prayerbook*, ed. J. H. Hertz (New York: Bloch Publishing, 1960), pp. 898–900 (hereinafter Hertz). The edition of the services that is more generally available is that of Morris Silverman, *High Holiday Prayerbook* (Hartford: Prayer Book Press, 1951; repr. 1963), pp. 267–268 (hereinafter Silverman). "The Prayer" is one of the centers of the liturgy. It recurs five times and is recited silently and then aloud, in personal and then in communal prayer. The middle part of The Prayer, the one dealing with the substance of Yom Kippur, is composed of five paragraphs: "You have chosen us," "You have given us the Day of Atonement," "May Israel be remembered," "Forbear punishment for our sins," and "Make us holy." This whole part, thus, is one unit; it ends with, "Blessed are You . . . King. . . ." I have omitted here the second and third paragraphs and have added a section to the fourth and inserted lines into the fifth. The invocation of the verses is rooted in the covenant.

Place yourself in the presence of God; acknowledge God's overwhelming sovereignty and transcendent power; and then pray these words.

For the Prayer

You have chosen us from among all the nations.
You have loved us and wanted us,
    and have raised us above all the other languages.
You have made us holy through Your commandments
    and have drawn us near, our King, to Your service.
And You have set Your great and holy Name upon us. . . .

Our God and God of our ancestors,
Forbear punishment for our intentional sins on this Day of Atonement;
Wipe away and remove our rebellious sins and our inadvertent sins from
        before Your eyes.[10]
As it is said, "I, I am the One Who wipes away your rebellious sins
      for My sake
    and I shall not take into account your inadvertent sins."[11]
And it has been said, "I have wiped away your rebellious sins like a haze
    and your inadvertent sins like a cloud;
    return to Me, for I have redeemed you."[12]
And it has been said, "For on this day, God will atone for you,
    to purify you from all your inadvertent sins;
    before the Lord you will be purified."[13]

Our God and God of our ancestors,
Ask forbearance for Your intentional sins on this Day of Atonement;
Wipe away and remove Your rebellious sins and Your inadvertent sins
        from before our eyes.

---

[10] I have translated the Hebrew *meḥal* as "forbear punishment" (noun, "forbearance"); *selaḥ* as "forgive"; *shuv* as "return" or "repent," the latter being its more rabbinic meaning; and *ḥazor* as "repent," also according to its rabbinic meaning. I have striven for the strongest possible phrasing; however, my choice of words in Hebrew and in English is a function of each context as well as of substance. For the distinction between rebellious, purposeful, and unintentional sins, see pp. 139–141 above on Ps. 109:14.

[11] Isa. 43:25.

[12] Isa. 44:22.

[13] Lev. 16:30.

כָּאָמוּר: עוּרָה! לָמָה תִישַׁן יְיָ!
הָקִיצָה! אַל תִּזְנַח לָנֶצַח!
וְנֶאֱמַר: שׁוּבָה יְיָ!
עַד מָתַי?!
וְהִנָּחֵם עַל עֲבָדֶיךָ!
וְנֶאֱמַר: מִתְרַצֶּה בְּרַחֲמִים
וּמִתְפַּיֵּס בְּתַחֲנוּנִים,
הִתְרַצֵּה וְהִתְפַּיֵּס לְדוֹר עָנִי
כִּי אֵין עוֹזֵר.

קַדְּשֵׁנוּ בְּמִצְוֹתֶיךָ
וְתֵן חֶלְקֵנוּ בְּתוֹרָתֶךָ.
שַׂבְּעֵנוּ מִטּוּבֶךָ
וְשַׂמְּחֵנוּ בִּישׁוּעָתֶךָ.
וְטַהֵר לִבֵּנוּ לְעָבְדְךָ בֶּאֱמֶת
כִּי אַתָּה סָלְחָן לְיִשְׂרָאֵל וּמָחֳלָן לְשִׁבְטֵי יְשׁוּרוּן
בְּכָל דּוֹר וָדוֹר;
כִּי אַתָּה אֱלֹהִים אֱמֶת, שׁוֹפֵט צֶדֶק
לָךְ וּלְעַמְּךָ עַד עוֹלָם;
וּמִבַּלְעָדֶיךָ אֵין לָנוּ מֶלֶךְ מוֹחֵל וְסוֹלֵחַ אֶלָּא אָתָּה.
בָּרוּךְ אַתָּה יְיָ
מֶלֶךְ מוֹחֵל וְסוֹלֵחַ לַעֲוֹנוֹתֵינוּ
וְלַעֲווֹנוֹת עַמּוֹ בֵּית יִשְׂרָאֵל
וּמַעֲבִיר אַשְׁמוֹתֵינוּ בְּכָל שָׁנָה וְשָׁנָה
מֶלֶךְ שָׁב לִבְנֵי בְרִיתוֹ
וְחוֹזֵר בִּתְשׁוּבָה לִפְנֵי עַמּוֹ
מֶלֶךְ עַל כָּל הָאָרֶץ
מְקַדֵּשׁ יִשְׂרָאֵל וְיוֹם הַכִּפּוּרִים.

As it is said, "Wake up! Why do You sleep, Lord?!
   Arise! Do not abandon forever!"[14]
And it has been said, "Do repentance, Lord!
   For how long?
   Change Your mind about Your servants!"[15]
And it has been said, "God, Who is conciliated through mercy and
      reconciled through pleas,
   be conciliated and reconciled to an impoverished generation,
   for there is no other help."[16]

Make us holy through Your commandments,
   and make our portion be in Your Torah.
Make us satisfied from Your goodness,
   and make us joyful with Your salvation.
Purify our hearts to serve You in truth
for You forgive Israel and forbear punishment for the tribes of Yeshurun
   in every generation;
for You are the true God, the righteous Judge
   for Yourself and for Your people, forever.
Besides You, we have no King Who forbears and forgives.
Blessed are You, Lord,
King, Who forbears and forgives our sins
      and the sins of God's people, the house of Israel,
   Who causes our guilt to pass away every year,
King, Who returns to the children of God's covenant
      and repents before God's people,
Ruler over the whole universe,
   Who sanctifies Israel and the Day of Atonement.

*

[14] Ps. 44:24.
[15] Ps. 90:13.
[16] Daily liturgy, Hertz, p. 184.

For Yom Kippur[17]

יְהִי רָצוֹן מִלְּפָנֶיךָ, יְיָ אֱלֹהֵינוּ וֵאלֹהֵי אֲבוֹתֵינוּ,
שֶׁתִּתְמַלֵּא תְפִלָּתֶךָ
שֶׁיִּכְבְּשׁוּ רַחֲמֶיךָ אֶת כַּעַסְךָ מֵעָלֵינוּ
וְתָשׁוּב לְפָנֵינוּ בֶּאֱמֶת וּבְתוֹם לֵבָב
כִּי אָנוּ עַמֶּךָ וְאַתָּה אֱלֹהֵינוּ
אָנוּ בָנֶיךָ וְאַתָּה אָבִינוּ.

For Yom Kippur

אָבִינוּ מַלְכֵּנוּ חָטָאנוּ לְפָנֶיךָ.
אָבִינוּ מַלְכֵּנוּ חָטָאתָ לְפָנֵינוּ.
אָבִינוּ מַלְכֵּנוּ אֵין לָנוּ מֶלֶךְ אֶלָּא אָתָּה.
אָבִינוּ מַלְכֵּנוּ אֵין לְךָ עַם סְגֻלָּה אֶלָּא אָנוּ.
אָבִינוּ מַלְכֵּנוּ עֲשֵׂה עִמָּנוּ לְמַעַן שְׁמֶךָ.

אָבִינוּ מַלְכֵּנוּ חַדֵּשׁ עָלֵינוּ שָׁנָה טוֹבָה.
אָבִינוּ מַלְכֵּנוּ בַּטֵּל מֵעָלֵינוּ כָּל גְּזֵרוֹת קָשׁוֹת.
אָבִינוּ מַלְכֵּנוּ בַּטֵּל מַחְשְׁבוֹת שׂוֹנְאֵינוּ.
אָבִינוּ מַלְכֵּנוּ הָפֵר עֲצַת אוֹיְבֵינוּ.
אָבִינוּ מַלְכֵּנוּ כַּלֵּה כָל צַר וּמַשְׂטִין מֵעָלֵינוּ.
אָבִינוּ מַלְכֵּנוּ סְתוֹם פִּיּוֹת מַשְׂטִינֵינוּ וּמְקַטְרְגֵינוּ.

אָבִינוּ מַלְכֵּנוּ כַּלֵּה דֶּבֶר וְחֶרֶב וְרָעָב וּשְׁבִי וּמַשְׁחִית
מִבְּנֵי בְרִיתֶךָ.
אָבִינוּ מַלְכֵּנוּ מְנַע מַגֵּפָה מִנַּחֲלָתֶךָ.

---

[17] The Prayer on Yom Kippur contains two confessions (Hertz, p. 920; Silverman, p. 273). After them, there are three paragraphs of personal meditation: "My God, until I was created," "My God, guard my tongue from evil," and "May it be Your will." This is for insertion between paragraphs one and two.

[18] "May it be My will that My compassionate love (mercy) predominate over My anger, overwhelming My other qualities, so that I comport Myself with the quality of compassionate love toward My children, engaging them beyond the requirements of the law" (Talmud, Berakhot 7a, cited above, p. 28). "Our God and God of our ancestors, call up a memory of us before You, a good memory, and take note of us in the most ancient heavens, a noting of deliverance and mercy. Remember for us, O Lord our God, the covenant, the grace, and the oath you took

AFTER CONFESSION

May it be Your will, O Lord, our God and God of our ancestors,
that Your prayer be fulfilled
    that Your mercy defeat Your anger against us,[18] and
that You repent before us, in truth and with a whole heart;
for we are Your people and You are our God,
    we are Your children and You are our Parent.

OUR FATHER, OUR KING[19]

Our Father, our King, we have sinned before You.
Our Father, our King, You have sinned before us.
Our Father, our King, we have no King other than You.
Our Father, our King, You have no special people other than us.
Our Father, our King, act with us for the sake of Your Name.

Our Father, our King, renew this year for us for good.
Our Father, our King, annul all harsh decrees against us.
Our Father, our King, annul the thoughts of those who hate us.
Our Father, our King, nullify the plans of our enemies.
Our Father, our King, banish every foe and adversary from us.
Our Father, our King, stop the mouths of those who plot against us and
       persecute us.

Our Father, our King, banish disease, war, hunger, captivity, and
       destruction from the children of Your covenant.
Our Father, our King, keep plague from Your inheritance.

---

to Abraham, our father, on Mt. Moriah. May the binding which Abraham, our father, bound
Isaac, his son, on the altar in which he suppressed his mercy to do Your will with a whole heart
appear before You. So, too, may Your mercy suppress Your anger from upon us and, in Your
great goodness, may Your wrath turn away from Your people, Your city, and Your portion" (Rosh
ha-Shana liturgy, "Remembrances"; Hertz, pp. 880–882; Silverman, p. 165; cited above, pp. 28
and 263).

[19] After The Prayer in the morning liturgy, "Our Father, Our King," is recited in front of the
open ark (Hertz, pp. 162–166; Silverman, p. 303). I have followed the sequence of the stichs
in Silverman since it is the more widely used version and I have inserted modifications to fit the
theology of protest.

אָבִינוּ מַלְכֵּנוּ סְלַח וּמְחַל
לְכָל עֲוֹנוֹתֵינוּ.
אָבִינוּ מַלְכֵּנוּ בַּקֵּשׁ סְלִיחָה וּמְחִילָה
לְכָל עֲוֹנוֹתֶיךָ.
אָבִינוּ מַלְכֵּנוּ מְחֵה וְהַעֲבֵר פְּשָׁעֵינוּ וְחַטֹּאתֵינוּ
מִנֶּגֶד עֵינֶיךָ.
אָבִינוּ מַלְכֵּנוּ בַּקֵּשׁ מְחִיָּה וְהַעֲבָרָה לִפְשָׁעֶיךָ וּלְחַטֹּאתֶיךָ
מִנֶּגֶד עֵינֵינוּ.
אָבִינוּ מַלְכֵּנוּ מְחוֹק בְּרַחֲמֶיךָ הָרַבִּים כָּל שִׁטְרֵי חוֹבוֹתֵינוּ.
אָבִינוּ מַלְכֵּנוּ הַחֲזִירֵנוּ בִּתְשׁוּבָה שְׁלֵמָה לְפָנֶיךָ.
אָבִינוּ מַלְכֵּנוּ עֲשֵׂה תְּשׁוּבָה שְׁלֵמָה לְפָנֵינוּ.
אָבִינוּ מַלְכֵּנוּ שְׁלַח רְפוּאָה שְׁלֵמָה לְחוֹלֵי עַמֶּךָ.
אָבִינוּ מַלְכֵּנוּ קְרַע רוֹעַ גְּזַר דִּינֵינוּ.

אָבִינוּ מַלְכֵּנוּ זָכְרֵנוּ בְּזִכָּרוֹן טוֹב לְפָנֶיךָ.
אָבִינוּ מַלְכֵּנוּ כָּתְבֵנוּ בְּסֵפֶר חַיִּים טוֹבִים.
אָבִינוּ מַלְכֵּנוּ כָּתְבֵנוּ בְּסֵפֶר
גְּאוּלָה וִישׁוּעָה.
אָבִינוּ מַלְכֵּנוּ כָּתְבֵנוּ בְּסֵפֶר
פַּרְנָסָה וְכַלְכָּלָה.
אָבִינוּ מַלְכֵּנוּ כָּתְבֵנוּ בְּסֵפֶר זְכֻיּוֹת.
אָבִינוּ מַלְכֵּנוּ כָּתְבֵנוּ בְּסֵפֶר
סְלִיחָה וּמְחִילָה.
אָבִינוּ מַלְכֵּנוּ כְּתֹב עַצְמְךָ בְּסֵפֶר סְלִיחָה וּמְחִילָה.

אָבִינוּ מַלְכֵּנוּ הַצְמַח לָנוּ יְשׁוּעָה בְּקָרוֹב.
אָבִינוּ מַלְכֵּנוּ הָרֵם קֶרֶן יִשְׂרָאֵל עַמֶּךָ.
אָבִינוּ מַלְכֵּנוּ הָרֵם קֶרֶן מְשִׁיחֶךָ.
אָבִינוּ מַלְכֵּנוּ מַלֵּא יָדֵינוּ מִבִּרְכוֹתֶיךָ.
אָבִינוּ מַלְכֵּנוּ מַלֵּא אֲסָמֵינוּ שָׂבָע.

אָבִינוּ מַלְכֵּנוּ שְׁמַע קוֹלֵנוּ חוּס וְרַחֵם עָלֵינוּ.
אָבִינוּ מַלְכֵּנוּ קַבֵּל בְּרַחֲמִים וּבְרָצוֹן אֶת תְּפִלָּתֵנוּ.
אָבִינוּ מַלְכֵּנוּ פְּתַח שַׁעֲרֵי שָׁמַיִם לִתְפִלָּתֵנוּ.
אָבִינוּ מַלְכֵּנוּ נָא אַל תְּשִׁיבֵנוּ רֵיקָם מִלְּפָנֶיךָ.

Our Father, our King, forgive and forbear punishment for all our purposeful sins.

Our Father, our King, ask forgiveness and forbearance for all Your purposeful sins.

Our Father, our King, wipe away and remove all our rebellious and inadvertent sins from before Your eyes.

Our Father, our King, ask erasure and removal of all Your rebellious and inadvertent sins from before our eyes.

Our Father, our King, efface in Your great mercy all record of our guilt.

Our Father, our King, cause us to do complete repentance before You.

Our Father, our King, do complete repentance before us.

Our Father, our King, send complete healing to the sick of Your people.

Our Father, our King, destroy the bitterness of our judgments against one another.

Our Father, our King, remember us well before You.

Our Father, our King, write us into the book of good life.

Our Father, our King, write us into the book of redemption and salvation.

Our Father, our King, write us into the book of livelihood and sustenance.

Our Father, our King, write us into the book of merits.

Our Father, our King, write us into the book of forgiveness and forbearance.

Our Father, our King, write Yourself into our book of forgiveness and forbearance.

Our Father, our King, bring us salvation quickly.

Our Father, our King, raise the banner of Israel, Your people.

Our Father, our King, raise the banner of Your messiah.

Our Father, our King, fill our hands with Your blessings.

Our Father, our King, fill our storehouses with plenty.

Our Father, our King, hear our voices; have pity and mercy upon us.

Our Father, our King, accept our prayer in mercy and in good will.

Our Father, our King, open the gates of heaven to our prayers.

Our Father, our King, do not send us away empty-handed from before You.

אָבִינוּ מַלְכֵּנוּ זָכוֹר כִּי עָפָר אֲנָחְנוּ.

אָבִינוּ מַלְכֵּנוּ תְּהֵא הַשָּׁעָה הַזֹּאת שְׁעַת רַחֲמִים
וְעֵת רָצוֹן מִלְּפָנֶיךָ.

אָבִינוּ מַלְכֵּנוּ חֲמוֹל עָלֵינוּ וְעַל עוֹלָלֵינוּ וְטַפֵּינוּ.

אָבִינוּ מַלְכֵּנוּ עֲשֵׂה
לְמַעַן הֲרוּגִים עַל שֵׁם קָדְשֶׁךָ.

אָבִינוּ מַלְכֵּנוּ עֲשֵׂה
לְמַעַן טְבוּחִים עַל יִחוּדֶךָ.

אָבִינוּ מַלְכֵּנוּ עֲשֵׂה
לְמַעַן בָּאֵי בָאֵשׁ וּבַמַּיִם עַל קִדּוּשׁ שְׁמֶךָ.

אָבִינוּ מַלְכֵּנוּ נְקוֹם לְעֵינֵינוּ
נִקְמַת דַּם עֲבָדֶיךָ הַשָּׁפוּךְ.

אָבִינוּ מַלְכֵּנוּ עֲשֵׂה לְמַעַנְךָ וּלְמַעֲנֵנוּ.

אָבִינוּ מַלְכֵּנוּ עֲשֵׂה לְמַעַנְךָ אִם לֹא לְמַעֲנֵנוּ.

אָבִינוּ מַלְכֵּנוּ עֲשֵׂה לְמַעַנְךָ וְהוֹשִׁיעֵנוּ.

אָבִינוּ מַלְכֵּנוּ עֲשֵׂה לְמַעַן רַחֲמֶיךָ הָרַבִּים.

אָבִינוּ מַלְכֵּנוּ עֲשֵׂה לְמַעַן שִׁמְךָ הַגָּדוֹל הַגִּבּוֹר וְהַנּוֹרָא
שֶׁנִּקְרָא עָלֵינוּ.

אָבִינוּ מַלְכֵּנוּ זָכוֹר לָנוּ זְכוּת אֲבוֹתֵינוּ וּמַעֲשֵׂה יָדֵינוּ,
וְשׁוּבָה אֵלֵינוּ.

אָבִינוּ מַלְכֵּנוּ חָנֵּנוּ וַעֲנֵנוּ כִּי אֵין בָּנוּ מַעֲשִׂים,
עֲשֵׂה עִמָּנוּ צְדָקָה וָחֶסֶד וְהוֹשִׁיעֵנוּ.

Our Father, our King, remember that we are but dust.

Our Father, our King, may this hour be one of mercy and good will in
    Your presence.

Our Father, our King, have pity on us and on our children and our
    infants.

Our Father, our King, act
    for the sake of those killed for Your holy Name.

Our Father, our King, act
    for the sake of those butchered for Your unity.

Our Father, our King, act
    for the sake of those who died by water and fire for You.

Our Father, our King, avenge the spilled blood of Your servants
    before our very eyes.

Our Father, our King, act for Your sake and for ours.

Our Father, our King, act for Your sake if not for ours.

Our Father, our King, act for Your sake and save us.

Our Father, our King, act for the sake of Your own great mercy.

Our Father, our King, act for the sake of Your great, powerful, and
    awesome Name which we bear.

Our Father, our King, remember for us the merit of our ancestors and
    our good deeds, and return to us.

Our Father, our King, be kind unto us and answer us, for we have no
    deeds;
        act in justness and grace with us, and save us.

For the Weekly Liturgy[20]

הַשִׁיבֵנוּ אָבִינוּ לְתוֹרָתֶךָ
וְקָרְבֵנוּ מַלְכֵּנוּ לַעֲבוֹדָתֶךָ
וְהַחֲזִירֵנוּ בִּתְשׁוּבָה שְׁלֵמָה לְפָנֶיךָ;
שׁוּבָה יְיָ מִלְּפָנֵינוּ
וּבַקֵּשׁ מְחִילָה מֵאִתָּנוּ.
בָּרוּךְ אַתָּה יְיָ הָרוֹצֶה בִּתְשׁוּבָה.

מִתְרַצֶּה בְּרַחֲמִים וּמִתְפַּיֵּס בְּתַחֲנוּנִים,
הִתְרַצֵּה וְהִתְפַּיֵּס לְדוֹר עָנִי
כִּי אֵין עוֹזֵר.
אָבִינוּ מַלְכֵּנוּ זְכוֹר לָנוּ זְכוּת אֲבוֹתֵינוּ וּמַעֲשֵׂה יָדֵינוּ,
וְשׁוּבָה אֵלֵינוּ.
אָבִינוּ מַלְכֵּנוּ חָנֵּנוּ וַעֲנֵנוּ כִּי אֵין בָּנוּ מַעֲשִׂים,
עֲשֵׂה עִמָּנוּ צְדָקָה וָחֶסֶד וְהוֹשִׁיעֵנוּ.

[20] The first selection is for use on Mondays and Thursdays as a substitute for the usual petition in The Prayer (Hertz, p. 138). The second selection is for use on Mondays and Thursdays
as an addition to the usual supplications. (*tahanun*, Hertz, pp. 184–188).

Place yourself in the presence of God; acknowledge God's overwhelming sovereignty and
transcendent power; and then pray these words in their proper place in the liturgy.

Return us, our Father, to Your Torah;
    bring us near, our King, to Your service;
    and cause us to do complete repentance before You.
Repent, Lord, before us;
    and ask forbearance from us.
Blessed are You, Who desires repentance.

God, Who is conciliated through mercy and reconciled through pleas,
    be conciliated and reconciled to an impoverished generation,
    for there is no other help.
Our Father, our King, remember for us the merit of our ancestors and
        our good deeds, and return to us.
Our Father, our King, be kind unto us and answer us, for we have no
        deeds;
    act in justness and grace with us, and save us.[21]

---

[21] It is not my place to suggest modifications to Christian liturgy, but in the interest of dialogue and without intending any offense whatsoever and in the spirit of the theology of protest, I offer the following inter-pretation of the Lord's Prayer: "Our Father, Who is heaven, hallowed be Your Name. Your kingdom come, Your will be done on earth as it is in heaven. Give us this day our daily bread. Forgive us our sins, as we forgive those who sin against us. Ask forgiveness of us, as we ask forgiveness of those who wrong us. Lead us not into temptation, but deliver us from evil. . . ."

A Private Meditation

אֱלֹהַי.

הֲרֵי אֲנִי לְפָנֶיךָ כִּכְלִי מָלֵא בּוּשָׁה וּכְלִמָּה שֶׁמָּא הֶעֱוִיתִי פָנִים וְכָפַרְתִּי
בְּךָ וּבְתוֹרָתֶךָ. גָּלוּי וְיָדוּעַ לִי שֶׁחָטָאתִי לְפָנֶיךָ וְשֶׁעוֹמֵד אֲנִי אָשֵׁם לִפְנֵי כִסֵּא
כְבוֹדֶךָ. מְרוּבִּים חֲטָאַי עֲוֹנַי וּפְשָׁעַי, בְּיָחִיד וּבְרַבִּים. מִתְחָרֵט וּמִתְנַחֵם אֲנִי
עֲלֵיהֶם. וְהִנְנִי מְבַקֵּשׁ סְלִיחָה וּמְחִילָה עֲלֵיהֶם.

אוּלָם הֲרֵי אֲנִי לְפָנֶיךָ מָלֵא תִמָּהוֹן לֵבָב וְתַדְהֵמָה עַל מַה שֶׁרָאוּ עֵינַי
וְשָׁמְעוּ אָזְנַי: "אֵיכָה יָעִיב בְּאַפּוֹ יְיָ אֶת בַּת צִיּוֹן, הִשְׁלִיךְ מִשָּׁמַיִם אֶרֶץ
תִּפְאֶרֶת יִשְׂרָאֵל, וְלֹא זָכַר הֲדוֹם רַגְלָיו בְּיוֹם אַפּוֹ." "אַף זָנַחְתָּ וַתִּכְלִימֵנוּ,
וְלֹא תֵצֵא בְּצִבְאוֹתֵינוּ. תְּשִׁיבֵנוּ אָחוֹר מִנִּי צָר, וּמְשַׂנְאֵינוּ שָׁסוּ לָמוֹ. תִּתְּנֵנוּ
כְּצֹאן מַאֲכָל, וּבַגּוֹיִם זֵרִיתָנוּ. תִּמְכֹּר עַמְּךָ בְלֹא הוֹן, וְלֹא רִבִּיתָ בִּמְחִירֵיהֶם.
תְּשִׂימֵנוּ חֶרְפָּה לִשְׁכֵנֵינוּ, לַעַג וָקֶלֶס לִסְבִיבוֹתֵינוּ . . . כָּל זֹאת בָּאַתְנוּ וְלֹא
שְׁכַחֲנוּךָ, וְלֹא שִׁקַּרְנוּ בִּבְרִיתֶךָ. לֹא נָסוֹג אָחוֹר לִבֵּנוּ, וַתֵּט אֲשׁוּרֵנוּ מִנִּי
אָרְחֶךָ. כִּי דִכִּיתָנוּ בִּמְקוֹם תַּנִּים וַתְּכַס עָלֵינוּ בְצַלְמָוֶת, אִם שָׁכַחְנוּ שֵׁם
אֱלֹהֵינוּ וַנִּפְרֹשׂ כַּפֵּינוּ לְאֵל זָר? . . . כִּי עָלֶיךָ הֹרַגְנוּ כָל הַיּוֹם, נֶחְשַׁבְנוּ כְּצֹאן
טִבְחָה."

אֵינֶנִּי כוֹפֵר לֹא בְּךָ וְלֹא בְּתוֹרָתֶךָ. אַתָּה כִּפַּרְתָּ בָּנוּ, כִּי נְקִיִּים הָיִינוּ.
אַתָּה הוֹבַשְׁתָּנוּ, וְאָנוּ חֲפֵי פֶשַׁע הָיִינוּ. אַתָּה עִנִּיתָנוּ, אַכְזָרִי הָיִיתָ, וְאָנוּ לֹא
חָטָאנוּ עַד כֹּה. עָלֶיךָ הָאַחֲרָיוּת, וְלֹא עָלֵינוּ. עָלֶיךָ לְבַקֵּשׁ מְחִילָה מֵאִתָּנוּ, וְלֹא
עָלֵינוּ לְבַקֵּשׁ סְלִיחָה מִמְּךָ. עָלֶיךָ לַחֲזוֹר אֵלֵינוּ, וְלֹא עָלֵינוּ לָשׁוּב אֵלֶיךָ.

וּבְכָל זֹאת נִתְחַזֵּק וְנִתְעוֹדֵד. נִבְנֶה אֶת עוֹלָמֵנוּ. נֹאהַב אֶת רֵעֵינוּ. נָגֵן
עַל עַמֵּנוּ וְעַל אַרְצֵנוּ. נַאֲמִין בְּךָ, נְקַוֶּה אֵלֶיךָ, נְיַחֵל לָךְ, נְחַכֶּה לָךְ, וּנְצַפֶּה
לִרְאוֹת שׁוּב אֶת פָּנֶיךָ.

אָמֵן.

UPON COMPLETION OF THIS BOOK

My God.

I come before you as a vessel filled with shame and disgrace lest I have been arrogant before You and have denied You or Your Torah. It is known and manifest to me that I have sinned before You, that I stand guilty before Your throne. My unintentional, purposeful, and rebellious sins are many, in private and in public. I regret and I repent of them. I ask forgiveness and forbearance of punishment for them.

Yet I also stand before You, my heart filled with pain and shock at what my eyes have seen and my ears have heard. "How can the Lord have spurned in His rage the daughter of Zion, casting the glory of Israel from heaven to earth and pushing the earthly embodiment of His power from His memory on the day of His rage?"[22] "Indeed, You deserted us and shamed us, and did not go out with our forces. You put us to flight from our enemies, and those who hated us tore us to pieces at will. You handed us over like sheep to be devoured, and cast us among the nations. You sold Your people for nothing, and did not make a profit on their sale price. You made us an object of shame for our neighbors, a thing of scorn and derision for those around us. . . . All this happened to us yet we did not forget You, nor did we betray Your covenant. Our hearts did not retreat, nor did our steps deviate from Your way. Though You crushed us into a desolate place and covered us with deep darkness, did we forget the name of our God or spread our hands in prayer to a strange deity? . . . Truly, for Your sake we were killed all day long, we were considered sheep to be butchered."[23]

I do not deny You or Your Torah; You denied us, for we were innocent. You crushed us, yet we were guiltless. You were the Abuser; our sins were not commensurate with Your actions. The responsibility is Yours, not ours. You must ask forbearance from us, not we ask forgiveness from You. You must return to us, not we come back to You.

In spite of all this, we will gather our strength and support one another. We will build our world. We will love one another. We will defend our people and our land. We will believe in You, we will place our hope in You. We will yearn for You, we will wait for You, and we will anticipate the time when we will see Your Face again.

Amen.

[22] Lam. 2:1 with the Targum, there, and Maimonides, *Guide of the Perplexed,* I:28, and the Targum, there.
[23] Ps. 44:10–23.

Glossary

For more technical definitions of the theological, psychological, and specifically Jewish terms given here, consult the appropriate literature, some of which is listed in the bibliography below.

affections Technical term in theology referring to ongoing emotional attitudes, as opposed to feelings and state of consciousness, which are transitory; also called "dispositions." See "Thematic Index."

anthropopathic Having human feelings and capacities; in contrast to "anthropomorphic," having human form.

attribute A quality said to be inherent in the subject it describes; for God, there are "essential" attributes without which one cannot understand God and "accidental" attributes which are metaphors. See "Thematic Index."

C.E. Of the current, or common, era; used in place of A.D. (in the year of our Lord), which is appropriate to Christians but not to others; complemented by B.C.E., before the current era.

Da capo al fine Italian phrase used in music, meaning return to the beginning and play the section again; here used to return the reader to the beginning of a section for re-reading with alternate wording.

din Torah Tradition of calling God to account for injustice in the form of a trial of God. See "Thematic Index."

dispositions See *affections*.

dissociation Process in human psychology in which a person cuts off emotional and/or intellectual contact with the surrounding world and withdraws sharply into the self because something in the environment appears very threatening.

grouped textual field Method for displaying text and various commentaries simultaneously.

halakha (1) Jewish law; the Jewish legal system; (2) a specific law; sometimes spelled *halacha*.

hasidism   A modern Jewish mystical movement, beginning in the eighteenth century, stressing joy, a central leader, community, and focusing on the immediacy of Jewish spirituality.

High Holidays   The season which includes Rosh ha-Shana and Yom Kippur (q.v.).

Ibn Ezra   Well-known Spanish medieval Jewish exegete (1089–1164).

kavvana   Process of focusing one's consciousness, especially during prayer. See "Thematic Index."

kedusha (adj. *kadosh*)   Holiness; the quality of sacredness inherent in objects, persons, events, places, or texts. See "Thematic Index, " under "holiness."

Kol Nidre   Formula annulling all vows recited as Yom Kippur begins; its haunting melody invokes the entire penitential attitude.

Luria   Rabbi Isaac Luria: key figure in the development of Jewish mysticism; lived in Sefat in Israel (ca. 1550 C.E.).

Maimonides   Leading authority of the Jewish middle ages in Cairo; legalist, philosopher, commentator; also known as Rambam, an acronym for his name: Rabbi Moses ben Maimon (1138–1204).

Malbim   Nineteenth-century biblical exegete and author; acronym of Rabbi Meir Loeb ben Yechiel Michael; adamant opponent of modern reform.

Mesudat David   Commentary by Rabbi David Altschuler, nineteenth-century Polish biblical exegete and author; this commentary develops the context of the text.

Mesudat Zion   Commentary by Rabbi David Altschuler, nineteenth-century Polish biblical exegete and author; this commentary explains the meaning of the words.

midrash   (1) An interpretation of a verse or part thereof; (2) the process of interpretation; (3) an anthology of such interpretations.

Mishna   Book of Jewish law, arranged topically; 50-220 C.E.; part of the Talmud.

mitsva (pl. *mitsvot*)   A commandment; an act which a Jew is obligated to do because it is commanded by God in the Torah as interpreted by the rabbis.

multiculturalism   Social philosophy that encourages and honors difference in groups and cultures.

multiple personality disorder (MPD)   A psychological defense in which a person splits himself or herself into separate personalities which may or may not have knowledge of one another; splitting is often a result of dissociation (q.v.).

mysterium tremendum et fascinans   The utter holiness sensed in a moment, object, or person; it overwhelms and fascinates one who experiences it.

plurisignification   Having many meanings at the same time; texts may be plurisignificative. See "Thematic Index."

plurivocity   Having many voices at the same time; traditions are plurivocal. See "Thematic Index."

providence The affirmation of God's continuing action in our personal and national lives.

Radak Rabbi David Kimhi; well-known Spanish medieval exegete, specialist in grammar and syntax (ca. 1200).

Rambam See *Maimonides.*

Rashi Most famous of medieval commentators on the Tanakh, Talmud, and other texts; acronym of his name: Rabbi Shelomo Yitzhaki; lived in northern France (1040–1105).

Rosh ha-Shana The New Year; also the Day of Judgment, which marks the beginning of the ten days of repentance that culminate in Yom Kippur.

Saadia Sa'adia Ga'on, prevailing authority in tenth-century Judaism; leader, exegete, philosopher, and liturgist; lived in Iraq.

Sefat Emet Writings of Rabbi Yehuda Aryeh Loeb, son of Rabbi Abraham Mordecai, of the hasidim of Gur; commentary on the Torah and Psalms.

sefirot The ten aspects of God's personality according to the Zohar. See "Thematic Index."

seriatim To do something one after another, in sequence; usually because the act requires differing or contradictory actions. See "Thematic Index."

Shabbat (pl. Shabbatot) The Sabbath; day of rest and surcease from pre-scribed forms of work.

Shekhina (1) The divine presence; (2) the feminine aspect of God, especially according to the Zohar and Jewish mystical tradition.

sukka (pl. sukkot) (1) A booth in which the Jews lived while in the desert; hence, a temporary dwelling; (2) plural serves as name of the holiday of Tabernacles during which Jews live in booths.

Talmud The major compendium of discussions on Jewish legal texts; com-posed of the Mishna (a law book compiled by topic, ca. 220 C.E.) and the Gemara (discussions of the Mishna, ca. 500 C.E.).

Tanakh Jewish word for what the Christians call the "Old Testament"; acronym for Torah, Nevi'im (prophets), and Ketuvim (Holy Writings).

teshuva Repentance; requires acknowledging one's sin, asking forgiveness, resolving not to commit the sin again; and being tested. See "Thematic Index."

Tetragrammaton The ineffable Name of God, of which only the consonants are known: YHVH; some read it Jehovah, Jahveh, Yahweh; traditionally translated as "Lord"; not pronounced by Jews but typically read as "'Adonay"; sometimes referred to as the "Name." See "Thematic Index."

theurgy See *tikkun.*

tikkun The process of meditatively bringing wholeness to persons, actions, the cosmos, and God.

transference The psychological process in which one projects one's experience of one's parent onto a third person and then reacts to that person as if she or he were one's parent; especially complicated when speaking of God as "Father," "Mother," or "King." See "Thematic Index."

Torah   (1) The first five books of the Bible; the Pentateuch; (2) a handwritten scroll containing the first five books of the Bible, which is read ritually in the synagogue.

Yom Kippur   The Day of Atonement; full day of fasting and prayer for forgiveness of sins.

Zohar   The key book of Jewish mysticism and theurgy; speaks of God in personal terms and of God's relationship to humankind in interactive terms; written in 1293 though ascribed to earlier sources. See "Source Index."

Bibliography

The Masoretic Text of the Hebrew Tanakh is used; the abbreviations for the various books are the standard ones.

Translations

Arabic. See Qafih.

Chouraqui, A., trans. *La Bible*. Desclée de Brouwer, n.p., 1985.

Feuer, A. C., trans. *Tehillim*. Artscroll Tanach Series. New York: Mesorah Publications, 1977. Reprint, 1985.

The Holy Bible, read by Efrem Zimbalist, Jr. Tapes by Maranatha Library, 1983.

Luther, M., trans. *Die heilige Schrift*. Berlin: Britische und Ausländische Bibelgesellschaft, 1933.

Miqra'ot Gedolot. New York: Tanach Publishing, 1959.

Qafih, T., ed. *Tehillim 'im tirgum ufeirush haGa'on Rabbenu Sa'adia*. Jerusalem: n.p., 1966.

Segond, L., trans. *La Sainte Bible*. Paris: Nouvelle édition revue, 1963.

Tanakh: An New Translation of the Holy Scriptures. Philadelphia: Jewish Publications Society, 1985.

Targum. See *Miqra'ot Gedolot*.

Commentaries

Buber, S., ed. *Midrash Tehillim/Shohar Tov*. 1891. Reprinted, Jerusalem, 1977.

Cohen, J. A., ed. *Osar haTehillim*. 5 vols. Chicago: n.p., 1947.

Hacham, A., comm. *Sefer Tehillim*. 2 vols. Jerusalem: Mossad Harav Kook, 1984, 1986.

Ibn Ezra. See *Miqra'ot Gedolot* above under "Translations."

Imrot Tehorot. See Rosenwald.

Kahn, Y. *Sefer Zera' Ya'akov*. Brooklyn: Moriah Offset, 1979.

Kirkpatrick, A. F., ed. *The Book of Psalms*. Cambridge: Cambridge University Press, 1906.

Mesudat David. See *Miqra'ot Gedolot* above under "Translations."

Mesudat Zion. See *Miqra'ot Gedolot* above under "Translations."

Rashi. See *Miqra'ot Gedolot* above under "Translations."

Rosenwald, D. Y., comm. *Sefer Tehillim, kolel 'Imrot Tehorot*. Haifa: n.p., 1978.

Sefat Emet. See *Sefer Tehillim 'im Sefat Emet*.

Sefer Tehillim 'im Sefat Emet. Jerusalem: n.p., 1976.

Zera' Ya'kov. See Kahn.

Classic Jewish Texts

Hertz, J. H., ed. *The Authorized Daily Prayerbook*. New York: Bloch Publishing, 1960. Cited by location in the liturgy.

Maimonides, *Guide of the Perplexed*. Translated by S. Pines. Chicago: University of Chicago Press, 1963. Cited by part and chapter.

———. *Mishne Torah*, "Hilkhot Teshuva." Cited by chapter and paragraph.

Saadia Ga'on. *The Book of Beliefs and Opinions*. Translated by S. Rosenblatt. New Haven, Conn.: Yale University Press, 1948.

Silverman, M., ed. *High Holiday Prayerbook*. Hartford: Prayer Book Press, 1951. Reprint, 1963.

Talmud. Edited by A. Steinsaltz. Jerusalem: Israel Institute for Talmudic Publications, 1967–.

Talmud. Standard editions, cited by tractate and folio.

Zohar. Venice edition, cited by volume and folio.

Studies

Amy. Paper written for a class on Psalms. Unpublished.

Bal, Mieke. *Lethal Love*. Bloomington, Ind.: Indiana University Press, 1987.

———. *Murder and Difference*. Translated by M. Gumpert. Bloomington, Ind.: Indiana University Press, 1988.

ben Iehuda, Elieser. *Thesaurus Totius Hebraitatis et Veteris et Recentioris*. 8 vols. New York: Thomas Yoseloff, Sagamore Press, 1960.

Benjamin, J. *The Bonds of Love*. New York: Pantheon Books, 1988.

Bettelheim, Bruno. *The Uses of Enchantment*. New York: Alfred A. Knopf, 1976.

Blumenthal, D. "Creation: What Difference Does It Make?" In *God and Creation,* edited by D. Burrell and B. McGinn, 154–172. Notre Dame, Ind.: Notre Dame Press, 1989.

———. *Emory Studies on the Holocaust.* 2 vols. Atlanta: Emory University Press, 1985, 1988.

———. "A Genesis of Faith." Review of J. Leehan, *Pastoral Care for Survivors of Family Abuse;* E. Gil, *Treatment of Adult Survivors of Childhood Abuse;* and P. Marcus and A. Rosenberg, *Healing Their Wounds: Psychotherapy with Holocaust Survivors and Their Familes. Religious Studies Review* 18:3 (July 1992) 209–211.

———. *God at the Center.* San Francisco: Harper & Row, 1988.

———. "Maimonides: Prayer, Worship, and Mysticism." In *Approaches to Judaism in Medieval Times,* edited by D. Blumenthal, 1–16. Atlanta: Scholars Press, 1988.

———. "Mercy." In *Contemporary Jewish Religious Thought,* edited by A. Cohen and P. Mendes-Flohr, 589–595. New York: Charles Scribner's Sons, 1987.

———. *The Place of Faith and Grace in Judaism.* Austin, Tex.: Center for Judaic-Christian Studies, 1985.

———. "Revelation: A Modern Dilemma." *Conservative Judaism* 31 (1977), 64–69.

———. "Speaking About God in the Modern World." *Conservative Judaism* 33 (1980), 49–59.

———. *Understanding Jewish Mysticism.* 2 vols. New York: KTAV Publishing House, 1978, 1982.

———. Various entries. In *A Dictionary of Jewish-Christian Dialogue,* edited by L. Klenicki and G. Wigoder. Ramsey, N.J.: Paulist Press, 1984.

Brueggemann, W. *The Message of Psalms.* Minneapolis: Augsburg Publishing House, 1984.

Carr, S. *Yet Life Was a Triumph.* Nashville: Oliver Nelson, 1991.

Chopp, R. *The Power to Speak: Feminism, Language, God.* New York: Crossroad, 1989.

Cowley, A. E. *Gesenius's Hebrew Grammar.* 2nd edition. Oxford: Clarendon Press, 1910.

Derrida, J. *Glas.* Translated by J. Leavy, Jr. Lincoln, Neb.: University of Nebraska Press, 1987.

———. "Living On: Border Lines." Translated by J. Hulbert. In *Deconstruction and Criticism,* 75–116.

———. *Positions.* Translated by A. Bass. Chicago: University of Chicago Press, 1981.

Des Pres, T. *The Survivor: An Anatomy of Life in the Death Camps*. Oxford: Oxford University Press, 1976.

Edwards, Jonathan. *The Nature of True Virtue*. Foreword by W. K. Frankena. Ann Arbor, Mich.: University of Michigan Press, 1960.

Ellwood, G. F. *Batter My Heart*. Wallingford, Penn.: Pendle Hill Pamphlets, 1988.

Farley, W. *Tragic Vision and Divine Compassion: A Contemporary Theodicy*. Louisville, Ky.: Westminster/John Knox Press, 1990.

Faur, J. "Jewish and Western Historiographies: A Post-Modern Interpretation." *Modern Judaism* 12 (1992), 23–37.

Fisch, H. *Poetry with a Purpose: Biblical Poetics and Interpretation*. Bloomington, Ind.: Indiana University Press, 1988. Reprint, 1990.

Foucault, M. *Power/Knowledge*. Edited by C. Gordon. New York: Pantheon Books, 1972. Reprint, 1980.

Foust, M. Paper written for class on Psalms. Unpublished.

Fraser, S. *My Father's House: A Memoir of Incest and Healing*. New York: Ticknor & Fields, 1988.

Gil, E. *Treatment of Adult Survivors of Child Abuse*. Walnut Creek, Calif.: Launch Press, 1988.

Gilligan, C. *In Another Voice*. Cambridge, Mass.: Harvard University Press, 1982.

Graetz, N. "The Haftarah Tradition and the Metaphoric Battering of Hosea's Wife." *Conservative Judaism* 45:1 (Fall 1992), 29–42.

Green, A. *Seek My Face, Speak My Words*. Northvale, N.J.: Jason Aronson, 1992.

Gunkel, H. *The Psalms*. Philadelphia: Fortress Press, 1930. Reprint, 1967.

Hartman, D. *A Living Covenant*. New York: Free Press, 1985.

Heschel, A. J. *God In Search of Man*. New York: Meridian Books, Jewish Publication Society, 1955.

———. *Man Is Not Alone*. Harper Torchbooks. New York: Harper & Brothers, 1951.

———. *The Prophets*. 2 vols. New York: Harper & Row, 1962.

———. *Who Is Man?* Stanford, Calif.: Stanford University Press, 1965.

Janowitz, N. See Wenig.

Jung, C. G. *Answer to Job*. Translated by F. C. Hull. Princeton, N.J.: Princeton University Press, 1958.

Kadushin, M. *The Rabbinic Mind*. New York: Jewish Theological Seminary, 1952. Reprint, New York: Bloch Publishing, 1977.

———. *Worship and Ethics*. Chicago: Northwestern University Press, 1964.

Kasher, M. *Torah Shelemah: Talmudic-Midrashic Encyclopedia of the Pentateuch*. 43 vols. New York: American Biblical Encyclopedia Society, 1949–.

Keller, C. *From a Broken Web*. Boston: Beacon Press, 1986.

Keshgegian, F. "'Whose Wounds are not the End of Anything': Concepts of Justice and the Process of Recovery from Childhood Sexual Abuse." AAR paper. Unpublished.

Koehler, L., and W. Baumgartner. *Lexicon in Veteris Testamenti Libros*. Leiden: E. J. Brill, 1953.

Laytner, A. *Arguing With God: A Jewish Tradition*. Northvale, N.J.: Jason Aronson, 1990.

Leehan, J. *Pastoral Care for Survivors of Family Abuse*. Louisville, Ky.: Westminster/John Knox Press, 1989.

———. *Defiant Hope: Spirituality for Survivors of Family Abuse*. Louisville, Ky.: Westminster/John Knox Press, 1993.

Levenson, Jon D. *Creation and the Persistence of Evil: The Jewish Drama of Divine Omnipotence*. San Francisco: Harper & Row, 1988.

Levinas, E. *Collected Philosophical Papers*. Translated by A. Lingis. Dordrecht: Martinus Nijhoff, 1987.

Lewis, C. S. *Reflections on Psalms*. New York: Harcourt Brace Jovanovich, 1958.

Marcus, P., and A. Rosenberg. *Healing Their Wounds: Psychotherapy with Holocaust Survivors and Their Families*. New York: Praeger Publishers, 1989.

Miller, A. *For Your Own Good*. Translated by H. and H. Hannum. New York: Farrar, Straus, Giroux, 1983.

———. *The Drama of the Gifted Child*. New York: Basic Books, 1981.

Muffs, Yochanan. *Love and Joy: Law, Language, and Religion in Ancient Israel*. New York: Jewish Theological Seminary, 1992.

Murray, J. C. *The Problem of God*. New Haven, Conn.: Yale University Press, 1964.

Newsom, C., and S. Ringe, eds. *The Women's Bible Commentary*. Louisville, Ky.: Westminster/John Knox Press, 1992.

Neusner, J. *The Glory of God is Intelligence*. Salt Lake City, Ut.: Brigham Young University, 1978.

———. *Invitation to the Talmud*. New York: Harper & Row, 1973.

———. *Judaism: The Evidence of the Mishnah*. Chicago: University of Chicago Press, 1981.

Otto, R. *The Idea of the Holy*. New York: Oxford University Press, 1958.

Reik, T. *Ritual: Four Psychoanalytic Studies*. Translated by D. Bryan. New York: Grove Press, 1946.

Saliers, D. *The Soul in Paraphrase: Prayer and the Religious Affections*. New York: Seabury Press, 1980.

———. *Worship and Spirituality*. Philadelphia: Westminster Press, 1984.

Scarf, M. *Battered Jewish Wives: Case Studies in the Response to Rage*. Lewiston, N.Y.: Edwin Mellen Press, 1988.

Shapiro, S. "Failing Speech: Post-Holocaust Writings and the Discourse of Postmodernism." *Semeia* 40 (1987), 65–91.

———. "Hearing the Testimony of Radical Negation." In *The Holocaust as Interruption*. Edited by Elisabeth Schüssler Fiorenza and David Tracy. *Concilium* 175 (1984), 3–10.

———. Review of E. Fackenheim. *Religious Studies Review* 13:3 (July 1987), 204–213.

Steele, K. "The Healing Pool." *Voices* 24:3 (1988), 74–78.

———. "Sitting With the Shattered Soul." *Pilgrimage: Journal of Personal Exploration and Psychotherapy* 15:6 (1989), 19–25.

Taylor, M. *Altarity*. Chicago: University of Chicago Press, 1987.

———. *Erring: A Postmodern A/theology*. Chicago: University of Chicago Press, 1981.

Tessier, L. J. "Women Sexually Abused as Children—The Spiritual Consequences." *Second Opinion* 17:3 (January 1992), 11–23.

Tishby, I. *The Wisdom of the Zohar*. Translated by D. Goldstein. 3 vols. Littmann Library. London: Oxford University Press, 1989.

Trible, P. *God and the Rhetoric of Sexuality*. Philadelphia: Fortress Press, 1978.

———. *Texts of Terror*. Philadelphia: Fortress Press, 1984.

Umansky, E., and D. A. Ashton. *Four Centuries of Jewish Women's Spirituality*. Boston: Beacon Press, 1992.

Weil, S. "Love of God and Affliction." In *Simone Weil Reader*, edited by G. Panichas. Mt. Kisco, N.Y.: Moyer Bell Limited, 1977.

Wenig, M., and N. Janowitz. *Siddur Nashim*. Unpublished.

Wiesel, E. *Ani Ma'amin*. New York: Random House, 1973.

———. *Messengers of God: Biblical Portraits and Legends*. New York: Summit Books, 1976.

———. *Night*. New York: Bantam Books, 1960. Reprint, 1982.

———. *The Trial of God*. New York: Schocken Books, 1979.

Wolstein, B. *Freedom to Experience*. New York: Grune & Stratton, 1964.

———. *Theory of Psychoanalytic Therapy*. New York: Grune & Stratton, 1967.

Wyschogrod, M. *The Body of Faith: Judaism as Corporeal Election*. New York: Seabury Press, 1983.

Zalman Schneur of Liadi. *Liqqutei Amarim [Tanya]*. Translated by N. Mindel. Brooklyn, N.Y.: Kehot Publication Society, 1965.

Source Index

The entries in this index have been selected; this is not a complete reference index.

Thematic Index

The entries in this index have been selected; this is not a complete reference index.